5/21/82

The Land Use Awakening
Zoning Law in the Seventies

ROBERT H. FREILICH
ERIC O. STUHLER

*A Publication
of the
American
Bar Association
Section of
Urban, State and
Local Government Law*

1981

Summary of Contents

Introduction

The Land Use Awakening: Zoning Law in the Seventies   1
    ROBERT H. FREILICH
    ERIC O. STUHLER

Exclusionary Zoning

Legal Assaults on Municipal Land Use Regulation   51
Vol. 5, No. 1, p. 1
    IRA MICHAEL HEYMAN

Procedural Reform

Fasano v. Board of County Commissioners of   75
Washington County: Is Rezoning an Administrative or
Legislative Function?
Vol. 6, No. 1, p. vii
    ROBERT H. FREILICH

A Tentative Guide to the American Law Institute's   81
Proposed Model Land Development Code
Vol. 6, No. 4, p. 928
    CYRIL A. FOX, JR.

Some Observations on the American Law Institute's   103
Model Land Development Code
Vol. 8, No. 3, p. 474
    FRED P. BOSSELMAN
    GEORGE M. RAYMOND
    RICHARD A. PERSICO

Growth Management and the "Taking" Issue

Golden v. Town of Ramapo: Establishing a   121
New Dimension in American Planning Law
Vol. 4, No. 3, p. ix
    ROBERT H. FREILICH

Impact Zoning: Alternative to Exclusion in the Suburbs   129
Vol. 8, No. 3, p. 417
    VICTOR JOHN YANNACONE, JR.
    JOHN RAHENKAMP
    ANGELO J. CERCHIONE

No-Growth and Related Land-Use Problems: An Overview   161
Vol. 9, No. 1, p. 122
    RONALD A. ZUMBRUN
    THOMAS E. HOOKANO

Flexible Zoning

Air Rights are "Fertile Soil"   197
Vol. 1, No. 3, p. 247
    EUGENE J. MORRIS

Transfer Development Rights—A Pragmatic View   218
Vol. 9, No. 3, p. 571
    HERSHEL J. RICHMAN
    LANE H. KENDIG

State Role in Land Use Planning

Institutionalizing the Revolution: Judicial Reaction   235
to State Land-Use Laws
Vol. 9, No. 1, p. 183
    DAVID E. HESS

Statewide Land Use Planning in Oregon with   247
Special Emphasis on Housing Issues
Vol. 11, No. 1, p. 1
    TERRY D. MORGAN
    JOHN W. SHONKWILER

Conclusion

The Public Control of Land Use: An Anglophile's View   281
Vol. 10, No. 1, p. 130
    VICTOR MOORE

Table of Cases   297

NOTE: The articles in this book have been reproduced from the original
volumes of *The Urban Lawyer*. Each entry in this Summary of Contents includes the volume, issue and page numbers of the original article for easy
access to cross-references in the footnotes.

Acknowledgments

We gratefully acknowledge each author's kind permission to reprint the articles contained in this anthology. It is through the contribution of our authors, who are each outstanding authorities in the land use field, that *The Urban Lawyer* has been established as the leading journal in the area of urban, state, and local government law.

Robert H. Freilich
Eric O. Stuhler

Table of Contents

INTRODUCTION

The Land Use Awakening: Zoning Law in the Seventies   1
    ROBERT H. FREILICH
    ERIC O. STUHLER

    I. Introduction   1
   II. Exclusionary Zoning   5
       A. Exclusionary Zoning Issues   7
       B. Regional General Welfare   14
       C. Federal Intervention   16
       D. The Future of Exclusionary Zoning   19
   III. Procedural Reform   21
       A. Introduction   21
       B. Zoning Referenda and the *Fasano* Rule   24
       C. The State and Federal Role in   28
         Land Use Planning
   IV. Growth Management   32
       A. Urbanization   32
       B. The New Approaches   33
       C. Efforts to Preserve and Revitalize   36
   V. The "Taking" Issue   39
       A. The Development of the Police Power   39
       B. Invalidation of Improper Regulations   42
       C. Implied Exercise of Eminent Domain   44
       D. Section 1983 Liability   47
   VI. Conclusion   48

EXCLUSIONARY ZONING

Legal Assaults on Municipal Land Use Regulation   51
    IRA MICHAEL HEYMAN

    I. A Brief History   51
   II. Attacks on Municipal Land-Use Regulation   54
       A. Environmentalists   54
       B. The Lawyers   57
       C. The Market   60
       D. The Use of the Courts by Proponents of   61
         Open Housing
       E. State Governments   64
       F. Federal Stimulants   66

III. Speculations on the Future   68
IV. Conclusion   73

PROCEDURAL REFORM

Fasano v. Board of County Commissioners of   75
Washington County: Is Rezoning an
Administrative or Legislative Function?
    ROBERT H. FREILICH

A Tentative Guide to the American Law Institute's   81
Proposed Model Land Development Code
    CYRIL A. FOX, JR.

    I. Introduction   81
    II. Grant and Extent of Regulatory Power   83
   III. Regulation   84
   IV. Planning   86
    V. Discontinuing Existing Uses   90
   VI. State Planning and Regulatory Activities in General   91
  VII. State Planning   92
      A. State Land Development Agency   92
      B. State Land Development Plan   92
      C. State Long-Range Planning Institute   93
VIII. State Intervention in Local Regulation   93
      A. State Land Adjudicatory Board   94
      B. "Areas of Critical State Concern" 94
      C. "Development of Regional Impact"   96
   IX. Conclusion   101

Some Observations on the American Law Institute's   103
Model Land Development Code
    FRED P. BOSSELMAN
    GEORGE M. RAYMOND
    RICHARD A. PERSICO

GROWTH MANAGEMENT AND THE "TAKING" ISSUE

Golden v. Town of Ramapo: Establishing a   121
New Dimension in American Planning Law
    ROBERT H. FREILICH

Impact Zoning: Alternative to Exclusion   129
in the Suburbs
    VICTOR JOHN YANNACONE, JR.
    JOHN RAHENKAMP
    ANGELO J. CERCHIONE

I. Introduction   129
   A. The "Taking" Issue   132
      1. Regulations that Protect the Public Health,   135
         Safety and General Welfare
      2. Regulations that Protect Significant   136
         Natural and Societal Resources
      3. Recovery of Property Vested with the   139
         Public Interest
   B. Land Use Regulation   142
   C. The Petaluma Plan   143
   D. Timed-Sequential Growth: Ramapo   148
   E. Impact Zoning   153
      1. Evolution of and Impact Zoning Plan   155
      2. Capacity and Allocation   156
      3. Regional Housing Allocation   157
II. Conclusion   160

No-Growth and Related Land-Use Legal Problems: 161
An Overview
   RONALD A. ZUMBRUN
   THOMAS E. HOOKANO

I. Introduction   161
II. Survey of Current Growth Control Activity: 162
    Direct and Indirect
   A. Direct Local Control Activity   162
      1. The Ramapo Plan—Timing and Sequential Growth   162
      2. The Petaluma Plan: 500-Unit Limitation   163
      3. Boca Raton, Florida: Housing Caps   165
      4. City of Eastlake v. Forest City Enterprises: 166
         Constitutionality of Referendum Zoning
      5. The Livermore Solution: Control by   167
         Initiative
      6. San Jose, California—Interim Controls   168
         by Initiative
   B. Indirect Local Control Measures   170
      1. Withheld Municipal Services   170
      2. Zoning Devices with Exclusionary Effects   171
   C. Regional Land Use and Federal Environmental   173
      Programs with Growth Control Effects
      1. Regional Land Use Control Programs   174
      2. Federal Environmental Legislation with   175
         Growth-Limiting Effects
III. A Brief Description of Primary Economics and   178
     Social Effects of Growth Control Measures
IV. Legal Arguments Relative to "No-Growth" Activity   182

A. The Equal Protection Clause of the   182
   Fourteenth Amendment
B. Right to Travel   184
C. Expansion of the General Welfare Concept   186
D. Substantive Due Process   189
E. Inverse Condemnation: A Postscript   192
V. Conclusion   195

FLEXIBLE ZONING

Air Rights are "Fertile Soil"   197
   EUGENE J. MORRIS

  I. Introduction   197
 II. Legal Aspects   199
     1. Ancient Origins   199
     2. The "Appurtenant" Theory   200
     3. The "Homogeneous Space" Theory   202
     4. Development into Modern Law   203
     5. Earlier Statutory Recognition of Air Rights   206
     6. Modern Statutory Developments   206
III. The Air Rights Transaction   211
     1. Conveyances of Air Rights   211
     2. Comparison of Methods   213
     3. Problems   215
 IV. Conclusion   217

Transfer Development Rights—A Pragmatic View   218
   HERSHEL J. RICHMAN
   LANE H. KENDIG

   I. Introduction   218
  II. Buckingham—The Setting and Planning for Agriculture 219
 III. Why TDR?   220
  IV. How Much Will It Preserve?   224
   V. Back-Up for TDR   226
  VI. Setting up a TDR System   227
 VII. Legal Constraints in Buckingham   229
VIII. Public Reaction   232
  IX. Conclusion   233

STATE ROLE IN LAND USE PLANNING

Institutionalizing the Revolution: 235
Judicial Reaction to State Land-Use Laws
   DAVID E. HESS

   I. Statewide Land-Use Management   236

II. Shoreland Management   237
III. Regional Agencies   240
IV. Legal Guidelines   243

Statewide Land Use Planning in Oregon with   247
Special Emphasis on Housing Issues
    TERRY D. MORGAN
    JOHN W. SHONKWILER

  I. Introduction   247
 II. The Goals of Statewide Planning   248
    A. The Judicial Framework: Primacy of the   248
       Comprehensive Plan
    B. Statewide Planning Legislation   251
    C. The Second Phase   260
    D. Regional Planning Legislation   261
III. The Effect of Statewide Planning on   264
    the Provision of Housing
    A. Housing Crisis in Progress   264
    B. Oregon's Response   267
    C. Scheme of the Statewide Housing Goal 269
    D. Judicial Activism in Other Jurisdictions: 270
       A Comparison
    E. Housing Goal Revisited   274
    F. Problems and Recommendations   277
IV. Conclusion   280

CONCLUSION

The Public Control of Land Use: An Anglophile's View   281
    VICTOR MOORE

  I. Introduction   281
 II. Legal Structure of Land Use Control: 282
    Britain v. United States
III. An Anglophile's View of Effectiveness of   288
    United States Land Use Controls
    A. Greater Regional, State and   290
       Federal Involvement
    B. How to Deal with the Windfalls Which 292
       Accrue to an Owner of Land Allowed to
       Develop It and the Wipeouts Which Are Suffered by
       Those Not Allowed to Do So

TABLE OF CASES   297

The Land Use Awakening: Zoning Law in the Seventies

Robert H. Freilich

Hulen Professor of Law in Urban Affairs,
University of Missouri–Kansas City School of Law;
Editor, *The Urban Lawyer;* A.B., University of
Chicago; J.D., Yale Law School; M.I.A., Columbia
University School of International Affairs; LL.M.
and J.S.D., Columbia University School of Law;
Member, Missouri and New York Bars.

Eric O. Stuhler

Executive Editor, *The Urban Lawyer;*
B.A. Busin. Admin., Lindenwood College II,
St. Charles, Missouri; J.D., University of
Missouri–Kansas City School of Law

I. Introduction

A REMARKABLE PROCESS HAS TAKEN PLACE in American land use law and practice over the past decade—an exciting awakening of innovative and flexible responses to problems whose solutions have mainly laid dormant for over forty years. The seventies were filled with the conception and development of countless major doctrines including exclusionary zoning, growth management, state and regional land use planning and regulation, flexible zoning (TDR's, impact, and performance zoning), environmental protection, historic preservation, the "taking" issue, civil rights liability, inverse condemnation, regional general welfare, and finally, major procedural reforms in standing, categorization of decision-making, and development of model codes.

The Urban Lawyer, the national journal on urban law of the American Bar Association, was born in the spring of 1969 and has just recently completed its tenth birthday celebration. During the decade of the seventies, *The Urban Lawyer* was the perfect mirror of the land use issues, crises, solutions, and predictions which developed. Land use was one of the major concerns of the journal during this period of infancy. Accordingly, the decision was made to publish in this anthology issue what the editors and the Section of Urban, State and Local Government Law consider to be the outstanding pieces published during the decade which helped us to shape our views and focus on the "land use awakening." As an interesting side note, in 1978, *Environmental Comment* published a list of the ten most significant state land use regulation cases[1] and eight of these cases not only arose during this past decade, but were fully surveyed, analyzed, and discussed in the pages of *The Urban Lawyer*. In this introduction we will be cognizant of these significant land use cases as well as the other dominant federal, state, and local government issues that arose. We are sure that the excellent articles included in this anthology capture the essence of the decade's excitement and we hope that you will enjoy our look back on this remarkable decade.

The beginning of land use ordinances, as we know them today, were originally enacted at the turn of the century. They were upheld as an extension of the well recognized governmental power to abate nuisances.[2] However, in the 1926 landmark decision of *Village of Euclid v. Ambler Realty Co.,*[3] the Court extended the umbrella of the police power to zoning to insure necessary flexibility and sensitivity in meeting society's overall needs:

> The constantly increasing density of our urban populations, the multiplying forms of industry and the growing complexity of our civilization make it necessary for the State, either directly or through some public agency by its sanction, to limit individual activities to a greater extent than formerly. With the growth and development of the state the police power necessarily develops, within reasonable bounds, to meet the changing conditions.[4]

---

1. Dozier & Hagman, *Ranking Land Development and Environmental Cases and Courts,* 4 ENVT'L COM. 4 (Aug. 1978). The cases ranked as follows: (1) Golden v. Planning Bd. of Ramapo, 30 N.Y.2d 359, 285 N.E.2d 291, 334 N.Y.S.2d 138, *appeal dismissed,* 409 U.S. 1003 (1972) (timing of development); (2) Boomer v. Atlantic Cement Co., 26 N.Y.2d 219, 257 N.E.2d 870, 309 N.Y.S.2d 312, (1970) (nuisance); (3) Southern Burlington County NAACP v. Township of Mt. Laurel, 67 N.J. 151, 336 A.2d 713, *appeal dismissed, cert. denied,* 423 U.S. 808 (1975) (exclusionary zoning); (4) Just v. Marinette County, 56 Wis. 2d 7, 201 N.W.2d 761 (1972) (environmental protection); (5) Cheney v. Village 2 at New Hope, Inc., 429 Pa. 626, 241 A.2d 81 (1968) (planned unit development); (6) Fasano v. Board of County Comm'rs, 264 Or. 574, 507 P.2d 23 (1973) (rezoning as administrative matter); (7) Associated Homebuilders of Greater East Bay, Inc. v. City of Walnut Creek, 4 Cal. 3d 725, 484 P.2d 606, 94 Cal. Rptr. 630 (1971) (subdivision exactions); (8) Spur Indus., Inc. v. Del E. Webb Dev. Co., 108 Ariz. 178, 494 P.2d 700 (1972) (nuisance); (9) Fred F. French Invest. Co. v. City of New York, 77 Misc. 2d 745, 352 N.Y.S.2d 762 (1973) (transferable development rights); (10) *In re* Girsh, 437 Pa. 237, 263 A.2d 495 (1970) (exclusionary zoning).
2. Mugler v. Kansas, 123 U.S. 623, 668–69 (1887); Hadacheck v. Sebastian, 239 U.S. 394 (1915).
3. 272 U.S. 365 (1926).
4. *Id.* at 392 (*quoting* City of Aurora v. Burns, 319 Ill. 84, 93, 149 N.E. 784, 788 (1925)).

As early as 1894, the bounds and limitations on the police power were being set by the Supreme Court. In *Lawton v. Steele*[5] they held that for an exercise of police power to be valid it must employ a reasonable means to a lawful end.[6] Some thirty years later, the *Euclid* Court established the general constitutionality of zoning within acceptable police power guidelines by stating that zoning ordinances must (1) not be exercised in an arbitrary or capricious way, (2) be found reasonable, and (3) not be confiscatory. In 1928, in the case of *Nectow v. City of Cambridge*,[7] limitations and guidelines were set on the specific constitutionality of zoning as applied to an individual landowner's property. The court mandated, that to be valid, a zoning ordinance must allow the property owner an adequate return on his investment and a reasonable use.[8] Thereafter, and until 1974, the Supreme Court did not decide a single zoning case. It thus left the shaping of land use law to the various state courts to deal with as they saw fit. Traditional police power which was used to meet problems associated with health, safety, and preservation of property values, was expanded by the state supreme courts to include such areas as aesthetics, elimination of blight, historic preservation, and growth management.[9] The Supreme Court left the field of land use regulation to the states for over forty critical years. Thus, state doctrines have inevitably been diverse in responding to the immediate problems of the day. However, there has been a general awakening to America's urban problems, and the development of innovative solutions has become the benchmark of the state courts during the seventies.

In 1974, the Supreme Court finally broke its self-imposed silence in *Village of Belle Terre v. Boraas*.[10] The Court upheld a zoning ordinance designed to eliminate group student housing by restricting all land use to one-family dwellings, and expanded the use of zoning to include protection of the character and environment of the community: "A quiet place where yards are wide, people few, and motor vehicles restricted are legitimate guidelines in a land use project

5. 152 U.S. 133 (1894).
6. *Id.* at 140.
7. 277 U.S. 183 (1928).
8. *Id.* at 187.
9. *See* Golden v. Planning Bd. of Ramapo, 30 N.Y.2d 359, 285 N.E.2d 291, 334 N.Y.S.2d 138, *appeal dismissed*, 409 U.S. 1003 (1972); Construction Industry Ass'n v. City of Petaluma, 522 F.2d 897 (9th Cir. 1975), *cert. denied*, 424 U.S. 934 (1976); Associated Homebuilders of Greater Eastbay, Inc. v. City of Livermore, 18 Cal. 3d 582, 557 P.2d 473, 135 Cal. Rptr. 41 (1976); Just v. Marinette County, 56 Wis. 2d 7, 201 N.W.2d 761 (1972).
10. 416 U.S. 1 (1974).

addressed to family needs. . . . The police power is not confined to
the elimination of filth, stench, and unhealthy places."[11] Two years
later, the Court spoke again in *Young v. American Mini Theatres*,[12]
when it reaffirmed local sovereignty by allowing Detroit to regulate
X-rated movie theaters which contributed to neighborhood deterioration. The police power continued its expansion in 1978 with the
Penn Central Transportation Company v. New York City[13] decision.
Here the Court found that the use of transfer development rights
(TDR's) to preserve historical landmarks was constitutional. The
New York Landmarks Preservation Commission used this technique
of assuring "fair" compensation in saving Grand Central Terminal
from becoming the base of a multistory office building. The Court in
1979 took a major action toward regulating the police power in
Lake Country Estates, Inc. v. Tahoe Regional Planning Agency.[14]
The Court opened a virtual Pandora's box when it created a section
1983 cause of action for depriving a landowner of property without
just compensation. However, in *Agins v. City of Tiburon*,[15] the
Court was once again protecting regulatory police powers by finding
no inverse condemnation absent limitation of all reasonable use of
an owner's property. The Supreme Court in this case also took a
giant step forward in recognizing that open space preservation and
prevention of urban sprawl were legitimate goals of a growth management system within the police power. Zoning, therefore, has become a delicate balance of the exercise of police powers and the right
of eminent domain. Whether these two governmental powers are
symmetrical and where the line between them will be drawn by the
Court is a major question as we leave the seventies.[16]

---

11. *Id.* at 9.
12. 427 U.S. 50 (1976).
13. 438 U.S. 104 (1978).
14. 440 U.S. 391 (1979).
15. _____ U.S. _____, 100 S. Ct. 2138 (1980).
16. As was stated in a recent and excellent article on the subject of regulatory takings "any attempt to formulate inverse condemnation criteria must be
prefaced with a vow of humility in view of the unsuccessful attempts of numerous scholars to foreclose debate on the subject." Morgan & Shonkwiler, *Regulatory Takings in Oregon: A Walk Down Fifth Avenue without Due Process*, 16
WILLAMETTE L. J. 591, 629 (1980). *See* Berger, *A Policy Analysis of the
Taking Problem*, 49 N.Y.U. L. REV. 165 (1974); Costonis, *"Fair" Compensation and the Accommodation Power: Antidotes for the Taking Impasses in
Land Use Controversies*, 75 COLUM. L. REV. 1021 (1975). Krasnowiecki &
Paul, *The Preservation of Open Space in Metropolitan Areas*, 110 U. PA. L.
REV. 179 (1961); Michelman, *Property, Utility and Fairness: Comments on
the Ethical Foundations of "Just Compensation" Law*, 80 HARV. L. REV. 1165
(1967); Sax, *Takings, Private Property and Public Rights*, 81 YALE L.J. 149

The crises which faced the nation during the decade were phenomenal. They included (1) the deterioration of central cities and closer-in neighborhoods, (2) the despoliation of environmentally sensitive lands, (3) the energy shortage, (4) the fiscal insolvency of cities, (5) the reduction of prime agricultural land, and (6) the spiraling cost of housing. These problems were dealt with in fragmented and isolated ways, and, as usual, no one technique became the awaited truth. It was not until comprehensive approaches and procedural reforms were implemented that American society began to realize that balanced approaches to these problems do exist. There was a need to view cities in greater perspective and with the advent of regional general welfare standards and progressive growth management techniques, a positive and effective approach was found. These developments, along with newer, faster, and more equitable procedures for the processing of land development proposals, have provided a balance of private and public concerns. This is the path we are destined to take. We have the power and knowledge to confront these crises, as we enter the eighties. The question now is: Do we have the willpower, as a society, to combat them?

In order to provide some connecting tissue to what otherwise might seem an endless web of interaction, we have provided this introductory essay which we hope will highlight the significance of the papers presented, link them to the other issues and solutions of the decade, and where appropriate, to supply data and information on subsequent decisions and statutes. In addition, however, this introduction will attempt to summarize the key events of the decade and to place them in a historical perspective. This we hope will be of great service, both in and of itself, but particularly to enable the reader to assess each article published in the anthology in a truly "retrospective" light to see how remarkably foresighted they were and remain.

II. Exclusionary Zoning

The decade of the seventies opened with an emphasis upon the socioeconomic problems of society. It was an inevitable outgrowth of the "War against Poverty," the racial riots of the late sixties, and the Kerner and Douglas Commission reports on racial discrimination in the nation. While it was the time of extreme racial impaction in the

---

(1971); Van Alstyne, *Taking or Damaging by Police Power: The Search for Inverse Condemnation Criteria*, 44 S. CAL. L. REV. 1 (1970); Waite, *Governmental Power and Private Property*, 16 CATH. U.L. REV. 283 (1967).

central cities and white flight to the suburbs, it also was the era of rapid conversion of agricultural and rural land, environmental awareness, and sensitivity to destruction of air and water resources, flood plains, and coastal zones. Population growth and the spiraling capital and service costs for meeting the demands of a sprawling society seemed to weigh as heavily on the nation's mind as the fear of socio-economic and racial invasion of suburban areas. As is generally true with any singular view of society's problems, those who saw the problems as solely racial, social, or economic, seemed to agree on the remedy: dismantling or severely reducing the planning and zoning powers of local government. Strange bedfellows were made between the exclusionary zoning advocates and the housing and development industry. In the middle of the seventies, the combination of regional general welfare strategies, public interest in the environment, growth management, energy, agriculture, and fiscal responsibility was able to be successfully assimilated with broader social and non-discriminatory goals.

In the *Euclid* case, the Supreme Court's first affirmation of comprehensive zoning as constitutional, the Court seemed unaware of the possible exclusionary potential of zoning.

> With particular reference to apartment houses, it is pointed out that the development of detached house sections is greatly retarded by the coming of apartment houses, which has sometimes resulted in destroying the entire section for private purposes; that in such sections very often the apartment house is a mere parasite, constructed in order to take advantage of the open spaces and attractive surroundings created by the residential character of the district. Moreover, the coming of one apartment house is followed by others, interfering by their height and bulk with the free circulation of air and monopolizing the rays of the sun which otherwise would fall upon the smaller homes, and bringing, as their necessary accompaniments, the disturbing noises incident to increased traffic and business, and the occupation, by means of moving and parked automobiles, of larger portions of the streets, thus detracting from their safety and depriving children of the privilege of quiet and open spaces for play, enjoyed by those in more favored localities,—finally, the residential character of the neighborhood and its desirability as a place of detached residences are utterly destroyed.[17]

Contrast this negative attitude toward apartment living in 1926 with such later cases as *In re Girsh*[18] in the seventies. The trial court which originally invalidated the *Euclid* ordinance in 1924 foresaw the potential exclusionary impact of exclusionary zoning when it wrote:

---

17. Euclid v. Ambler Realty Co., 272 U.S. 365, 394 (1926).
18. 437 Pa. 237, 263 A.2d 395 (1970).

The plain truth is that the true object of the ordinance in question is to place all the property in an undeveloped area . . . in a strait-jacket. The purpose to be accomplished is really to regulate the mode of living of persons who may hereafter inhabit it. [T]he result to be accomplished is to classify the population and segregate them according to their income or situation in life. The true reason why some persons live in a mansion and others in a shack, why some live in a single-family dwelling and others in an apartment, or why some live in a well-kept apartment and others in a tenement, is primarily economic. Aside from contributing to these results and furthering such class tendencies, the ordinance has also an esthetic purpose; . . . to make this village develop into a city along lines now conceived by the village council to be attractive and beautiful.[19]

Here, the court was attempting to ascertain the real purpose of the particular regulation. Did such laws promote the public health, safety, morals, and general welfare, or were they simply mechanisms to keep persons out of certain neighborhoods or even entire communities?

This basic question remains the pivotal lever for resolving exclusionary zoning issues in the contemporary world. In the decades of the fifties and the sixties many suburban communities were struggling as much to control environmental, fiscal, and energy problems as with efforts to avoid black suburbanization. Unfortunately, without the modern tools of growth management, communities utilized the old two-dimensional techniques of large lot zoning, minimum building size, and exclusive use zones in order to seize control of their destiny over growth issues. The net effect was to skew both the racial composition of the community through the socio-economic differential impact while at the same time unwittingly exacerbating the major problems of sprawl and lack of balance in the production of housing. This imbalance has been significantly rectified in the seventies through the use of modern growth management processes (which we will explore later in the growth management section). These methods fully assimilate regional housing and population allocations with techniques that focus on equitable and efficient capital needs while allowing the timing, sequencing, and management of growth.

A. *Exclusionary Zoning Issues*

Ira Michael Heyman, in his article "Legal Assaults on Municipal Land Use Regulation,"[20] reflects the growing concern over exclusionary zoning in the late sixties and throughout the seventies. In a

---

19. Ambler Realty Co. v. Village of Euclid, 297 F. 307, 316 (N.D. Ohio 1924).
20. 5 URB. LAW. 1 (1973) (also reprinted in this anthology).

series of decisions reflecting the parochial nature of many suburban zoning systems and the reluctance to assimilate population growth, low- and moderate-income housing, and racial/ethnic groups, the courts threw out invidious large lot zoning,[21] minimum floor area requirements,[22] exclusion of multiple-family housing,[23] excessive industrial zoning,[24] and intolerance to mobile homes and manufactured housing,[25] which had undesirable exclusionary effects. Doctrines establishing preferences for quasi-public uses such as day care centers, halfway houses, and public-subsidized housing were developed.[26] However, an attempt to fashion a "preferred use" doctrine for almost anything other than single-family housing failed.[27] The courts were careful as the decade wore on to recognize that such exclusionary systems were only invalid where they attempted to skew actual population assimilation and growth in developing areas. Police power restrictions were recognized as valid in non-urban or rural areas,[28] to preserve family values,[29] protect agricultural areas,[30] meet environ-

21. National Land and Inv. Corp. v. Kohn, 419 Pa. 504, 215 A.2d 597 (1965); In re Kit-Mar Builders, 439 Pa. 466, 268 A.2d 765 (1970); Oakwood at Madison, Inc. v. Township of Madison County, 128 N.J. Super. 438, 320 A.2d 223 (1974).

22. Southern Burlington NAACP v. Township of Mt. Laurel, 119 N.J. Super. 164, 290 A.2d 465 (1972); Home Builder's League, Inc. v. Township of Berlin, 157 N.J. Super. 586, 385 A.2d 295 (1978).

23. In re Girsh, 437 Pa. 237, 263 A.2d 395 (1970); Ridge Realty Co. v. Oldham County Plan. Comm'n, 495 S.W.2d 432 (Ky. 1973); Malmar-Assocs. v. Board of Comm'rs, 260 Md. 292, 272 A.2d 6 (1971); see also Molino v. Borough of Glassboro, 116 N.J. Super. 195, 281 A.2d 401 (1971), which invalidated limits on the number of bedrooms in multi-family developments.

24. Southern Burlington NAACP v. Township of Mt. Laurel, 67 N.J. 151, 336 A.2d 713 (1975).

25. High Meadows Park, Inc. v. City of Aurora, 112 Ill. App. 2d 220, 250 N.E.2d 517 (1969); Johnson County Plan. Comm'n v. Fayette Bldg. Corp., 156 Ind. App. 557, 297 N.E.2d 899 (1973); Derry Borough v. Shomo, 5 Pa. Commw. Ct. 216, 289 A.2d 513 (1972).

26. Freilich & Bass, Exclusionary Zoning: Suggested Litigation Approaches, 3 URB. LAW. 344 (1971); Cameron v. Zoning Agent of Bellingham, 357 Mass. 757, 260 N.E.2d 143 (1970); Abbott House v. Village of Tarrytown, 34 A.D.2d 821, 312 N.Y.S.2d 841 (1970); DeSimone v. Greater Englewood Hous. Corp., 56 N.J. 428, 267 A.2d 31 (1970).

27. Kropf v. City of Sterling Heights, 391 Mich. 139, 215 N.W.2d 179 (1974), reversing the "preferred use" doctrine announced in Bristow v. City of Woodhaven, 35 Mich. App. 205, 192 N.W.2d 322 (1971).

28. DeCaro v. Washington Township, 21 Pa. Commw. Ct. 252, 344 A.2d 725 (1975); Steel Hill Dev., Inc. v. Town of Sanbornton, 469 F.2d 956 (1st Cir. 1972).

29. Village of Belle Terre v. Boraas, 416 U.S. 1 (1974); Ybarra v. Town of Los Altos Hills, 503 F.2d 250 (9th Cir. 1974).

30. SAVE Centennial Valley Ass'n v. Schultz, 284 N.W.2d 452 (S.D. 1979); Gisler v. County of Madera, 38 Cal. App. 3d 303, 112 Cal. Rptr. 919 (1974); Meyer v. Lord, 37 Or. App. 59, 586 P.2d 367 (1978).

mental problems,[31] to time and sequence growth,[32] and limit housing starts where other opportunities within the region existed.[33]

Significant differences also existed between the federal and state courts in the granting of access to the courts for the litigation of such issues. Under the rubric of "standing," the federal courts limited zoning litigation to developers and occupants of actual housing projects.[34] Generic attacks on the validity of suburban zoning systems were disallowed as the federal courts refused to become "super zoning boards," or to disallow exclusionary referenda.[35] The states, on the other hand, were constantly expanding access to the courts to nonresidents, associations, and low- and moderate-income groups residing in central cities.[36]

Despite these differences, it soon became apparent to all intelligent observers that even state judicial solutions to fair housing in America were not adequate to overcome the denial of social, racial, and economic housing opportunities.[37] Litigation, even where suc-

---

31. Salamar Builders Corp. v. Tuttle, 29 N.Y.2d 221, 275 N.E.2d 585, 325 N.Y.S.2d 933 (1971); Smoke Rise, Inc. v. Washington Suburban Sanitary Comm'n, 400 F. Supp. 1369 (D. Md. 1975); Just v. Marinette County, 56 Wis. 2d 7, 201 N.W.2d 761 (1972).

32. Golden v. Planning Bd. of the Town of Ramapo, 30 N.Y.2d 359, 285 N.E.2d 291, 334 N.Y.S.2d 138 (1972); Associated Homebuilders v. City of Livermore, 18 Cal. 3d 582, 557 P.2d 473, 135 Cal. Rptr. 41 (1976).

33. Construction Indus. Ass'n v. City of Petaluma, 522 F.2d 897 (9th Cir. 1975), cert. denied, 424 U.S. 934 (1976); Coalition for Los Angeles County Planning v. Board of Supervisors, 76 Cal. 3d 241, 142 Cal. Rptr. 766 (1975); but see Boca Villas Corp. v. City of Boca Raton, 45 Fla. Supp. 65 (1976), aff'd, 372 So. 2d 485 (Dist. Ct. App. 1979) (setting aside population cap unrelated to comprehensive planning standards).

34. Warth v. Seldin, 422 U.S. 490 (1975); Construction Indus. Ass'n v. City of Petaluma, 522 F.2d 897 (9th Cir. 1975); City of Hartford v. Glastonbury, 561 F.2d 1032 (2nd Cir. 1977).

35. City of Eastlake v. Forest City Enterprises, Inc., 426 U.S. 668 (1976); James v. Valtierra, 402 U.S. 137 (1971); Ranjel v. City of Lansing, 417 F.2d 321 (6th Cir. 1969); but see Hunter v. Erickson, 393 U.S. 385 (1969); Reitman v. Mulkey, 387 U.S. 369 (1967).

36. Douglaston Civic Ass'n v. Galvin, 36 N.Y.2d 1, 324 N.E.2d 317, 364 N.Y.S.2d 830 (1974); Citizens for Washington Square v. City of Davenport, 277 N.W.2d 882 (Iowa 1979); Suffolk Hous. Servs., Inc. v. Town of Brookhaven, 63 A.D.2d 731, 405 N.Y.S.2d 302 (1978); City of Wilmington v. Lord, 378 A.2d 635 (Del. 1977).

37. Rose, Myths and Misconceptions of Exclusionary Zoning Litigation, 8 REAL EST. L.J. (1979); Burchell, Listokin and James, Exclusionary Zoning: Pitfalls of the Regional Remedy, 7 URB. LAW. 262 (1975). It was at this time in 1975 that the American Bar Association, Special Committee on Housing and Urban Development Law organized a special project with the assistance of Dep't of HUD funds to investigate comprehensive solutions—legislative, judicial and executive—to the development of anti-exclusionary housing techniques. The resulting study is excellent in its treatment of the effective role that the judiciary can play in exclusionary zoning litigation. See R. FISHMAN, HOUS-

cessful, dragged on for years with little suburban housing to show for the efforts. It became obvious that courts would have to develop answers to difficult problems concerning the separation of legislative-judicial powers,[38] characterization of rezoning as administrative,[39] appointment of hearing examiners, special masters, or administrative law judges to develop facts,[40] and to retain jurisdiction over cases to

---

ING FOR ALL UNDER LAW (1978). For a particularly exhaustive critique of the study, see Silverman, Housing for All Under the Law: The Limits of Legalist Reform, 27 U.C.L.A. L. REV. 99 (1979). [Prof. Freilich was a member of the Advisory Commission on Housing and Urban Development which undertook the study.]

38. See Krasnowiecki, Securing Definitive Relief for the Developer: An Overview, 3 ZONING & PLAN. L. REP. 1 (Jan. 1980) for an excellent article on the need for courts to supervise zoning cases and to establish the delicate boundary line between the legislative and judicial roles. For example, in the well-known exclusionary zoning case, In re Girsh, 437 Pa. 237, 263 A.2d 395 (1970), after the plaintiff won his case in the Pennsylvania Supreme Court establishing the general unconstitutionality of the total exclusion of apartment houses, the township rezoned someone else's property to multi-family rather than Mr. Girsh's. After all, Mr. Girsh did not establish that his property necessarily was the most suitable for that zoning. Should a successful plaintiff be rewarded for his social diligence regardless of the land use considerations attached to his specific site? Can the court without violating separation of powers doctrine order that the legislative body so zone the property? Generally, this site-specific relief is restricted to specific constitutionality cases where the plaintiff has demonstrated unique hardship or lack of a reasonable use for his own site. For an incredible tale of the developer who won the battle but lost the war, see Fiore v. City of Highland Park, 76 Ill. App. 2d 62, 221 N.E.2d 323 (1966), aff'd, 93 Ill. App. 2d 24, 235 N.E.2d 23 (1968).

39. Fasano v. Board of County Comm'rs, 264 Or. 574, 507 P.2d 23 (1973); West v. City of Portage, 392 Mich. 458, 221 N.W.2d 303 (1974); Arnel Dev. Co. v. City of Costa Mesa, 98 Cal. App. 3d 567, 159 Cal. Rptr. 592 (1979); Leonard v. City of Bothell, 87 Wash. 2d 847, 557 P.2d 1306 (1976). In Snyder v. City of Lakewood, 542 P.2d 371 (Colo. 1975), the court held that a review of a rezoning ordinance is an administrative proceeding, and the 30 day statute of limitations for the writ of certiorari will apply and a plenary declaratory judgment will not lie if commenced more than 30 days after the filing of the ordinance. Since a complete record will have to be made at the city council level, including requisite findings, [see Topanga Assn. v. County of Los Angeles, 11 Cal. 3d 506, 552 P.2d 12, 113 Cal. Rptr. 836 (1974)] receipt of additional evidence at the trial level would be inappropriate since the reviewing body on certiorari may not substitute its judgment for that of the administrative body. Sullivan, From Kroner to Fasano: Judicial Review of Land Use Regulation in Oregon, 10 WILLAMETTE L. J. 358, 370–74 (1974). This should result in speedier judicial processing and appeal, as well as eliminating the hazard of a referendum for the developer of low-income housing. City of Eastlake v. Forest City Enterprises, Inc., 426 U.S. 668, 693 (1976) (dissent of Stevens, J.); West v. City of Portage, 392 Mich. 458, 221 N.W.2d 303 (1974); Leonard v. City of Bothell, 87 Wash. 2d 847, 557 P.2d 1306 (1976).

40. For a detailed analysis of the utilization of the hearing examiner in zoning and land use administration, see R. FISHMAN, HOUSING FOR ALL UNDER LAW at 287–303 (1978).

assure compliance.[41] Two examples in the federal courts will illustrate the problems. Federal court cases in the seventies pertaining to housing revolved around two specific and highly separate problems in American society. The first involved the invalidation of efforts by the federal and local governments under Title VI of the Civil Rights Act of 1964 and Title VIII of the Civil Rights Act of 1968 to build all subsidized housing in existing racially impacted areas, thus furthering segregation.[42] In the famous *Gautreaux* litigation, begun in the 1960s, not one single unit of housing had been built in non-impacted areas of Chicago despite thirteen years of vigorous litigation with innumerable court orders.[43] Similarly, in specific attacks on suburban cities' refusals to zone low- and moderate-income housing projects, the results have been equally ineffective. The U.S. Supreme Court has required that a showing of "intent" to discriminate, rather than "discriminatory impact," be shown in suits brought under the fourteenth amendment.[44] Even where a blatant intentional violation is shown, as where a suburban city was incorporated to block a multi-family federal subsidized project authorized by St. Louis County, the litigation has dragged on for years and the housing is yet to be built.[45]

---

41. Federal litigation was commenced in 1966 in an effort to prohibit the Chicago Housing Authority's racially unconstitutional site selection and tenant assignment procedures which resulted in a judgment against the CHA in 1969. After years of frustration in enforcing the judgment, the U.S. District Court appointed a U.S. magistrate to serve as a special master. The role of the master was to determine the precise causes of the five year delay in implementing the orders of the Court and to recommending a plan that would expedite compliance with these orders. Gautreaux v. Chicago Housing Authority, 384 F. Supp. 37 (N.D. Ill. 1974). As of 1980, the plaintiffs in the case were still awaiting substantial compliance with the Court's orders and requested the appointment of a receiver for the Chicago Housing Authority. *See* A. Freilich, Gautreaux v. The Chicago Housing Authority, A Study in Implementation (May 1980) (unpublished paper, Public Affairs Dep't, at the University of Chicago).

42. Shannon v. Dep't of HUD, 436 F. Supp. 809 (3d Cir. 1970); Gautreaux v. Chicago Housing Auth., 503 F.2d 930 (7th Cir. 1974); El Cortez Heights Ass'n v. Tucson Housing Auth., 10 Ariz. App. 132, 457 P.2d 294 (1969); Mahaley v. Cuyahoga Metropol. Hous. Auth., 500 F.2d 1087 (6th Cir. 1974); Crow v. Brown, 457 F.2d 788 (5th Cir. 1972).

43. In Hills v. Gautreaux, 425 U.S. 284 (1976), the U.S. Supreme Court affirmed the federal district court decision mandating a metropolitan remedy for the dispersal of federally subsidized housing units to avoid minority concentration. A detailed summary of the litigation in Hills v. Gautreaux is contained in R. FISHMAN, HOUSING FOR ALL UNDER LAW at appendix 3 (1978).

44. Village of Arlington Heights v. Metropolitan Hous. Dev. Corp., 429 U.S. 252 (1977); Washington v. Davis, 426 U.S. 229 (1976).

45. In the suit brought by the United States, the Court held that the incorporation of the city with the immediate aim of blocking a housing project with enactment of a single-family zoning ordinance had a racially discriminatory

Faced with these difficulties, it is clear that individual and legislative remedies prove to be more satisfactory. Armed with the awesome power of section 1982 suits and Title VIII of the Housing Act of 1968, black suburbanization through the purchase of existing housing has proven to be far more efficacious.[46] Legislative requirements, built into the community development block grant program to require local, suburban, and area housing opportunity plans, have been somewhat successful[47] despite lack of standing in central cities to enforce the requirements.[48] State housing programs to eliminate suburban zoning restrictions have been only partially effective,[49] but

---

effect. United States v. City of Black Jack, 508 F.2d 1179 (8th Cir. 1974), cert. denied, 422 U.S. 1042, rehearing denied, 423 U.S. 584 (1975). Although the city's zoning action was held invalid, the delay from the adjudication of the question rendered the housing project economically infeasible. The plaintiff, Park View Heights Corp., was the nonprofit sponsor of the § 236 project and prospective residents, suing as a class, then sought damages and equitable relief from the city. That action led to a consent judgment under which the city agreed to pay $450,000 in damages to the sponsor (in effect, buying the land). The consent decree barred further damages but left open further equitable relief. In 1976, the plaintiffs moved for relief directing the city to build at least 108 multi-racial, moderate-income, housing units to replace the last project. The trial court found that there was no causal connection between the city's discriminatory action and the demise of the project, Park View Heights Corp. v. City of Black Jack, 454 F. Supp. 1223 (E.D. Mo. 1978). This was reversed by the Court of Appeals, which held that the city must provide affirmative housing opportunities to overcome the past discrimination. 605 F.2d 1033 (8th Cir. 1979), cert. denied, _____ U.S. _____, 100 S. Ct. 1081 (1980). The city, which had run up a large legal bill and had been forced to buy an unwanted parcel, is now confronted by the probability that a § 8 development will take the place of the frustrated moderate-income § 236 project and will in all probability be occupied by a lower-income group.

46. Jones v. Alfred H. Mayer Co., 392 U.S. 409 (1968).

47. The Housing and Community Dev. Act of 1974 mandates an affirmative duty to plan for the community's low-cost housing needs. 42 U.S.C. § 5304 (a) (4) (A) (1977). The housing assistance plan required in the local application for the funds should include the locality's fair share of the region's housing needs. 24 C.F.R. § 570.303 (b) (2).

48. City of Hartford v. Town of Glastonbury, 561 F.2d 1032 (2d Cir. 1977).

49. The most famous of the programs was the establishment by New York of the Urban Development Corporation with the power to override local zoning and planning in the establishment of low- and moderate-income housing. See Floyd v. New York State Urban Dev. Corp., 33 N.Y.2d 1, 300 N.E.2d 704, 347 N.Y.S.2d 161 (1973). When the Urban Development Corporation attempted to utilize these powers in Westchester County to create substantial numbers of low-income units, the legislature withdrew the power. 1973 N.Y. Laws ch. 446, § 3. Another state program involves the Massachusetts Zoning Appeals Law, MASS. GEN. LAWS ANN. ch. 40B, §§ 20–23 (West 1973), which allows a state override of local zoning to assure that 1.5% of a locality's land area is utilized for low- and moderate-income housing. The act was upheld as constitutional in Board of Appeals v. Housing Appeals Comm., 294 N.E.2d 393 (Mass. 1973). The passive nature of the Act, however, has indicated that

mandatory comprehensive planning to include housing seems far more successful.[50] The greatest achievement, however, was the realization in the state courts that individual localities may too often yield to temptation and consider only their own territorial or parochial needs and not those of the region. Early decisions began to formulate "regional" standards that zoning had to meet, although these decisions were primarily utilized negatively to exclude unwarranted regional effects rather than affirmatively to achieve regional needs.[51]

The breakthrough, however, came with the formulation of the innovative concept of "regional general welfare" as an aspect of substantive due process. Since the state has delegated its power to

---

it has been a failure. Austin, Yoshida & O'Connor, *Subsidized Housing and the Anti-Snob Zoning Act*, in The Land Use Controversy in Massachusetts: Case Studies and Policy Options 111–123 (L. Susskind ed. 1975). Local attempts to mandate that developers build a percentage of low-income housing, known as "inclusionary" zoning, have generally not been favorably accepted in the courts. Board of Supervisors v. DeGroff, 214 Va. 235, 198 S.E.2d 600 (1973); Middlesex and Boston St. Ry. Co. v. Newton, 371 Mass. 849, 359 N.E.2d 1279 (1977); Oakwood at Madison, Inc. v. Township of Madison, 72 N.J. 481, 371, A.2d 1192 (1977) (expressing doubts as to the validity of bonuses awarded developers for price concessions to build low- and moderate-income housing as not being related to land use considerations). Similar reservations have been expressed by the British courts. *See* R. v. Hillington London Borough Council *ex. p.* Royco Homes Ltd. [1974] 2 W.L.R. 805, 2 All E.R. 643, in which the court held that a planning permission could not be conditioned on the developer furnishing a percentage of low-income housing since such a requirement is "ultra-vires" the planning act. *See* Brown, Garner, Leach & Moore, *The Hillington (Royce) Case*, J. Plan & Env'tl L. (Sept. 1974) at 507.

50. Cal. [Gov't] Code § 65860(a) (West Supp. 1980), requires every city and county to adopt a general plan that must contain certain mandatory elements including a housing element. The housing element must make adequate provision for the housing needs of all economic segments of the community. *See also* the Florida Local Government Comprehensive Planning Act of 1975, Fla. Stat. ch. 75–257 (1975); Minn. Stat. §§ 462.355, 473.121, and 473.175 (West Supp. 1980) (local governments within the Minneapolis-St. Paul Region are required to prepare comprehensive plans including mandatory housing elements). The American Law Institute's Model Land Development Code does recognize the need for the state to declare "areas of state concern" and to provide for state review of "developments of regional impact" which includes housing for low- and moderate-income persons as one of the categories so designated. A Model Land Development Code § 1–301 (4) (a-c). *See* Fox, *A Tentative Guide to the American Law Institute's Model Land Development Code*, 6 Urb. Law. 928, 945 (1974) (also reprinted in this anthology). The Code, however, does not mandate that a locality adopt a comprehensive plan.

51. For an early formulation of the "negative" regional factors test, *see* Freilich & Bass, *Exclusionary Zoning: Suggested Litigation Approaches*, 3 Urb. Law. 344, 363–373 (1971); Huttig v. City of Richmond Heights, 373 S.W.2d 833 (Mo. 1963); Wrigley Properties, Inc. v. City of Ladue, 369 S.W.2d 397 (Mo. 1963); Township of Riverdale v. Town of Orangetown, 403 F.2d 684 (2d Cir. 1964). The primary emphasis of the negative test was the exclusion of a use because of its incompatibility with the land use of surrounding municipalities, rather than the inclusion of a use because of regional needs.

the municipality, an exercise of zoning authority must be in accordance with the needs and welfare of the state as a whole rather than limited to the territorial confines of the jurisdiction itself. Thus regional interests, including primarily housing needs, must be fully reflected in the decisions of the localities within our fragmented metropolises,[52] although the doctrine has also been extended to the consideration of environmental and energy concerns.[53]

B. *Regional General Welfare*

The concept of regional general welfare on the state level has taken on two basic schools of thought. The first school believes that the zoning of a developing municipality must incorporate a mandatory "fair share" of low- and moderate-income housing. The second school believes that regional considerations are only one factor when deciding zoning and planning issues. The "fair share" idea was best exemplified by the landmark decision of *Southern Burlington County NAACP v. Township of Mount Laurel*,[54] which is ranked third in overall state land use planning decisions.[55] The New Jersey Supreme Court held that a developing community must use zoning to make realistically possible an appropriate variety and choice of housing to low- and moderate-income families. The municipality had to meet the "fair share"[56] of the present and prospective regional housing needs. The court put both an affirmative obligation on municipalities to insure a variety of housing opportunities and a heavy burden in showing particular circumstances when such obligations are not met.[57] The Mount Laurel area was almost 65 percent undeveloped with the other 35 percent containing extensive residential development. The residential area zoning required a minimum lot size of one-half acre and excluded townhouses, most apartments, and other

---

52. Southern Burlington NAACP v. Township of Mt. Laurel, 67 N.J. 151, 336 A.2d 713 (1975); Surrick v. Zoning Hearing Bd., 476 Pa. 182, 382 A.2d 105 (1977); Berenson v. Town of New Castle, 38 N.Y.2d 102, 341 N.E.2d 236, 378 N.Y.S. 672 (1975); Associated Homebuilders v. City of Livermore, 18 Cal. 3d 582, 557 P.2d 473, 135 Cal. Rptr. 345 (1976).

53. Save a Valuable Environment v. City of Bothell, 89 Wash. 862, 576 P.2d 401 (1978); Glenview Dev. Co. v. Franklin Township, 164 N.J. Super. 563, 397 A.2d 384 (1978).

54. 67 N.J. 151, 336 A.2d 713, *appeal dismissed, cert. denied*, 423 U.S. 808 (1975).

55. Dozier & Hagman, *Ranking Land Development and Environmental Cases and Courts*, 4 ENVT'L COM. 4 (Aug. 1978).

56. Other communities now also use the "fair share" test. *See* Surrick v. Zoning Hearing Bd., 476 Pa. 182, 382 A.2d 105 (1977).

57. Crawford & Yokley, *Land Use Planning and Zoning*, 7 URB. LAW. 727 (1975).

multi-family dwellings. The homes in Mount Laurel appealed primarily to middle-income families and the apartments that were built were accompanied by limitations on family size and high rent schedules.[58] The court found that the township was attempting to protect its local tax structure by excluding categories of housing contrary to the general public welfare. The "general welfare" concept requires zoning regulations to reflect the "fair share" of the housing needs for all categories of people. The court stated that these needs extend beyond the township's boundaries to the regional and state level.[59]

As later cases revealed, the "fair share" concept did not embrace fully developed communities or require premature growth into non-developed areas. In *Pascack Association, Ltd. v. Mayor and Council of Washington Township*,[60] the New Jersey Supreme Court held that communities included under *Mount Laurel* are those that are developing, and those which are fully developed or almost fully developed were excluded. In *Glenview Development Co. v. Franklin Township*,[61] the court held that fair share housing requirements should not be made applicable to rural, agricultural, or nondeveloped communities so as to prematurely stimulate growth. The court also found that exclusionary density requirements, when removed, do not always provide housing for low- and moderate-income families. The New Jersey courts have upheld such density ordinances where developers were simply proposing to increase the value of their developments and not producing low- and moderate-income housing. *Oakwood at Madison, Inc. v. Township of Madison*[62] modified the *Mount Laurel* decision by no longer requiring affirmative measures to provide housing. The newly adopted standard stated that "a municipality need only modify its zoning ordinance so that land will be available on which a private developer could if he wanted to, build housing at the least cost."[63] It seems that the New Jersey courts are now beginning to realize the true economic ramifications of *Mount Laurel:* that invalidating exclusionary zoning ordinances does not magically produce adequate housing for all members of a community. The many economic, practical, and social issues must be viewed

---

58. Bagne, Curtin, Gunter, Werner, Gorlick, Goldner, Spokes, Abrams, Crawford, Solomon, Sullivan & Gehrke, *Land Use Planning and Zoning*, 8 URB. LAW. 747, 751–52 (1976).

59. *Id.*

60. 74 N.J. 470, 378 A.2d 6 (1977).

61. 164 N.J. Super. 563, 397 A.2d 384 (1978).

62. 72 N.J. 481, 371 A.2d 1192 (1977).

63. Rose, *Myths and Misconceptions of Exclusionary Zoning Litigation*, 8 REAL EST. L.J. 99, 123 (1979).

together, and solutions to housing problems should be found after new practices in zoning take the initial step.

The second school of thought in the regional general welfare concept is that regional needs are only one factor in considering whether a zoning ordinance is valid. Here, contrary to the possible fixed quotas of the "fair share" idea, the requirements are much more flexible. Accordingly, the state of New York did not follow New Jersey's lead when it decided *Berenson v. Town of New Castle*.[64] The court decided that for a zoning ordinance to be valid, it must provide needed housing opportunities. The test required (1) a properly balanced and well-ordered plan for the community and (2) that consideration be given to regional needs. In one respect *Berenson* did not go as far as *Mount Laurel* and require New Castle to provide a "fair share" of housing. In fact, if neighboring communities are meeting regional needs, New York would allow exclusionary practices in that municipality's ordinances. However, they went farther than *Mount Laurel* in requiring that a town board must consciously consider the regional needs of the area before excluding certain types of multifamily housing.[65] The California courts in *Associated Homebuilders v. City of Livermore*[66] also require that consideration be given to regional welfare if a municipal ordinance has an impact on the region. The state of Washington in *Save a Valuable Environment v. City of Bothell*[67] invalidated a municipal land use ordinance which rezoned farmland to accommodate a shopping center. The court found illegal spot zoning and failure to serve the welfare of the regional community. As can be seen by the efforts of the state courts, their fight to curb exclusionary zoning practices has been a massive one. The attempt of state legislatures is exemplified by Oregon's practices in "Statewide Land Use Planning in Oregon with Special Emphasis on Housing Issues,"[68] written by Terry Morgan and John Shonkwiler.

C. *Federal Intervention*

During the seventies, exclusive use zones, rather than the traditional all higher inclusive use zones, left their mark amid many constitutional attacks. In *Village of Belle Terre v. Boraas*,[69] the Supreme

---

64. 38 N.Y.2d 102, 341 N.E.2d 236; 378 N.Y.S. 672 (1975), *rehearing,* 67 A.D.2d 506, 415 N.Y.S.2d 669 (1979).
65. Berenson, 415 N.Y.S.2d at 672.
66. 18 Cal. 3d 582, 557 P.2d 473, 135 Cal. Rptr. 345 (1976).
67. 89 Wash. 2d 862, 576 P.2d 401 (1978).
68. 11 URB. LAW. 1 (1979) (also reprinted in this anthology).
69. 416 U.S. 1 (1974).

Court upheld an ordinance that permitted only single-family dwellings and prohibited more than two unrelated people from living together. The Court based its findings on the premise that promotion of family values and lifestyles was a valid zoning purpose. "The police power is not confined to elimination of filth, stench, and unhealthy places. It is ample to lay out zones where family values, youth values, and the blessings of quiet seclusion and clean air make the area a sanctuary for people."[70] The boundary as to how far municipalities could go in this regard was laid in *Moore v. City of East Cleveland.*[71] Here the Court held a zoning ordinance unconstitutional because it defined a "single-family" as only the husband and wife, unmarried children of either, and the spouses' parents. The Court found that such a restrictive ordinance violated substantive due process and intruded too deeply into family life.[72] The present federal guidelines seem to allow municipalities to bar three or more unrelated individuals in one house; however, groups related by blood, adoption, or marriage must be allowed to stay together.[73]

Racial exclusionary zoning practices brought much heated debate and received much attention during the decade of the seventies. *United States v. City of Black Jack, Missouri*[74] was one important example of a suit brought under Title VIII of the Civil Rights Act of 1968. The Eighth Circuit found that the city's zoning ordinance was in violation of federal law because it did not allow construction of townhouses for low- and moderate-income families. Even though the lower federal court found no discriminatory effect or motive, the circuit court found that the effect of the ordinance was that of excluding minorities. One year later, a community in the neighboring state of Illinois found itself under similar racial attack. In *Village of Arlington Heights v. Metropolitan Housing Development Corporation,*[75] the U.S. Supreme Court held that zoning laws are not unconstitutional simply because they tend to keep out minorities and low-income groups. There could be racial impact without a finding of unconstitutionality. Arlington Heights is one of the many suburbs of Chicago. The municipality's planning board denied the application of a housing developer to build a federally assisted housing project

70. *Id.* at 9.
71. 431 U.S. 494 (1977).
72. *Id.* at 502.
73. Curtin & Shirk, *Land Use Planning and Zoning,* 10 URB. LAW. 441, 445 (1978).
74. 508 F.2d 1179 (8th Cir. 1974), *cert. denied,* 422 U.S. 1042 (1975).
75. 429 U.S. 252 (1977).

for racially integrated low- and moderate-income families.[76] The Court found a basis for its decision in *Washington v. Davis*[77] when it said "official action will not be held unconstitutional solely because it results in a racially disproportionate impact."[78] A pattern has to form because impact alone is not determinative. The *Washington v. Davis* case was decided after *Black Jack* but prior to *Arlington Heights*. The burden of proof does not shift from the plaintiffs to the municipality since there must be a showing of racially discriminatory intent or purpose. The Court requires other evidence such as disproportionate impact, the historical background, specific antecedent events, departure from normal procedures, or contemporary statements of the decision makers[79] to prove a fourteenth amendment equal protection violation. No additional evidence was shown in *Arlington* and the Court upheld the ordinance as far as due process and equal protection arguments were concerned. However, the case was remanded to determine if Fair Housing Act requirements would affect the zoning classification. The Seventh Circuit established that under the Fair Housing Act, criteria could be imposed that would fall short of discriminatory intent when a Title VIII allegation occurs.[80] The end result is that the Constitution is not violated unless there is clear discriminatory intent. However, federal legislatures and the states are free to impose more stringent rules to discourage racially biased exclusionary practices if they feel the necessity.

The legal right of a person or group to challenge a land use ordinance in a judicial forum is probably the single most important preliminary step in any zoning controversy. In comparison, the forums are generally less restrictive on the state level than on the federal level. For example, in *Mount Laurel*,[81] New Jersey broke with established precedent and opened its courts to plaintiffs not actually owning the property in controversy. The court held that those who could claim a deprivation of housing opportunities resulting from restrictive municipal land use regulations had standing. The various state standing rules during the seventies fill an entire spectrum ranging

---

76. Curtin & Shirk, *Land Use Planning and Zoning*, 9 URB. LAW. 724, 733–34 (1977) [hereinafter cited as *Land Use Planning and Zoning* (1977)].
77. 426 U.S. 279 (1976).
78. *Id.* at 283.
79. *Land Use Planning and Zoning* (1977) at 734.
80. Metropolitan Hous. Dev. Corp. v. Village of Arlington Heights, 558 F.2d 1283 (7th Cir. 1977).
81. 67 N.J. 151, 336 A.2d 713, *appeal dismissed, cert. denied*, 423 U.S. 808 (1975).

from restrictive to liberal, however, the trend seems to be the opening of courtroom doors to more persons than ever before.

The federal standing cases during the seventies seemed to follow another path. Even though both state and federal jurisdictions require that the plaintiff (1) have a personal stake in the outcome or injury in fact and (2) they are within the zone of interests protected by the statute,[82] recent federal cases reflect an increased judicial scrutiny of standing for zoning challenges.[83] In *Warth v. Seldin*,[84] a group consisting of members of minority groups who were excluded from living in Pennfield, New York; a taxpayer association from both Rochester, New York and Pennfield; local home builders, and a local housing council were denied standing in federal court. The minority group lacked standing because they could show no causal relation between the zoning ordinance and their inability to gain housing. The taxpayers were denied standing because they could not show personal injury and both the home builders and council were also refused because they could show no denial of any proposed developments. The Supreme Court found there could be no standing without injury in fact, stating the plaintiffs could not meet the "zone of interest" standard. Later that same year, the Ninth Circuit in *Construction Industry Association of Sonoma County v. City of Petaluma*[85] held that building contractors could not assert right to travel violations for unknown third parties. The *Petaluma* court reversed a decision holding that a five-year zoning plan violated the fundamental right to travel by limiting the natural growth of population. Petaluma only issued five hundred development-unit permits annually. The court found that protecting the small town character and preserving open space was a legitimate government interest, and that the plaintiff builders did not meet the "zone of interest" requirements for standing. The trends of both *Warth* and *City of Petaluma* reflect the strictness of the federal courts in the area of standing and it seems that exclusionary zoning will continue to receive the intense scrutiny it does now.

D. *The Future of Exclusionary Zoning*

The basic lessons of the decade seem to be in the nature of caveats avoiding singular and all-embracing solutions to societal problems. It

---

82. Data Processing Serv. v. Camp, 397 U.S. 150 (1970); Sierra Club v. Morton, 405 U.S. 727 (1972).

83. *Land Use Planning and Zoning* (1977) at 776.

84. 422 U.S. 490 (1975).

85. 522 F.2d 897 (9th Cir. 1975).

is important, for socio-economic purposes, that zoning be put into proper perspective. First, all zoning by its very nature is, in some form, exclusionary. What we should be concerned with is zoning that has racial overtones or is designed by intent or effect to keep out low-income groups. Economic segregation should constitute a suspect classification particularly where occasioned through an exercise of the police power. Exclusionary zoning has gained a negative reputation because it has traditionally been thought of as an evil that must be thwarted at all costs. Yet against the backdrop of socio-economic exclusion in the suburbs it is the felt necessity of planners to encourage middle-income families to remain in or move back to the cities in an effort to promote vitalization of urban areas which would otherwise be lost to decay.[86] Failure to do so would result in housing, schools, facilities, and services declining even further with the breakdown of the municipal tax structure. The purpose and effect of present national policy is not simply to keep people out of the suburbs, but to keep them in the cities where they are vitally needed. The cities, suburbs, and agricultural land would all suffer tremendously if no zoning or planning were allowed to preserve aesthetic, environmental, and cultural features of a community.[87]

One must remember that housing is just one aspect of a host of problems confronting cities. Inflation makes it nearly impossible for low- and moderate-income families to acquire housing without government subsidies. It is the role of the government to make available land to accommodate a fair share of the housing and provide the necessary subsidies. Housing for such income groups is not cheap housing and it cannot be without adequate services and facilities. The impression of low-income housing is housing without adequate sewers, plumbing, or electricity, missing toilet seats, no grass or shrubbery, high crime, and an inadequate school system. The need for these social, physical, and environmental necessities is even more imperative in low- and moderate-income neighborhoods and this need must be met.

Suburbs cannot become single-family domains. The elderly, singles, and young married couples need housing too, and the need should be mixed with a selection of housing types. Inflation and its effects should stimulate diverse housing types. For example, new multi-fam-

---

86. For an excellent discussion on the necessity of exclusionary zoning, *see* Rose, *Myths and Misconceptions of Exclusionary Zoning Litigation*, 8 REAL EST. L.J. 99 (1979).

87. Herman v. Parker, 348 U.S. 26 (1954); Village of Belle Terre v. Boraas, 416 U.S. 1 (1974).

ily duplex and fourplex units which keep costs down should be blended in with single-family dwellings. However, localities must be allowed to adopt restrictive practices where they have urban sprawl, loss of agricultural land, and fiscal problems. To ban all restrictive zoning would in effect throw the baby out with the bath water. National policy dictates that cities must be saved, agricultural land preserved, and uneconomic sprawl halted; therefore, urban planning cannot be arrested simply because some of its effects impact on housing. Restrictive zoning is not necessarily exclusionary. What is exclusionary is the intent to keep people out simply because of their color, nationality, or economic status in life.

The decade began with a concern to give minorities their fair share of this country's affluence coming out of the sweeping reforms of the 1960's. Indeed we seemed like a rich society and the only apparent reason for restrictive zoning was to exclude. Realizing, however, that we are a limited society with dwindling natural resources and many pressing needs, places us in a dilemma concerning the exclusionary zoning question which is not clearly and neatly resolvable. The federal courts have taken a too simplistic "intent versus effect" approach which relates too far over to the police power side. The state courts, however, are learning to balance the problems by requiring comprehensive plans and placing issues into a regional setting. Exclusionary zoning practices are a legitimate concern, however, it is only one of the major crises confronting our society. A comprehensive regional approach must provide the balance needed so that we can deal with these multi-faceted problems as we move on to the eighties.

III. Procedural Reform

A. *Introduction*

The seventies witnessed major innovations in the administration of land use as well as in the substantive expansion of zoning power. The lack of procedural safeguards in zoning use has finally been confronted by a combination of new techniques and policies on both the state and federal level. The traditional view of zoning as a legislative function is a result of state enabling statutes with few procedural standards. In response to this problem farsighted cases, such as *Fasano v. Board of County Commissioners*,[88] offer many procedural

---

88. 264 Or. 574, 507 P.2d 23 (1973).

reforms. In the future, the process will need even more stimulus. The American Law Institute's Model Land Development Code has incorporated many of the newly conceived procedural reforms. Cyril A. Fox, Jr., in his article, "A Tentative Guide to the American Law Institute's Proposed Model Land Development Code,"[89] discusses many of the new safeguards such as notice requirements, written findings of fact and law, and quasi-judicial type hearings. Fred Bosselman, George Raymond, and Richard Persico add useful insight in their article, "Some Observations on the American Law Institute's Model Land Development Code."[90] Both articles give novice and expert alike a useful background to this major milestone in procedural reform.

The decade of the seventies will be noted for its vast improvements in the administration of land use controls including the important developments of procedural safeguards for discretionary zoning decisions, the increasing use of hearing examiners, and the decentralization of land use decision making. In the area of procedural safeguards, the California courts in *Topanga Association for a Scenic Community v. County of Los Angeles*[91] required that administrative agencies must render findings sufficient to enable all parties to determine whether and on what basis they should seek review. An adequate record is now required and must be provided to the reviewing court, giving the judge a basis for the board's action.[92] The judiciary now has expanded its role in reviewing administrative decision making and the demand for a full record allows the scrutiny of agency findings to the fullest degree.

Due to the ever increasing sophistication of the regulatory process there has been a virtual "explosion" in the use of permits, variances, and special-use zoning.[93] The length and delay of processing such requests is rapidly taking its effect in the form of increased housing costs. One major innovation to alleviate slow and inefficient administration of applications is the growing use of zoning hearing examiners. Many of the responsibilities of a local legislative body, board of appeals, and planning commission can be delegated to the hearing examiner, thus enabling the holding of quasi-judicial hearings on

---

89. 6 URB. LAW. 928 (1974) (also reprinted in this anthology).
90. 8 URB. LAW. 474 (1976) (also reprinted in this anthology).
91. 11 Cal. 3d 506, 113 Cal. Rptr. 836 (1974).
92. *Id.* at 840.
93. F. BOSSELMAN, D. FEURER & C. SIEMON, THE PERMIT EXPLOSION (1976).

applications for variances, special-use permits, and single parcel re-zonings.[94] The examiner forwards the facts and his recommendations to the official governing body for its final decision. The role which the hearing examiner plays in a community can be expanded to fit the area's need and the amount of funds available to finance such a system. The advantages of using the hearing examiner in a quasi-judicial type atmosphere are the fulfillment of due process notice requirements, a more formal presentation of evidence and arguments by interested parties, the use of factual findings, a written determination of the basis of the decision, and an accurate record. Most important is the reduction of the council's workload in evaluating rezoning matters because of the refinement by the hearing examiner of the determinative issues.[95]

Citizen participation in the land use administration system is also being recognized as an effective means of handling neighborhood rezoning decisions. Tasks which may be included in such a decentralization of decision making range from attending general public hearings to the establishment of institutionalized advisory boards that address such issues as subdivisions, zoning review, neighborhood planning, historic preservation, and the development of central business districts.[96] While groups may be given actual authority, the political reluctance of city councils to turn over "power" and their lack of confidence in community group proficiency, usually results in the creation of only advisory roles. A growing realization that the comprehensive plan establishes broad goals, objectives, and programs while utilizing community and area plans for determination of neighborhood issues is fostering this movement.

These three approaches serve to improve the administration and application of land use control. Of all reforms, however, the most critical is that of recasting the rezoning process affecting individual parcels of land from a legislative to a quasi-judicial function. The legislative categorization serves to obstruct meaningful judicial review. The existing process tends to mask the problems of exclusionary practices, parochialism, poor planning, and individual bias. A change to an administrative or quasi-judicial process will assure adequate review by the courts and is the beginning of a trend to eliminate abuses.

---

94. R. FISHMAN, HOUSING FOR ALL UNDER LAW at 290 (1978).
95. *Id.* at 302.
96. *Id.* at 305.

B. *Zoning Referenda and the* Fasano *Rule*

Rezoning referenda and initiative is the practice of referring zoning measures to the voters for approval or rejection. This principle is premised upon the democratic principle that the people of a community should be allowed to approve or initiate legislative acts. The determination of a municipality to use the initiative or referendum is based on political, socio-economic, and legal considerations. The major issues which have created the most controversy are whether the enactment of zoning or rezoning is an administrative or legislative function, and whether the processes of planning are stifled, particularly by the initiative.

The traditional view of zoning and rezoning is that such acts are deemed legislative and therefore carry a presumption of validity[97] which may be overturned only upon a showing that the legislative body acted totally arbitrarily or capriciously. This "fairly debatable" test was first expounded by the Supreme Court in *Village of Euclid v. Ambler Realty Co.*[98] and places a tremendous burden upon the opponent of the legislative action. A recent illustration can be seen in *Board of County Commissioners, Hillsborough County v. Ralston.*[99]

> Judicial authority to order zoning change is limited to those circumstances in which the maintenance of the existing classification is arbitrary, capricious, confiscatory in its effect: in short, unconstitutional. The basic authority to zone lies with . . . (the) commissioners, and so long as their prescribed limitations are fairly debatable, we are powerless to intervene.[100]

This traditional view of zoning should be viewed in light of the Supreme Court's recent reaffirmation of local sovereignty. In *Young v. American Mini Theatres*[101] the court allowed Detroit to regulate X-rated movie theaters even against first amendment attack. Various urban planners and real estate experts gave findings that such establishments contributed to neighborhood deterioration. The Court accorded high respect to the city's interest in preserving the character of its neighborhoods and the quality of urban life. The Court has resolved to grant cities flexibility in solving their urban problems.

---

97. Fasano v. Board of County Comm'rs, 264 Or. 574, 507 P.2d 23, 26 (1973).

98. 272 U.S. 365, 388 (1926): "If the validity of the legislative classification for zoning purposes be *fairly debatable,* the legislative judgment must be allowed to control." (Emphasis added.) *See* Board of County Comm'rs, v. Ralston, 284 So. 2d 456 (Fla. App. 1973).

99. 284 So. 2d at 456.

100. *Id.* at 457.

101. 427 U.S. 50 (1976).

The result of this reaffirmation of local sovereignty has threatening potential, for such power may also be used to further parochial interests and practice exclusion.[102]

In our look at the top ten land use planning and development cases we find that *Fasano v. Board of County Commissioners of Washington County*[103] is ranked sixth. It is a tribute to the state of Oregon which is now considered one of the leaders in finding solutions to urban law problems. The decision provides a rational basis for judicial review of zoning, holding that rezoning specific pieces of property is no longer a legislative function but a judicial one.[104] The Oregon Supreme Court removed the legislative cloak of presumed validity and made a marked departure from the majority view. In *Fasano* the Board of County Commissioners approved a zoning change from single-family residential to a Planned Residential according to a planned unit development (PUD) type ordinance. The ordinance was of the "floating zone" variety and was passed after adoption of the county's comprehensive plan. The zone change allowed the erecting of mobile home parks which was contested by adjoining property owners. The trial court reversed the board's order and the decision was affirmed by the court of appeals.

The Oregon Court of Appeals, with several jurisdictions following suit,[105] developed a new approach in handling rezoning matters. The application or amendment of a zoning ordinance to a specific piece of property, affecting a limited number of people and based on contested facts, results in an administrative or quasi-judicial function rather than a legislative function. Subsequently, the court held that the passage of the original comprehensive plan and zoning ordinance is not administrative but that narrowly confined zoning amendments are. The original plan is legislative because it affects the entire community, whereas rezoning usually affects only an individual parcel

---

102. *See* City of Eastlake v. Forest City Enterprises, Inc., 426 U.S. 668 (1976).
103. 264 Or. 574, 507 P.2d 23 (1973).
104. The characterization of "judicial" is that of the Oregon Supreme Court. Ordinarily actions of a legislative body which address a specific set of facts and issuance of a license, approval or permit are denominated "quasi-judicial," or "administrative." *See* Jehovah's Witnesses v. Mullen, 214 Or. 281, 292, 330 P.2d 5 (1958); Chrobuck v. Snohomish County, 78 Wash. 2d 884, 480 P.2d 489, 495–96 (1971); Ward v. Village of Skokie, 26 Ill. 2d 415, 186 N.E.2d 529, 533 (1962); Belclaire Holding Corp. v. Klingher, 28 App. Div. 2d 689, 280 N.Y.S.2d 942 (1967).
105. Fasano v. Board of County Comm'rs, 264 Or. 574, 507 P.2d 23 (1973).

thus approximating a licensing, franchising, or administrative task.[106] A further reason for interpreting zoning board decisions as administrative or quasi-judicial rather than legislative is the resultant increase in due process safeguards accorded judicial type proceedings.[107]

Even less stringent alternatives to *Fasano*[108] end up rejecting in some form the proposition that the judicial review of rezoning is limited to "whether the change is arbitrary or capricious" by rejecting the presumption of validity. The count in *Fasano* further established that the power to zone is conditioned upon consistency with the comprehensive plan.[109] There must be both a public need for the zoning change and that need must be served by changing the zone of that particular property as opposed to alternative property.[110] The burden of proof is on the party seeking the change, and the greater the proposed change, the greater the burden of proof.[111] In the *Fasano* ruling, these burdens of proof were not met and the lower court's ruling not to allow the change was affirmed.

The controversy over whether rezoning is an administrative or legislative function was not settled by *Fasano*. The parochial and exclusionary interests of residents of suburban municipalities coupled with reaffirmed local sovereignty provides further reason why *Fasano* reasoning is essential. The threat of the mandatory referendum on the practice of exclusion of subsidized housing was fulfilled in the instance of *City of Eastlake v. Forest City Enterprises, Inc.*[112] The U.S. Supreme Court in this case allowed a mandatory requirement in the city's charter that, after city council approval, all changes to the zoning ordinance must also pass a referendum by 55 percent. In the lower court opinion, the Ohio Supreme Court did not follow *Fasano*'s lead and held that rezoning is a legislative function.[113] It also

---

106. Comment, *Zoning Amendments—The Product of Judicial or Quasi-Judicial Action*, 33 OHIO ST. L.J. 130, 137 (1972). *See also* Dillon Companies, Inc. v. City of Boulder, 183 Colo. 117, 515 P.2d 627 (1973); Fleming v. City of Tacoma, 81 Wash. 2d 292, 502 P.2d 327 (1972).

107. Comment, *supra* note 106.

108. *See* Beaver Gasoline Co. v. Zoning Hearing Bd., 445 Pa. 571, 285 A.2d 501 (1971). Pennsylvania in circumstances of exclusion of uses from a jurisdiction reverses the presumption of validity and places on the municipality the burden of proving that a rational basis exists for the zoning regulation.

109. Fasano, 507 P.2d at 27–30.

110. *Id.*

111. *Id.*

112. 426 U.S. 668 (1976).

113. Forest City Enterprises, Inc. v. City of Eastlake, 41 Ohio St. 2d 187, 324 N.E.2d 740 (1975).

held that the referendum was not a proper delegation of legislative authority and violated the fourteenth amendment's due process clause since the owner could not be assured of a rational decision by voters who had no interest in or knowledge of the property. If Ohio had held that rezoning was an administrative rather than a legislative function, the decision would not have been reversed. Chief Justice Burger said that: "A referendum cannot however be characterized as a delegation of power. [Since] . . . all power derives from the people, . . . the people can reserve to themselves power to deal directly with matters which might otherwise be assigned directly to the legislature."[114]

If it had been characterized as an administrative act, then a referendum would have been an improper delegation of authority. As it stood, the legislative power could rest with the people. The *Eastlake* opinion was laden with praise for the referendum process and its promotion of democracy and afforded referenda presumptive validity.[115]

Eastlake leaves us with several pressing problems and the case itself contains many flaws. A property owner who wishes a zoning change must submit his request to apathetic, disinterested, or biased voters, even though his proposition may conform to the comprehensive plan and already have been approved by the city council. The possibility of arbitrary results was discussed only to the extent that the substantive result of a particular referendum would not be reviewable.[116] The Court failed to address the issue of a mandatory versus a permissive referendum requirement. If every rezoning would require a mandatory referendum, the system would become unwieldly and costly to developers leading to even more exclusionary practices.[117] The dissent in *Eastlake* recognizes the problems of mislabeling an administrative act as legislative. Justice Stevens points out "the obvious difference between the adoption of a comprehensive city-wide plan by legislative action and the decision of particular issues involving specific uses of specific parcels."[118] He believes, as do a growing number of state courts, that the referendum requirement is "manifestly unreasonable."[119] Another aspect of *Eastlake,* which may be more disturbing, is that while many communities utilize new

---

114. 426 U.S. at 672.
115. *Id.* at 670–79.
116. *Id.* at 677.
117. *See* 324 N.E.2d at 748.
118. 426 U.S. at 683.
119. *Id.* at 694.

found authority to deal with a variety of urban problems,[120] the referendum requirement might significantly strengthen the power of local authorities to shirk regional responsibilities and engage in exclusionary housing practices.

Attacks on the referendum procedure have very little chance of success. There is, of course, the duty to consider regional needs;[121] however, a challenge to the substantive result of a referendum based on the misuse of police power would not be successful. *Washington v. Davis*[122] refused to find an equal protection violation based solely on statistical showings of disproportionate impact along racial lines. Adding the Court's reluctance to examine the intent of voters in a referendum,[123] broad-based police power challenges to referenda seem unlikely. For a more in-depth look at the rezoning referenda controversy, see Professor Freilich's comment, *"Fasano v. Board of County Commissioners of Washington County:* Is Rezoning an Administrative or Legislative Function?"[124] The traditions of democracy hold referenda and initiative an essential part of the process. However, they can be used, and have been in cases such as *Eastlake,* to subvert solutions to pressing urban problems and add a democratic gloss to suburban communities' desire to keep out minorities. The local sovereignty approach is a well-intentioned effort to expedite solutions to urban problems, however, there are inherent dangers which must be reconsidered. It would be tragically ironic if at a time local governments are given the tools to deal with urban problems they are also given the means to compound them.

C. *The State and Federal Role in Land Use Planning*

States have traditionally delegated their land use planning powers to local government. The recent recognition of regional needs has made comprehensive planning mandatory in several states and has

---

120. *See* Freilich, Golden v. Town of Ramapo: *Establishing a New Dimension in American Planning Law,* 4 URB. LAW. ix (Summer 1972) (also reprinted in this anthology).

121. *See* Southern Burlington NAACP v. Township of Mt. Laurel, 67 N.J. 151, 336 A.2d 713 (1975), *cert. denied,* 423 U.S. 808 (1975); Township of Williston v. Chesterdale Farms, Inc., 462 Pa. 445, 341 A.2d 466 (1975); Berenson v. Town of New Castle, 38 N.Y.2d 102, 341 N.E.2d 236, 378 N.Y.S. 672 (1975).

122. 426 U.S. 229 (1976).

123. James v. Valtierra, 402 U.S. 137 (1971).

124. Freilich, Fasano v. Board of County Commissioners of Washington County: *Is Rezoning an Administrative or Legislative Function?,* 6 URB. LAW. vii (Winter 1974) (also reprinted in this anthology).

encouraged the development of state regional programs. David Hess, in his article, "Institutionalizing the Revolution: Judicial Reaction to State Land-Use Laws,"[125] discusses the recent involvement of states in growth and shoreland management and the expanding powers of regional agencies. The American Law Institute Model Development Code[126] also encourages a comprehensive plan which would place under state control or review "areas of critical state concern," such as environmentally significant areas, inland wetlands, agricultural lands, areas where major public facilities or investments are present, and developments of regional impact or regional benefit. State or regional growth management policies which provide stability and standards on which to base long range decisions have gained favor by the court. There seems to be forming a judicial presumption of constitutionality of state or regional programs, because all challenged state land use programs have been upheld.[127] Terry Morgan and John Shonkwiler address the adoption of progressive programs on the state level in their article, "Statewide Land Use Planning in Oregon with Special Emphasis on Housing Issues."[128] Here the Land Conservation and Development Commission was established to control, plan, and coordinate all land use in the state. Other states, including California[129] and Massachusetts,[130] have also accepted the regional responsibility doctrine, which has been developed to combat urban sprawl.

On the federal level, the President's Urban and Regional Policy Group (URPG) has recognized the critical issues of urban sprawl, energy, and the environment in their 1978 report.[131] Even though the federal government has been a major contributor to urban sprawl

---

125. 9 URB. LAW. 183 (1977) (also reprinted in this anthology).

126. *See* Fox, *A Tentative Guide to the American Law Institute's Proposed Model Land Development Code,* 6 URB. LAW. 928 (1974); Bosselman, Raymond & Perisco, *Some Observations on the American Law Institute's Model Land Development Code,* 8 URB. LAW. 474 (1976) (both reprinted in this anthology).

127. Colorado—City of Louisville v. District Court, 190 Colo. 33, 543 P.2d 67 (1975); Hawaii—Town v. Land Use Comm'n, 55 Hawaii 538, 524 P.2d 84 (1974); Maine—*In re* Spring Valley Dev., 300 A.2d 736 (1973); Vermont—*In re* Wildlife Wonderland, Inc., 133 Vt. 507, 346 A.2d 645 (1975).

128. 11 URB. LAW. 1 (1979) (also reprinted in this anthology).

129. *See* Urban Development Strategy for California (State Office of Plan. and Research 1977).

130. *See* City and Town Centers: A Program for Growth, The Massachusetts Growth Policy Report (Massachusetts Office of State Plan. 1977).

131. The President's Urban and Regional Policy Group Report, A New Partnership to Conserve America's Communities, III-4 (March 1978) [hereinafter cited as URPG 1978].

through suburban guaranteed loan programs, tax breaks for home-owners, federal highway systems, and other federal agency projects, national studies have encouraged urban planning and the develop-ment of new growth controls.[132] The URPG briefly examined past federal efforts to assist urban areas and found the programs to be piecemeal, without coordination, complicated, and not easily admin-istered. They concluded that many important programs fail to reach the cities or people in distress and encourage sprawl,[133] stating that less than one out of every five federal dollars goes for aid to state and local government.[134] In acknowledgment of the URPG report and based on the premise that it is in the national interest to save and strengthen American cities and urban communities, President Carter announced a community conservation program in his Urban Policy on March 29, 1979. It was not until eight months later that the full impact of a portion of that policy became evident. At that time, the secretary of transportation disapproved completion of a section of an interstate highway around Dayton, Ohio, on which a shopping center had been proposed (thus the "shopping center" policy), citing the Urban Policy as a basis for the decision.[135] The president, in his address delivering his Urban Policy to Congress, described imple-mentation of the policy as a partnership of local, state, and federal government with private industry and citizens. Noting the abrupt swings of policy by the federal government in the past, the president suggested that this policy provided a "consistent" and "coherent" approach. He stated:

> For those who live in our urban areas, the gravest flaw in past Federal policy was not that we failed to spend money, it was that too many of the programs were ineffective and too many that did work had their benefits cancelled by other conflicting Federal and State Activities.[136]

In submitting the policy, President Carter acknowledged that at least 150 changes in existing programs would be required, some needing legislation and others requiring only administrative action.[137] A key

---

132. THE NATIONAL COMMISSION ON URBAN PROBLEMS (the Douglas Com-mission), BUILDING THE AMERICAN CITY; THE ADVISORY COMMISSION ON INTERGOVERNMENTAL RELATIONS (ACIR), URBAN AND RURAL AMERICA, POLICIES FOR FUTURE GROWTH, Document A-32, 1968.
133. URPG 1978, *supra* note 131 at I-66–67.
134. *Id.* at I-67.
135. We gratefully acknowledge the research contained in J. Werholtz, A "Shopping Center" Policy (May 7, 1980) (unpublished article at the Uni-versity of Missouri–Kansas City Law School).
136. Remarks Announcing the Policy, President Jimmy Carter, March 27, 1978.
137. *Id.*

component to the shopping center policy is "a continuing mechanism, . . . to analyze the effects of new federal policies and programs on our communities."[138] That mechanism is entitled Urban and Community Impact Analysis. Regarding that mechanism, the Urban Policy reads:

> I am implementing a process through my Domestic Policy Staff (DPS) and Office of Management and Budget (OMB) to ensure that we do not inadvertently take actions which contradict the goals of the Urban Policy. Each agency submitting a major domestic initiative must include its own urban and community impact analysis. DPS and OMB will review these submissions and will ensure that any anti-urban impacts of proposed Federal policies will be brought to my attention.[139]

To implement the Urban Policy, the president issued four executive orders on August 16, 1978, which have the force and effect of statutes.[140] One of those four executive orders is especially relevant to the shopping center policy: E.O. No. 12074, Urban and Community Impact Analyses. That order established an internal management procedure for identifying aspects of proposed federal policies that may have impact on cities, counties, and other communities. It orders the director of the Office of Management and Budget to develop criteria for identifying major policy proposals to be analyzed, formulate standards regarding the content and format of impact analyses, and establish procedures for the submission and review of such analyses. The director of OMB and the assistant to the president for the Domestic Affairs Policy are to review the analyses.[141] The order also provides that all executive agencies prepare urban and community impact analyses for major policy initiatives as identified by OMB, DPS, or the agencies themselves. Each agency "to the extent permitted by law," shall cooperate with OMB and DPS in their function under the order and comply with the prescribed procedures.[142] The effectiveness of federal governmental policies in land use control is examined and compared to that of Great Britain's in Victor Moore's article, "The Public Control of Land Use: An Anglophile's View."[143] Now that the federal government has begun to change its approach toward effective land use planning and growth

---

138. *Id.*
139. National Urban Policy, President Jimmy Carter (March 27, 1978) (message to Congress).
140. Feliciano v. United States, 297 F. Supp. 1356 (D.P.R. 1969), *aff'd*, 422 F.2d 943 (1st Cir. 1970), *cert. denied*, 400 U.S. 823 (1970).
141. Executive Order 12074, August 16, 1978, 43 FR 36875, § 1-1.
142. *Id.* at § 1-2.
143. 10 URB. LAW. 130 (1978) (also reprinted in this anthology).

management the old inconsistent and fragmented policies may begin
to move in the right direction.

IV. Growth Management

The United States has traditionally been thought of as a place of
seemingly limitless land and resources. However, this abundance is
rapidly disappearing because of the extraordinary loss of rural and
agricultural land to the encroachment of urban sprawl.[144] The conversion of non-urban land is producing many serious effects including diminishment of domestic and export food capacity, destruction
of rural and open space environments, stimulating wasteful expenditure of suburban capital improvements with concomitant high tax
rates, and increased energy and utilization cost. These complex problems have been significantly offset in many communities and metropolitan areas during the decade of the seventies with the development of new and innovative growth management techniques.
Municipal, regional, and state governments now have the knowledge
and the power to deal with urban sprawl, however, the question still
remains: Does our society have the will to pool its resources and
institutional arrangements to solve the problem?

A. *Urbanization*

Most of the national growth in America during the post-war era has
taken place in the urban-rural fringes of major metropolitan areas.
At the same time that moderate- to middle-income white families
developed the economic capacity to seek single-family suburban
homes, the cities suffered increased migration of poor nonwhite
families to our rural areas. Cities became less desirable places to live
because of deterioration, abandonment, high crime, and racially
impacted housing and school systems. The federal government accelerated this process through its various housing, taxation, and
highway policies. Incentives for the construction of low density,
detached single-family housing were provided by federally insured
mortgage money and the many tax advantages of home ownership.[145]
The interstate highway system further provides access to suburban

---

144. Freilich & Davis, *Saving the Land: The Utilization of Modern Techniques of Growth Management to Preserve Rural and Agricultural America*, 13
URB. LAW 27 (1980).

145. Weaver, *National Land Policies—Historic and Emergent*, 12 U.C.L.A.
L. REV. 719, 721 (1965); Grad, *The City Is Here to Stay*, URB. L. ANN. 3,
13. *See also* I.R.C. §§ 163–64 (1954).

areas where land is cheaper for industrial and commercial uses and taxes are lower.[146] The net effect of these centrifugal and centripetal forces was to leave the central city with even more severe housing, educational, and environmental problems while depleting and degrading the important natural land resources in the path of suburban development.

Intelligent reexamination of the philosophy of unlimited growth indicates the direction society must go. Combating urban sprawl by an inward redirection of growth would halt the depopulation of central city areas and would encourage the rehabilitation and revitalization of bypassed city neighborhoods. Preventing sprawl would benefit environmental concerns by leaving open space and not offsetting delicate ecological balances. Energy consumption would be reduced by limiting the area over which facilities and services must be extended. The fiscal crisis would be helped by reducing the costs of capital and operational services while increasing central city ratables. Effective growth management is a major key to solving the crises affecting America today.

B. *The New Approaches*

From its inception to the early seventies, zoning has traditionally used a two-dimensional approach. The community was zoned into residential, commercial, or industrial use zones which could be developed at will even though essential facilities were lagging far behind the area's needs. Many communities relied upon zoning techniques, mentioned in the previous sections, such as large lot zoning, minimum floor areas, exclusive industrial zoning, and the exclusion of mobile homes and multi-family housing to slow growth. These zoning practices were actually counterproductive by exacerbating suburban sprawl by encouraging low density development and many were held invalid as exclusionary. The sophisticated technique of growth management, which for the first time was to involve the timing and sequencing of development to coincide with adequate public facilities and orderly development of suburban areas, began in 1972 with the number one state land use case of the decade,[147] and clearly one of the most important cases in land use planning, *Golden v.*

---

146. *See* Reiter, *The Impact of the Federal Highway Program on Urban Areas,* 1 URB. LAW. 76 (1969).
147. Dozier & Hagman, *Ranking Land Development and Environmental Cases and Courts,* 4 ENVT'L COM. 4 (Aug. 1978).

Planning Board of Town of Ramapo.[148] In the editor's comment, *"Golden v. Town of Ramapo:* Establishing a New Dimension in American Planning Law,"[149] the purpose and implementation of development timing and sequential control are discussed along with their significance. Ramapo in 1966 was the first municipality to implement a comprehensive local growth control plan.[150] After being upheld by both the New York Court of Appeals and the U.S. Supreme Court, the plan is now a model for other municipalities. The town required residential development to proceed in accordance with the timing, sequencing, and provision of adequate municipal facilities as established by a long term comprehensive plan and capital improvement program. The due process requirement of a "reasonable return within a reasonable period of time" was met because restraints on development of land were measured by the eighteen-year period set by the capital improvement program and the comprehensive plan. The ordinance provided that all areas of the municipality would be improved within the plan period and there were interim development controls to aid in its implementation.[151] Later growth management techniques which have been accepted by the courts include subdivision controls based on the adequacy of off-site public facilities,[152] landbanking and development easements,[153] preferential

---

148. Golden v. Planning Bd. of Ramapo, 30 N.Y.2d 359, 285 N.E.2d 291, 334 N.Y.S.2d 138, *appeal dismissed,* 409 U.S. 1003 (1972).

149. Freilich, Golden v. Planning Board of Town of Ramapo: *Establishing a New Dimension in American Planning Law,* 4 URB. LAW. ix (Summer 1972) (also reprinted in this anthology).

150. The Ramapo Plan and decision have been the subject of many articles. *See, e.g.,* Freilich & Greis, *Timing and Sequential Development, Ramapo and the Control of Growth,* in FUTURE LAND USE 59–106 (Rutgers Center for Urban Policy Research 1975); Bosselman, *Growth Management and Constitutional Rights—Part I: The Blessings of Quiet Seclusion,* 8 URB. L. ANN. 3 (1974); Bosselman, *Can the Town of Ramapo Pass a Law to Bind the Rights of the Whole World?,* 1 FLA. ST. L. REV. 234 (1973); Clark & Grable, *Growth Control in California: Prospects for Local Governmental Implementation of Timing and Sequential Control of Residential Development,* 5 PAC. L.J. 570 (1974); Elliott & Marcus, *From Euclid to Ramapo: New Directions in Land Development Controls,* 1 HOFSTRA L. REV. 56 (1973).

151. *See* Almquist v. Town of Marshan, 245 N.W.2d 819 (Minn. 1976); Freilich, *Interim Development Controls: Essential Tools for Implementing Flexible Planning and Zoning,* 49 J. URB. L. 65 (1971).

152. *See, e.g.,* Freilich & Levi, *Model Subdivision Regulation,* ASPO (1975); Freilich & Levi, *Model Regulations for the Control of Land Subdivision,* 36 Mo. L. REV. 1 (1971); Note, *Control of the Timing and Location of Government Utility Extensions,* 26 STAN. L. REV. 945 (1974).

153. *See, e.g.,* Freilich, *Development Timing, Moratoria and Controlling Growth,* 1974 INST. ON PLAN., ZONING AND EMINENT DOMAIN 172–78.

assessment and green acres laws,[154] urban/rural demarcation lines,[155] and population quotas.[156]

In *Ramapo,* the court recognized the fundamental constitutional principle that development of the urban fringe may be controlled by linking development with the planned extension of capital improvements, the lifetime of the comprehensive plan being the "reasonable time" required. The purpose of the plan is to assimilate population growth into the developing areas while allowing nondeveloping areas to use traditional zoning techniques to limit growth. The effect of such measures would be that a "reasonable use" in rural areas would differ from those considered reasonable in urban areas.[157] This would allow some techniques that would be considered exclusionary in urbanizing areas to satisfy due process requirements and preserve rural-agricultural areas. It was natural that this concept would be extended to operate on a larger regional and metropolitan level.

One effective way to deal with regional needs while controlling sprawl is through the regional "tier" system. This system utilizes the Ramapo principle through the delineation of functional areas within the region for identification of goals, objectives, and implementation of growth management techniques. The system creates five planning areas which geographically and functionally segment the region. Tier I consists of the inner city downtown areas; Tier II consists of the residential neighborhoods of the central city and older suburban areas; Tier III consists of the developing fringe set aside for urbanization and intense development; Tier IV consists of rural and agricultural areas which are premature for active development; and

---

154. *See, e.g.,* Hady, *Differential Assessment Programs for Agricultural Land,* in LAND USE; TOUGH CHOICES IN TODAY'S WORLD 114 (1977) (Spec. Pub. No. 22, S.C.S.); Comment, *Assessment to Preserve Agricultural Land: With Application to the Four-State Region of Iowa, Kansas, Missouri and Nebraska,* 47 U.M.K.C. L. REV. 629 (1979).

155. *See, e.g.,* Rodo Land, Inc. v. Board of County Comm'rs, 517 P.2d 873 (Colo. Ct. App. 1974).

156. Boca Villas Corp. v. City of Boca Raton, 45 Fla. Supp. 65 (Civ. Ct. 1976), *aff'd,* 372 So. 2d 485 (Fla. Dist. Ct. App. 1979); Construction Indus. Ass'n v. City of Petaluma, 375 F. Supp. 574 (N.D. Cal. 1974) *rev'd,* 522 F.2d 897 (9th Cir. 1975), *cert. denied,* 424 U.S. 934 (1976).

157. DeCaro v. Washington Township, 21 Pa. Commw. Ct. 252, 344 A.2d 725 (1975) (upholding large lot rural zoning if population growth will be accommodated in urban growth areas); Coalition for Los Angeles County Plan. v. Board of Supervisors, 76 Cal. 3d 241, 142 Cal. Rptr. 766 (1975) (setting aside L.A. county plan to develop 1.5 million acres in urban sprawl where growth can be accommodated in compact area); SAVE Centennial Valley Ass'n. v. Schultz, 284 N.W.2d 452 (S.D. 1979) (subdivision approval in agricultural area violates comprehensive plan and is void); Steel Hill Dev., Inc. v. Town of Sanbornton, 469 F.2d 956 (1st Cir. 1972).

Tier V incorporates an environmental overlay zone to designate land permanently not suited for development or which requires partial protection because of environmental considerations.[158] The regional tier system must be used with the area's comprehensive or regional plan and should be adapted to meet local and municipal autonomy within the regional guidelines.

C. *Efforts to Preserve and Revitalize*

Preserving agricultural land and the rural environment, revitalizing central cities, controlling urban sprawl, and harnessing high suburban tax expenditures requires the use of many interrelated techniques including regulatory, taxing, and compensatory approaches. Regulatory techniques include large lot zoning which would be constitutional in Tier IV regions where development is premature[159] and has been upheld for indefinite periods.[160] Other regulatory techniques include exclusive agricultural use zones.[161] In such agricultural districts, all non-agricultural uses may be excluded if the land meets prime agricultural soil type, productivity, and location criteria.[162] Population quotas which take into account regional needs may be upheld even though permanent city-wide population caps are usually held invalid.[163] Under impact zoning techniques, zoning approvals

---

158. The comprehensive regional approach to growth management is illustrated by the five-tier development framework established by the Metropolitan Council of Minneapolis–St. Paul in which Professor Freilich served as legal consultant. *See* Freilich & Ragsdale, *Timing and Sequential Controls—The Essential Basis for Effective Regional Planning,* 58 MINN. L. REV. 1009 (1974). Similar systems were also developed by Professor Freilich in Baltimore County, San Diego, and Lexington-Fayette County. *See* EINSWEILER, FREILICH, *et al.,* THE DESIGN OF STATE, REGIONAL AND LOCAL GROWTH MANAGEMENT SYSTEMS (National Science Foundation, 2 vols., 1978).

159. Steel Hill Dev., Inc. v. Town of Sanbornton, 469 F.2d 956 (1st Cir. 1972).

160. Ybarra v. Town of Los Altos Hills, 503 F.2d 250 (9th Cir. 1974).

161. *See* Wilcox v. Zoning Bd. of Appeals, 17 N.Y.2d 249, 217 N.E.2d 633, 270 N.Y.S.2d 569 (1966); N.Y. [AGRIC. & MKTS.] LAW. §§ 300–07 (McKinney 1972 & Supp. 1975); Siegel, *Illinois Zoning: On the Verge of a New Era,* 25 DEPAUL L. REV. 616 (1976); Tomain, *Land Use Controls in Iowa,* 27 DRAKE L. REV. 254 (1978).

162. City Planning Dept. of San Diego, Population, Housing and Land Absorption Report for 1979; R. FREILICH, M. GLEESON & M. LEITNER, THE DESIGN OF STATE, REGIONAL AND LOCAL GROWTH MANAGEMENT SYSTEMS, Technical Report prepared under Grant No. ENV76–06857 from National Science Foundation, Research applied to National Needs Program (Mar. 1978); Urban Development Strategy for California (State Office of Planning and Research 1978).

163. Construction Indust. Ass'n v. City of Petaluma, 375 F. Supp. 574 (N.D. Cal. 1974), *rev'd,* 522 F.2d 897 (9th Cir. 1975), *cert. denied,* 424 U.S. 934 (1976); Bocas Villas Corp. v. City of Boca Raton, 45 Fla. Supp. 65 (1976), *aff'd,* 372 So. 2d 485 (Fla. 1979).

would be assigned based upon contiguity with economic productivity and environmental sensitivity. Victor Yannacone, Jr., John Rahenkamp, and Angelo Cerchione take a closer look at these techniques in their article, "Impact Zoning: Alternative to Exclusion in the Suburbs."[164]

The acquisition of parks, open spaces, and flood plains, together with the provision of mixed use housing developments encouraging alternative life styles and housing savings, have been accomplished with planned unit development, clustering, and average density.[165] In *Cheney v. Village 2 at New Hope, Inc.*,[166] the fifth ranked state land use case of the decade,[167] the Pennsylvania Supreme Court upheld the validity of planned unit development (PUD) even before the adoption of enabling legislation. PUD allows developments to be planned and built as a unit using innovative arrangements of buildings to preserve the natural surroundings and open space. Other innovative techniques to preserve both rural character and to utilize underdeveloped urban areas are explored in "Air Rights are 'Fertile Soil,' "[168] by Eugene Morris.

Budgetary techniques coupled with innovative approaches as to capital improvements can also be used to control the direction, timing, location, and type of development in an area. The requirement of availability of utilities, roads, parks, and other public facilities has been successfully upheld,[169] although some states are still following the common law utility extension rules.[170] *Associated Homebuilders of Greater East Bay, Inc. v. City of Walnut Creek*,[171] the number eight ranked state land use case, significantly advanced growth management by holding that impact fees may be charged to new development for its pro-rata share of capital costs rather than being charged back to the general community.

Taxation techniques have also been implemented to preserve

---

164. 8 URB. LAW. 417 (1976) (also reprinted in this anthology). U.S. Advisory Commission on Intergovernmental Relations, ACIR State Legislative Program, 1970 Cumulative Supp. 31–36–00 at 5 (1969); Comment, *Planned Unit Development*, 35 MO. L. REV. 27 (1970).

165. *See* Dykman, *Book Review*, 12 U.C.L.A. L. REV. 991 (1965).

166. 429 Pa. 626, 241 A.2d 81 (1968).

167. Dozier & Hagman, *Ranking Land Development and Environmental Cases and Courts*, 4 ENVT'L COM. 4 (Aug. 1978).

168. 1 URB. LAW. 247 (1969) (also reprinted in this anthology).

169. Wilson v. Hidden Valley Municipal Water Dist., 256 Cal. App. 2d 271, 63 Cal. Rptr. 889 (1967); Associated Homebuilders of Greater Eastbay v. City of Livermore, 18 Cal. 2d 582, 557 P.2d 473, 135 Cal. Rptr. 41 (1976).

170. Robinson v. City of Boulder, 547 P.2d 228 (Colo. 1976).

171. 4 Cal. 3d 633, 484 P.2d 606, 94 Cal. Rptr. 630 (1971).

farmland, although with mixed success. Preferential assessments, which assess land according to its present use value, allow agricultural landowners to benefit from lower taxes. Unfortunately, in most states, the land may be sold immediately for development when profitable.[172] Farmland conversion may be discouraged by aggressive capital gains taxes,[173] penalties levied when the land use changes, and taxing at one rate for urban service districts and a lower rate for general service districts.[174]

Compensatory techniques such as landbanking[175] may also be used to preserve the nature of the rural environment. The government could purchase agricultural land and lease it back to the farmers[176] or simply purchase the development rights.[177] Limitations to these techniques include fiscal prudence and the public purpose requirements of eminent domain.[178] Recent decisions in Hawaii, however, indicate that major advances in authorizing eminent domain for agricultural land purchase and either retention or redistribution will be found to be constitutional.[179]

Transfer development rights (TDR's) have been used in a variety of instances to avoid eminent domain. The separation of the right to develop property from other property rights is one of the major developments of the seventies. In Hershel J. Richman and Lane H. Kendig's article, "Transfer Development Rights—A Pragmatic View,"[180] the authors develop the idea of preserving open space

---

172. *See* T. Hady & A. Sibold, *State Programs for the Differential Assessment of Farm and Open Space Land,* 2 U.S. ECON. RESEARCH SERVICE AG. ECON. RPT. No. 256 (1974).

173. VT. STAT. ANN. tit. 32, §§ 10001–10 (1973).

174. *See* Frazer v. Carr, 210 Tenn. 565, 360 S.W.2d 449 (1962).

175. *See, e.g.,* Note, *Judicial Review of Land Bank Dispositions,* 41 U. CHI. L. REV. 377 (1974); *Public Land Banking, A New Praxis for Urban Growth,* 23 CASE W. RES. L. REV. 897, 899 (1972).

176. W. Bryant, *Farmland Preservation Alternatives in Semi-suburban Areas,* A.E. EXT. 75–5, DEPT. OF AG. ECON. (Cornell 1975); Young, *The Saskatchewan Land Bank,* 40 SASK. L. REV. 1 (1975).

177. N.Y. Suffolk County adopted a development rights program pursuant to N.Y. [GEN. MUN.] LAW 247 (McKinney 1974), by passing Local Law No. 19, Local Law Relating to the Acquisition of Development Rights on Agricultural Lands, Suffolk County, New York (1974).

178. *See* LETWIN, MUNICIPAL LAND BANKS: LAND RESERVE POLICY FOR URBAN DEVELOPMENT 236–376 (1975).

179. *See* Midkif v. Tom, 483 F. Supp. 62 (D. Hawaii 1979) for a major expansion of public purpose in allowing acquisition of agricultural areas for land redistribution. Echoing the result achieved in urban renewal, Berman v. Parker, 348 U.S. 26 (1954). *See also* People of Puerto Rico v. Eastern Sugar Assocs., 156 F.2d 316 (1st Cir. 1946), *cert. denied,* 329 U.S. 772 (1946).

180. 9 URB. LAW. 571 (1977) (also reprinted in this anthology).

through the sale of development rights from the restricted parcel to incentive areas.

The problems of urbanization and its accompanying sprawl can be met with an effective growth management plan. These problems are delineated and analyzed by Ronald A. Zumbrun and Thomas E. Hookano in their article, "No-Growth and Related Land-Use Legal Problems: An Overview."[181] It must be realized that growth can be orderly in accordance with comprehensive planning. The housing needs of the population can be met without devouring agricultural land, and the best combination of land use devices for any given locality will depend upon the community's resources and legislative flexibility. The will to control urban sprawl is the key to combating the problem. Changing governmental attitudes along with citizens' interest in conservation, preservation, rehabilitation, and fiscal solvency have launched the area of growth management into the eighties with a desire to succeed in providing an acceptable place for all to live by balancing all the various interests of the nation.

V. The "Taking" Issue

A. *The Development of the Police Power*

Since the early decisions of *Euclid* and *Nectow*,[182] municipalities have had the power to zone and thereby regulate permissible land uses in conformance with a general community plan. This power is a grant of state government's police power to local government in an effort to promote the public health, safety, morals, and general welfare.[183] Valid zoning must be a reasonable exercise of this delegated police power.[184] A zoning ordinance must, by the police power's definition, utilize a reasonable means to a lawful end as well as allow a "reasonable use" for the property. If a regulation has a non-public objective (general constitutionality) or as applied denies the private property owner a reasonable use (specific constitutionality), the zon-

---

181. 9 URB. LAW. 122 (1977) (also reprinted in this anthology).

182. *See* Village of Euclid v. Ambler Realty Co., 272 U.S. 365 (1926); Nectow v. City of Cambridge, 277 U.S. 183 (1928).

183. The "police power" is defined as the inherent power of the states to enact laws and otherwise promote the public health, safety, morals and general welfare. Day-Brite Lighting Inc. v. Missouri, 342 U.S. 421, 424 (1952); Euclid v. Ambler Realty Co., 272 U.S. at 395.

184. Goldblatt v. Town of Hempstead, 369 U.S. 590 (1962).

ing law deprives the landowner of property without due process of law and constitutes an invalid exercise of the police power.[185]

This, however, is only the beginning of the quandary. Such regulatory invalidity has also been categorized as a "taking" of the property.[186] Does it also authorize the payment of damages or compensation? Does it in fact result in an exercise of eminent domain? Are the due process and eminent domain powers symmetrical—one beginning where the other leaves off—the inverse of each other? These questions as to what constitutes a "taking" and the consequences which follow the determination that a "taking" has occurred, have been questions which the courts and constitutional analysts have been pondering for a century.[187] Deciding at what point a governmental entity has overstepped its police power is an uncertain proposition in itself. In an era of increasingly acceptable regulation of private property,[188] when a reasonable use can be innovatively calculated,[189] a valid exercise of police power can sometimes be found even in extreme circumstances.[190]

---

185. Lawton v. Steele, 152 U.S. 133 (1894); Nectow v. City of Cambridge, 277 U.S. at 183.

186. Pennsylvania Coal Co. v. Mahon, 260 U.S. 393 (1922).

187. Lawton v. Steele, 152 U.S. 133 (1894); Pennsylvania Coal Co. v. Mahon, 260 U.S. 393 (1922); Penn Cent. Transp. Co. v. City of New York, 438 U.S. 104 (1978); Agins v. City of Tiburon, _____ U.S. _____, 100 S. Ct. 2138 (1980); Binder, *Taking vs. Reasonable Regulation, A Reappraisal in Light of Regional Planning and Wetlands,* 25 FLA. L. REV. 1 (1972); Sax, *Takings and the Police Power,* 74 YALE L.J. 36 (1964); Sax, *Takings, Private Property and Public Rights,* 81 YALE L.J. 149 (1971); Johnson, *Constitutional Law and Community Planning,* 20 LAW & CONTEMP. PROB. 199 (1955); F. BOSSELMAN, D. CALLIES, J. BANTA, THE TAKING ISSUE (1971); Morgan, *Regulatory Takings in Oregon, A Walk Down Fifth Avenue without Due Process,* 16 WILLAMETTE L.J. 591 (1980).

188. The steady expansion of the police power in zoning and planning has been witnessed in the following areas: (a) Growth management—Golden v. Planning Bd. of Ramapo, 30 N.Y.2d 359, 285 N.E.2d 291, 334 N.Y.S.2d 138, *appeal dismissed,* 409 U.S. 1003 (1972); (b) Urban renewal—Berman v. Parker, 348 U.S. 26 (1954); (c) Aesthetics—New Orleans v. Duke, 427 U.S. 297 (1976); (d) Environmental regulation—Just v. Marinette County, 56 Wis. 2d 7, 201 N.W.2d 761 (1972); (e) Transfers of development rights—Penn Cent. Transp. Co. v. City of New York, 438 U.S. 104 (1973); (f) Preservation of open space and prevention of urban sprawl—Agins v. City of Tiburon, _____ U.S. _____, 100 S. Ct. 2138 (1980); (g) Control of pornography— Young v. American Mini Theatres, 427 U.S. 50 (1976).

189. *See* Fred F. French Investing Co. v. City of New York, 39 N.Y.2d 587, 350 N.E.2d 381, 385 N.Y.S.2d 5 (1976); Costonis, *Fair Compensation and the Accommodation Power,* 75 COLUM. L. REV. 1021 (1975); Penn Central Transp. Co. v. City of New York, 42 N.Y.2d 324, 366 N.E.2d 1271, 397 N.Y.S.2d 914 (1977), *aff'd,* 438 U.S. 104 (1978).

190. Agins v. City of Tiburon, _____ U.S. _____, 100 S. Ct. 2138 (1980); Avco Community Developers, Inc. v. South Coast Regional Commission, 17

But far more vexatious is the question of what the consequences for such a "taking" should be. The remedies for overregulation of property come from three basic schools of thought. The majority, which includes mostly state decisions, deals with improper exercise of police power by rendering the regulation invalid. Under the majority view in states such as New York and California, going "too far" does not constitute a "taking." Under this view, an overly broad police power regulation can never constitute inverse condemnation, absent specific dominion and control over the property by the governmental authority. The regulation merely becomes null and void.[191] Since no "taking" results and no damages are required, the states are very favorable to this idea because of obvious financial considerations. The minority view, which seems to be gaining recognition by the Supreme Court, is that the improper use of police power is an implied exercise of eminent domain and requires the payment of just compensation. The Supreme Court is overlapping the doctrines of "taking" and invalidating regulations, the end result being a blend or symmetry of the eminent domain and police powers. This "fairness approach" will no doubt be reflected in future decisions.[192] The third and newest alternative is implementation of section 1983 liability,[193] since municipal qualified immunity is no longer a safeguard.[194] Liability is involved for constitutional violation consisting of taking property without due process by persons acting under the

---

Cal. 3d 785, 553 P.2d 546, 132 Cal. Rptr. 386 (1976); SAVE Centennial Valley Ass'n, Inc. v. Schultz, 284 N.W.2d 452 (S.D. 1979); County Council v. District Land Corp., 274 Md. 691, 337 A.2d 712 (1975).

191. *See* Fred F. French Investing Co. v. City of New York, 77 Misc. 2d 199, 352 N.Y.S.2d 762 (1973); HFH, Ltd. v. Superior Court, 15 Cal. 3d 508, 542 P.2d 237, 125 Cal. Rptr. 365 (1975), *cert. denied,* 425 U.S. 904 (1976). Agins v. City of Tiburon, 24 Cal. 3d 266, 598 P.2d 25, 157 Cal. Rptr. 372, *aff'd,* ____ U.S. ____, 100 S. Ct. 2138 (1980).

192. *See generally* Penn Cent. Transp. Co. v. City of New York, 438 U.S. 104 (1978); Kaiser-Aetna v. United States, 444 U.S. 164 (1980), blending navigation servitude with compensation.

193. *See* Lynch v. Household Finance Corp., 405 U.S. 538 (1972); Lake Country Estates, Inc. v. Tahoe Regional Planning Agency, 440 U.S. 391 (1979).

194. Owen v. City of Independence, ____ U.S. ____, 100 S. Ct. 1398 (1980). *See also* Monell v. Department of Social Services, 436 U.S. 658 (1978). The Court held that municipalities and other sub-state regional and local governments are "persons" under § 1983 and could be used for monetary, declaratory, and injunctive relief where the action alleged to be unconstitutional implements an official city policy or ordinance. Lake Country Estates, Inc. v. Tahoe Regional Planning Agency, 440 U.S. 391 (1979).

color of state law.[195] What this may mean in terms of zoning regulations has not yet been felt, however, municipal regulations that infringe upon constitutional or federal rights now have unlimited possibilities for liability.

B. *Invalidation of Improper Regulations*

The basis for the majority viewpoint was firmly established in *Fred F. French Investing Co. v. City of New York*.[196] This state case was ranked ninth in overall importance in land development cases.[197] The decision held that there can be no cause of action in inverse condemnation absent specific control of, or physical encroachment on the property by the government.[198] The court held a New York City zoning resolution invalid because it rezoned two private parks exclusively as parks open to the public. A distinction was drawn between the actual "taking" of the land which was viewed as an enterprise capacity and regulation of the land which was viewed as a legislative capacity. Anything within the municipality's enterprise capacity required compensation; whereas, the legislative capacity required no inverse condemnation, the remedy being the regulation declared an unreasonable exercise of police power and thereby invalid. The court set three standards for an unreasonable ordinance any of which would force the reviewing court to render it invalid. (1) If it "encroaches on the exercise of private property rights without substantial relation to a legitimate governmental purpose,"[199] (2) if it has no reasonable relationship to the end being sought,[200] or (3) if it "renders the property unsuitable for any reasonable income production or other private use for which it is adapted and thus destroys its economic value or all but a bare residue of its value."[201]

The California Supreme Court agreed with New York in *HFH*,

---

195. *See* Freilich, Rushing & Noland, *1978–79 Annual Review of Local Government Law: Undermining Municipal and State Initiative in an Era of Crisis and Uncertainty*, 11 URB. LAW. 547, 550 (1979) [hereinafter cited as *1978–79 Annual Review*].

196. 77 Misc. 2d 199, 352 N.Y.S.2d 762 (1973).

197. Dozier & Hagman, *Ranking Land Development and Environmental Cases and Courts*, 4 ENVT'L COM. 4 (Aug. 1978).

198. Freilich, Growcock & Ungar, *1977–78 Annual Review of Local Government Law: Judicial and Constitutional Intervention in Municipal Fiscal Affairs*, 10 URB. LAW. 573 (1978) [hereinafter cited as *1977–78 Annual Review*].

199. 350 N.E.2d at 386.

200. *Id.*

201. *Id.* at 387.

Ltd. v. Superior Court of Los Angeles County.[202] The court gave several reasons for denying inverse condemnation. It stressed that the interests of private property owners are subordinate to the interests of society as a whole. The California Supreme Court felt that uncompensated hardships are a necessary part of the regulatory system. The court also felt that landowners have no vested rights in current or future zoning regulation and that the landowner also receives the benefits from zoning as well as the burdens.[203] In a related case decided in 1980, *Agins v. City of Tiburon,*[204] the United States Supreme Court had the opportunity to decide whether an alleged inverse condemnation cause of action properly pleads damage relief or merely injunctive or declaratory relief invalidating the ordinance. The question, however, was never resolved since the U.S. Supreme Court found that no inverse condemnation existed. The California Supreme Court had ruled that even with an unconstitutional limitation the remedy called solely for declaratory relief in the form of mandamus.[205] The California court wanted to avoid "a chilling effect upon the exercise of police regulatory powers at the local level because the expenditure of funds would be to some extent within the power of the judiciary,"[206] even if the regulation deprives the owner of "substantially all reasonable use of his property."[207] However, California is already carving out exceptions to this stringent rule as evidenced by *Toso v. City of Santa Barbara.*[208] Here, Santa Barbara had used precondemnation tactics to lower the value of the plaintiff's property and denied him a rezoning application. This "bad faith" exercise prompted a "special circumstance" test which allowed inverse condemnation. *Toso* reiterated that the appropriate remedy for arbitrary and discriminatory zoning is mandamus, however, "where the zoning is so arbitrary or oppressive as to constitute a compensable taking or where inequitable zoning action is undertaken as a prelude to public acquisition"[209] the process is actually inverse condemnation.

---

202. 15 Cal. 3d 508, 542 P.2d 237, 125 Cal. Rptr. 365 (1975), *cert. denied,* 425 U.S. 904 (1976).

203. *See 1978–79 Annual Review, supra* note 195, at 554.

204. Agins v. City of Tiburon, 24 Cal. 3d 266, 598 P.2d 25, 157 Cal. Rptr. 372, *aff'd,* _____ U.S. _____, 100 S. Ct. 2138 (1980).

205. 598 P.2d at 28, 24 Cal. 3d at 270–71, 157 Cal. Rptr. at 373.

206. *Id.* at 30.

207. *Id.*

208. 102 Cal. App. 3d 934, 162 Cal. Rptr. 210 (1980).

209. *Id.* at 944, 162 Cal. Rptr. at 220.

C. Implied Exercise of Eminent Domain

The "taking" issue will continue to remain vexatious as long as the Supreme Court reserves judgment and fails to elucidate the key factors in the regulatory taking-inverse condemnation controversy. The U.S. Supreme Court view can be seen in the pre-*Euclid* decision of *Pennsylvania Coal Co. v. Mahon.*[210] The general rule at least is, that while property may be regulated to a certain extent, if regulation goes too far it will be recognized as a "taking."[211] In *Goldblatt v. Town of Hempstead*[212] the Court found that a use restriction on real property may constitute a "taking" if not reasonably necessary to effectuate a substantial public purpose or if it has an unduly harsh impact upon the owner's use of property.[213] This joint exercise of the eminent domain and police powers can be seen in *Penn Central Transportation Co. v. City of New York.*[214] The Landmarks Preservavation Commission denied Penn Central a permit to construct a fifty-nine story office building atop the Grand Central Station Terminal. The reason given was that an addition was inconsistent with the terminal's status as a landmark. The terminal owner brought suit claiming a deprivation of property without due process and that the commission's action constituted a "taking" requiring just compensation. The Supreme Court affirmed the New York City Court of Appeals decision that the enforcement of the Landmarks Preservation Law[215] was a legitimate and reasonable exercise of the police power.[216] By finding this a reasonable exercise the Court expressly reserved the option to find a sufficiently drastic zoning regulation to constitute a "taking." It also reserved judgment on the question of whether a "taking" can occur absent the government's actual physical control over the property, suggesting that the eminent domain and police powers are amenable to joint consideration.[217] What the Court might be saying is that severe and unduly harsh zoning regulations may give rise to damages pursuant to the eminent domain clause.[218] The Court is hinting at the minority view, as was seen in *Agins v. City of Tiburon,*[219] but it is not yet prepared to go that route.

---

210. 260 U.S. 393 (1922).
211. *Id.* at 414.
212. 369 U.S. 590 (1962).
213. *See id.*
214. 438 U.S. 104 (1978).
215. N.Y.C. AD. CODE, ch. 8–A, § 205–1.0 *et seq.* (1976).
216. Penn Cent., 438 U.S. at 138 (1978).
217. *1977–78 Annual Review, supra* note 198, at 580.
218. *Id.* at 575.
219. _____ U.S. _____, 100 S. Ct. 2138 (1980).

It implies that if the property owner is denied a "reasonable return"[220] the regulation may be struck as void, however, the denial of a reasonable return has never been expressly held to be an exercise of eminent domain. There is now direct evidence that the Supreme Court intends to blend the eminent domain and police powers. The Court mentions several factors when finding a "taking" such as the regulation's economic impact, whether there is physical or abstract governmental action, and the public purpose behind the regulation.[221] The Court has, for the time being, decided to adhere to no set formula in determining whether a taking has occurred but is content to resolve these matters on an ad hoc basis.[222]

Other vexing issues involving inverse condemnation have arisen during the decade. If the courts in "balancing" the interests of "growth" versus "pollution" refuse to grant injunctive relief against large scale employers, they are granting eminent domain powers. This "public interest" issue received widespread attention during the seventies and can be exemplified by two landmark cases. The state land use case which is ranked second[223] overall is *Boomer v. Atlantic Cement Company.*[224] Here the majority allowed a cement plant to continue operations even though it was a continuing nuisance and substantially impaired the property rights of neighboring residences. The court granted a remedy solely of damages consisting of the fair market value of the houses and refused to grant an injunction against the company. The dissent argued against the logic in which the public good was not the critical lever but rather the private gain. They pointed out that the court in essence was breaking new ground by giving a violator the right of inverse condemnation against the residents not for a "public purpose" but for illegal use. *Just v. Marinette County,*[225] which is ranked fourth,[226] reflected stringent regula-

---

220. *See* Penn Cent. Transp. Co. v. City of New York, 42 N.Y.2d 324, 366 N.E.2d 1271, 397 N.Y.S.2d 914 (1977). The New York Court of Appeals went to great lengths to assure Penn Central a "reasonable return" on their investment by entitling the owners only to return on the "private increment" adding neighboring Penn Central property to the return; and allowing transfer development rights in exchange for the non-use of the airspace.

221. Penn Cent., 438 U.S. at 122–28.

222. *Id.*

223. Dozier & Hagman, *Ranking Land Development and Environmental Cases and Courts,* 4 ENVT'L COM. 4 (Aug. 1978).

224. 26 N.Y.2d 219, 257 N.E.2d 870 (1970).

225. 56 Wis. 2d 7, 201 N.W.2d 761 (1972).

226. Dozier & Hagman, *Ranking Land Development and Environmental Cases and Courts,* 4 ENVT'L COM. 4 (Aug. 1978).

tion in the area of flood plains and wetlands. Flood control and preserving an ecological balance between shoreland and the water are obvious public needs which have been demonstrated during the seventies. Shoreland and water resources are areas subject to enormous pressure for development as our population continues to grow and our society urbanizes at an ever-increasing pace. As a city expands toward a lakefront or riverside, developers are naturally presented with an opportunity to realize profits on what might once have been marginally valuable land, building in the face of potential flood damage,[227] or by dredging and filling wetlands, ignoring the ecological consequences, or worse, denying the legitimacy of environmentalist warnings. In any event, the "improvement" goes up and the public loses thereby.

Marinette County enacted a Shoreland Zoning Ordinance in 1967, as authorized by the Wisconsin Water Quality Act of 1965.[228] The ordinance prohibited, inter alia, filling wetlands without a conditional use permit which limited the land to natural uses only, and severely limited any economic use of the land for nonnatural structural improvements. The Justs, however, proceeded with filling their land without the necessary permit, and when they were brought into court, claimed that the statute was unconstitutional because it authorized a taking of their land for a public purpose without providing for just compensation. The court framed the issue as: ". . . a conflict between the public interest in stopping the despoliation of natural resources, which our citizens until recently have taken as inevitable and for granted, and an owner's asserted right to use his property as he wishes."[229] In holding that the regulation of the use of shoreland was a valid exercise of the police power, the court relied on what the Council on Environmental Quality has termed the "critical natural features theory," i.e., certain areas of land in their natural state serve a function vital to the general well-being of the public. The theory implicitly recognizes that as long as there are some reasonable uses still remaining to the owner, regulations which require him to keep the land in its natural state, or substantially so, do not cause a taking

---

227. Council on Environmental Quality, *Fourth Annual Report* (1973) reports at 313 the alarming fact that federal flood plain insurance, covering annual losses of 2 billion dollars across the nation, has actually "had the effect of encouraging new development projects which increased flood plain occupancy," even though the intent had been to protect only existing properties.
228. WIS. STAT. ANN. §§ 144.26, 59.971 (West Supp. 1980).
229. 201 N.W.2d at 767.

without compensation, even though there might be a severe diminution in the value of the land due to his inability to develop it.

D. *Section 1983 Liability*

The most important development, and perhaps the most distressing for municipal treasuries, is the Supreme Court's acceptance of inverse condemnation as a cause of action under section 1983.[230] No longer can localities hide behind a curtain of absolute immunity. Awaiting definitive criteria for an eminent domain "taking" may be futile in light of the consequences of section 1983 liability. The Supreme Court decided in *Monell v. Department of Social Services*[231] that local governments and municipalities are "persons" under section 1983 and thereby could be sued for monetary, declaratory, and injunctive relief where an unconstitutional action implements official city policy.[232] There are three basic requirements for a cause of action under section 1983. There must have been (1) an act taken under color of state law which results in a (2) deprivation of a constitutional or federal statutory right and such deprivation must have resulted in (3) injury to the plaintiff.[233]

Deprivation of property under section 1983 is either property taken without due process or taken property for which there has been unjust compensation. *Lynch v. Household Finance*[234] holds that taking property without due process by persons acting under the color of state law was a violation of the Constitution and therefore a section 1983 cause of action. *Lake Country Estates, Inc. v. Tahoe Regional Planning Agency*[235] created a section 1983 cause of action for deprivation of property without compensation under environmental and zoning regulation. The Agency adopted a Land Use Ordinance and General Plan which the corporation plaintiff alleged destroyed the value of its land. The Court accepted the inverse condemnation

---

230. 42 U.S.C. § 1983 (1970) reads as follows:

Every person who, under color of any statute, ordinance, regulation, custom, or usage, of any State or Territory, subjects, or causes to be subjected, any citizen of the United States or other person within the jurisdiction thereof to the deprivation on any rights, privileges, or immunities secured by the Constitution and laws, shall be liable to the party injured in an action at law, suit in equity, or other proper proceeding for redress.

231. 436 U.S. 658 (1978).

232. *Id.* at 691. The court further held that such official policy could be represented by custom even though such custom had not received formal approval.

233. *1978–79 Annual Review, supra* note 195, at 550.

234. 405 U.S. 538 (1972).

235. 440 U.S. 391 (1979).

claim as a section 1983 cause of action.[236] There are now unlimited possibilities for liability.[237]

The *Lake Tahoe* decision may mark the beginning of the end of the "taking" issue as far as municipalities are concerned. "A holding that a regulation is constitutionally invalid provides little protection if the same invalidity can in turn be the basis for a section 1983 cause of action for damages."[238] The future of municipal planning and implementation hangs in the balance as cities begin surveying the newly established risks. Redefinition and clarification of section 1983 issues are desperately needed and until they are resolved city planners must enter into the eighties with some trepidation.

VI. Conclusion

The state and federal courts are the ultimate arbiters in any land use dispute and there are several keys to creating acceptable land use programs. The consensus of recent court decisions seems to indicate the presence of three basic requirements to be met by land use programs in order to avoid serious challenge in the courts.[239] First, there must be legitimate, nondiscriminatory goals. The purpose for which the land use restrictions are imposed must fall reasonably within the scope of the police power, and the restriction cannot be so onerous as to amount to a "taking." The restrictions cannot have a racially discriminatory intent or purpose, although an impact which falls along racial lines will not necessarily invalidate the ordinance if

---

236. *Id.* at 399.

237. *See* Searles, *An Overview of Inverse Condemnation*, THE RECORD 20 (1978); Kanner, *The Consequences of Taking Property by Regulation*, 24 PRAC. LAW. 75 (1978); Fulham and Scharf, *Inverse Condemnation: Its Availability in Challenging the Validity of a Zoning Ordinance*, 26 STAN. L. REV. 1439 (1974).

If a Section 1983 cause of action does lie for inverse condemnation, a plaintiff may be able to recover for damages as a result of downzoning, excessive and intolerable aircraft noise, zoning that deprives property owners of the reasonable use of their land, unreasonable delay in condemnation resulting in blight, withholding of government services to an owner's property, and injury to property as a result of construction, blasting or excavation.

1978–79 Annual Review, supra note 195, at 553. Moreover, under two additional U.S. Supreme Court decisions in 1980, cities will be liable for attorney's fees under 42 U.S.C. § 1988 if the city settles the matter short of a defendant's verdict. Maher v. Gagne, _____ U.S. _____, 100 S. Ct. 2570 (1980). Liability will extend to violations of federal statutory law such as the National Environmental Policy Act, and not solely constitutional deprivations. Maine v. Thiboutot, _____ U.S. _____, 100 S. Ct. 2502 (1980).

238. *1978–79 Annual Review, supra* note 195, at 555.

239. Freilich, *Courts: The Ultimate Arbiters in Land Use Disputes*, in LAND USE: TOUGH CHOICES IN TODAY'S WORLD 22 (1977).

other valid reasons are present.[240] Second, there must be development of, and adherence to a comprehensive plan. Although the presence of a separate overall plan for the community is not necessarily essential to the approval of an individual ordinance, such a plan carries great weight in a courtroom because it shows that the enacting community has given careful study to the preparation of its land use controls and the ordinance being challenged is not merely a spur-of-the-moment, stopgap idea. In *Ramapo*,[241] the court was obviously impressed with the study and preparation which preceded adoption of a growth control plan:

> The plan's preparation included a four-volume study of the existing land uses, public facilities, transportation, industry and commerce, housing needs and projected population trends. The proposals appearing in the studies were subsequently adopted . . . and implemented by way of a master plan. The master plan was followed by the adoption of a capital budget, providing for the development of the improvements specified in the master plan within the next six years. . . . The Town Board adopted a capital program which provides for the location and sequence of additional capital improvements for the 12 years following the life of the capital budget. The two plans, covering a period of 18 years, detail the capital improvements projected for maximum development and conform to the specifications set forth in the master plan, the official map and drainage plan.[242]

An important adjunct to such in-depth planning is the use of interim development controls, during the study/planning period, to enable the community to maintain the status quo while it collects data and formulates plans. By preventing the new vesting of rights during the planning process, the community can prevent an onslaught of building permit applications by builders fearful of more stringent requirements.[243] Finally, there must be a regional approach. As discussed earlier, courts are beginning to test the reasonableness of land use restrictions not only by their impact on residents of the enacting community but also by the impact on people in the surrounding areas. To pass judicial muster, it is increasingly necessary that land use plans cater to area-wide needs rather than on narrowly focused local issues.[244] Within this framework, the progress in the seventies will continue into the new decade of the eighties.

---

240. *See* Village of Arlington Heights v. Metropol. Hous. Dev. Corp., 429 U.S. 252 (1979).

241. Golden v. Planning Bd. of Ramapo, 30 N.Y.2d 359, 285 N.E.2d 291, 334 N.Y.S.2d 138, *appeal dismissed,* 409 U.S. 1003 (1972).

242. *Id.* at 362.

243. Freilich, *Interim Development Controls: Essential Tools for Implementing Flexible Planning and Zoning,* 49 J. Urb. Law. 65 (1971).

244. *See* Freilich & Ragsdale, *Timing and Sequential Controls—The Essential Basis for Effective Regional Planning,* 58 Minn. L. Rev. 1009 (1974).

Legal Assaults on Municipal Land Use Regulation*

Ira Michael Heyman

Professor, University of California
—Berkeley School of Law; B.A.,
Dartmouth College; LL.B., Yale
Law School; Member, New York
and California Bars.

FOR GOOD OR ILL, the institution of land use regulation is far from being a dead letter. I firmly believe that we are, or will be, relying more heavily on regulation as time progresses[1] especially to protect environmental goals. But a major trend away from the municipal monopoly on the land-use regulatory powers has emerged and there are strong tendencies towards the reorganization of governments at the state and local levels and the assignment of land-use regulatory powers to higher echelons. This trend should have important impacts on future land development processes.

A Brief History

Zoning and subdivision regulation on any real scale came into being in the United States during the first quarter of the twentieth century. The objectives were relatively benign, and the assumptions were simplistic.[2] The most important objectives were threefold: to segregate inconsistent uses; to prevent congestion; and to provide for the economical provision of public services. To accomplish these, within the then conceived limitations of governmental structure and constitutional prohibitions, zones would be established at

---

*This paper was prepared as a speech intended to provoke discussion among the participants of an RFF conference held in March, 1972. Thus, many of the ideas are not fully worked out and the author cautions the reader that the purpose of the exercise is to paint a relatively broad picture and discern probable major trend lines. The investigation is far from definitive.

[1] IRA MICHAEL HEYMAN, INNOVATIVE REGULATION AND COMPREHENSIVE PLANNING, THE NEW ZONING, (1971) spells out the reasons for this.

[2] This matter is reviewed and analyzed at much greater length in HEYMAN, *Innovative Regulations supra* note 1.

the municipal level within which certain uses (with attendant bulk and yard requirements) would be permitted as "of right," that is, without need for individualized administrative treatment and merely by proof of compliance with the stated law. Zones would be cumulative from single family homes to relatively unrestricted use. They would also be few in number and large in size. A minimum of legislative and administrative flexibility was envisioned. Amendments, especially boundary changes, would occur when conditions changed, but only on an extraordinary vote in the case of protest. An individualized administrative variance might be issued, but only for unique hardship cases.

There were at least five crucial assumptions upon which the original system was built. First, a simplistic segregation of uses would result in a quality urban environment. Second, it would be possible, in drawing the zoning map, to formulate an intelligent all-at-once decision to which the market would conform. Third, the governors of the system would rarely change the rules. Fourth, nonconforming uses would go away. Fifth, municipal power would accomplish the goals. Most of these have proved to be wrong.

Undoubtedly, land-use control at the municipal level has had some beneficent effects, especially as it has become much more sophisticated. It has reduced some situations of potential land use conflicts and has thus aided certainty of expectations and marketability of property—especially residential property. It has permitted somewhat better planning for the provision of public services. It has been increasingly useful for various environmental ends. It has permitted a local neighborhood majority to act in concert in situations where one or two landowners could destroy neighborhood values. It has helped to maintain the special character of selected areas, such as ones of historic importance. It has provided a vehicle for shifting some public costs to development, especially through subdivision exactions.

But land-use control at the municipal level has largely failed to accomplish many of the original and emerging goals. It has not been able to withstand pressures created by an active market. The extraordinary congestion in downtown Manhattan and San Francisco attests to this. It has not been able to withstand inter-municipal competition for tax revenues and business activity. Shortages of strategically placed open spaces in metropolitan areas are the result. A host of other examples could be mentioned.

Perhaps one of the principal effects of land-use control at the municipal level has been to buttress exclusionary tendencies. This objective was undoubtedly unintended, at least consciously, by the fathers of land-use control. But it was not wholly unanticipated. It is instructive to recall the words of the District Judge in the famous *Euclid* case who, as we know, was reversed in the United States Supreme Court:

> The plain truth is that the true object of the ordinance in question is to place all the property in an undeveloped area of 16 square miles in a strait-jacket. The purpose to be accomplished is really to regulate the mode of living of persons who may hereafter inhabit it. In the last analysis, the result to be accomplished is to classify population and segregate them according to their income or situation in life.[3]

It seems safe to say that a great many people prefer to live in the midst of cultural homogeneity. The typology of homogeneity is difficult to state. In its simplistic forms: many whites want to live apart from blacks, or at least low-income blacks; many blacks want to live apart from whites; many middle- and upper-income people want to live apart from lower-income people; ethnic enclaves have a tendency to persist, for both inclusionary and exclusionary reasons.

Presuming that the generalization is roughly true, how do groups of relatively homogeneous people seek to assure relative cultural isolation? The very wealthy can often buy exclusivity in large estates protected by restrictive covenants. Those who reject main-stream values can depart for rural communes. But the middle class, especially the white middle class, does not have these options. It seeks to rely on governmental, quasi-governmental, and private institutions.

The most accessible governmental institutions are local ones. And the ones most amenable to such use are the rich profusion of suburban general purpose municipal governments that abound, and can still be created, in our metropolitan regions. And, as previously stated, it is to these governments that we have heretofore entrusted general jurisdiction over land-use controls.

We should not be surprised, therefore, that land-use controls, together with a number of other manipulations of legal institutions at the local level (such as the refusal to create a public housing

---

[3]297 F. 307, 318 (N.D. Ohio 1924), *rev'd.* 272 U.S. 365 (1926).

authority) have played an important part in barring low-income persons, especially members of minority groups, from access to many suburban areas.

The sum result has been that while municipal land regulation has been far from a total success in accomplishing many of its more benign objectives, but as Robert Weaver reports,[4] and as the National Commission on Urban Problems (Douglas Commission) suggested earlier,[5] it has been fairly successful as an exclusionary tool.

Attacks on Municipal Land-Use Regulation

Six of the major sources of assault on municipal land-use regulation are explored in this paper: the environmentalists, the lawyers, the market, the manifold proponents of open housing (especially the civil rights movement), state governments, and the federal government.

The Environmentalists

The Council on Environmental Quality recently published *The Quiet Revolution in Land-Use Control*,[6] in which the authors review nine new innovative land-use regulatory systems, most of which have been fashioned and adopted to protect physical environmental values. The striking feature of all of them is that they interfere, often substantially, with the municipal land-use control monopoly.

The systems are premised on the realization that a municipality cannot provide rational treatment for ecological systems that transcend local boundaries. Moreover, many of the systems reflect the evident fact that a local jurisdiction, because of perceived self-interest will take actions that are harmful to the combined interests of a larger constituency. California provides two striking examples.

The San Francisco Bay Conservation and Development Commission now has almost exclusive jurisdiction over development in San Francisco Bay.[7] This amounts largely to regulating the filling and

---

[4]ROBERT WEAVER, HOUSING AND ASSOCIATED PROBLEMS OF MINORITIES.
[5]Building the American City, 211, 217 (House Doc. No. 91–34, December 12, 1968).
[6]Fred Bosselman and Davis Callies, *The Quiet Revolution in Land-Use Control* (Council on Environmental Quality, December 15, 1971) (hereafter *The Quiet Revolution*).
[7]*Id.* at 108. *See also*, Jack Schoop and John Hirten, *San Francisco Bay*

dredging of the Bay and adjoining tidelands. Prior to the creation
of this regional agency, nine counties and a host of cities, whose
geographical boundaries extended into the Bay, were the sole
determiners of whether shallow portions of the Bay would be filled.[8]
Such filling was proceeding at a rapid rate for various types of
development. No local government saw reason to interfere (action
by a single would simply deprive that jurisdiction of revenue and
business-producing activities with no assurance that its competitors
would act similarly). Moreover, no locality perceived that its
sanctioned fill would create large problems. This situation resulted
in the transfer of a rather important quantum of land control power
to the San Francisco Bay agency, an upper echelon of government,
which could at least consider regional benefits and costs in its regulatory decisions.

   The Tahoe Regional Planning Agency[9] is an even more significant innovation because it has almost full power to supersede the
land-use regulations of local governments (some six in the Tahoe
Region). It has already adopted a plan and ordinances that significantly control zoning, subdivision standards, grading, and shoreline
development. Additional ordinances are under preparation. Again,
the reason for the shifting of power upward was the realization that
local governments, practically speaking, were unable individually
to withstand the extraordinary development pressures that were
bound to result in significant decay of the total regional environment.

   California is far from unique. Bosselman and Callies analyze
the Massachusetts Wetland Protection Program, the Maine Site
Location Law, the Wisconsin Shoreland Protection Program, the
Twin Cities Metropolitan Council, the Vermont Environmental
Control Law, the Hawaii State Land-Use Commission, and other
systems. A brief review of some aspects of these systems will illustrate the point.

   An important ingredient of the Massachusetts legislation is state
agency control of coastal wetlands.[10] The Massachusetts Depart-

---

Plan—Combining Policy with Police Power, 37 J. AM. INSTIT. OF PLAN-
NERS 2 (1971).
   [8]See, Note, *Saving San Francisco Bay—A Case Study in Environmental
Legislation*, 23 STAN. L. REV. 349 (1971).
   [9]Pub. L. No. 91–148, 83 Stat. 360 (91st Cong. Dec. 18, 1969). *See*, Report of the Lake Tahoe Joint Study Committee (March 1967).
   [10]The Quiet Revolution, *supra* note 6, at 205.

ment of Natural Resources is authorized to issue protective orders defining the boundaries of the coastal wetland areas and prohibiting any development except under carefully controlled circumstances. As the study reports, "the orders are filed in the title records and become binding restrictions on the use of land. To date about one-third of the state's coastal wetlands have been covered by protective orders and another one-third are in various stages of public hearings."[11] While the legislation permits stricter regulation by local entities, it interestingly makes no provision whatsoever for local government participation in the state's regulatory program. The state agency is directed to hold its own public hearings and to work directly with private landowners in the issuance of protective orders and to administer its own permit system. As might be expected, local officials if they are interested, are consulted by the Department and the few town boards that desired direct involvement were accommodated. Generally speaking, however, primary (and nearly complete) land-use control over vast areas of coastal wetlands has passed from local to state control.

Vermont's Environmental Control Law[12] is much more pervasive. This 1970 Act created a State Environmental Board of nine members and seven regional commissions of three members each. Any residential subdivision consisting of ten or more lots of less than ten acres, any housing, commercial or industrial development of substantial size, and any development above the elevation of 2,500 feet requires a permit from the State Environmental Board. Application for permits are reviewed by a state interagency committee, which sends recommendations to the regional commission. The commission holds a public hearing at which comments may be offered by local planning commissions. The regional commission then decides whether or not to issue the permit. In order to grant a permit, ten conditions must be met. Some of these relate to environmental characteristics—water pollution, waste disposal, water availability, soil erosion, scenic and aesthetic values. Some relate to other matters—burden on governmental services, highway congestion, conformance with local and state plans. Appeals from commission decisions can be made to the State Environmental Board by the applicant, state agencies, and local governments. The Vermont Environmental Control Law also calls for the State Board

---

[11]*Id.* at 209.
[12]*Id.* at 54.

to adopt a state capability and development plan and a state land-use plan.

The Vermont system, which is a model for state and regional assumption of land-use control, was stimulated by a boom in second homes and ski resorts and a backdrop of very little local exercise of land regulatory powers. Vermont had a perfectly adequate set of enabling acts, however, and the local decisions to forgo use of them was a choice for market dictation of the development process. But when it became clear that environmental values were seriously jeopardized, the state intruded in a manner that substantially undercut the probabilities of future local control.

The other examples in the Bosselman-Callies monograph tell much the same stories. And the examples they give are only the seminal undertakings. Similar agencies are now being created or proposed in nearly all the states, even those with mature local governments and an historic bias towards home rule. It is only a matter of time, for instance, before California creates a state coastal commission and multipurpose environmental agencies with jurisdiction over open-space preservation, among other matters, in her great metropolitan areas such as the San Francisco Bay area, Los Angeles County, and San Diego County.[13]

The lesson of this trend line is clear. Municipal governments will increasingly be shorn of significant land-use control powers in order to protect environmental values.

The Lawyers

Another assault on municipal land use regulation is coming from the legal fraternity through one of its most prestigious (and conservative) institutions—the American Law Institute [ALI]. The Institute, which has been the sponsor of a variety of restatements of the law and of model and uniform statutes that have had considerable impact, has been struggling with a Model Land Development Code for nearly four years.[14] There is a good reason to believe that the effort will produce a product that is acceptable to the Institute membership and that will be adopted in the near future. Whether

---

[13]Bills have been introduced and vigorously debated concerning both matters.

[14]American Law Institute, *A Model Land Development Code*. Tentative Draft No. 1 (4–24–68); Tentative Draft No. 2 (4–24–70); Tentative Draft No. 3 (4–22–71). Citations below are at Tentative drafts No. 2 and No. 3 (hereinafter ALI Draft 2 and ALI Draft 3).

or not this occurs, the draft sections already circulated are affecting lawyers' attitudes and are providing bases for new legislation in a number of states. Three major sets of provisions contained in the circulated drafts of the Code are of importance to the subject of this paper.

First, the draft Code's planning section, which replaces the old Standard Planning Enabling Act, calls for what might be called an impact statement relating to social concerns.[15] The Code provides for long-range planning and short-run programming, with emphasis on the latter. In both instances, the Code suggests (although perhaps it should require) text analyzing the probable social and economic consequences of provisions of a proposed plan or program, including the impact on population distribution by characteristics (such as race and income) and an evaluation of the consequences of alternative plans and programs. While this direction is addressed to local governments, the identification of these outcomes could have powerful influences upon extra-municipal review, and internal municipal politics.

The second set of provisions of particular relevance appears in the section on land-use regulation and represents an attempt to "legalize" land-use control, which as practiced, consists largely of *ad hoc* or piecemeal decision-making despite the facade of pre-stated standards and certainty.[16] These provisions therefore, impose explicit and detailed procedures for making rules and for granting permits. The latter provisions require records as well as hearings and written findings. Again, these sections are directed at local governments, but the disclosure of the actual reasons for local decisions is intended to facilitate extra-local review.

Finally, and of most importance, the Code provides the detailed machinery for state planning, state regulation, and state administrative review of local land-use decisions.[17] It is unnecessary to review these provisions in detail here, for many of the features have already been discussed in connection with the Massachusetts and Vermont statutes. But three aspects deserve mention.

First, the Code provides for a State Land Planning Agency with power to designate geographical areas of critical concern to the

---

[15]ALI Draft 2, §§ 3–102(5); 3–103(2); 3–104(2); 3–105(2)(e).
[16]*Id.* at §§ 2–303—2–305.
[17]ALI Draft 3, Articles 7 and 8.

state and to subject local regulation in such areas to state review and approval.[18]

Second, the Code identifies four types of development of special "state or regional benefit" and requires local governments to approve such developments, even if they are inconsistent with local land-use regulations, if the "probable net benefit . . . exceeds the probable net detriment" as determined under ten explicit factors stated in the Code.[19] The State Planning Agency may be a party to the proceeding, and the local decision is appealable to a State Land Adjudicatory Board. One of the four catagories is "development by any person receiving state or federal aid designed to facilitate a type of development specified by the State Planning Agency by rule." The notes to the section make it clear that this category includes subsidized housing, such as public housing and sections 235 and 236 housing. This provision follows to some extent the Massachusetts Zoning Appeals Law,[20] which authorizes developers of low-income housing to apply to the local government for a "comprehensive permit" in lieu of all other permits. If the permit is denied, the developer can appeal to a state board—the Housing Appeals Committee—which has the power to vacate the denial and direct the issuance of a permit if the denial was not "reasonable and consistent with local needs." Under another portion of the statute, local regulations are consistent with local needs if they are "reasonable in view of the regional need for low- and moderate-income housing." This, and a succeeding sentence, are a bit of legislative legerdemain that result in the setting of quotas the local government is then protected if it refuses permits once the quota has been reached.[21]

Finally, under the Model Code, the State Planning Agency is empowered to define large scale development that is likely to present issues of state or regional significance, and to subject such development to special review processes somewhat similar to the processes applicable to development of special state or regional benefit.[22]

The American Law Institute Code does not go nearly as far as

---

[18]*Id.* at §§ 7–201—7–208.
[19]*Id.* at §§ 7–301, 7–502.
[20]40B MASS. LAWS ANN. §§ 20–23 (Supp. 1971).
[21]The Quiet Revolution, *supra* note 6 at 167, 168.
[22]ALI Draft 3, §§ 7–401—7–405.

the Vermont statute, for instance, in superseding local land-use controls. Nor does it go so far in selected areas of regulation as do the two California regional agencies previously discussed or the Massachusetts wetlands legislation. Nevertheless, it sets up the general machinery for significant state intrusion upon local land-use control by setting forth specific criteria against which to judge whether particular local land-use decisions make regional and state-wide sense and by subjecting such decisions to state administrative review where the presumptions of regularity and validity that normally attend judicial review are largely unavailable to the local government. Finally, the Model Code, unlike the environmental statutes, permits the state agency to supersede local vetos; in other words, to license certain development over the objections of local governments.

The Market

A third assault on municipal land-use regulation will predictably come from the new participants in the land development market. Richard Babcock has pointed out that in the past fifteen years the "housing industry has undergone evulsive change" with "corporations, national in scope, immense in capital, and diversified in market ambitions, announcing . . . entry into the housing field by acquisition or by internal expansion. . . . These sophisticated aggregates are chagrined to discover that village codes are a major barrier to marketing their dwelling-related products,"[23] many of which, for various reasons, consist of all or component parts of low-income housing.

The participants as Prototype Site Developers under "Operation Breakthrough," for instance include such national firms as Aluminum Corporation of America, General Electric, and Republic Steel.[24] These firms, and others such as Westinghouse's Urban Systems Development Corporation and Aerojet-General Corporation are investing considerable money in a variety of innovative housing techniques both with and without the sponsorship of the Department of Housing and Urban Development [HUD].[25] By February 1970, the National Corporation for Housing Partnerships had

---

[23]Richard Babcock, *The Courts Enter the Land Development Market*, 5 CITY 58 (1971).

[24]Carter Burgess and Sidney Friedberg, *NHP—A New Opportunity for Housing*, 39 GEO. WASH. L. REV. 870, 888–89 (1971).

[25]Business Week, 32–36, (March 17, 1970).

raised over 12 million from an impressive array of corporate sponsors including Armco Steel, Kennecott Copper, Reynolds Aluminum, and Boise-Cascade.[26] *Standard and Poor* in 1971 reported that "A development of major significance in recent years has been the growing penetration of the total [housing] market by the large, well-financed, and often publicly owned tract and community builders."[27]

Babcock concludes that "the impact of this change in the housing industry on the allocation of governmental power can be profound.[28] This conclusion seems warranted. First, these new participants can effectively seek state and federal legislative and administrative intervention to override municipal bars to their products. A good example is the recent spate of legislation creating state boards to license prefabricated housing, thus overriding inconsistent local code provisions.[29]

Second, well-capitalized industrial entities are in a position to invoke judicial review of local exclusionary regulations and to test their validity. They can finance the delay, especially if big projects are involved. This will create opportunities for repetitive judicial reflections on the rationality of local regulations that are inconsistent with regional needs.[30]

The Use of the Courts by
Proponents of Open Housing

A fourth attack on municipal land-use regulation has come from litigation by proponents of open housing. Dan Fessler's presentation at the RFF Conference addresses the legal questions raised in the vast number of law suits brought mainly by lawyers deeply involved in the civic rights movement. Some noteworthy battles have been won. If federal or state courts could be convinced to adopt legal theories that should be easily relied upon to strike down municipal land-use regulations that operated to exclude low-income persons

---

[26]Business Week, 83, (Feb. 14, 1970).

[27]The Outlook—Building for the Future (Standard and Poor's Corporation, 1971).

[28]*Supra*, note 23.

[29]*See*, Automation in Housing, 42–43 (Sept. 1971) reporting the adoption of such acts in nineteen states, and consideration of such acts in nearly every other state. *See also*, Note, *An Analysis of the Probable Impact of the California Factory-Built Housing Law*, 23 STAN. L. REV. 978 (1971).

[30]*See e.g., In re* Kit Mar Builders, 439 Pa. 466, 268 A. 2d 765 (1970); *In re* Girsh, 437 Pa. 237, 263 A.2d 395 (1970).

from residency, the utility and impact of municipal land regulation would be seriously undercut. It seems somewhat doubtful at this point in time, however, that doctrines with such sweeping impact will be embraced by the judiciary.

Fessler discusses three potential basis for federal court negation of local regulations such as large lot zoning, exclusion of multiple dwellings, and prohibition of mobile homes: equal protection, supremacy, and substantive due process.

A successful equal protection attack might proceed from a judicial determination (1) that the purpose of a particular regulation was to exclude members of racial minorities; (2) that a regulation that produces such an effect, regardless of purpose, is invalid; or, more broadly (3) that a regulation having the effect of discriminating on the basis of wealth is invalid. Judicial acceptance of the third proposition would seriously weaken the validity of much zoning, especially in the suburbs. And the cases would not be difficult to litigate because the factual basis could be proved statistically. But, for the reasons Fessler indicates, it is highly doubtful that the federal courts (or state courts) will embrace this view. Similarly, it is doubtful that the courts will adopt the second position, although there is some arguable precedent for it.[31] More likely, the federal courts will only interdict local regulation on the basis of equal protection when it is shown that the locality adopted or perpetuated a regulation for the purpose of excluding (or ghettoizing) a racial minority.[32] Such a judicial position would require individualized proofs of a difficult order in each case and would seriously blunt the efficacy of the judiciary as a tool for achieving open housing.

The supremacy doctrine—that state and local laws that are inconsistent with federal law based on express powers (in this case, the Thirteenth Amendment) are invalid—offers an attractive opportunity, as Fessler establishes, to the federal executive and legislature to sweep away a variety of local regulations that exclude

---

[31]Dailey v. City of Lawton, 425 F.2d 1037 (10th Cir. 1970); Kennedy Park Homes v. City of Lakawanna, 436 F.2d 108 (2nd Cir. 1971); *But see*, James v. Valtierra, 91 S. Ct. 1331 (1971) where "motive" or "purpose" was not found, and despite "effect" of racial exclusion the local regulation was upheld.

[32]Dailey v. City of Lawton; *supra*, note 31; Kennedy Park Homes v. City of Lackawanna, *supra*, note 31; Crow v. Brown, 332 F. Supp. 382 (N.D. Ga. 1971).

disadvantaged minorities. But the judiciary alone will not do this, it will require the action of the political arms of government.[33]

Finally, Fessler investigates the doctrine of substantive due process. This doctrine essentially asks the judges to substitute their value judgments for those of the legislature on matters not treated directly in constitutions (*i.e.*, matters other than speech, religion, search and seizure, and criminal procedure). The judges are importuned to rule that a particular regulation is invalid, usually as applied, because it does not accomplish a particularly important purpose and/or it unreasonably interferes with other values. Thus, for instance, a litigant attacking a zoning ordinance that completely excludes mobile homes entirely from a town might argue seriatim that the exclusion serves no useful purpose, that the exclusion is inconsistent with other town regulations (permitting, for instance, semi-permanent occupation of motel units), that the exclusion is inconsistent with the regional need for locations for lower-income residents, and that the regulation thus arbitrarily interferes with the rights of the owner to use his property.[34]

Fessler concludes, properly in my view, that it is unlikely that federal courts will make free use of the substantive due process approach in reviewing local regulation.[35] On the other hand, as Fessler argues, it is much more likely that state judges will be willing to find local regulations with exclusionary impacts "unreasonable," especially if the state constitution, or state legislation, contains language leading generally in that direction. Some recent cases might indicate a trend line.[36]

---

[33]In Shannon v. HUD, 436 F.2d 809 (3rd Cir. 1970), the court read the history of housing and civil rights legislation to create a national policy requiring HUD to take into account racial concentration in dispersing federal housing subsidies. It is quite doubtful, however, that a federal court on supremacy grounds would invalidate local laws that exclude without a direct and bold congressional statement to that end. The probabilities for such legislation do not seem high.

[34]*See, e.g.*, Judge Hall's classic dissent in Vickers v. Gloucester Township, 37 N.J. 232, 251, 181 A.2d 129, 148 (1962).

[35]*But see*, Southern Alameda Spanish Speaking Organization v. City of Union City, 424 F.2d 291 (9th Cir. 1970) and the district court's subsequent determination, No. 41490 Memo. of Decision by Sweigert, J. filed July 31, 1970.

[36]*E.G., In re* Girsh, 437 Pa. 237, 263 A. 2d 395 (1970); *In re* Kit Mar Builders, 439 Pa. 466, 268 A.2d 765 (1970); Board of County Comm. v. Casper, 200 Va. 653, 107 S.E. 2d 390 (1959).

What the foregoing indicates is that judicial attack on municipal land-use regulation will most likely continue to exert a pressure towards either regionalization of the low income access problem or at least selected judicial vetoes of particular municipal policy decisions that operate to deny access to low income residents. The frequency of such suits will increase as the new participants in the market find such grounds effective. But judicial attack will not produce rapid across-the-board change, because the courts appear unwilling to premise decisions on sweeping doctrinal grounds.

Before leaving this topic, reference at least should be made to the recent decision of the California Supreme Court in *Serrano v. Priest*.[37] *Serrano* held the California scheme for financing public education to be unconstitutional as a denial of equal protection of the laws, under the Federal and California Constitutions, in discriminating on the basis of wealth in the provision of public education. The culprit was reliance on the property tax, at least for a good portion of the local education bill. The solution will probably be to greatly increase the financing of public secondary and primary education from the state level. Such a solution would have interesting implications on exclusionary land regulation, even if restricted solely to education. At least in California about one-half of the local property tax goes to local school districts. Shifting this revenue drain to the state level would deprive the municipality of its principle public *raison d'etre* for exclusion, the shortage of local funds. If *Serrano* is extended to other municipal services, the argument for exclusionary zoning becomes even weaker. Adoption of the *Serrano* doctrine *might* make some suburban cities less unfriendly to the dispersion of some of the disadvantaged to their jurisdictions; it would certainly make it harder to justify refusal to accommodate newcomers. It *might* make laws like the Massachusetts quota system unnecessary. It *might* make negotiations carried out by regional entities more fruitful. But the extension of the *Serrano* doctrine to other states or to other municipal services is highly uncertain.[38]

State Governments

The environmental movement is largely responsible for the creation of a number of state (and regional) agencies that are playing an

---

[37] 5 Cal. 3d 584, 96 Cal. Rptr. 601, 487 P.2d 1241 (1971).
[38] *But see*, Kenneth Karst, *Serrano v. Priest—A State Court's Responsibility's and Opportunities in the Development of Federal Constitutional Law*, 60 CAL. L. REV. 720 (1972).

increasingly important role in land regulation. These agencies have usually been given negative powers and can do no more than veto land-uses and development licensed by local governments. But we are beginning to witness, the evolution of state agencies that function positively. The state planning agency proposed in the ALI Model Land Development Code, for instance, is given power to override local development vetoes in selected cases. And developments in New York provide a good example of state efforts with the potential for positive action.[39]

Nelson Rockefeller, when first elected in 1958, moved rapidly to strengthen the office of the Governor as a policy planning center.[40] Then came a number of steps that have made state planning and implementation more effective in two regards. First, the activities of state functional agencies are better coordinated. Second, a variety of state public benefit corporations have been created which have facilitated financing, programming, and construction of capital facilities, including low- and moderate-income housing.

In the course of Rockefeller's first three terms (1958–1970), New York created the Office of Planning Coordination, a series of multi-county regional planning boards, a planning programming-budgeting (PPB) system, a number of "super departments," and a series of public benefit corporations, as mentioned above. The regional planning boards have become neither regional general purpose governments nor state instruments operating regionally with some local representation, as originally hoped.[41] The rest of the apparatus, however, has clearly strengthened the state hand and, concomitantly, drained some powers away from local government. Continuation of this trend seems probable.[42]

The public benefit corporation is a central feature in the New York approach. One example is the State University Construction Fund. The other, of particular interest to this paper, is the New York State Urban Development Corporation (UDC), the board of which is appointed by the governor. UDC has the authority and capacity to undertake four types of projects: residential projects consisting of low- and moderate-income housing; industrial projects;

---

[39]This text is based largely on Vincent I. Moore, *Politics, Planning and Power in New York State—The Path from Theory to Reality*, 37 J. AM. INSTIT. PLANNERS, 66 (March 1971).

[40]*Id.*

[41]*Id.* at 70.

[42]*Id.* at 76.

civic projects; and land-improvement projects. It is empowered to acquire land by purchase or condemnation, to override local zoning and building codes, and to build, sell, manage, or lease any of its projects.[43]

As of October 1, 1970, two years after its establishment, UDC had seventeen projects underway, including 7,500 housing units, and had also committed another 43,000 units in twenty-six different localities. While its policy has been to go into a city only when invited by local officials (although this has meant a mayor's invitation even over the objection of city council members), this might change, at least in degree, when UDC becomes financially independent.[44]

New York has a record of pioneering with innovative techniques, many of which are later adopted in other states. A successful program of the sort described will undoubtedly be copied by other urban states. Thus, we see another source of erosion of the municipal monopoly on land-use regulation.[45]

Federal Stimulants

From the great variety of federal programs ranging from planning grants to river basin commissions, I have selected only a few prominent undertakings, or prospects, that bear particularly on the continued vitality of municipal land use regulation.

There are two especially noteworthy programs that have been adopted and one prospective program, that if adopted, will further erode the municipal monopoly over land use controls: metropolitan clearing house A–95 type review; and HUD policy regarding the distribution of subsidy funds for housing,[46] and pending measures involving a national land-use policy.

The Office of Management and Budget Circular A–95, Title IV of the Intergovernmental Cooperation Act of 1968, provides for review of applications for assistance under more than 100 federal grant and loan programs by state, regional and metropolitan clear-

---

[43]*Id.*

[44]*Id.* at 77.

[45]A variety of other laws shifting licensing power to state levels have been passed, especially concerning installations which localities resist but which are deemed necessary for the general welfare. Siting of power generation plants is a good example.

[46]Revenue sharing, with payments directly to local governments, if it comes to pass, will exert a contrary pressure.

inghouses.[47] The reviews, which are advisory only, seek to identify the relationship of the proposed project to area comprehensive plans. The review requirements, originally established for metropolitan areas by a 1966 statute,[48] have stimulated the creation of numerous councils of government and the preparation of regional and metropolitan plans.

A–95 review, as practiced, will obviously not regionalize land-use regulation. But it does provide an evolutionary base, for negotiation between a regional agency and local governments regarding municipal exclusion of developments of regional consequence. The experience of the Dayton, Ohio, area exemplifies this possible trend.[49] There, the Miami Valley Regional Planning Commission devised a plan "to disperse in four years 14,000 units of federally subsidized housing throughout the Dayton, Ohio, Metropolitan area on a 'fair share' basis, computed on the basis of both community needs and capacities—in other words, a plan to build low- and moderate-income housing, including public housing, in white suburbs."[50] The plan was unanimously adopted in 1970 by the local elected officials who constitute the Commission, and its chances of success appear substantial.[51] A–95 type review was one of the levers for Commission implementation, but, more important, it appears to have been the prime stimulant for the creation of the regional commission that provided the crucial framework for building a metropolitan consensus.

In *Shannon v. HUD*[52] the Third Circuit Court of Appeals held that federal statutes have created a national housing policy which mandates that HUD act affirmatively to eradicate residental segregation, both *de jure* and *de facto*, in federally assisted housing.[53] HUD has issued project criteria for public housing funds and housing subsidies that favor projects located away from areas of minor-

---

[47]WILLIAM BRUSSAT, *Realizing the Potentials of A–95*, PLANNING 1971 (ASPO 1971); Vincent Smith, The Intergovernmental Cooperation Act of 1968; Opportunity for State Government, *id.* at 61.

[48]Section 204, Demonstration Cities and Metropolitan Development Act of 1966, Pub. L. No. 89–754, 80 Stat. 1255.

[49]Lois Craig, *The Dayton Area's "Fair Share" Housing Plan Enters the Implementation Phase*, 6 CITY 50 (1972).

[50]*Id.*

[51]*Id.*

[52]436 F.2d 809 (3rd Cir. 1970); Noted 46 N.Y.U.L. REV. 561 (1971).

[53]*See also*, Gautreaux v. Chicago Housing Authority, 296 F. Supp. 907 (N.D. Ill. 1969).

ity concentration.[54] In addition, HUD is seeking to give priority funding on water, sewer, urban renewal, and model cities grants to communities that adopt area-wide planning goals and provide housing accessibility on a nondiscriminatory basis.[55] Secretary Romney reported in December 1971 that of 117 low-income housing projects started during the latter half of 1970 in six metropolitan areas (Baltimore, Washington, San Diego, San Antonio, Pittsburgh, and Jacksonville), 77 were in suburban areas and 40 within the central city areas. Whether or not these figures are significant, it seems apparent that HUD is making serious effort to disperse low-income housing. The political future of such efforts is problematic.[56] But recent legislative activity gives reason to expect more, rather than less, federal action in the future.[57]

A variety of legislation has been introduced in the past few years with the objective of requiring the states to engage in land-use planning and regulation. In their latest embodiments,[58] states would be induced to create state land planning processes and land-use programs[59] to control the siting of key growth inducing facilities, the construction of large scale developments, and the protection of areas of critical environmental concern.[60] Such legislation can be seen as a part of an emergence of a nascent "national urban growth policy" discussed in 1971 by Norman Beckman.[61] Serious interventions of these sorts will by necessity undercut municipal self-determination.

Speculations on the Future

What are the probable land development consequences of today's broad trend toward regionalization? At the outset two points should be noted. First various sources of pressure towards change have different goals and strengths. The environmental movement, for instance, is not centrally concerned with the dispersion of low-

---

[54]30 CONG. Q. 50–55 (Jan. 8, 1972).

[55]*Id.* at 64.

[56]The Ashley proposal, H.R. 9688, 92nd Cong. 2d Sess., for instance, for metropolitan housing councils patterned on the Dayton experience, 30 CONG. Q. 55 (Jan. 8, 1972), was recently defeated in the House.

[57]See survey, of legislative activity in 30 CONG. Q. 50–55 (Jan. 8, 1972).

[58]30 CONG. Q., 297 (Feb. 12, 1972).

[59]For a broad treatment of these matters *see*, HERMAN RUTH, *Elements of a National Policy for Land-Use*, PLANNING 1971. (1971).

[60]*See also*, Melvin Levin, *The Big Regions*, 34 J. AM. INSTIT. PLANNERS 66 (1968).

[61]Beckman, *Development of National Urban Growth Policy—Legislative Review* 1970, 37 J. AM. INSTIT. PLANNERS 146 (1971).

income persons throughout a metropolitan area, as is the civil rights movement. Second, it is considered less of an invasion of local prerogatives. In addition, to create a regional or state agency that can veto a development licensed by a local government is characteristically perceived as less of an invasion than to empower such an agency to license a development that local government has traditionally had authority to veto.[62] Therefore, objectives that can be accomplished through a system that reviews local determinations, and weeds out unacceptable development, stand a better chance for implementation than objectives that require imposing a regionally important development on unwilling localities.

The seemingly most powerful stimulant towards regionalization of land-use regulation is the environmental movement. Four chief reasons support this assertion. First, the conditions it opposes are concretely perceived as ones requiring extra-local control: air and water pollution, loss of open space, disappearance of undeveloped shoreline, and freeway traffic. Second, these conditions are part of everyday life and not visited primarily on deprived classes or racial groups. Third, a large constituency of politically able and influential persons are interested in these problems. Finally, for many people the costs of environmental quality do not enter into the calculus of decision-making because the trade-offs involved are remote or the added costs as distributed do not seem consequential. There are few persons, for instance, who consider the probable increase in electricity rates occasioned by regulations prohibiting the use of low-grade fuel oil with a high sulfur content. Similarly, there has been very little public concern with the cost consequences of the automobile emission standards promulgated under the Clean Air Act of 1970.

If the recent past evidences what is likely to occur in the near future, we can predict the creation of numerous regional and state agencies empowered to veto locally licensed development.[63] The veto power will take the form of both zoning-type regulations (such as the Hawaii state conservation zone where urban development is prohibited in advance) and performance standards (such as the regulations of the Tahoe Regional Planning Commission requiring

---

[62]This statement excludes, of course, subject matters that traditionally have been administered at the state level; such as highway location and construction.

[63]Nearly every environmental agency studied by Callies and Bosselman exercises this type of authority.

elaborate mechanical systems to preclude siltation otherwise produced by land development). Such regulations will almost invariably render development more expensive by internalizing costs that previously were externalized. Thus in the Tahoe example, for instance, the developer and his buyers will have to pay the cost of cleaning up storm runoff rather than having discharged wastes cause pollution that is harmful to other users of the Lake. And the probabilities are substantial that the regulations will be considerably more onerous than at present, especially as the regulating agencies will, at the outset at least, be devoted to the single goal of environmental protection and will not be charged with responsibility for solving associated social problems, such as housing and employment.

If these predictions are correct, the environmental movement will produce agencies that will slow down development and make it more expensive—thus increasing the exclusionary effects of present local land-use regulations. (Low- and moderate-income housing projects, for instance, will have to satisfy two reviews, not the single local one as at present.) Local government resistance to regional edicts involving these subjects will not be intense because the local constituencies, at least in the suburbs, will generally agree with the regional goals. Agreement, in fact, will be easy because the regional regulations will operate primarily to the disadvantage of nonresidents who might like to move in; existing homes and business will be largely unaffected. The acceptability of tough regional environmental regulations will be even more pronounced where courts embrace the *Serrano v. Priest* doctrine. For if the states assume a larger share of fiscal responsibility for schools and other local services, suburban governments will find it less necessary to attract industry (and provide housing for workers) to solve their fiscal problems.

Four of the other pressures for change will act at variance with the environmental stimulant, in form and, to an extent, in goals. Open housing proponents are seeking to emasculate local veto powers. Market pressures operate similarly. State efforts of the sort exemplified in New York and provided for the ALI Model Land Development Code authorize state licensing of regionally important development over local objection. Federal policy is conflicting, but HUD dispersion policies and metropolitan clearinghouses for federal subsidies seek to overcome the potency of local opposition to development of regional importance.

The proponents of open housing, while seemingly well-organized, do not appear to be nearly as powerful politically as the environmental movement. Their constituency is considerably smaller. The goals are central to a relatively small group; in fact, dispersion is viewed ambivalently by many minority persons, and resisted in the suburbs.

Despite the foregoing, it is possible that the proponents of open housing will occasionally be able to wrest concessions from suburban representatives, perhaps as the price for supporting the creation of an environmental agency at the regional level. This might be demonstrated by some theorizing about the San Francisco Bay Region. The minority population in central cities of the region continues to grow. Political organization within this population has become much firmer. More minority members occupy offices of considerable influence. Many minority members are quite suspicious of proposals to create regional agencies of any kind. These are seen as part of a strategy to strip local governments of power just at the point when minority voters are likely to take over controls of some of these governments. (Oakland and Richmond are good examples.) These fears, whether real or imagined, jibe nicely with the fears of some suburbanites who equate regional government with central city rule. The attitudes of the minority population also could lead to cooperative relationships with groups whose economic interests are most endangered by effective environmental controls. Given a situation where minority political leaders control an important swing vote, it is not inconceivable that the price for creating a regional entity with powers to protect environmental values will be the assignment to such an agency of power and responsibility involving social concerns as well. If the San Francisco Bay Conservation and Development Commission were being proposed today, the quid pro quo might well be access by minorities to housing near new industrial employment opportunities in the suburbs. This would make particularly good sense because a strict prohibition on filling in the Bay has made it increasingly difficult to locate new industry in the central cities where minority concentrations are highest.[64] While coalition political efforts of the sort described will be success-

---

[64]The mayors of large cities, for obvious reasons, have also been active in supporting legislation to permit metropolitan dispersion of low-income residents.

ful only occasionally, combinations of housing producers and state
and federal officials might prove to have greater vitality.

Open housing proponents will undoubtedly continue to bring
court actions that will exert pressure in selected instances. Judicial
intervention alone will not seriously undercut municipal land regulatory power on a national scale unless, as is doubtful, federal
courts adopt a position that equal protection renders invalid regulations that have the *effect* of excluding persons on the basis of
wealth or race. In the absence of such a holding, litigation will be
successful where discriminatory purpose can be shown and, more
broadly, in those states where courts are willing to judge the reasonableness of a particular regulation by taking into account its
regional implications. In most instances, this will require case-by-
case litigation with each determination based on the particular
mixture of facts that are proved. Such litigation creates opportunities for upsetting a particular regulation hitherto invulnerable to
attack, but case-by-case assaults in expensive law suits will not
alone produce sweeping change. The availability of judicial remedies, however, might be a useful political lever in a number of negotiations.

The strength of open housing proponents should be augmented
by the resources of the new participants in the housing market. If
the present trend continues (and it might well be furthered by federal programs like "Operation Breakthrough") large politically influential corporations will have a financial stake in breaking down
parochial barriers to low- and moderate-income housing. Such corporations should perceive the advantages of state and regional
agencies that can license development barred by local regulation,
and should be willing to spend money and exert influence in support
of the creation of such agencies. Moreover, to the extent that litigation can play a useful role, such corporations predictably will be
willing and able to pursue judicial remedies. Their cases will be
strengthened because they will be "representing" not only their
shareholders but also the consumers of their products.

State governments might well follow the lead of New York in
creating instrumentalities with authority to supersede local decisions for selected types of development. They will be importuned
to do so by housing producers, open housing proponents, and central city politicians. Moreover, especially in the large urban states,
the plight of the disadvantaged is increasingly viewed as a state
problem. One must not discount, however, the large suburban

representation in state legislatures and the vitality of suburban resistance to the erosion of "home rule" powers.

The federal government might play an important role. The most realistic possibility is through metropolitan planning and review agencies of the sort stimulated by the A–95 process. William Wheaton in 1967[65] called for a metropolitan allocation agency with power to negotiate with local governments concerning population placement by racial and economic classes, the location of metropolitan facilities, and the location of revenue and employment generating sources. The agency's stick would be the control over state and federal grants-in-aid. Such an instrumentality is only one step away from the emerging A–95 agencies and could be an effective means for implementing a variety of federal policies including the HUD principles guiding the location of federally subsidized housing. Other means are also available.[66]

The other pressure for change is coming from the lawyers as reflected in the ALI Model Land Development Code. An intriguing aspect is the attempt to legalize planning decisions—by the establishing and enforcing of procedures that require disclosure of the reasons underlying decisions to permit or bar a proposed development, and by requiring estimates of the social and environmental effects of such decisions. Such a system of required disclosure would affect local planning determinations in two important ways. Local officials would have to face up to the moral and regional consequences of their actions. And local decisions would be more vulnerable when subject to effective extra-local judicial or administrative review. Both effects tend to impose *de facto* limitations on parochial decision-making.

Conclusion

We are witnessing a substantial transfer of land-use control from the local to regional and state levels. Professionals, both lawyers and planners, have long called for this move, and lawyers, as well as the planners, are now beginning to act institutionally to achieve it. More important, however, there are new participants in the process, and the groups exerting the greatest contemporary pressure are involved in the environmental movement. As power moves up-

---

[65]William Wheaton, *Metro-Allocation Planning*, 33 J. AM. INSTIT. PLANNERS 103 (1967).
[66]*See* notes 56 and 57, *supra*.

ward in response to this pressure, newly created state and regional agencies are likely to exercise their negative powers to prevent development that would have adverse physical environmental impacts. The strongest exercise of these powers will probably restrict the actions of land owners far more than zoning does now. If rulings are based upon environmental considerations alone and social goals are ignored, development will become more expensive, thus heightening exclusionary impacts.

The new agencies will provide a governmental framework which could be used to achieve social outcomes. Whether they will be so used will depend upon the vitality of the new participants in the housing market and the proponents of open housing. The ability of the housing groups to secure state and federal interventions which override local development vetos will determine the substantive outcome of the movement of land regulation power upward.

Editor's Comments

Fasano v. Board of County Commissioners of Washington County: Is Rezoning an Administrative or Legislative Function?

Robert H. Freilich

Editor, *The Urban Lawyer*
Hulen Professor of Law in
Urban Affairs
University of Missouri—Kansas City
School of Law

HAVING ARISEN from a relative quiesence, the State of Oregon in the last several years has found itself among the leaders in finding solutions to various urban law problems such as the environment, gas rationing, growth control and coastline development. Last year was no exception, as the Supreme Court of Oregon handed down its decision in *Fasano v. Board of County Commissioners of Washington County.*[1] In my opinion, this decision finally provides a rational basis for judicial review of zoning by holding a zoning board's actions in rezoning specific pieces of property is a *judicial* rather than a legislative function.[2] By removing the legislative cloak of presumed validity, the Oregon supreme court has made a marked departure from the majority view.

The case involved a challenge to the approval by the Board of County Commissioners of a zone change from single family residential to Planned Residential which allowed mobile home parks.

---

1. 507 P.2d 23 (Ore. 1973), digested in 5 URB. LAW. 771 (1973).
2. The characterization of "judicial" is that of the Oregon supreme court. Ordinarily actions of a legislative body which address a specific set of facts and issuance of a license, approval or permit are denominated "*quasi-judicial*," or "administrative." *See* Jehovah's Witnesses v. Mullen, 214 Ore. 281, 292, 330 P.2d 5 (1958); Chrobuch v. Snohomish, 78 Wash. 2d 884, 480 P.2d 489, 495–96 (1971); Ward v. Village of Skokie, 26 Ill. 2d 415, 186 N.E.2d 529, 533 (1962); Belclaire Holding Corp. v. Klingher, 28 App. Div. 2d 689, 280 N.Y.S.2d 942 (1967).

The PUD type ordinance which was passed subsequent to the county's comprehensive plan, was of the "floating zone" variety in that specifications and procedures were established for those wishing to qualify their property, but no land was placed on the zoning map.[3] Adjoining property owners had contested the change and the trial court's reversal of the board's order was affirmed by the court of appeals.

Traditionally, the majority view has been that a county governing board's action in adopting a zoning ordinance or amendment (rezoning) is legislative. As a result, the actions of the legislative body are accorded a presumption of validity[4] which may only be overturned by a court on a showing that the board acted arbitrarily or capriciously. Because of the "fairly debatable" test of *Village of Euclid v. Ambler Realty Co.*,[5] the opponent of the legislative action has a tremendous burden on judicial review. As recently illustrated in *Board of County Commissioners, Hillsborough County v. Ralston*:[6]

> Judicial authority to order zoning change is limited to those circumstances in which the maintenance of the existing classification is arbitrary, capricious, confiscatory in its effect: in short, unconstitutional. The basic authority to zone lies with . . . (the) commissioners, and so long as their prescribed limitations are fairly debatable, we are powerless to intervene.[7]

However, a very few jurisdictions, such as Oregon, are beginning to realize that the process of applying a zoning ordinance or amendment to a specific piece of property which affects a limited number of people and is based on contested facts, more nearly approximates an administrative or quasi-judicial function than a legislative function. As Justice Howell states in *Fasano*:

---

3. *See* Rodgers v. Village of Tarrytown, 202 N.Y. 115, 96 N.E.2d 731 (1950), which originated the "floating zone" concept.

4. The court in Fasano, *supra* note 1, at 26 states:
The majority of jurisdictions state that a zoning ordinance is a legislative act and is thereby entitled to presumptive validity.
Previously, in Smith v. County of Washington, 241 Ore. 380, 406 P.2d 545 (1965), the Supreme Court of Oregon had apparently applied the same presumption of validity to an amendment to a zoning ordinance.

5. 272 U.S. 365, 388 (1926): "If the validity of the legislative classification for zoning purposes be *fairly debatable*, the legislative judgment must be allowed to control." (emphasis added)

6. 284 So.2d 456 (Fla. App. 1973).

7. *Id.* at 457. *See also* Beaver Gasoline Co. v. Zoning Hearing Board of the Borough of Osborne, 445 Pa. 571, 285 A.2d 501, 503 (1971): ". . . a challenge to the constitutionality of a zoning ordinance must overcome a presumption of its validity."

. . . we would be ignoring reality to rigidly view all zoning decisions by local governing bodies as legislative acts to be accorded a full presumption of validity and shielded from less than constitutional scrutiny by the theory of separation of powers. Local and small decision groups are simply not the equivalent in all respects of state and national legislatures.[8]

There can be no dispute that the original passage of comprehensive plans and zoning ordinances is a legislative function since these actions are classified as general policy decisions which apply to the entire community. However, a zoning amendment may be differentiated on the basis that such a determination is narrowly confined to a particular piece of property and the use will generally affect only a small number of people, thus approximating an administrative exercise. In making the ultimate decision as to whether a zoning board exercises legislative or quasi-judicial action, one commentator has suggested that the test to be applied:

> Basically . . . involves the determination of whether action produces a general rule or policy which is applicable to an open class of individuals, interests or situations, or whether it entails the application of a general rule or policy to specific individuals, interests, or situations. If the former determination is satisfied, there is legislative action; if the latter is satisfied, the action is judicial.[9]

Other jurisdictions have developed various modes of discarding the legislative presumption in certain instances, but without going to the extent of *Fasano* where it has been altogether eliminated. Pennsylvania, in circumstances of exclusion of uses from a jurisdiction (which are not a nuisance per se) reverses the presumption of validity and places on the municipality the burden of proving that a rational basis exists for the zoning regulation.[10] Another ap-

---

8. Fasano, *supra* note 1, at 26. Further, Justice Howell, in stating that judicial recognition of such fact of life is growing, quotes Justice Klingbiel's often cited specially concurring opinion in Ward v. Village of Skokie, *supra* note 2, 186 N.E.2d at 533:
   It is not a part of the legislative function to grant permits, make special exceptions, or decide particular cases. Such activities are not legislative but administrative, quasi-judicial, or judicial in character. To place them in the hands of legislative bodies, whose acts as such are not judicially reviewable, is to open the door completely to arbitrary government.
9. Comment, *Zoning Amendments—The Product of Judicial or Quasi-Judicial Action*, 33 OHIO ST. L.J. 130, 137 (1972). *See also* Dillon Companies, Inc. v. City of Boulder, 515 P.2d 627 (Colo. 1973); Fleming v. City of Tacoma, 81 Wash. 2d 292, 502, P.2d 327 (1972).
10. Beaver Gasoline Co., *supra* note 7; Appeal of Girsh, 437 Pa. 237, 263 A.2d 395 (1970); Exton Quarries, Inc. v. Zoning Bd. of Adjustment, 425 Pa. 43, 228 A.2d 169 (1967). Note the similarity to the fundamental interest test of Shapiro v. Thompson, 394 U.S. 618 (1969) where the state must show a "compelling interest" for the regulation.

proach is that utilized by Michigan. The courts of that state have developed a classification of "preferred uses" (hospitals, schools, churches, multi-family housing and mobile homes) which may not be excluded from a community unless some overriding public interest is shown. Thus, although the Michigan courts use the so called "antipresumption," the focus is on the type of land use involved.[11] A number of states also grant a preferred status to uses which accord with state policy, particularly public or subsidized housing.[12] An important factor in the New York Court of Appeals upholding of the concept of timed and sequential zoning in the *Ramapo* case,[13] was the key provision of the ordinance permitting public housing to be exempt from the provisions of the zoning ordinance.[14]

In rejecting the proposition that judicial review of a zoning change by a local governing body is not limited to a determination of "whether the change is arbitrary or capricious," the court in *Fasano* established the following principles and standards for review:[15]

1. The power to zone is conditioned on the comprehensive plan; therefore any change in zoning must be shown to be in accord with the comprehensive plan. In making such a showing, it must be proved that:
   a. There is a public need for the change;
   b. Such need is served by changing the zone of the particular property in question rather than other available property;

---

11. Bristow v. City of Woodhaven, 35 Mich. App. 205, 192 N.W.2d 322 (1971); Simmons v. City of Royal Oak, 38 Mich. App. 496, 196 N.W.2d 811 (1972); Baker v. City of Algonae, 39 Mich. App. 526, 198 N.W.2d 13 (1972); Binkowski v. Township of Shelby, 46 Mich. App. 451, 208 N.W.2d 243 (1973). *See also* Feiler, *Metropolitanization and Land-Use Parochialism—Toward a Judicial Attitude*, 69 MICH. L. REV. 655 (1971); Fisher, *The General Public Interest vs. The Presumption of Zoning Ordinance Validity: A Debatable Question*, 50 J. URB. L. 129 (1972).

12. *See* Freilich & Bass, *Exclusionary Zoning: Suggested Litigation Approaches*, 3 URB. LAW. 344, 372 (1971); Cameron v. Zoning Agent of Bellingham, 357 Mass. 757, 260 N.E.2d 143 (1970); DeSimone v. Greater Englewood Housing Corp. No. 1, 56 N.J. 428, 267 A.2d 31 (1970).

13. Golden v. Planning Board of the Town of Ramapo, 30 N.Y.2d 359, 334 N.Y.S.2d 138, 285 N.E.2d 291 (1972), *appeal dismissed*, 409 U.S. 1003 (1972).

14. Matter of Greenwald v. Town of Ramapo, 35 App. Div. 2d 958, 317 N.Y.S.2d 839 (1970); Matter of Farrelly v. Town of Ramapo, 35 App. Div. 2d 957, 317 N.Y.S.2d 837 (1970); Fletcher v. Romney, 323 F. Supp. 189 (S.D.N.Y. 1971).

15. Fasano, *supra* note 1, at 27–30.

2. The burden of proof is on the party seeking the change since it involves an exercise of judicial authority. The greater the change, the greater will be the burden in showing such change is in accord with the comprehensive plan, that there is public need for the change, and that such need will best be met by the change.

In *Fasano,* since the procedures outlined and burdens of proof were not met, the supreme court affirmed the determinations of the lower courts not to allow the change.

Another compelling reason for interpreting the decisions of zoning boards as judicial rather than legislative actions, is the greater due process safeguards accorded a judicial proceeding.[16] However, when considering local legislative bodies which are in many instances partially composed of and subject to the influence of developers, one of the greatest reasons for judicial review on rezoning is cogently stated by Justice Howell:

> By treating the exercise of authority by the commission in this case as the exercise of judicial rather than of legislative authority and thus enlarging the scope of review on appeal, and by placing the burden of the . . . level of proof upon the one seeking change, we may lay the court open to criticism by legal scholars who think it desirable that planning authorities be vested with the ability to adjust more freely to changed conditions. *However, having weighed the dangers of making desirable changes more difficult against the dangers of the almost irresistible pressures that can be asserted by privated economic interests on local government, we believe that the latter dangers are more to be feared.* (emphasis added)[17]

The recent move towards statewide zoning, hailed by some as the "quiet revolution" in land use controls, has been mainly focussing on environmental concerns in rural and critical environmental areas (lakes, ponds, shorelines, flood plains, etc.). Moves towards statewide zoning in *urban* areas have proved to be less than satisfactory. Massachusetts' anti-snob zoning housing law has produced little public or subsidized housing of note, while New York State's Urban Development Corporation has had its powers of overriding local planning and zoning in township areas deleted by the legislature. It seems unlikely that there will be any major movement to statewide control over urban areas. The process would reverse the entire struggle of the 1960's for citizen participation and decentralization of

---

16. Comment, *supra* note 9.
17. Fasano, *supra* note 1, at 29–30.

governmental decision-making functions. If powers are given to states to control local zoning and planning processes two major factors will become apparent (1) the states are likely to be as exclusionary or *more exclusionary than localities* (witness Vermont's new land use control law, Oregon, New York); and (2) judicial review of state decisions will not be possible except under extreme circumstances of arbitrariness and capriciousness (a resort to the early 1930's concept of "substantive due process"). Most state capitals are located in nonmetropolitan areas (Albany, Sacramento, Trenton, Tallahassee, etc.) and the experience with reapportionment in state legislatures shows that they are likely to become more representative of exclusionist suburban attitudes than the suburbs themselves. Municipalities and regions, however, will have far greater flexibility to adapt innovative planning approaches (timing and sequential controls; transfer of development rights; cluster zoning) and because of the delegation of power from the state to a sub-state governmental body, the Courts will have the opportunity to review local and regional decisions to require that decisions be in accordance with enabling act standards, such as a regional or local comprehensive plan. Decisions like *Golden* and *Fasano*, by placing strict procedures and standards on local communities in making planning decisions are far more likely to result in better planning, greater responsiveness to public needs, concerns, and participation, than a resort to state systems of land use control in urban areas. Surely one experience with the disaster of FHA housing programs in urban areas indicates that simply being "higher" does not mean "better."

Although *Fasano* has not, to this point, been given the attention which it deserves, I believe it represents a rational approach to review of zoning cases. For all of us interested in planning and zoning, I am of the opinion that the protections which judicial review provides in controlling development and in preserving the desired and compatible uses of land in our local communities far outweigh any disadvantages that might result.

A Tentative Guide to the American Law Institute's Proposed Model Land Development Code*

Cyril A. Fox, Jr.

Assistant Professor of Law
University of Pittsburgh School of
Law; A.B., The College of Wooster
(1958); J.D., University of
Pittsburgh (1965); Member,
Pennsylvania Bar.

I. Introduction

I MUST ADMIT to feeling a bit uncomfortable talking about the American Law Institute's Model Land Development Code when, technically, it will not exist until next year at the earliest. When completed, the Code will be the result of more than twelve years of "critical re-examination and re-working of the law relating to public control of land use and land development." Undertaken by the ALI in 1963 with the aid of a grant from the Ford Foundation, the Code is being prepared under the guidance of Professor Allison Dunham of the University of Chicago Law School as Chief Reporter, aided initially by three Assistant Reporters and, since 1969, by Fred P. Bosselman, Esquire, of Chicago, as Associate Reporter. In addition, an Advisory Committee of distinguished judges, lawyers, and academicians, chaired by Richard F. Babcock, Esquire of Chicago, has worked with the Reporters from the beginning.

Since 1968 the Council and full membership of the ALI have discussed six "Tentative Drafts" of various provisions of the Code. This year Proposed Official Draft No. 1, containing six of the twelve projected final articles, was considered by the Institute at its annual meeting. It is expected that the other six articles, along with the few recommended changes in P.O.D. No. 1, will be presented to next year's annual meeting for final approval.

---

*Remarks before the Local Government Law Section Session on Land Use Policy at the Annual Meeting of the American Bar Association, August 14, 1974, Honolulu, Hawaii.

Although not yet completed, work on the Code has progressed sufficiently to permit discussion of many of its features. In fact, "Tentative Draft No. 3," covering state involvement in land regulation has already had a significant impact. Florida's Environmental Land and Water Management Act of 1972[1] is based largely upon that Draft. Senator Jackson's proposed "Land Use Policy and Planning Assistance Act of 1973," S. 268, borrows extensively from that Draft as, to a lesser extent does H.R. 10294, the "Land Use Planning Act of 1973," sponsored by Representative Udall and others.

The Model Code will be the first major revision of development legislation since publication of the Standard State Zoning Enabling Act, and its companion, the Standard City Planning Enabling Act almost fifty years ago. In its present form, the Code covers four substantive areas of land development control law. Using familiar terminology, which the Code often seeks to avoid, these are: (1) the use of land, or zoning; (2) the division of land into parcels, or subdivision; (3) re-planning and development of improperly or inadequately planned and used land, or urban redevelopment; and (4) direct governmental intervention in the land market for planning and development purposes, or eminent domain.

The regulatory and planning authority for local governments is set forth in Articles 1 through 5 of the proposed Code. Article 6, still in "Tentative Draft" form, provides authority for the state to engage in "land banking," the acquisition and disposition of property and property interests for future private and public development. Articles 7 and 8 provide the framework for state planning activities and intervention in local development decision-making. Articles 9 through 12 are essentially procedural articles, dealing with judicial review of development decisions (Article 9), enforcement of development regulations (Article 10), public records of regulations and permits (Article 11), and financing and coordinating public development activities (Article 12).

Only Articles 1 through 5 and 7 have reached "Proposed Official Draft" form. Therefore, Article 6 and Articles 9 through 12 will not be discussed. Discussion of Article 8, although also still in "Tentative Draft," is essential to an understanding of the role of state government in development planning under the Proposed Code.

---

1. 14 Fla. Stat. Ann. §§380.012 et seq. (1974).

Despite tne recent surge in federal and state legislation directly involving state or regional agencies in land development regulation, the Model Code places the primary authority for this activity in the existing units of local government. The Reporters believe that as much as ninety-five per cent of all land use decisions do not have regional or state-wide impact. Decisions directly affecting the growth and development of a community are best made by that community through its own political processes, not by some bureaucrat far removed from the scene of the actual controversy.[2]

Since the Code places the primary responsibility for regulation in the local government, we should first examine how local regulation will occur before turning to the means by which the state may become involved in the regulatory and planning process.

II. Grant and Extent of Regulatory Power

Article 1 contains the basic grant of regulatory authority and defines, among other terms, the scope of activities which may be regulated. Local governments are authorized "to plan or otherwise encourage, regulate or undertake the development of land" in accordance with the powers and procedures set forth in the Code.[3] Here, the Code seeks to emphasize that planning and regulatory actions can operate positively to encourage and direct future development of a community, not only in the negative fashion envisioned by the Standard Acts, in order to conserve the value of existing land uses.[4]

Consistent with the proposition that all land use decisions should be made at the local level, at least initially, the Code includes the federal, state and other local governments and their instrumentalities,[5] as "developers" subject to local regulation, unless exempted by the local ordinance.

The definition of "development," those activities which may be regulated, is so complicated and so extensive that it requires a lengthy section of its own.[6] This definition is largely adapted from

---

2. A Model Land Development Code, Commentary to Article 7, at 286 (Proposed Official Draft No. 1, 1974) [hereinafter cited as Code. All references are to P.O.D. No. 1 unless otherwise indicated.].

3. Code, §1–102.

4. Note to Code §1–102, at 11. Compare Standard Zoning Enabling Act (Final ed. 1926) §3 n.25 as to the purpose of zoning under SZEA.

5. Code, §§1–201 (1) and (4).

6. Code, §1–202.

the English Town and Country Planning Act.[7] "Development" is defined as "the performance of any building or mining operation, the making of any material change in the use or appearance of any structure or land, the division of land into two or more parcels, and the creation or termination or any rights of access or riparian rights." "Land" is defined as "the earth, water and air, above, below or on the surface."[8]

This broad definition of development sets what the Reporters regard as the "outer limits of local regulatory power."[9] A municipality need not exercise this power to its full extent. The definition also represents an effort to reduce disputes over the existence of power to regulate particular activities. In this effort, however, the Code introduces a new term which has eluded precise definition in many other contexts, that of a "material change." The next battle over the extent of municipal power will undoubtedly center upon the materiality of a change which a municipality is seeking to regulate. Unfortunately, neither the Code nor the Reporters' Notes offer any real indication of the intended meaning of this term.

III. Regulation

Having established that almost any activity associated with land may be regulated as "development," Article 2 sets forth the manner in which local regulations are to be imposed and administered. It is in this Article that the pragmatism of the Code is most apparent. The basic regulatory philosophy of Article 2 is that most land development decisions today are the result of an exercise of discretion and are made on an *ad hoc* basis, usually in response to some developer's proposal. Typical of the current techniques which allow *ad hoc* exercise of discretion are area rezonings, special or conditional use permits, special exceptions and variances. The Code adopts the view that an *ad hoc* approach to development regulation is not all that bad, provided particular decisions are subject to some

---

7. English Town and Country Planning Act, 1971, §22. The philosophy embraced by this definition and by the Code's *ad hoc* approach to regulations is sufficiently parallel to the English system to have prompted an article discussing an earlier draft of these provisions by Professor Donald G. Hagman of U.C.L.A. entitled *Articles 1 and 2 of a Model Land Development Code: The English Are Coming*, 1971 ASPO LAND USE CONTROLS ANNUAL 3. Professor Hagman suggests that widespread adoption of the Code may result in a dramatic increase in American subscriptions to several English legal treatises and periodicals.

8. Code, §1–102(b).

9. Code, §1–102, Note at 23.

minimal requirements of rationality and that all competing interests are afforded an opportunity to participate in the decision-making process. Thus, Article 2 creates a framework within which *ad hoc* decisions can occur while, at the same time, requiring that all parties having an interest be heard before the initial decision is made.

Traditional development controls, zoning and subdivision, are to be incorporated into a single ordinance called the "development ordinance."[10] These regulations are administered by a local Land Development Agency designated in the development ordinance.[11] The local Land Development Agency may exercise a wide range of powers now divided among the planning commission, planning department, zoning officer, board of adjustment and local governing body.

The development ordinance establishes the regulatory scheme for the municipality.[12] It may authorize "general development" for types of uses whose approval requires no exercise of discretion. This is similar to the present concept of the "permitted use." It also may authorize the local Land Development Agency to permit other activities as "special development" where substantial discretion must be exercised in approving applications.

"Special development permits" are the heart of the sophisticated regulatory techniques authorized by the Code.[13] Discretion may be delegated to the local Land Development Agency to approve permits similar to, but not identical with, bulk and use variances, special exceptions, conditional uses and the like. That discretion is controlled by any substantive standards in the ordinance and Code, and by a mandatory administrative hearing process.[14] The Agency's decision in these situations, its "development order," must be in writing and must be based upon the record made at the hearing.[15] Notice of the hearing must have been given to a wide range of potentially interested parties, as listed in the Code. All material findings of fact must be supported by substantial evidence in the record; all conclusions must be supported with reasons that do not simply echo the language of the Code or development ordinance.

To the extent that the local governing body wishes to retain or otherwise exercise control over individual development applica-

---

10. Code, §2–101.
11. Code, §§2–301 *et seq.*
12. Code, §§2–102 and 2–103.
13. Code, §§2–201 to 2–212.
14. Code, §2–304.
15. Code, §2–306.

tions, by special permits or area rezoning procedures, it may act only after the local agency has held a similar administrative hearing and made a report to the governing body. In any subsequent review, the governing body's action is treated as administrative, not legislative, action subject to the same evidentiary requirements as administrative decisions of the local Agency. This is one of the Code's devices for discouraging legislative "tinkering" with the regulation process after adoption of the ordinance.[16]

The local Land Development Agency may be authorized to adopt regulations of general effect, called "rules."[17] Most often these would be in the nature of supplemental criteria for the issuance of development permits, although the governing body may delegate the preparation of all development regulations to the agency. Here, a non-adversary "legislative hearing,"[18] as distinguished from an adjudicative "administrative hearing" resulting in a specific "development order," must be held before the rule can become effective.

The local Land Development Agency is an administrative agency. The traditional tests of administrative law, as supplemented by specific provisions of the Code, will determine the validity of its actions.

Unlike the Standard Zoning Enabling Act and its progeny, the Code is careful not to straightjacket the types of development controls which a municipality may impose.[19] The extent and manner of regulation is largely left to the municipality. It may divide its territory into use districts and impose controls based upon traditional zoning practice, but need not encompass the entire area of the municipality. So-called "non-Euclidean" development controls, e.g., performance standards, would appear to be allowed instead of use districts, as would a blend of use and performance controls. The municipality might choose to regulate only certain types of development activity, such as heavy industry, multi-family dwellings or traffic-oriented business.

IV. Planning

Article 3, which deals with physical planning, is one of the more interesting, and also more disappointing, provisions of the proposed

---

16. Code, §§2–311 and 2–312.
17. Code, §2–303.
18. Code, §2–305.
19. Code, §2–101.

Model Code. Despite strong opposition from professional planning organizations, the ALI has rejected the idea that regulation of development must be preceded by some form of "comprehensive" or "master" planning, as had been required under the Standard Acts.[20] The regulation of development is thought to be too important to have to wait until the planning process described in Article 3 has been completed.[21] That planning process may be too expensive or too sophisticated for many similar municipalities. If forced to engage in the process as a prerequisite to the control of development, many of these might choose to forego regulation altogether.

These reasons for allowing regulation on as broad a scale as the Code authorizes without any formal planning effort do not seem persuasive. The planning process envisioned by the Code does require a significant degree of sophistication and can require the commitment of substantial funds, time and effort if it is to be carried out adequately. But to pretend that the regulation of development ever can proceed rationally without some consideration of its purpose and effect and of the policies and value judgments it represents is to ignore those practical realities which the Code so often invokes in other situations. No municipality should adopt land development regulations simply for the purpose of having land development regulations. Municipalities adopt regulations in order to accomplish some purpose considered important by the local governing body. Even regulations simply to preserve the status quo are the result of a planning decision.

Courts are just now demonstrating an awareness of the importance of planning to development regulation. By "planning" in this context, I mean something which evidences the rationale of particular controls and the public purpose served by those controls. Courts are rewarding municipalities which can demonstrate that a challenged regulation is based upon some legitimate, ascertainable public policy, even though reasonable minds may differ as to the wisdom of the policy.[22] At the same time, they are becoming far

---

20. SZEA, §3 ("comprehensive plan"); SPEA, §6 ("master plans").
21. Code, §3–101, Note at 142–44.
22. See, e.g., Town of Bedford v. Village of Mt. Kisco, 33 N.Y.2d 178, 351 N.Y.S.2d 129, 306 N.E.2d 155 (1973); Golden v. Planning Board of Town of Ramapo, 30 N.Y.2d 359, 285 N.E.2d 291, 334 N.Y.S.2d 138 (1972), app. dismissed, 409 U.S. 1003; Steel Hill Development, Inc. v. Town of Sanbornton, 469 F.2d 956 (1st Cir. 1972).

less willing to uphold a regulation whose purpose or reasonableness cannot be established.[23]

A better solution to the problem of prior planning might be to require that any development ordinance contain, in some minimal form, the reasons for its adoption and the policies its regulations are intended to serve.[24] This process need not be as sophisticated or as expensive as that contemplated by Article 3. It would provide a touchstone for the local Land Development Agency, the governing body, developers, other property owners and users and, eventually, a reviewing court to test the reasonableness of particular regulatory actions. It is unfortunate that the Code does not provide a simple, expedient technique for meeting this need.

Instead of requiring planning as a prerequisite to the power to regulate development, the Code offers incentives to those municipalities which choose to engage in planning. Only these municipalities are permitted to allow planned unit developments as "special development;"[25] to engage in development activities, including the exercise of eminent domain, in "specially planned areas" similar to urban redevelopment projects;[26] "special development for plan implementation;"[27] to order the discontinuance of certain existing land uses[28]; and to exercise "official map" powers.[29]

The planning process of Article 3 represents a compromise between the two prevalent theories of the proper function of physical planning. The Standard Act regarded planning as the formulation of specific long term goals for physical development, an "end-state" activity. Many critics of this "end-state" theory of planning view the proper function of planning as a continuous process for evaluating physical, social, economic and other changes in the community and reconciling these conflicting interests through an ongoing decision-making process, often without regard to pre-set long term

---

23. *E.g.*, Fasano v. Board of County Commissioners of Washington Co., 507 P.2d 23 (Ore. 1973); Concord Township Appeal, 439 Pa. 466, 268 A.2d 765 (1970) (also known as Appeal of Kit-Mar Builders, Inc.).

24. *See* PA. STAT. ANN. tit. 53, §10606 (1972), which requires that all local zoning ordinances contain a "statement of community objectives" indicating "those factors which the community believes relevant in describing the purpose and intent" of the ordinance. *See also* CAL. GOV'T CODE §§65302 (West 1966).

25. Code, §2–210.

26. Code, §2–211.

27. Code, §2–212.

28. Code, §§4–101 and 4–102.

29. Code, §§3–201 and 3–202.

goals. The proposed Code provides for both long term goal setting and a process by which these goals will be accomplished, evaluated and adjusted over time.

The local Land Development Agency, or any other agency designated by the governing body, prepares a Local Land Development Plan, a "statement . . . (of) objectives, policies and standards to guide public and private development of land within its planning jurisdiction and including a short term program of public actions . . . (designed to bring about those objectives, policies and standards)."[30] The Plan, then, has two substantive components, the "statement of objectives, policies and standards" and the "short term program of public actions." Significantly, the Code requires that the Local Land Development Plan, including the short term program and its periodic revisions, be adopted by the local governing body. Unlike the "zoning plan" of the SZEA or the "master plan" of the SPEA, the Local Land Development Plan is to be the official land development policy of the municipality.[31]

The process of preparing the statement of objectives, policies and standards is treated as more important than its final content, which is always subject to change.[32] That purpose is to create a municipal capability for observing what has happened, is now happening, and may happen in the future with respect to the municipality's physical development, and the physical, social and economic consequences of that development. The Code lists at least 10 types of studies which the local Agency should consider in preparing the Plan, including, among others, demographic studies, studies of present and future land use patterns and relationships and municipal finance.[33] The Plan also must identify present problems of development and physical deterioration, that is, it must deal with the total community, warts and all. Finally, it must analyze the probable social and economic consequences of its proposals and evaluate alternative strategies with respect to those probable consequences. The Plan may include many other elements as well.[34]

The key to the planning process is the short term program, a program of public actions to be undertaken over a one to five year period, identifying the order in which these actions should occur and the appropriate public agency to undertake each action and

---

30. Code, §3–101.
31. Code, §3–106.
32. Code, §3–102.
33. Code, §3–103.
34. Code, §3–104.

specifying how each action will serve to accomplish the objectives, policies and standards of the Plan.[35] A short term program may provide for actions to be taken over a period of more than five years, but a new program must be adopted, as part of a periodic Local Land Development Report, at least every five years if the municipality is to continue to exercise the additional powers granted by the Code to those local governments engaging in planning.[36]

V. Discontinuing Existing Uses

Article 4 provides a limited power to compel the discontinuance of existing uses which do not comply with the general development regulations of the area in which they are located. Included are the traditional nonconforming use and its many relatives.[37] The Code rejects the cherished belief of many zoning officers that all such uses are *per se* evil and must be eliminated. Instead, the power to eliminate these uses is made to depend upon the existence of a municipal policy to preserve other, inconsistent characteristics of the neighborhood for a substantial period of time, as evidenced by the Local Land Development Plan.[38] Discontinuance of individual uses is a matter for the local Land Development Agency.[39] In addition to ordering immediate discontinuance, the agency may exempt a use from discontinuance, grant a "special development permit" for the use where it meets the special development requirements, or grant an extension of the time for discontinuance, applying reasonable standards for amortization. Further, the Agency may recommend that the municipality acquire the property, or an interest in the property, by eminent domain under provisions of Article 5 to obtain an earlier discontinuance than the principles of amortization would allow.

The Code does not alter a municipality's common law and statutory powers to define and abate public nuisances. Moreover, even non-planning municipalities are permitted to require the discontinuance of existing uses found by the local governing body to be "offensive to the public or users of neighboring land" and to perform "no essential public function that cannot readily be performed at more appropriate sites in the region."[40]

---

35. Code, §3–105.
36. Code, §3–107.
37. Code, §4–101.
38. Code, §4–102(1) (a).
39. Code, §§4–201 and 4–202.
40. Code, §4–102(1) (e).

VI. State Planning and Regulatory Activities in General

Articles 7 and 8 should be considered together. They provide for state land planning and involvement in those local decisions which may have regional or statewide impact. Despite the Code's emphasis on local decision-making, these two articles will probably receive the most attention from planners, legislators and academicians in the immediate future.

A number of recent federal statutes have required that the states become directly involved in various aspects of land use regulation.[41] Many states are jumping into these waters without any federal push. No others have yet gone as far as the Hawaiian legislation[42] but many may be headed along a similar path. Vermont's Environmental Control Law[43] is not too far removed in purpose. Oregon has recently created a Conservation and Land Development Commission to prepare uniform land use policies, goals and guidelines for the entire state.[44] Other states are injecting themselves into the local decision-making process with respect to particular types of uses or the development of particular geographic areas.

The Code will provide machinery flexible enough to accomplish any of these diverse objectives. A state may become as deeply involved in regulation and control as Hawaii, may limit its intervention to specific regions or "critical areas," as the California-Nevada Tahoe Regional Planning Agency,[45] New Jersey's Hackensack Meadowlands Development Commission[46] or New York's Adirondack Park Agency;[47] or it may choose to provide protection for necessary types of development not usually popular with local communities, as Massachusetts' Zoning Agency Appeal Law[48] for moderate and low income housing. The degree of state involvement, then, is essentially a political decision, with implementation of that decision to be governed by the processes set forth in the Code.

---

41. *E.g.*, The Clean Air Act of 1970, 42 U.S.C. §§1857 *et. seq.* (1970); The Coastal Zone Management Act of 1972, 16 U.S.C.A. §§1451 *et. seq.* (Supp. 1974); The Water Pollution Control Act Amendments of 1972, 33 U.S.C.A. §§1251 *et. seq.* (Supp. 1974).

42. Hawaii Rev. Stat., ch. 205 (Supp. 1973).

43. 10 Vt. Stat. Ann. §§6001–6091 (Supp. 1974) (commonly known as "Act 250.").

44. Ore. Rev. Stat. ch. 273 (1973).

45. Calif. Code §66800 (West Supp. 1974); 10 Nev. Rev. Stats. tit. 22, ch. 277 *et seq.* (1973).

46. N.J. Stat. Ann. §§13:17.1 *et seq.* (Supp. 1974).

47. N.Y. Exec. Law §§800–819 (McKinney 1972).

48. Mass. Gen. Laws Ann. ch. 40B, §§20–23 (Supp. 1974).

VII. State Planning

A. *State Land Development Agency*

Article 8, not yet in "Proposed Official Draft" form, provides the administrative structure for state land development planning while Article 7 authorizes state involvement in the local regulatory process. Article 8 creates the State Land Planning Agency whose functions and duties, although not its powers, are quite similar to those of the local Land Planning Agency.[49] In addition to its substantive powers of intervention under Article 7, it may prepare regional or state Land Development Plans, assist local communities in land development planning and create regional planning divisions to carry out its functions in various parts of the state. The State Land Development Agency may intervene in proceedings before local agencies or the courts where there is a controversy over the meaning or validity of a state Plan, or over other actions of the State Agency or the Code. The Agency must intervene when so requested by a local agency or court.[50]

Where no local Land Development Agency exists, the State Agency is authorized to appoint one.[51] This appointed local agency has all of the powers and duties of any local agency under Article 2, including the power to adopt and enforce its own development regulations. This ability to intervene so directly in local matters should act as a powerful incentive for municipalities to adopt development regulations and create their own regulatory agencies, staffed by persons of their own choosing. Any state-appointed agency functions only until the municipality adopts its own development ordinance.

B. *State Land Development Plan*

The State Land Development Plan is quite similar to the Local Land Development Plan, both in scope and purpose.[52] Preparation is optional and is necessary only if the state wants to engage in official mapping. The State Plan may encompass the entire state or only one or more regions. Like the local plan, the State Plan must contain a statement of objectives, policies and standards to guide development and a short term program of public actions designed to achieve those objectives, policies and standards. The factors to be

---

49. Code, §§8–101 to 8–103.
50. Code, §8–203.
51. Code, §8–206.
52. Code, §§8–401 to 8–405.

considered in preparation of the State Plan are similar to those recommended for local plans. Most of the same factors must be considered, although on a grander scale appropriate to the greater area covered by the State Plan. There is somewhat less discretion as to the number and character of studies to be made in preparation of the plan. An even greater degree of sophistication is required as the State Plan must contain projections of the nature and expected rate of change in physical, economic and social conditions, and the consequences of changes in these conditions. The State Plan also must demonstrate consideration of environmental factors not mentioned in Article 3. Local Land Development Plans also are to be considered in preparing the State Plan.

As with local Plans, the most important element of the state planning process is the short term program of public actions. The provisions of Article 8 are similar to those of Article 3 for local Plans, but, again, on a somewhat grander scale. The State Plan is to become the official land development policy of the state, with the Code suggesting optional methods of accomplishing this, from executive order to formal legislative adoption of the plan.

C. *State Long-Range Planning Institute*

Article 8 also authorizes the creation of a State Long Range Planning Institute.[53] The Institute is a "think tank" whose function is to engage in research, analysis and the examination of long-range policies for the development of land within the state. It may provide technical assistance to the state and local land planning agencies, but has no administrative or regulatory function.

VIII. State Intervention in Local Regulation

Article 7 is the substantively more important of the two, giving the State Land Planning Agency the power to interfere with or intervene in local land development regulation. Consistent with the Code's philosophy that most land use decisions do not involve significant regional, state or national interests, it is designed to minimize the need for state intervention unless the state finds intervention to be necessary or appropriate because of the potential impact of some development activity.

Two techniques are employed to identify situations which can justify state intervention: (1) by identifying geographic areas where

---

53. Code, §§8–601 and 8–602.

development can affect significant state or regional interest—"Areas of Critical State Concern"—and (2) by identifying types of development which, by their very existence, can affect these interests—"Developments of Regional Impact."

All local Land Development Agencies and development ordinances are subject to the procedures, standards and criteria adopted by the State Agency under Article 7.[54] However, the local agency still administers the development regulations in ACSA or for a DRI. In this way, the Code tries to minimize the size of the state planning bureaucracy, reduce the expense of the proceedings to private parties and eliminate forum shopping.

A. *State Land Adjudicatory Board*

Any decision of a local agency involving substantial issues under Article 7 may be appealed by any party to the State Land Adjudicatory Board, which is a state-wide body created for this express purpose.[55] On appeal, the Board has all of the powers of the local agency. It may grant or deny a requested permit, modify the local agency's decision or remand it to the local agency for further proceedings. Its decisions are based on the record made before the local agency, and must be in writing and supported by findings, conclusions and reasons. Judicial review of the board's actions is available in the same manner as review of any state administrative agency action.

This is one of the primary ways in which the Code protects state and regional interests from parochialism on the part of local agencies. While the local agency has the power to make the decision in the first instance, that decision is subject to review by a state administrative agency and then by a court of state-wide, not local, responsibility. Presumably, both will put the broader public interest ahead of those peculiar to the municipality.

B. *"Areas of Critical State Concern"*

The State Land Planning Agency, after holding a "legislative type hearing," may designate a geographic portion of the state as an "Area of Critical State Concern," (ACSC) where it meets certain criteria set forth in the Code.[56] An ACSC might have environmental or ecological significance. Sites for certain major public activities,

---

54. Code, §7–101.
55. Code, §§7–501 to 7–503.
56. Code, §7–201.

such as airports, limited access highway interchanges, educational facilities for residents of more than one community and the like may either be designated as ACSC or treated as "Developments of Regional Impact," (DRI) at the election of the State Agency. A site for a "new community" may be treated as an ACSC if designated on an existing State Land Development Plan. This is the only ACSC designation which requires prior planning. Land not subject to any local development ordinance may be designated as an ACSC.

The foregoing are the types of land use considerations which the Code suggests as appropriate for ACSC treatment. The Reporters point out, however, that particular states might wish to add to the list of factors or situations to meet particular problems or concerns.[57]

In the designation of an ACSC, the State Agency must give its reasons for the designation, indicate the dangers which could result from a failure to coordinate development controls and the benefits which may result from their coordination and must set forth general regulatory principles for guiding development in the area. It may also specify types of development to be permitted pending the preparation of appropriate final regulations.

The Code offers a great amount of flexibility to the State Agency in the extent of its control of development in an ACSC. For example, if the purpose of the designation is to protect a watershed from pollution, the Agency may permit development not involving potential pollution without any further state consideration, only requiring coordinated regulation of potential pollution sources. Or, if the purpose is to provide control over traffic generating activities under a "clean air" plan, the State might require regulation of development of a certain size or type, leaving all other matters in the sole control of the individual municipalities.

When an ACSC has been designated, the local governments within that area are afforded an opportunity to propose their own development regulations consistent with the guidelines established in the designation.[58] When approved by the State Agency, these regulations govern development. If any municipality fails to propose acceptable regulations, the State Agency may promulgate regulations for that portion of the ACSC, which will supersede, to the extent specified by the State Agency, local regulations.[59] The mu-

---

57. Note to Code, §7–201 at 295.
58. Code, §7–203.
59. Code, §7–204.

nicipality may regain control by subsequently adopting acceptable regulations of its own.

Once approved, the regulations, whether local or state-imposed, are administered by the local land development agencies in the ACSC in the same manner as any other development regulations. The State Agency must be given notice, however, of any applications for "special development permits" affecting state or regional interest so that it may review the application and determine if it should intervene as a party in the proceeding.[60]

The ACSC technique enables the state to become directly involved in local development policy to protect specific regional or state interests. At the same time, the Code makes every effort to allow the local political process to operate in the formulation and administration of individual regulations, consistent with protection of these larger interests. Only when a municipality has demonstrated that it is unable or unwilling to give what the state regards as due consideration to other than local interests need the state intervene more forcefully and dictate the actual content of those regulations.

C. *"Development of Regional Impact"*

1. IN GENERAL

The State Land Development Agency is also authorized to define categories of development which, because of their size, nature or effect on surrounding land, constitute "Developments of Regional Impact" (DRI).[61] Among the considerations proposed by the Code for determining those activities which may be considered as DRI is the extent to which the development will create or alleviate environmental problems, the amount of vehicular and pedestrian traffic to be generated by the activity, the number of persons who may be on the site at any one time, the physical size of the site and the likelihood that the development will generate additional or subsidiary development.

2. "DEVELOPMENTS OF REGIONAL BENEFIT"

Certain types of development may qualify as DRI even though they are not among the categories defined by the State Agency. Called "Developments of Regional Benefit" (DRB),[62] these include development by other governmental agencies, developments for religious, charitable, educational or public utility purposes which will

---

60. Code, §7–208.
61. Code, §7–301.
62. Code, §7–301(4).

serve a substantial number of non-residents of the community in which they are located, and the construction of low and moderate income housing. This last activity, as presently proposed, represents a significant revision of the DRB concept contained in Tentative Draft No. 3 of the Code.[63] The Tentative Draft would have permitted a broad category of activities receiving state or federal aid to seek the special treatment afforded a DRB. The developer of a DRB which would not otherwise be a DRI may proceed either under the existing development regulations of the municipality or seek to have the development treated as a DRI under Article 7 of the Code.

3. WHEN OTHERWISE PERMITTED DEVELOPMENT MAY BE REFUSED

If a qualified DRI is of a type allowed under the local development ordinance, the local Land Development Agency may refuse a permit only if it finds that "the probable net detriment from the development exceeds the probable net benefit."[64] For example, a regional sanitary land-fill or a "clean" incinerator, neither particularly sought-after land uses, might have to be approved by a community despite strong local opposition if of a type of use generally permitted under the development ordinance.

The primary question raised by this standard—net benefit and net detriment to whom?—is left unanswered by the Code. The Code provides an extensive and excellent list of factors to be considered in determining the benefit-detriment effect of the proposed development, essentially a greatly expanded cost-benefit analysis. Unfortunately, the local agency is permitted to determine the areas over which "benefits" and "detriments" are to be allocated. While the reasonableness of that determination is subject to review by the State Land Adjudicatory Board and the courts, the Code should establish some guidelines as to the areas to be considered. Presumably, the area for allocating "benefits" should be greater than the municipality itself or there would be no real state or regional interests requiring the protection of DRI treatment.

4. WHEN NON-PERMITTED DEVELOPMENT MUST BE ALLOWED

Where a proposed development is not permitted under local regulations,[65] the permit may not be granted unless the applicant estab-

---

63. Tentative Draft No. 3, 1971, §7–401 (now consolidated with §7–301 in P.O.D. No. 1).
64. Code, §7–304(1).
65. Code, §7–304(2).

lishes that (1) "the probable net benefit from the development exceeds the probable net detriment"; (2) the development will not prevent achievement of the objective of any local or state Land Development Plan; and (3) the development will deviate from the local regulations only to that extent reasonably necessary to meet certain public needs, that is, "to enable a substantial segment of the population of the state to obtain reasonable access to housing, employment, educational or recreational opportunities." This last requirement serves two purposes. First, it imposes a concept of public purpose or public need on a DRI to justify overriding local controls. The proponents of the development must establish the existence of that need. Second, it enables the local Agency to impose appropriate conditions upon the development so as to minimize adverse effects. This is another example of the Code's policy of protecting the in tegrity of local decision-making against unnecessary interference by outsiders.

5. WHERE A DEVELOPMENT OF REGIONAL IMPACT MAY PROVIDE SUBSTANTIALLY INCREASED EMPLOYMENT OPPORTUNITIES

The Code places an additional qualification on those DRI which will "substantially increase employment opportunities" within a municipality.[66] Even though otherwise qualified, a local Agency may not grant a development permit for the DRI without finding that adequate housing reasonably accessible to the site exists for future employees, or that a local Land Development Plan has been adopted which will make that housing available within a reasonable time. Where a State Land Development Plan indicates that the site is a desirable location for the development, this finding is not necessary. The Reporters' Note indicates that this provision is intended to work equity among municipal neighbors. "The local government that seeks to attract industry to improve its tax base but refuses to provide the housing that is a necessary concomitant to the new job is throwing an unreasonable burden on neighboring communities that should not be permitted lightly."[67]

It is difficult to argue with the inter-municipal morality of this proposition in the abstract. However, there is nothing presently in the Code to prevent a municipality from granting special treatment to desirable industries under the development ordinance, eliminating the need of these developers to seek DRI treatment altogether.

---

66. Code, §7–305.
67. Note to Code, §7–305 at 318.

Only those industrial developments specified by the State Agency, or those seeking special DRB treatment, would have to satisfy this Code requirement. I suspect that most often use of the DRI provision will be by developers whose projects are not among those specified by the State Agency and who themselves are unable to negotiate satisfactory regulations with the municipality. They will seek to establish that the development is "of regional benfit," and entitled to DRI treatment. Where the project involves a less desirable activity which may generate substantial employment, *e.g.*, a stone quarry, asphalt plant or atomic electric plant, the local Agency will find this requirement most helpful in denying a permit which the "benefit-detriment" test might otherwise require. If the availability of adequate housing is a proper limitation on local land development regulations for a DRI, it seems equally applicable to all development which may generate substantially increased employment opportunities, not only those seeking or subjected to special treatment.

The purpose of the DRI provisions appears to be to require the local Agency to consider qualified development proposals in a broader frame of reference than it otherwise might. They also allow a developer or the State Agency to establish that a particular project will bring substantially greater benefit to an area of the state than the costs or other burdens it will impose upon a particular municipality. Where this can be established, it then becomes unreasonable to allow the municipality to deny those benefits to the greater area.

6. ANALYSIS OF "BENEFITS" AND "DETRIMENTS"

One of the most significant overall contributions of the Code is the method provided for determining the extent and value of local and regional interests, the "net benefits" and "net detriments."[68] That method is far from perfected, but it is an excellent beginning. Once there has been sufficient experience, through trial and error, with the process, we can expect to understand much more about the relationships between local land uses and the larger regions in which they are located. The system can be improved. Until that time, however, the proposed method is well worth trying.

I have already commented on what I believe to be the major defect of the proposal, the lack of any standards for determining the minimum area whose interests must be considered in allocating ben-

---

68. Code, §§7–401 and 7–402.

efits and detriments. At present, the size of these areas is a question
of fact to be decided by the local agency. This is to allow the local
Agency to examine the effect of the proposal upon a larger area
than its own territory. However, the lack of standards also allows
the agency to limit the area under consideration to its own municipality or some other smaller area. True, the proponents may offer
evidence over as large an area as will produce a favorable result.
Whether that area is the proper one to consider, however, is largely
a matter of guesswork at present. It would be better to provide some
criteria for selecting a "reasonable area" over which the effects of
the development must be considered, thereby eliminating much of
that guesswork.

Despite this suggested defect, the Code's provisions for balancing
benefits and detriments once the areas have been selected is both
interesting and exciting. The questions of what effects are beneficial
or detrimental are questions of fact for the local agency, as is the
weighing of those facts to determine whether there is a "net benefit"
or "net detriment." Proponents and opponents are permitted to submit any evidence they believe relevant or material. The agency cannot refuse to consider suggested effects of the proposal because those
effects may be indirect or intangible or not readily quantifiable. In
addition to preparing more traditional cost-benefit analyses, the
agency may evaluate the social and environmental consequences of
the proposal.

Specifically enumerated factors which may be considered include
the potential effects upon the immediate and larger areas of granting or denying the requested permit. The Code suggests that the
Agency ask itself such questions as: Will the "absence of such development deny adequate facilities to the surrounding areas in respect to employment opportunities, charitable facilities or other
amenities related to the general welfare"? How will the proposal
affect the ability of people to find adequate housing reasonably accessible to their places of employment? How will the proposed development relate to any present state or local Land Development
Plan? The local agency may consider whether alternate locations or
methods of development would be more appropriate, have a more
favorable impact on the environment, be less likely to have an adverse impact on other persons or property or the provision of municipal services and the costs of those services, or relate more effi-
ciently to present or proposed public transportation facilities and
other existing or proposed public or publicly assisted development.

Where the development imposes immediate costs upon the municipality, one of the most interesting questions which the Agency may ask, in the light of recent court decisions involving "exclusionary zoning,"[69] is: Has the municipality already received more than its fair share of this type of development in terms of regional needs? Again, we can expect local Agencies to ask this question most often when they want to deny a permit. True, a municipality's "fair share" of an unwanted activity is only one of the many factors which the Agency is authorized to consider. It was undoubtedly included in the Code for the most humanitarian of motives. However, it will require vigorous and forceful advocacy by the developer or the State Agency if this "fair share" approach is to become an effective mechanism for providing adequate housing and other facilities for persons of low and moderate income; one of its obvious purposes. Unless that type of leadership is forthcoming from the State Agency, we can expect the "fair share" provision to be used to exclude more than to include needed but unwanted development.

It is important to keep in mind that the State Land Planning Agency is notified of all applications for a DRI. It may intervene in the proceedings and submit a report of its views of the issues involved in balancing benefits and detriments.[70] Indeed, the State Agency must intervene and submit such a report if requested to do so by the local agency. I am not sure what status the report has in the local agency proceedings. The Code does not indicate whether it can be considered as evidence upon which the local agency may rely in making its final decision, or whether it constitutes only an advisory opinion by the State Agency. This could be an important issue and should be clarified before final approval of the Code.

IX. Conclusion

In summary, the Code places primary responsibility for the regulation of land development in the local governments. However, it does provide for recognition of state or regional interests in specific situations which, in the judgment of a particular state, justify or require consideration of larger areas and larger issues than the in-

---

69. Oakwood at Madison, Inc. v. Township of Madison, 117 N.J. Super. 11, 283 A.2d 353 (1971), *cert. granted*, 62 N.J. 185, 299 A.2d 720 (1972), *on remand*, 128 N.J. Super. 438, 320 A.2d 223 (1974); *see also* Williston Twp. v. Chesterdale Farms, Inc., 7 Pa. Cmwlth. 453, 300 A.2d 107 (1973) (Mencer, J.) (equally divided court).

70. Code, §7–403. While Florida's Environmental Land and Water Conservation Act, *supra* note 1, was modeled after T.D. No. 3, it is interesting to note that this provision was added to P.O.D. No. 1 because of a similar provision of the Florida Act, FLA. STAT. ANN. §380.06(8) (1974).

terest of a single municipality. The Code makes very few value judgments of its own as to when the state should intervene in the local decision-making process. That is left to the political processes of the particular state. This is a very pragmatic solution to a very difficult problem. If I had to make one general criticism of the Code's overall philosophy, it is this: The Code concentrates overmuch on process and offers little guidance to those charged with the responsibility of regulating development at the state or local level on the very substantial question of how value choices should be made.

In any critical examination of the Codes, two points should alway be kept in mind. The Code is intended as enabling legislation, a grant of power to the state and local governments to regulate the physical use and development of land. Therefore, it need not contain a detailed set of substantive rules. It provides the basic policy within which regulatory agencies may act in the formulation and execution of policy.

Second, the proposed Code is a "model code" not intended to be adopted wholesale by every state in the Union. As Herbert Wechsler, Director of the ALI has said of the Code:

> [T]he product here envisaged is a model code and not a uniform enactment. The analogue of our work is not, in other words, the [Uniform] Commercial Code, where uniformity of law was deemed a basic value, but the Model Penal Code, designed as a source material for the legislative re-examination and improvement of prevailing law. It is not, therefore, integral to this effort that the Code should be enacted as a whole. The criterion of judgment rather is whether the formulations proposed point the way toward genuine advance.[71]

To the extent that the Code, when completed, is read with this perspective, as "pointing the way toward genuine advance," it should be most successful. It is, as were the SZEA and the SPEA before it, a treatise on the present state of land planning and development law. It should be read and considered by anyone concerned with this area of the law. It should not, however, be accepted as gospel or as the final word in the field. It has its flaws as well as its occasional aspects of brilliance. But it is addressed to a particular society in a particular state of legal and social development. Hopefully, it will not be another fifty years before someone undertakes so thorough an examination of planning and development control.

---

71. A Model Land Development Code, Foreword vii (Tent. Draft No. 2, 1970).

Some Observations on the American Law Institute's Model Land Development Code

(At the Association of the Bar of the City of New York, June 2, 1975)*

Fred P. Bosselman

Associate Reporter of the Model Land Development Code; member, Ross, Hardies, Babcock, and Parsons; University of Colorado, A.B. (1956), Harvard University, LL.B. (1959).

George M. Raymond

Raymond, Parish & Pine, Inc.; member American Institute of Planners and American Institute of Architects; Columbia University, B.A. (1946).

Richard A. Persico

Executive Director of the Adirondack Park Agency; State University of New York at Albany, B.A. (1955); Albany Law School J.D. (1961); Member of the New York Bar.

FRED P. BOSSELMAN: At the annual meeting of the American Law Institute in May, 1975, the Institute gave final approval to the Model Land Development Code.[1] The process of drafting this Code began about twelve years ago and its evolution has coincided with a period in the history of American land law that is remarkable for the changes that have taken place in public attitudes and in the laws reflecting those attitudes. Drafting a model code over the last twelve years has not in any way resembled the task of codifying a stable body of law. It has been more like trying to write sonnets in a hurricane.

Given this continual state of flux it is important to note that the ALI is not proposing this Code as a uniform law; there is in fact

---

*Submitted for publication and edited by Ms. Shirley Adelson Siegel, Assistant Attorney General, State of New York; chairman, Committee on Housing and Urban Development, The Association of the Bar of the City of New York; member of the Local Government Section, American Bar Association; A.B., Barnard College; J.D., Yale University.

1. All footnotes are references to the Proposed Official Draft of the American Law Institute's, A Model Land Development Code (April 15, 1975, submitted by the Council to the members of the A.L.I. on May 20, 21, 22, and 23, 1975).

no great value in having a uniform approach. It is not even a traditional model law; no one conceives that any state will adopt the whole Code as a package. It is more like a Sears and Roebuck Catalogue with a lot of quite separable provisions, and many of them in a variety of alternatives, so that the individual state may pick and choose the items that appeal to them.

The major credit or blame for instituting this project belongs to Richard Babcock and Paul Ylvisaker, who recognized the need for a reexamination of the traditional statutory law that governed the use of land. They formulated the basic principle for which the Code is probably best known—the idea that the state should retake some of the power to control the use of land from the local governments to which the power had been completely delegated in the twenties.

Article VII of the Code[2] embodies this principle and has been used as the basis for a wide variety of state legislation and for the proposed national land use legislation now pending in Congress. In general, this article of the Code operates on the assumption that although the great majority of land use decisions are properly made at the local level of government, a small percentage requires solution at a state or regional level in order to produce an equitable and rational result. The problem lies in defining criteria for deciding which of the land use decisions fall in the category that requires state or regional participation. We concluded that there were three factors which might put a land use decision into that category: one, the size of the proposed development; two, the type of the proposed development; and three, the nature of the area in which it is located.

I would like to describe a few aspects of the Code that have not attracted the same attention as Article VII, but that I believe contain ideas worth serious consideration.

One of the basic principles we followed in drafting the Code was that governmental development ought not to be given the immunity from regulation that is so typically found under present law. At the present time, there are many state agencies, special districts and authorities which have the power to construct highways, bridges, tunnels, sewers, public buildings and other public works without

---

2. This Article is designed to assist the states in finding a workable method for state and regional involvement in land development regulation. Although the increased state and federal concern with the consequences of land development is welcome, it is important to channel this concern into areas where it will be effective in dealing with important problems without unnecessarily increasing the cost of the land development process. A time-consuming and inefficient procedure requiring the approval of state or federal agencies for decisions of minor importance could have serious social consequences, especially for development in which cost is a key factor, such as housing. Commentary to Article VII at 289.

consideration of comprehensive planning concepts of the neighborhood level concerns of the people who would be affected by the projects. On the other hand, to give a veto power to local government over development that may serve important state or regional needs could have equally adverse consequences.

The Code proposes a compromise solution. The government agency must submit its proposal to the local land regulatory agency in the same manner as any private developer; having the same rights, going through the same hearings and subject to the same type of decisions.[3] However, if the development is in fact designed to serve the needs of people in the region, Article VII's appellate procedure[4] comes into play. The state (or regional) land adjudicatory board would bring a statewide perspective to the problem, a comprehensive planning perspective as opposed to the functional perspective typically found in development agencies. Where a state land development plan has been adopted (and as used in the Code that term can include either a state plan or a regional plan) the Code goes even farther and requires the governmental development to be consistent with the state or regional plan.[5]

---

3. Section 1–201. *Definitions*
(1) "Developer" means any person, including a governmental agency, undertaking any development as defined in § 1–202 of this Code and as further explained in the Notes following the Section;
1. "Developer." This term is intended to describe the actor performing the acts defined as developments in § 1–202. It expressly includes a "governmental agency" (defined in subsection (3)) in order to make clear that, contrary to tradition in some jurisdictions, development undertaken by government is subject to local ordinances regulating development unless specifically exempted.) *See* § 2–101(4).

4. Section 7–502. *Appeals*
(1) An order of a Land Development Agency may be appealed to the State Land Adjudicatory Board if it involves a substantial issue arising under Article VII.
(2) An appeal may be made by any person having standing to seek judicial review as of right under § 9–103.
(3) No appeal may be taken unless a notice of appeal is transmitted to the Land Development Agency whose order is challenged within four weeks after notice of the order has been given under § 2–306.
(4) The appellant shall furnish a copy of the notice of appeal to all parties to the proceeding before the Land Development Agency and to the local government that created the Land Development Agency.
(5) The State Land Adjudicatory Board shall establish rules designating the contents of appeals and all other matters relating to the procedures for appeal.
(6) The parties shall be entitled to make written submissions on the record and propose findings and conclusions. The State Land Adjudicatory Board may grant oral argument on any appeal.

5. Section 12–203. *Conformance with State Land Development Plans*
If a current State Land Development Plan is applicable no governmental

I think that these provisions of the Code are consistent with one of the most promising trends that has been developing in this field— the dissatisfaction with the traditional concept of the plan as a purely advisory document having no legal effect. There is a search for stability in the process, for some standards on which to base long-range decisions. The national growth rate appears to be leveling off, which makes this a good time to give planning an importance and credibility that it has lacked, by requiring that land use decisions be consistent with any comprehensive plan.

Another interesting part of the Code is found in Part Four of Article II.[6] It provides that where a development requires multiple permits from various local and state agencies or special districts, the developer may ask for a consolidated hearing on his application. The proposed Code does not suggest any change in the substantive decision-making powers of any existing agencies, but merely requires that they participate in a common hearing, base their decisions on the common record to be made before the panel of hearing examiners, and issue their decision according to a common time schedule.

Article VI, dealing with land banking, is another interesting and potentially important part of the Code.[7] This concept which may

---

agency shall undertake any development, and no person shall undertake any development with funds furnished by a governmental agency, if the development is inconsistent with that plan.

6. Section 2–402. *Joint Hearing*

(1) A developer seeking to undertake development requiring multiple permits may apply for a joint hearing on some or all of the permits by filing an application on forms to be provided by the State Land Planning Agency, accompanied by applications for each of those initial development permits listed in the permit register on which he seeks a joint hearing. The developer shall also file a copy of each application with the appropriate permit-issuing agency to which the application is directed and shall notify the agencies that an application for joint hearing has been filed. Development shall be treated as requiring multiple permits under this Part if it

(a) requires a special development permit or special amendment to a development ordinance pursuant to this Article; and

(b) requires one or more other initial development permits listed in the permit register. [, and]

[(c) is development of regional impact pursuant to § 7–301 of this Code.]

7. Selected portions of Article VI.

Section 6–101. *Land Reserve as a Public Purpose*

The acquisition of interests in land for the purpose of facilitating future planning to maintain a public land reserve, and the holding and disposition thereof in accordance with the purposes of this Code, are hereby declared to be for the public purpose of achieving the land policy and land planning obbe defined as the large scale purchase of interests in land by a governmental agency for the purpose of having the land available for undetermined future uses, is widely used in a number of other countries and is being used increasingly in Canada. At the 1973 Annual Meeting of the Institute the membership expressed considerable support for land banking and directed us to prepare such an Article. We did so and the concept is now approved as part of the Code.

Article VI is somewhat different from what has been tried in places like Suffolk County and Fairfax County. Under the Code all land banking would be done by a state land reserve agency having power to acquire land anywhere in the state, hold it and resell it, as needed. It could contract with local governments to perform land banking functions for them. But local governments would not be authorized to engage in this directly without state supervision. This is primarily out of a concern that this is a technique that is possibly subject to abuse by communities that are concerned with keeping

---

jectives of this State whether or not at the time of acquisition or expenditure of funds for acquisition or maintenance any particular future use, public or private, is contemplated for the land. Appropriations for, issuance of bonds for, taxation for a land reserve system, acquisition of land for a land reserve by gift, purchase or condemnation, management of land so acquired, and disposition of land so acquired, are hereby declared to be for a valid public purpose.

Section 6–102. *Organization of State Land Reserve Agency*

(1) There is hereby created a State Land Reserve Agency which is authorized to exercise the powers granted to it by this Article.

Section 6–103. *Land Reserve Policy*

(1) The State Land Reserve Agency shall adopt by rule and may amend from time to time a land reserve policy describing the general purposes for which it intends to acquire, hold and dispose of land under this Article.

(2) Before adopting any land reserve policy the Agency shall submit the proposed policy for review and comment to the State Land Planning Agency and any appropriate advisory committee created under Section 6–102.

(3) The State Land Reserve Agency shall not adopt any land reserve policy which the State Land Planning Agency had [disapproved] [determined to be inconsistent with a currently effective State Land Development Plan].

Section 6–301. *Purposes of Acquisition*

(1) The State Land Reserve Agency may acquire any land that is used or is capable of being used to carry out the Agency's land reserve policy, and which the Agency by resolution finds necessary and proper in carrying out the policy. The land may be acquired from private owners and from governmental agencies of this State and of the United States.

(2) The State Land Reserve Agency may acquire land for any lawful purposes of a local government pursuant to a contract authorized by § 6–501. Such acquisition must be consistent with the Agency's land reserve policy unless the acquisition is made solely with funds supplied by the local government.

(3) The power granted by this Article to acquire land includes the power to acquire any interest in land as defined in § 5–101.

(4) Land acquired under this Article shall be treated, for purposes of

people out and using it in a discriminatory fashion. There has been, within the last couple of years, a growing interest in land banking, particularly in many of the western states, motivated by various interests. In some cases it's to preserve agricultural land. In others, it's largely from a recreational or open space standpoint. I think this is an aspect of the Code that is going to get a lot of attention in the next couple of years.

Another section of the Code that is particularly interesting is Section 9–111,[8] which attempts to provide a mechanism for better resolution of disputes in which a property owner alleges that his property is being taken without just compensation because a land development regulation is unduly restrictive on his use of the land. Section 9–111 suggests that a court that finds a regulation to be unduly restrictive in the constitutional sense should delay holding the regulation invalid until the governmental agency has had time to decide whether it wishes to use the land acquisition powers given by the Code to purchase or condemn some interest in the property,

---

future disposition, as land acquired for planning purposes under § 5–401.
Section 6–304. *Condemnation Power*

(1) The State Land Reserve Agency shall have the power to condemn land, subject to the conditions of this Section and the [general eminent domain statute].

(2) The condemnation shall comply with the provisions of § 5–303 governing assumptions regarding development permission made in valuing the land, with the provisions of § 5–304 governing the valuation of temporary interests, and with the provisions of § 5–301 regarding compliance with local regulations if the condemnation is for the purpose of undertaking specific development.

8. Section 9–111. *Judicial Relief Available; Consolidation of Actions*

(1) Except as limited by § 9–111, the Court may, in a proceeding which does not involve the validity of an order, sustain the rule or ordinance, declare the rule or ordinance to be invalid in whole or in part, or grant such other relief as the court deems appropriate.

(2) Except as limited by § 9–111, the Court may, in a proceeding involving an order, affirm the decisions of the agency, set aside the order, remand the matter for further proceedings before the agency in accordance with directions contained in the opinion or order of the Court, or enter an order which might have been entered by the agency issuing the order and which the court could order the agency to issue.

(3) If an application for a development permit is pending at the time a proceeding seeking a declaration as to the validity of an ordinance or rule as commenced and the court is satisfied that a judicial declaration as to any order issued on the application will dispose of the issues raised in the pending proceeding, it may stay the declaratory proceeding until final action on the application for a development permit has been taken. If a proceeding to review an order granting or denying a development permit is pending, the court may consolidate or stay other proceedings in the interest of a speedy determination of the issues.

which would have the effect of eliminating the unconstitutionality of the regulation.

I should note that the land acquisition powers granted to local governments by the Code are very extensive (short of land banking) and authorize local government to use the power of land acquisition to accomplish virtually any purpose consistent with its own planning policies.[9] I realize that at the present time there are not many local governments in a position economically to think about acquiring large amounts of land, but hopefully the Code will survive these

---

9. Section 5–101. *Nature of Powers Granted*

(1) A local government and [enumerate any other governmental agencies to which power is to be granted] may acquire an interest in land for the purposes set forth in this Article subject to the terms of this Article.

(2) The grant of power under this Article to a local government and [other enumerated governmental agencies] to acquire an interest in land is in addition to any powers to acquire an interest in land under any other law.

(3) An "interest in land" includes a fee simple, leasehold interest, option, development right, right of first refusal, easement and any other interest in land less than a fee simple.

(4) Whenever a governmental agency is authorized by this Article to acquire an interest in land it may acquire the interest by exercising the power of eminent domain (hereinafter called condemnation) or by purchase, gift, exchange, interagency transfer, devise or other means.

(5) The grant of power by this Article to acquire an interest in land does not imply any lack of power to accomplish the same objective by regulation or any other means.

Section 5–102. *Discontinuance of Existing Land Uses*

A governmental agency authorized to acquire interests in land under this Article may acquire an interest in land as a means of securing the discontinuance of an existing use for which an order of discontinuance has been or could be issued under Article IV.

Section 5–103. *To Facilitate Development or Conservation of Specially Planned Areas*

A local government may acquire an interest in land for the purpose of facilitating development or conservation of a specially planned area designated by the local government if the acquisition is consistent with a precise plan adopted under § 2–211.

Section 5–104. *To Provide Replacement Land or Facilities*

(1) A governmental agency that is acquiring interests in land for any public or publicly-aided project may acquire such other interests in land as may be necessary or appropriate for the purpose of

(a) offering substitute sites or facilities to replace sites or facilities the usefulness of which has been impaired by the project; or

(b) making available dwelling units suitable to the reasonable requirements of persons within the jurisdiction of the agency who are displaced or are to be displaced by the project or by any common disaster or other casualty.

(2) The power of condemnation shall be used to acquire interests in land under this Section only if

(a) the acquisition of replacement property under this Section will not cause substantial uncompensated hardship, other than hardship for which compensation is available, to persons affected; and

(b) the acquisition is reasonably necessary to alleviate hardship caused

economic conditions, at which time local government will have the economic capability to take advantage of the broad powers.

In this connection, Part (2) of Article V of the Code[10] is also quite interesting. It contains sweeping authorization for the use of the urban renewal type powers, but not limited to the traditional urban renewal areas, namely areas where there is a finding that the present conditions in the area requires improvement. The public purpose of the use of the power relates to what is being built, rather than the problem that is being remedied. In other words, the position of the Code is that large scale development is desirable in and of itself. It serves a public purpose in that it fosters improved econo-

---

by a public or publicly-aided project or by a common disaster or other casualty.

Section 5–105. *To Preserve or Improve the Condition of Landmark Sites or Special Preservation Districts*

A governmental agency authorized to acquire interests in land under this Article may acquire an interest in land for the purpose of preserving or improving the condition of a landmark designated under § 2–208 or of a structure or land in a special preservation district designated under § 2–209.

Section 5–106. *To Achieve Planning Objectives*

A local government may, when reasonably necessary, acquire an interest in land to achieve the objectives of a state or local Land Development Plan or the objectives of permissible regulation under this Code including the following purposes

(1) to protect or improve environmental values including ecological balance;

(2) to preserve historical or archeological structures or sites;

(3) to minimize potential damage from floods, earthquakes, hurricanes or other natural disasters;

(4) to protect existing scenic or recreational values or to preserve open space;

(5) to facilitate the future construction of, or the continued usefulness of, needed public facilities.

Section 5–107. *Extraterritoriality*

Any power to acquire an interest in land granted to a governmental agency by this Part may be exercised outside its territorial boundaries, but the development of the land is subject to compliance with

(1) this Code;

(2) any applicable development ordinance of the local government in whose jurisdiction the land is located; and

(3) all other laws and ordinances otherwise applicable to the agency exercising the power of acquisition.

10. Section 5–201. *Public Purpose*

The assembly of land for large scale development is a public purpose for which the State Land Planning Agency may acquire land subject to the provisions of this Part. Before exercising the power of condemnation the State Land Planning Agency shall adopt a rule, identifying the categories of large scale development that should be encouraged in order to accomplish improved patterns of land development, and for which the Agency intends to acquire land pursuant to this Part.

Section 5–202. *Eligibility of Applicants*

The State Land Planning Agency may acquire an interest in land within a

mies, improved environmental considerations, and other forms of "social balance." Therefore, the condemnation power, for example, may be used to encourage new communities or other large scale development proposals, regardless of the existing conditions in the area.

---

development site in accordance with this Part if such acquisition is requested by

(1) a private developer who has already acquired control by purchase, option, agreement with a governmental agency or otherwise of over [60] percent of a development site for development meeting the standards of rules adopted under § 5–201; or

(2) a developer that is a governmental agency having the authority under other law to undertake development meeting the standards of rules adopted under § 5–201.

Section 5–203. *Application and Hearing Procedure*

(1) The State Land Planning Agency shall by rule specify the form and contents of an application requesting that it acquire land under this Part for large scale development. Each application shall contain a description of the development site of the proposed large scale development which is adequate to identify it.

(2) Before issuing an order concerning the application the State Land Planning Agency shall hold a hearing under [insert appropriate section of State Administrative Procedure Act] in the jurisdiction of the local government within which the land is located. In addition to any other requirements for notice of a hearing on orders, notice of a hearing on an application under this Part shall be published in a newspaper of general circulation in the community of the development site and shall be given individually to

(a) the applicant;

(b) the local government within whose jurisdiction the development is to be located; and

(c) the owner of each parcel of land within the site of the proposed development.

(3) The State Land Planning Agency shall publish notices of all applications filed under this Part in the weekly land development notice issued pursuant to § 8–208.

Section 5–204. *Order Directing Land Acquisition*

(1) The State Land Planning Agency shall issue an order directing the acquisition of land under this Part only if it finds that

(a) the proposed development will be large scale development meeting the standards of rules adopted under § 5–201;

(b) the developer is an eligible developer under § 5–202 and there is reasonable assurance that he is capable of completing the project according to his plan;

(c) the development is not inconsistent with any state or local Land Development Plan;

(d) the development will contribute to better patterns of growth for the area than would be likely to result in the absence of the development;

(e) there is reasonable assurance that the public facilities necessary to serve the development will be constructed at the appropriate time.

(2) An order authorizing the acquisition of land under this Part shall contain

(a) a description of the development site;

(b) the name and address of the developer for whom the acquisition is being made;

(c) the findings required by this Section; and

Another rather technical but quite important section of the Code dealing with land acquisition is Section 5–303,[11] which attempts to resolve the problem of how land development regulations are to be treated in valuing property being acquired in eminent domain proceedings. At the present time the landowner is entitled to inflate his land values by presenting evidence, in the condemnation proceeding, of the prospect of changing the existing regulations in order to allow virtually any type of land development. The only limitation on the owner is that he present a witness willing to testify that he would be interested in building on the land. Realistically this has presented a small hurdle, seriously hampering the land acquisition programs of many agencies, as well as weakening the land regulatory system. The proposed Code would eliminate this practice by restricting the landowner to the value of the property under the regulations currently effective at the date of the award. However, if these regulations are found by the Court to be so restrictive as to constitute an unconstitutional taking of the property, the court is restricted to value the property at its value for the minimum development necessary to eliminate the unconstitutional taking. These

---

(d) any reasonable conditions or restrictions relating to the use of the acquired land as are necessary to assure better patterns of growth for the area.

(3) A copy of the order shall be recorded with the appropriate filing officer under § 11–102.

Section 5–205. *Valuation of Land for Large Scale Development*

In valuing real property acquired under this Part no court shall exclude evidence of value on the ground that the value was generated by acts of the condemnor or of the developer who applied for the land acquisition.

11. Section 5–303. *Assumptions Regarding Development Permission*

If any interest in land is condemned under this Article the court shall assume for purpose of valuation that development would have been permitted on the land only in accordance with such combination of the following assumptions as shall produce the highest market value

(1) any development for which the landowner can obtain a general development permit under the terms of the development ordinance then applicable to the land; or

(2) any development for which the landowner can obtain a special development permit under the terms of the development ordinance then applicable to the land, except to the extent that the Land Development Agency prior to the date of the award has limited its willingness to issue a special development permit for the land by the issuance of a declaratory order under § 2–308; or

(3) any development for which the landowner can obtain a general or special development permit under an amendment to the ordinance adopted after the valuation date but prior to the date of the award; or

(4) any development permit previously granted which has not by its terms expired; or

(5) if the assumptions in the previous subsections would result in an unconstitutional taking of property, the minimum development necessary to eliminate the unconstitutional taking.

provisions are not likely to be popular with landowners, but we believe they provide substantial savings to governmental agencies acquiring land for public projects and eliminate some of the windfalls that now are provided to lucky owners.

GEORGE M. RAYMOND: First, and of greatest import, is the Code's suggestion that the primary responsibility for all important land use decisions belongs to the state notwithstanding lip service to the idea that local governments should remain "the primary authorities for planning and regulating development."[12] This conclusion is based on an evaluation of the areas which the Code would specifically place under state control. "Areas of critical state concern," as defined in the Code, could cover a very substantial proportion of the state's entire land area. They could include environmentally significant areas, which are considerable; all agricultural lands; all inland wetlands; and, beyond these, any topographically varied terrain and any open spaces "environmentally critical" to the proper shaping of urban development or which local interests can convince regional or county planners to declare as of more than local interest.[13]

---

12. Section 1–101. *Purposes*

(1) the designation of the local governments of this State as the primary authorities for planning and regulating development in this State according to a system of uniform statewide procedural standards.

13. Section 7–201. *Designation of Areas of Critical State Concern*

(1) The State Land Planning Agency may by rule designate specific geographical areas of the state as Areas of Critical State Concern and specify the boundaries thereof. In the rule designating an Area of Critical State Concern the State Land Planning Agency shall set forth

(a) the reasons why the particular area designated is of critical concern to the state or region;

(b) the dangers that might result from uncontrolled or inadequate development of the area;

(c) the advantages that might be achieved from the development of the area in a coordinated manner;

(d) general principles for guiding the development of the area; and

(e) the type of development, if any, that shall be permitted pending the adoption of regulations under §§ 7–203 or 7–204.

(2) Prior to adopting any rule under this Section, in addition to any notice and hearing otherwise required under § 8–201, the Agency shall hold a hearing under § 2–305 in a location or locations within an area proposed to be designated under the rule, or, if such location is not feasible, at a location convenient to people affected by the proposed rule. The Agency shall give notice to all local governments that include within their boundaries any part of any Area of Critical State Concern proposed to be designated by the rule, and shall publish notice of the proposed rule and the time and place of the hearing thereon in the weekly land development notice issued pursuant to § 8–208. The Agency shall either adopt, with or without modifications, or reject the proposed rule within [3 months] after notice is initially published.

(3) An Area of Critical State Concern may be designated only for

(a) an area significantly affected by, or having a significant effect upon,

The Code also proposes to give the state jurisdiction over all areas affected by, or significantly affecting, "existing or proposed major public facilities or other area(s) of major public investment." This could give the state a say in the use of all lands located adjacent to, or affected by, all interchanges between limited access and land service highways (most authorities suggest, as a minimum, that all lands within a one-mile radius be included); county or area-wide sewer or water supply systems; any major public facilities (such as hospitals, colleges, or universities); any regional, county, or State recreational area; and any airport, railroad station, or multi-model transportation center.

In addition to the lands which all of this would cover, the state's jurisdiction would also embrace all developments defined as of *regional impact*.[14] These could include a broad range of developments, and, what is more, the definition could vary, area by area. Thus, for instance, to be "of regional impact" in New York City a housing development might have to contain 500 units or more, whereas near Waddington, along the St. Lawrence River, a development with as few as 25 units might be deemed to exert a "regional impact."

---

an existing or proposed major public facility or other area of major public investment;

    (b) an area containing or having a significant impact upon historical, natural or environmental resources of regional or statewide importance;

    (c) a proposed site of a new community designated in a State Land Development Plan, together with a reasonable amount of surrounding land; or

    (d) any land within the jurisdiction of a local government that, at any time more than [3 years] after the effective date of this Code, has no development ordinance in effect.

(4) A "major public facility" means any publicly-owned facility of regional significance but does not include

    (a) any public facility operated by a local government, or any agency created by it, primarily for the benefit of the residents of that local government;

    (b) any street or highway except an interchange between a limited access highway and a frontage access street or highway;

    (c) any airport that is not to be used for instrument landings; or

    (d) any educational institution serving primarily the residents of a local community.

14. Section 7–301. *Development of Regional Impact*

(1) The State Land Planning Agency shall by rule define categories of development which, because of the nature or magnitude of the development or the nature or magnitude of its effect on the surrounding environment, is likely in the judgment of the Agency to present issues of state or regional significance.

(2) In adopting rules under this Section the State Land Planning Agency shall include in its consideration:

Finally, the Code would give the State control over the location of all developments defined as *of regional benefit*.[15] These would include all public projects other than those sponsored by the locality itself; all charitable institutions and utilities serving a broad area; and all publicly-assisted housing.

The possibility of enactment of legislation reflecting only selected parts of the ALI Code raises some difficult problems. For instance, among the states which have enacted statutes inspired by, if not entirely modeled upon, the ALI Code, none has accepted the concept of state jurisdiction over the regional distribution of assisted housing. The Code shied away from conditioning state control over "critical areas" upon the prior enactment of a state land development plan. Enactment of only the environmental protection features of the Code would make the task of those concerned with equitable housing distribution more, rather than less, difficult. For this reason a serious question can be raised as to whether support of "critical area" legislation is justifiable in the absence of a simultaneous statutory guarantee that regional housing responsibilities will be fairly

---

(a) The extent to which the development would create or alleviate environmental problems such as air or water pollution or noise;

(b) The amount of pedestrian or vehicular traffic likely to be generated;

(c) The number of persons likely to be residents, employees, or otherwise present;

(d) The size of the site to be occupied;

(e) The likelihood that additional or subsidiary development will be generated; and

(f) The unique qualities of particular areas of the state.

(3) Rules adopted under this Section may vary in different areas of the state to respond to differing conditions in these areas.

(4) Any development of regional benefit, as defined in this subsection, which is not otherwise included within the category of development of regional impact in the rule adopted under this subsection (1), shall nevertheless be treated as development of regional impact if the developer notifies the Land Development Agency at the time of his application for a development permit that he elects to proceed under this Part. "Development of regional benefit" means:

(a) development by a governmental agency other than the local government that created the Land Development Agency or another agency created solely by that local government;

(b) development which will be used for charitable purposes, including religious or educational facilities, and which serves or is intended to serve a substantial number of persons who do not reside within the boundaries of the local government creating the Land Development Agency;

(c) development by a public utility which is or will be employed to a substantial degree to provide services in an area beyond the territorial jurisdiction of the local government creating the Land Development Agency; and

(d) development of housing for persons of low and moderate income.

15. *Id.*, Section 7–301(4).

assumed by all local governments in the region. In this "post-Mt. Laurel"[16] age which is now just beginning, it may in fact be entirely justifiable to ask that, just as the Code mandates state identification of environmentally critical areas and the assumption by the state of responsibility for their protection, it should also mandate the preparation, as part of a required state land development plan, of a housing allocation system.

A similar type of problem arises with respect to the probable effectiveness of state control in areas impacted by major public facilities. We are gradually learning that a purely environmental approach to the distribution of major employment centers tends to scatter them all over the landscape in order to avoid polluting the air beyond acceptable federally-imposed, secondary standards. Under the Code, in an area defined as "critical" by reason of its being affected by a major public facility, the state could theoretically establish an acceptable land use intensity "floor" as well as "ceiling." Such a "floor" could vary on a case-by-case basis to capitalize on site-specific development opportunities. The thrust of the Code's commentary, however, and certainly the statutory precedents to which it has already given birth, suggest that this is not likely to happen.

The Code recognizes that purely advisory, appointed, regional planning agencies are totally ineffective, irrespective of the possible membership thereon of elected officials from all or some of their constituent local jurisdictions. Its recommendation is that the regional planning function be discharged by the state through the intermediary of Regional Planning Divisions established by it and to which it would delegate all or some of its own powers.[17] This is a welcome recognition of the futility of expecting results, of greater than marginal success, from regional agencies, which, although lacking any constituency, are nevertheless expected to perform in a highly controversial area in conflict with the still highly venerated doctrine of "home rule."

---

16. Township of Mt. Laurel v. So. Burlington Co. NAACP, 67 N.J. 151, 336 A.2d 713 (1975), *appeal dismissed*, __U.S.__, 96 S. Ct. 18 (1975).

17. Section 8–102. *Regional Planning Divisions*

(1) The State Land Planning Agency by rule may create one or more Regional Planning Divisions, designate the boundaries of the region in which each Division is to operate, and assign to a Division any of the functions granted to the State Land Planning Agency under this Code with regard to its region, subject to such review by the Agency as it deems appropriate. In addition to the requirements for adoption of rules under § 8–201, the State Land Planning Agency shall give notice to every local government having

Unfortunately, the Code would continue the traditional practice of granting local authorities the power to regulate land use even if they refuse to base such regulations on a land development plan. The inducements which the Code offers localities to develop such plans are not very enticing. The principal ones are: (1) the power to authorize planned unit development;[18] (2) the power to develop "precise plans;"[19] and (3) the power to acquire land for the imple-

---

jurisdiction over some portion of the territory in the proposed region and to every local government having jurisdiction over land adjacent to the territory in the proposed region, and it shall hold at least one hearing at a convenient place within the region. The Agency by rule may revoke any assignment of functions or revise the boundaries of any region.

(2) Upon the written petition of at least [2] local governments, or of at least [___] residents of the State requesting the creation of a Regional Planning Division or requesting a change of the boundary of an existing Division, the State Land Planning Agency shall consider the desirability of issuing the requested rule and shall prepare and issue a written statement of its conclusions and grant or deny the request within 120 days after its receipt. No request for a boundary change shall be acted upon until [6] months has expired since the last designation of that boundary was adopted.

18. Section 2–210. *Planned Unit Development*

(1) A development ordinance may authorize the Land Development Agency to grant special development permission for planned unit development by specifying the types or characteristics of development that may be permitted, which may differ from one part of the community to another.

(2) Special development permits may be granted for planned unit development, including combinations of land uses within the project area, and may be based on site planning criteria relating to the project as a whole rather than to individual parcels, if the Land Development Agency finds that the development:

(a) will be consistent with a currently effective Land Development Plan; and

(b) is likely to be compatible with development permitted under the general development provisions of the ordinance on substantially all land in the vicinity of the proposed development; and

(c) will not significantly interfere with the enjoyment of other land in the vicinity.

19. Section 3–101. *Local Land Development Plan*

(1) Using the procedures of § 3–106 a local government may adopt a Local Land Development Plan which shall be a statement (in words, maps, illustrations or other media of communication) setting forth its objectives, policies and standards to guide public and private development of land within its planning jurisdiction and including a short-term program of public actions as defined in § 3–105.

(2) Whenever any power exercised under this Code is required to bear some relationship to a Local Land Development Plan, a "Local Land Development Plan" means a statement adopted under § 3–106 appropriate for the objective, policy, or standard which the local government indicates will be achieved by the particular governmental action involved.

(3) Sections 3–102 through 3–104 are only guidelines concerning the purposes and contents of Local Land Development Plans and a Local Land Development Plan may not be reviewed by any court as to compliance with this Code on the ground that the contents or purposes are not consistent with this Code. Nothing in this subsection is intended to prevent a court in its

mentation of such "precise plans."[20] In contrast to these advantages, the disadvantages of adopting a plan under the Code are enormous. Such adoption would make all land use policies of the local government subject to *a priori* state review. By contrast, in the absence of a plan, the state's jurisdiction would be limited only to "critical areas" and to developments of more than local significance.

RICHARD A. PERSICO: Let me begin by pointing out in rapid succession what I think are probably the major improvements the Code provides over current enabling land use regulation. First of all, it is a credit to the Code and to the drafters to have brought such a degree of precision into the definition of terms used in land use planning. The definitions of variances, the special permit and the variety of nonconforming uses will all be highly beneficial. Secondly, I think that the broad grant of power given to local governments, in place of the traditional specific regulatory powers we are all familiar with, will provide flexibility that will encourage and facilitate land use regulation at the local level.

My most serious concerns are about the implementation of Article VII, which is the state land development system established in the Code. As I understand it, its thrust even where the state has established a state land development system, and you're dealing with uses which are of state or regional concern, is to leave the initial stages of enforcement and administration of that system to the localities. My reservations are based upon practical experience in a rural area in the State of New York.

The justification given in the commentary to the Code for the establishment of this system of local reliance is mainly the burden of time, cost and inconvenience to the state and to the developer. As to cost, experience in the Adirondacks shows that if you are going to give the ball to the local governments to do the initial enforcement, to conduct the first formal hearings, they are going to be completely without fiscal resources to do it, even where they operate with the best of intentions. We see this surfacing now. After two years we have gotten over half the communities in the Adirondacks involved in various stages of planning programs. With several now

---

consideration of any governmental action concerning development from considering the reasonableness of the Plan or its appropriateness and completeness in relation to the governmental action under consideration.

(4) A local government may designate any agency, committee, commission, department, or person to prepare the Local Land Development Plan.

20. Note 8, *supra*, Section 5–106.

about to adopt these they are awakening to the reality that they don't have the ways and means, particularly financially and expertise-wise, to administer the programs effectively.

In addition, based upon our experience, there is little willingness on the part of local governments to assume the cost, responsibilities and political headaches that go along with the enforcement of state mandates, except perhaps in the more sophisticated urban areas.

Editor's Comments

Golden v. Town of Ramapo: Establishing a New Dimension in American Planning Law

ON MAY 3, 1972 the New York Court of Appeals decided the case of *Golden v. The Planning Board of the Town of Ramapo* (no official citation at this writing) and by doing so opened up a whole new era in American planning law. This is perhaps the most important advance in zoning law since the watershed case of *Euclid v. Ambler*. As the attorney for the Town of Ramapo having conceived and developed the "timing and sequential control ordinances" for the Town and having written the brief and orally argued the case through the Court of Appeals, I would like to amplify the background and significance of the case.

The great movement of people and industries to the suburbs after World War II, with its resultant accelerated and rapid growth has led to wasteful and inefficient urban sprawl and leap-frog development. As a concomitant most suburban communities have been unable to develop adequate municipal facilities, particularly for residential development, as developers continually looking for cheaper land sites built outside of areas with adequate sewage, drainage, improved roads, firehouses, school sites, park and recreation facilities and other urban functions and services. The burden of capital investment is then shifted to the public sector and the general tax rate soars to meet the need for public facilities to catch up to the development. This transfer of the true cost of development from the developer to the public sector has led to a series of unfortunate effects on the urban fringe:

(a) imbalance of growth between types of uses;

(b) inability to provide public services to match private development;

(c) soaring tax rates on property due to inefficient provision of public services;

(d) poor quality of services provided due to rapid growth;

(e) land speculation, poor design, uncontrolled character and quality of private development, destruction of the natural landscape;

(f) inability to implement the planning process, lack of time to develop solutions, inadequate administrative and legal mechanisms;

(g) development of negative policies concerning social, racial and metropolitan solutions, formation of defensive incorporations and annexations, unwillingness to provide proper housing and facilities for diverse economic, racial and ethnic groups and irrational tax policies.

The traditional law of zoning and subdivision has been unequal to the task. Communities may regulate and divide the territorial area of the community into use zones or even flexible planned development but under traditional interpretation of the zoning and planning enabling acts, as well as the due process clause, regulating the timing and sequence of the development process was thought to be impermissible as a taking of the land without compensation. If the developer was deprived of any reasonable use of his land under a permanent zoning ordinance, the due process clause would fashion a remedy. Any direct remedy for the communities was never considered. Many communities, therefore, have sought to remedy the defects through devious devices. Holding zones (agricultural or industrial), numerical quotas, excessive large lot zoning, minimum floor area restrictions, have all been tried and despite their stated health and safety objects, they have all been related to the problem of excessive and scattered growth with its destructive effects. The by-product of exclusion of racial groups and low and moderate income families is another disastrous and unfortunate result of the desperate search for relief.

As attorney for a new administration in one of the fastest growing suburban communities in New York, in 1965, I was convinced that a direct resort to development timing and sequential control was not only possible under the enabling acts but also constitutional. The standard zoning enabling act already provided: "Such zoning regulations . . . shall be made . . . to prevent the overcrowding of land; to avoid undue concentration of population; *to facilitate the adequate provision of transportation, water, sewerage, schools, parks and other public requirements.*" The problem was: how do you utilize such provision and apply it to development so as to avoid confiscations. The solution was to relate residential development to capital investment, linking the private initiative to the public capacity. If the public, through its comprehensive planning process could develop capital programming so as to bring public facilities over a reasonable time to all areas of the community, the constitutional question could be solved. Since the restrictions on the land were only temporary — limited to a foreseeable period — the period of the plan — it would not be a permanent restriction on development—and since the public would be under a correlative duty to fulfill the capital budget and plan the restrictions would be reasonable, linked to necessity and obviously because of the planning, the antithesis of arbitrariness. Secondly, by limiting development to areas served with public facilities, we could avoid the use of low density exclusionary measures and develop a broad mix of housing.

So in 1965, with the courageous leadership of Supervisor John McAleney, a Columbia Law School graduate, a new town administration and a far-sighted planner, Manuel Emanuel, we began.

Ramapo was growing faster than almost any community in the nation. From 1940 to 1963 the population of New York State increased by 31.3%, Rockland County by 118.2% and Ramapo by 285.9%. In 1960 Ramapo's population was 35,000. By 1970 it reached 76,702. At that rate the Town would (89 square miles) reach a population saturation of 125,000 by 1979 with almost all of the growth in unbelievable urban sprawl, totally inadequate municipal facilities and no housing for low and moderate income families. From 1964 to 1969 we did Herculean work to bring planning to Ramapo. From 1964 to 1966 we developed a comprehensive master plan under funds authorized by § 701 of the Housing Act of 1954, for the growth and development of the Town. In implementing the master plan, we utilized interim development controls to prohibit development inconsistent with the plan. The interim development controls which we pioneered in Ramapo were upheld by the Courts as constitutional for the

first time in New York in *Rubin v. McAlevey,* 54 Misc.2d 338, 282 N.Y.S.2d 564 (1967) *aff'd* 29 A.D.2d 874, 288 N.Y.S.2d 519 (1968). In my article "Interim Development Controls: Essential Tools for Implementing Flexible Planning and Zoning" 49 Journal of Urban Law (1971), I point the necessity of these tools for developing a continuing and vital planning process.

We then began the process of implementing the comprehensive plan. We established the housing authority; we adopted an official map identifying all roads, parks and drainage systems to be preserved, we adopted model subdivision regulations to protect the housing consumer and to provide parks, boulevards and open space. The subdivision regulations which were adopted in 1966 have been used nationally and were published as model regulations in my article, "Model Regulations For The Control of Land Subdivision," 36 Mo. L. Rev. 1 (1971). The American Society of Planning Officials is publishing an annotated set of the regulations as a national model, publication date set for January, 1973. We simultaneously developed average density, cluster zoning and development easements, so as to preserve open space and provide community amenities. Ramapo's average density, cluster zoning and development easement laws are cited and appended to Charles Little's book "The Challenge of the Land" (1969) published by the Open Space Action Institute as model ordinances for the nation.

We then developed our 18 year capital budget and capital plan which committed the Town to developing adequate municipal facilities, including public sewers, drainage systems, improved roads, parks, recreational areas and firehouses for all areas of the Town and at rational densities for development. The Town spent hundreds of thousands of dollars in developing sewerage and drainage studies which provided information and engineering for these systems in all parts of the Town and for maximum development. We completely adopted the anti-thesis of the concept of writing in large lot zoning requirements to exclude low and moderate income housing and to exclude population growth. We planned for maximum development of the Town in 18 years instead of 7 years but at densities to encourage flexible and economically mixed development. Rather than avoiding development we had an ongoing capital improvement commitment to faster development but at a pace and with densities to assure adequate municipal facilities. At this juncture in 1969 we amended the zoning ordinance to provide the legal controls to regulate the timing and sequence of development in accordance with the availability and adequacy of municipal facilities. The 1969 zoning amendments did not "up zone" or "reclassify" residential land into non-residential uses. Rather it established a special permit use for residential development requiring a special permit for the Town Board prior to issuance of building permits or subdivision plat approval. The ordinance provides explicit standards for the issuance of the special permit. The standards are based upon the availability to the proposed residential development of the five essential facilities or services: (1) public sanitary sewers; (3) drainage facilities related to ade-

quate runoff capacity at maximum development; (3) improved parks and recreational facilities; (4) improved major, secondary and collector roads and (5) firehouses within appropriate distances. The ordinance provides that no special permit shall be issued unless the residential development has sufficient points (15) based on a sliding scale of values assigned under each of the five categories. The development points are related to the Town's capital plan under which the Town is committed to completion of public capital improvement to assure development of all areas of the Town within a maximum period of 18 years. Simultaneously the ordinance provides for variance relief if the subdivision is consistent with the Town's comprehensive planning; provides for reduction of assessed valuation on land to reflect the temporary restrictions on use of land; provides that the special permit may be issued presently for development at such time as the capital plan indicates that development is available and that the special permit is fully assignable and vested. Thus if the plan indicates facilities available for 15 points within 5 years in an area, the permit can be presently issued for development in five years. The developer is also accorded the right to advance development date by agreeing to provide such improvements as will bring the development within the number of development points required.

What we have fought for and won was the right of a community to chart its own destiny within for framework of reasonable planning. Until we initiated the program in 1964 the pattern was for the developers and speculators to make the decisions as to where growth would take place. The only factor in their decision was the profit motive. It is not their concern as to how their development will affect demands for government service which will be reflected in higher taxes and will have a tremendous impact on the lack of required secondary government investment. Nor are they especially concerned with the effects of their development on the environment or in the social and economic composition of the community.

The argument before the Court of Appeals lasted the entire afternoon of November 17, 1971 and the Court of Appeals recognized the importance of the case by giving counsel time to fully explain all of the full panoply of planning instituted by the community as well as the developers arguments that the case ended "exclusionary" zoning, citing *Girsh* and *Kit-Mar* and the exclusionary zoning cases. In recognizing that the delay in development is temporary (maximum of 18 years based on capital plan), the Court held that there was no denial of the right to subdivide, but rather that the refusal was a condition of that right, temporary in nature and supported by enabling legislation and legitimate zoning purposes. In the language of the Court, "where it is clear that the existing physical and financial resources of the community are inadequate to furnish the essential services and facilities which a substantial increase in population requires, there is a rational basis for "phased growth" and hence the challenged ordinance is not a violation of the Federal and State Constitutions. The Court went on to say:

"Experience over the last quar-

ter-century, with greater technological integration and drastic shifts in population distribution, has pointed out serious defects . . . in land use control. . . . Although the issues are found in the developers due process rights, those rights cannot realistically speaking, be viewed separately and apart from the rights of others. . . ."

The majority of the Court explicitly rejected the argument that the Ramapo ordinance was exclusionary. In the first place, Ramapo is not an "exclusionary" zoning case. Ramapo was the first suburban town in New York State to voluntarily, as part of its planning process, develop integrated public housing for low income families, over the objection of thousands of its citizens. As attorney for the Town and the Public Housing Authority, we were successful in developing two public housing areas with several hundred units of public housing for low income families which have now been built and are cited as models for the county, Planning for additional units is now taking place. One public housing area involves industrialized housing and both are located in landscaped, treed areas of incredible beauty, with integrated public schools and neighborhoods. We had to bring and fight several law suits in establishing the public housing under our zoning ordinance, see *Greenwald v. Town of Ramapo*, 35 A.D.2d 958 (1970); *Farrelly v. Town of Ramapo*, 35 A.D.2d 957, 317 N.Y.S.2d 837 (1970) and *Fletcher v. Romney*, 323 F. Supp. 189 (S.D. N.Y. 1971). The Supervisor of the Town, John F. McAlevey, stood by the public housing and won a sweet victory in

November 1971 in which the public housing was the key issue.

The confusion of many attorneys in the battle against exclusionary zoning is unfortunate. There is a tendency to see all zoning and planning as enemies simply because some communities utilize these tools in an exclusionary manner. The argument goes back to Richard Culers article, "Legal and Illegal Means For Controlling Community Growth on the Urban Fringe," 1961 Wis. L. Rev. 370. Should we go back to no zoning at all, to unlimited urban sprawl and development chaos in surburban areas because some of the tools being developed are being used erroneously? All zoning and planning tools are essentially neutral. They can be used correctly or incorrectly depending upon the motivation of the regulators. Our efforts must be to eliminate the abuses, while simultaneously developing stronger efforts to preserve the quality of our communities and of the environment and to assure economic and racial equality *in* planning not *without* planning.

In fact *Golden,* is a great victory for opponents of exclusionary zoning. For the first time the New York Court of Appeals expressly states that:

(1) Any scheme which restricts free mobility of people will be considered inherently suspect; and

(2) We will not countenance under any guise community efforts at immunization or exclusion.

Thus the language of the Court will be instrumental in overturning exclusionary zoning throughout the State of New York where it appears. The Court, however states:

"But far from being exclusionary, the present amendments merely seek, by the implementation of sequential development and timed growth to provide a balanced cohesive community dedicated to the efficient utilization of land."

The fact that you failed to note to your readers is that Ramapo, under the timing and sequential controls, is still growing at a rapid rate, in fact faster than the State of New York, and that the areas available for development each year are extensive and are being built without exclusion and at densities much higher than large-lot zoning. The community is being built, however, with proper planning and facilities and a mix of housing.

The dissent expressed concern that some communities may attempt to misread the decision and use it to erect legal barriers against people who are desirous of moving into the suburbs. I am of the firm opinion that the Court has expressly noted the mandatory requirement of prior comprehensive planning which is reasonable and equitable and reflective of all the social needs of society not only the disadvantaged but the overtaxed. No other community or region can adopt sequential and timing controls and succeed in withstanding a similar legal assault if they have not also done all of the other things necessary to demonstrate that what they are doing is a part of and consistent with rational community planning and not an effort to halt growth or exclude people. Ramapo at the end of the 18 year capital plan will have greater population and density and economic mix than most suburban communities. It is not excluding growth but timing and sequencing its growth. As the Court of Appeals put it: "The answer which Ramapo has posed can by no means be termed definitive; it is, however, a first practical step toward controlled growth achieved without foresaking broader social purposes."

Finally, the truly significant and landmark aspects of the case is that it represents the first time that any court in the United States has upheld the concept of restricting development in metropolitan areas through comprehensive planning or an exercise of the zoning power without compensation. Now for the first time regions, states and the federal government, as well as municipal governments, have the tool to develop a rational urban growth policy that can balance suburban developments with inner city revitalization and new community development. The recognition that timing and sequential controls, even over a period of 18 years, is a necessary concomitant of the police power to regulate urban growth finally provides us with the tool for controlling the direction of growth and the public capital investment in metropolitan areas. The necessity to use condemnation to purchase land areas in order to regulate their development is of doubtful validity under eminent domain in any event, is avoided. The need for timing controls in land use planning has been recognized for many years and by eminent national authorities:

(1) Douglas Commission, *Alternatives to Urban Sprawl,* Report No. 15, 1968 — "The prevention of urban sprawl should therefore qualify on a valid public purpose justifying the use of valid zoning and timing regulations";

(2) ACIR, *Urban and Rural* *America, Policies for Future Growth,* Document A-32 pp. 12–15 (1968)

(3) *New York State Planning Law Revision Study,* Document No. 4, Feb. 1970;

(4) *American Law Institute, A Model Land Development Code,* Tent. Drafts Nos. 1 and 2, 1968 and 1970; and

(5) Bair, *ASPO Report No. 243,* "Toward a Regulatory System for Use, Development, Occupancy and Construction" (1969); and

many other cited in the brief and in the court decisions that are too numerous to incorporate.

It is a compelling fact that many of our eminent judges, dissenting in exclusionary zoning cases, have pleaded that communities should use timing and sequential controls as alternatives to exclusion. In his brilliant dissenting opinion in *Vicker v. Township Committee of Gloucester Township,* 181 A.2d 129 (N.J. 1962), the case upholding entire exclusion of mobile homes from a township, Justice Hall wrote that as an alternative for exclusion, timing and sequential controls be validly used. He recognized that rapid growth is often the fiscal rationale for large lot zoning and exclusion used on a desperate measure to control haphazard urban sprawl.

"Such municipalities above all others, vitally need and may legally exercise comprehensive planning and implementing zoning techniques to avoid present haphazard development which can only bring future grief. They are entitled to aim thereby for a sound and balanced area with varying uses confined to specified districts and appropriately regulated. *They may even limit the pace of growth to coincide with the availability of the necessary additional facilities and services so as to minimize growing pains.* See Fagin, Regulating the Timing of Urban Development, 20 LAW AND CONT. PROB. 298 (1955). They do not have to permit an Oklahoma Landrush or a western boom town.

Similarly the Pennsylvania Supreme Court in *In Re Kit-Mar Builders* 268 A.2d 765 (Pa. 1970) in striking down large lot zoning cited the New York case of *Westwood Forest Estates, Inc. v. Village of South Nyack,* 23 N.Y.2d 424 (1969) which in dicta suggested the use of timing controls as a device alternative to exclusion:

> This is not to say that ... pursuant to its other powers ... the village ... may not impose restrictions on conditions on

the *granting of building permits in stages or perhaps even a moratorium on the issuance of any building permits, reasonably limited as to time.*

It should be pointed out that the dissent was not troubled by the use of timing and sequential controls or an attribute of the zoning and police power, but rather that it should be states and regions that are granted this power through specific legislation. Thus the historic principle was recognized both by the majority and minority judges. Whether, in fact, the national response to Ramapo, does indeed lead to a regional and metropolitan approach, as urged by the majority judges, nevertheless we are indeed on the threshold of a new era in planning law.

That in a nutshell is Ramapo. One of the most interesting and far-reaching examples of the intelligent application of planning in a community.

Impact Zoning:
Alternative to
Exclusion in the Suburbs

Victor John Yannacone, Jr.

Yannacone & Yannacone, Patchogue, N.Y.;
Past Co-Chairman Environmental Law Committee
American Trial Lawyers Association; Co-Founder
Environmental Defense Fund; Past Chairman
Environmental Law Committee Section of Insurance,
Negligence and Compensation Law, American Bar
Association; LL.B, 1959 Brooklyn School of Law.

John Rahenkamp, ASLA, AIP

Rahenkamp, Sachs, Wells & Associates, Phila., Pa.;
Chairman, Penjerdel Open Space Committee;
Former Chairman and Member Mt. Laurel Township
New Jersey Planning Board; B.S., Michigan State
University; M.A., University of Pennsylvania.

Angelo J. Cerchione

Associate, Benham, Blair, Winesett, Duke, Inc., Falls Church, Va.

Introduction

A FUNDAMENTAL ISSUE FACING many American communities today
is how to foster local development while protecting the public interest in land, landscape and natural resources—the capital assets
of our civilization. Community officials should recognize that impact zoning is the best method by which to preserve these capital
assets and to stabilize local growth. Through impact zoning, planners assess the needs of a locality in relation to the economic environmental and sociological capacity of a region to absorb future development. The impact of a proposed development project can be
scientifically researched before construction. The primary advantage
of impact zoning is that each locality assumes its fair share of the
ecological and housing needs of the region.

Municipal governments must depend on state authorization in
order to enact impact zoning laws. However, in the United States,
local governments already are authorized to exercise sovereign
powers to enhance the general welfare.[1] Impact zoning, which re-

---

1. Village of Euclid v. Ambler Realty, 272 U.S. 365 (1926).

flects the emerging public interest in regional growth, is without
question, a proper exercise of sovereignty by a municipality.

The concept of sovereignty in the United States has evolved considerably in 200 years, reflecting changes in society's perception of
the public interest. Unlike the English common law where sovereign
powers were confined to the monarch, the sovereign in the United
States is the people. In 1793, Chief Justice Jay explained the change
in the concept of sovereignty under the new republic:

> From the crown of *Great Britain*, the sovereignty of their country passed
> to the people of it. . . . [T]he people, in their collective and national ca-
> pacity, established the present Constitution. It is remarkable that in estab-
> lishing it, the people exercised their own rights, and their own proper
> sovereignty, and conscious of the plentitude of it, they declared with be-
> coming dignity, "We the *people* of the *United States*, do ordain and estab-
> lish this Constitution." Here we see the people acting as sovereigns of the
> whole country. . . .
>   . . . [T]he sovereignty of the nation is [in] the people of the nation. . . .
>   . . . Sovereignty is the right to govern; a nation or State-sovereign is the
> person or persons in whom that resides. In *Europe* the sovereignty is gen-
> erally ascribed to the *Prince*; here it resides with the people. . . . Their
> *Princes* have personal powers, dignities, and preeminiences, our rulers
> have none but *official*; nor do they partake in the sovereignty otherwise,
> or in any other capacity, than as private citizens.[2]

An essential difference in the concept of sovereignty in the United
States from the English absolute view is that the power of the majority is subject to the rights of the minority. A limitation on the
individual's right to private property imposed by the people collectively may constitute a "taking" under the Fifth Amendment.[3] However, the Constitution does not bar the exercise of sovereign power
by the Government, the People, to protect the public health, safety
or general welfare. Restriction of some individual rights to preserve
the common good is justified as a proper use of sovereignty in a
republic.

Some shudder at the temerity of those who would challenge the
ius abutendi[4] that sacrosanct bundle of rights usually associated

---

2. Chisholm v. Georgia, 1 U.S. (2 Dall.) 17, 60 (1793).
3. U.S. CONST. amend V.
4. Roscoe Pound, in 1958, after a lifetime of reflection on the nature of
law and jurisprudence and the rights of man notes, prophetically,
". . . There has been a progressive tendency to restrict the *ius abutendi*
which the maturity of law attributed to owners. A crowded and hungry
world may yet weigh this interest against individual claims of free action
still further by preventing destruction of commodies in order to keep up
prices, or even cutting off the common-law liberty of the owner of land to
sow it to salt if he so desires [citing a 1912 French article]. At times over-
production of agricultural products has led to proposals for restriction of

with nominal title to private property upon which great fortunes have been built, governments established, legislatures suborned, and the courts misled. Nevertheless, in the United States, all the power over land and natural resources once held by the Kings of England, France and Spain has been acquired by the people of the United States, collectively, and is exercised, on behalf of the sovereign people, by the executive, legislative, judicial and administrative branches of government. In the United States, government acts as trustee of the power of the people, and agent of the people for the benefit of the people.

While the Constitution strengthened the rights of individual property owners to an extent beyond that which could be tolerated by European monarchs, at no time did the sovereign people of the United States relinquish their collective right to determine the highest and best use of the land and the natural resources which they had wrested from the crowned heads of Europe. Just as the sovereign people of the United States by the Ninth Amendment to the Constitution[5] retained the essential sovereignty of the new nation to themselves, so the people of the individual states by the Tenth Amendment[6] retained their collective right to provide for the common good within each state and insist that land be used according to its intrinsic suitability rather than merely a substrate for local development.

---

the owners *ius utendi* by regulation of what crops he may raise [citing a 1932 *Yale Law Journal* article which may have influenced New Deal agricultural policy]. At other times there are projects for administrative appointment of receivers of agricultural land cultivated or managed by the owner 'in such a manner as to prejudice materially the production of food thereon. . . .' [citing a 1920 *English Law Review* article]. Restrictions with respect to housing proceed on another aspect of this same social interest [. . . in conservation of social resources, that is, the claim or want or demand involved in social life in civilized society that the goods of existence shall not be wasted; that where all human claims or wants or desires may not be satisfied, in view of infinite individual desires and limited natural means of satisfying them, the latter be made to go as far as possible; and, to that end, that acts or courses of conduct which tend needlessly to destroy or impair these goods shall be restrained. In its simplest form this is an interest in the use and conservation of natural resources and is recognized in the doctrines as to *res communes* may be used, but not owned, . . .]" 3 R. POUND, JURISPRUDENCE 305 (1959). *See also* V. Yannacone, *Agricultural Lands, Fertile Soils, Popular Sovereignty, The Trust Doctrine, Environmental Impact Assessment and the Natural Law*, N.D.L. REV. 615 (1975).

5. U.S. CONST. amend. IX. For a thorough discussion of the Ninth Amendment, see, V. YANNACONE & B. COHEN, 1 ENVIRONMENTAL RIGHTS AND REMEDIES 61 (1972).

6. U.S. CONST. amend. X.

Today, confinement of land use regulation to a municipal area may be an improper exercise of sovereign powers. The people, who elect governmental officials to exercise sovereign powers in their behalf, are no longer benefited by traditional land use regulations which fail to preserve the land and natural resources. Municipal zoning, confined to promoting local growth, not only conflicts with regional and national governmental interests but may also be exclusionary.

In response to this change in the urbanization process, planners have devised new tools to rationally structure local development. Among these tools are the housing unit cap of Petaluma, California[7] and the timing and sequential growth development program of Ramapo, New York.[8] However, the decisions in these cases indicate that local zoning must be designed to accommodate regional demands in the future. A municipal government serves the public interest best through the proper use of its sovereign powers by enacting impact zoning laws.

An example of proper exercise of sovereign powers is the use of impact zoning which forces a municipality to consider regional needs in order to benefit all the people. Under impact zoning, municipal officials plan local growth as well as accept a fair share of the burdens of regional growth. The carrying capacity of the resources of the community must be assessed before further development is allowed. Preparation of assessment statements by local planners have assisted government officials in developing regional housing allocation programs. Through the use of impact zoning, the exercise of sovereign powers in the area of land use regulation can continue to be retained by the people in their collective capacity.

A. The Taking Issue

At the heart of most controversies over land use regulation is the basic legal question: "What are the constitutional limitations to the public regulation of private property?" The taking clause of the Fifth Amendment has been and continues to be the principal barrier to unfettered regulation of private property. After years of litigation and hundreds of cases the extent and strength of the barrier remains

---

7. Construction Indus. Ass'n v. City of Petaluma, 522 F.2d 897 (9th Cir. 1975).

8. Golden v. Planning Board, 30 N.Y.2d 359, 285 N.E.2d 291, 334 N.Y.S.2d 138 (1972).

uncertain. EPA Administrator Russell Train, when chairman of the President's Council of Environmental Quality (CEQ), stated ". . . few subjects are more fraught with emotion and less understood than the rights of private property and the constitutional limits to the public control of those rights."[9]

In an introductory note, the authors of the 1973 CEQ report claim that:

> The taking issue is a weak link. All over the country attempts to solve environmental problems through land use regulation are threatened by the fear that they will be challenged in Court as an unconstitutional taking of private property without just compensation.[10]

Whether the taking clause is considered a weak link depends on one's orientation, interests, and portfolio. For many years attorneys retained by real estate and corporate interests have advised that the Fifth Amendment as interpreted by the United States Supreme Court [ever since that august body in the aptly named *Slaughter House Cases*[11] first personified big business by endowing corporate persons with all the rights, privileges, and immunities of human beings] was written to encourage and protect private enterprise. Indeed some legal scholars and judges also have adopted the view that any government regulation of land use is taking private property without just compensation. However, adherents of this anachronistic position of non-governmental interference of land use should examine the warning of the CEQ report.

> Many people seriously believe that the Constitution gives every man the right to do whatever he wants with his land. That foreign concepts like environmental protection and zoning were probably sneaked through by the Warren Court. Many more people recognize the validity of land use regulation in general, but believe that it may never be used to reduce the value of a man's land to the point where he can't make a profit on it. After all, what good is land if you can't make a profit on it?[12]

The Report reviews both judicial interpretation and scholarly commentary of the taking issue, and concludes that the Court has never adopted the philosophies of non-governmental interference or absolute right to make the highest profit from land.

---

9. TRAIN, FOREWORD TO F. BOSSELMAN, D. CALLIES & J. BANTA, THE TAKING ISSUE (1973).

10. *Id.* at iv.

11. 83 U.S. (16 Wall.) 36 (1872). *See also* 1 R. POUND, JURISPRUDENCE 95 (1959).

12. F. BOSSELMAN, D. CALLIES & J. BANTA, *supra* note 9 at 1.

The right to make money buying and selling land is a cherished American folkway, and one that cannot be lightly ignored. But in an increasingly crowded and polluted environment can we afford to continue circulating the myth that tells us that the taking clause protects this right of unrestricted use, regardless of its impact on society? Obviously not.[12a]

The potency of these comments in light of the concurrent energy, population, and environmental crises is unmistakable, and the language of the New York Court of Appeals in Ramapo prophetic:

Every restriction on the use of property entails hardships for some individual owners. Those difficulties are invariably the product of police regulation and the pecuniary profits of the individual must in the long run be subordinated to the needs of the community. . . . The fact that the ordinance limits the use of, and may depreciate the value of the property will not render it unconstitutional, however, unless it can be shown that the measure is either unreasonable in terms of necessity or the diminution in value is such as to be tantamount to a confiscation. . . . Diminution, in turn, is a relative factor and though its magnitude is an indicia of a taking, it does not of itself establish a confiscation. . . .
. . . Where it is clear that the existing physical and financial resources of the community are inadequate to furnish the essential services and facilities which a substantial increase in population requires, there is a rational basis for "phased growth," and hence the challenged ordinance is not violative of the Federal and State Constitutions.[13]

In the Anglo-American judicial system the owner of land taken for public use historically has been entitled to just compensation. About this tenet there is little question. Frequently litigated, however, is the question of what amount of compensation is just: the owner's expectation interest at the highest and best use of the land or the owner's restitution interest, reimbursing him for the reasonable value of the property.

Aside from taking outright the limitation of the landowners unrestrained right to the use of property has never required compensation. Government exercising the police powers to protect the public health and safety is a long acknowledged uncompensable limitation. Along the spectrum between compensated taking and uncompensable safety regulations different classes of "taking" may be identified.

1. Taking which arises from protection of the public health, safety and welfare;

2. Taking which results from protection of significant natural and societal resources;

12a. *Id.* at 2.
13. Golden v. Planning Board, *supra* note 8.

3. Taking which is occasioned by property becoming vested with the public interest.

1. *Regulations that Protect the Public Health, Safety and General Welfare*[14]

AIRPORTS, AIR TRAVEL, SAFETY AND NOISE

Regulation of airports, air travel, safety and noise are prototypical of the exercise of police powers to protect the public health, safety and general welfare. Judicial notice has been taken of two apparently competing propositions:

1. The air traveler is entitled to the safest flight available under the current state of the art in aviation technology;
2. The homeowner and the man on the street are entitled to protection from the hazards and noise of aircraft operations.

The location of an airport or any other major industrial or transportation facility irrevocably determines the environmental characteristics of the region. Some areas in the vicinity of airports and aircraft operations are inherently dangerous. Once designated residential housing should not be permitted in the zone of maximum hazard from aircraft. There is no constitutional right to live in the zone of maximum danger. Similarly, developments may be proscribed that increase the risk to aircraft operation.

Governmental limitation of the use of private property in an airport area may constitute a *de facto* "taking"; but not a *de jure* taking which requires the government, as representative of the sovereign people, to pay the fair market value of the property at its highest and best commercial use. These limitations on land use represent reasonable efforts to protect the public health, safety and welfare, and are within the police power of representative government acting on behalf of the sovereign people.

Noise is another characteristic of airports and certain industrial operations which irrevocably determines the uses which should be permitted in their neighborhood. All residential development should be prohibited in high noise areas around airports and other heavy industrial operations. Such restrictions can be justified for physiological, psychological, medical and aesthetic reasons.

---

14. Yannacone & Francella, Environmental Concern—The Law and Aviation, in MASTER PLANNING THE AVIATION ENVIRONMENT (A. Cerchione ed. 1969). *See also,* Cerchione & Sinis, *Protecting Airports and their Neighbors Through the Environmental Land Use Planning Process,* in PLANNING, ENVIRONMENTAL SCIENCE, AVIATION (V. Yannacone ed. 1974).

2. Regulations that Protect Significant Natural and Societal Resources

THE DEFENSE OF FLORISSANT

Courts of Equity were established to temper the rigidities of the common law, to allow it to bend to the realities of society. In the realm of private property, the rights of landowners have always been subject to modification in the public interest by equity. The protection of basic human rights is the lodestar of the United States Constitution. While the constitutional guarantees may never vary, the scope of their application must expand or contract to meet new and different conditions. Equity has provided a degree of elasticity not to the meaning but to the application of constitutional principles. It is this ability to accommodate the public interest, in order to meet the exigencies of each generation that has been the boost and excellence of the common law. Unbridled property rights, useful in the 19th century to a sparsely settled country with an expanding population must be reigned by modern appreciation of irreplaceable natural resources. Judicial intervention in the Florissant fossil bed dispute illustrates the expansion of the law to accommodate newly perceived public interests.

The preservation of the Florissant fossil beds in 1969[15] indicates how the courts may impose a public trust on private property. The Florissant fossil beds are located a short distance west of Colorado Springs, Colorado. The beds contain seeds, leaves, plants and insects from the Oligocene period (approximately 34 million years ago) which are remarkably preserved in paper-thin layers of volcanic shale throughout more than 6,000 acres of an ancient lake bed. Unfortunately, these fossil shales begin to disintegrate when the thin layer of soil protecting them from the weather is disturbed.

For many years scientists, conservationists, naturalists, the National Park Service, and individual congressmen worked to protect the fossil beds by establishing a Florissant Fossil Beds National Monument. When the bill passed the Senate in 1969, a Colorado Springs real estate company had contracted to purchase approximately 1,800 acres of the monument. During the House of Representatives' deliberation on the bill, the land company brazenly announced it would bulldoze a road through the fossil beds to open the area for second home development. A group of Colorado con-

---

15. For a complete discussion, see V. YANNACONE & B. COHEN, 1 ENVIRONMENTAL RIGHTS & REMEDIES §§ 2:9–2:14 (1972).

servationists attempted to persuade the land company to wait until the House of Representatives acted on the bill, or at least to confine excavation and development to the area outside the fossil beds. The land company refused. The company offered to sell the land containing the fossil beds to the conservationists for cash at a higher price than the company had paid.

The conservationists, fearing the land company would irreparably damage the fossil beds, formed a nonprofit, public benefit corporation called the Defenders of Florissant. An action for declaratory judgment and injunctive relief was filed against the land company and other landowners and contract vendees in the area to be included within the national monument.

A United States District Court heard the application for a temporary restraining order on July 9, 1969. Although the Defenders of Florissant established that the excavations for roads and culverts threatened by the land company would damage valuable areas within the proposed national monument, the District Court ruled that the land company might use the property within any manner proper under the law. The application for a temporary restraining order and a subsequent application for a stay pending appeal was denied. The District Court did note in passing that the fossil beds ought to be preserved.

Following this decision, the land company agreed to postpone excavation for a few days to give the Defenders an opportunity to raise funds to buy the land. The conservationists, unable to raise the ransom for the fossil beds, appealed to the Tenth Circuit Court of Appeals.

The appellate judges questioned whether they had the authority to protect a natural resource by issuing a restraining order in the absence of any statute protecting the fossils. The Defenders of Florissant argued that the right to preservation of the unique fossils, a national, natural resource treasure, was an unenumerated right retained by the people of the United States in the Ninth Amendment of the Constitution.[16] While recognizing the right of the landowners to make reasonable use of their land and to profit from their nominal title, the Defenders claimed that a court of equity could impose a public trust on that portion of the property which had become vested with the public interest—the 34 million year old fossils.

---

16. U.S. CONST. amend. IX.

Counsel for the Defenders of Florissant then picked up a fossil palm leaf that had been unearthed at Florissant, and concluded:

> The Florissant fossils are to geology, paleontology, paleobotany, palynology and evolution what the Rosetta Stone was to Egyptology. To sacrifice this 34 million year old record, a record you might say written by the mighty hand of God, for 30 year mortgages and the basements of the A-frame ghettos of the seventies is like wrapping fish with the Dead Sea Scrolls.

The Court of Appeals issued an order restraining the land company and other landowners in the area from ". . . disturbing the soil, subsoil, or geological formations of the Florissant fossil beds by any physical or mechanical means. . . ."

After an evidentiary hearing on July 29, 1969, the District Court denied the Defenders' application for a preliminary injunction again upholding the land company's private property rights. The land company announced it would begin excavation that afternoon although Congress had not yet completed action on the National Monument Bill. Several hours later, the Defenders filed a motion for an emergency stay with the Tenth Circuit Court of Appeals. The Court of Appeals immediately issued an order extending its prior temporary restraining order indefinitely.

The Florissant fossil beds were saved by the invocation of the Court's equitable powers to avert a wrong to the public. Although the Court order prohibiting excavation of the fossil beds may have deprived the landowners of the most profitable use of their land, the company could still develop the area for tourism, recreation, scientific research or other uses compatible with protection of the fossils. The speculators were not denied the opportunity to earn a reasonable return on their investment. Further, the fact that the land company did not wish to use its land for less profitable purposes did not make the judicial restraint on development a taking without due process of law.

The public's interest in the fossil beds was dormant. But once awakened by the roar of the developers' bulldozer it grew to a magnitude that justified limitation on the privately held land. The importance of the Florissant litigation is the judicial restriction of heretofore absolute private rights to protect the sovereign people's natural resource treasure.

Limitations on the use of private property may only be judicially imposed when a petitioner establishes that the action challenged represents an imminent danger of irreparable damage to some unique and essentially irreplaceable resource. The resource must be vested with the public interest so that beneficial ownership is in all the people not only for this generation but for generations yet unborn.

3. Recovery of Property Vested with the Public Interest

a. JUST COMPENSATION

Equity can be called upon to protect the rights of the people in property which becomes vested with public interest subsequent to its acquisition by private owners. Although, the owner of land taken for public use is entitled to just compensation, "just compensation" for property vested with public interest does not mean fair market value for the land's most profitable use.

No individual or corporation can be considered the absolute owner of property that has become vested with a substantial public interest since if we trace the claim of title back far enough title was originally in the sovereign.[17] In England, William took title to all the land after Hastings and then parceled it out among his lieutenants. Before constitutional protection against seizure of private property the sovereign could simply take back property at will. In the United States title originally lay with the people, collectively dispursed to private owners subject to reclamation as the need arose. The Fifth Amendment insures that the sovereign people pay compensation for such a reclamation or taking.

b. WHO MAY ASSERT THE PUBLIC INTEREST?

Although some commentators contend that the National Environmental Policy Act (NEPA) expanded the basis for standing, others

---

17. There is a rather famous tale, probably apocryphal, that aptly illustrates the origin of title to real property, at least in the United States. It seems that shortly after the Civil War, a large New York City law firm requested a title abstract on property in New Orleans. A Louisiana lawyer traced the chain of title back to 1803, and certified title in the present owner. The Wall Street law firm, however, was not satisfied with the short time covered by the abstract and haughtily demanded a further search of the title prior to 1803, and recertification of the title in the present owner. The Louisiana lawyer replied,

"On December 20, 1803, the United States purchased Louisiana from Napoleon, who acquired it on November 30, 1803 from the Count of Casa Calvo, Spanish Governor of the Louisiana Territory who was the duly authorized agent of the King of Spain who claimed title by discovery, exploration and conquest exercising his Divine Right as King and successor in interest to the Holy Roman Emperor whose title to all the World came from Jesus Christ, Son of God, through his vicar on earth, the Pope of Rome, exercising the power of God on earth, and God, as we all know, made Louisiana."

argue that NEPA cannot confer standing on any party not "aggrieved" in equity or under the Administrative Procedure Act.[18] Any party who wishes to protect the public interest in natural resources must have standing. The legal concept of "standing" evolved to insure that a plaintiff has sufficient interest in the outcome of the litigation to vigorously represent his position. Under Article III of the Constitution the Court may only rule on cases and controversies and may not give advisory opinions. Thus under the Administrative Procedure Act only an aggrieved party or his representative may bring suit. However, standing is not a procedural rule to be rotely applied but a legal concept that must be re-examined in the context of each controversy presented to a court.

In *Sierra Club v. Morton*,[19] an environmental group sought to enjoin Walt Disney Enterprises, Inc., from converting the beautiful Mineral King Valley in the Sierra Nevada mountains into a ski resort. The Supreme Court held that the Sierra Club lacked standing to bring suit. Though the basis of the Court's decision was the Club's failure to show that it was an aggrieved party, the decision is not to be interpreted as an inflexible judicial denial of standing to all environmental groups representing the public interest. Rather, it was a failure of the environmentalists to prove in this instance that they represented an aggrieved party.

The Supreme Court ruled that the Sierra Club had failed to establish sufficient direct interest in the controversy to be accorded standing. The Club had not shown that the organization would suffer "injury in fact" from the action challenged.

> . . . [A] mere 'interest in a problem,' no matter how long-standing the interest and no matter how qualified the organization is in evaluating the problem, is not sufficient by itself to render the organization 'adversely affected' or 'aggrieved' within the meaning of the APA.[20]

---

18. Administrative Procedure Act, 5 U.S.C. § 702. *See also* V. YANNACONNE & B. COHEN, 1 ENVIRONMENTAL RIGHTS & REMEDIES 440 (1972); Yannacone & Davison, *Natural Environmental Policy Act of 1969*, 1 ENVIRONMENTAL LAW 8 (1970); Yannacone, *The Origins of a National Environmental Policy*, in THE ENERGY CRISIS: DANGER AND OPPORTUNITY § 11 (V. Yannacone ed. 1944); Yannacone, *The Origins of Our National Environmental Policy*, in FUTURE LAND USE 145 (Burchell & Listokin ed. 1975).

19. In Sierra Club v. Morton, 405 U.S. 727 (1972), Mr. Justice Stewart stated that: "The requirement that a party seeking review [of agency action] must allege facts showing that [they are] adversely affected does not insulate executive action from judicial review, nor does it prevent any public interests from being protected through judicial process. . . ."

20. *Id.* at 739.

The Court indicated that aesthetic and environmental interests if sufficiently established could provide a basis for standing. Further, the Court rejected the claim that standing required special damages. Thus, the Court held that once a party is established as a proper representative of a party aggrieved or adversely affected it may assert the interests of the general public in environmental litigation, without the difficulty of showing special damages.

The real tragedy of the case was the failure of the Sierra Club to establish the basic requisites for equitable relief in environmental litigation—imminent danger of serious, permanent and irreparable damage to a national, natural resource treasure. Had the Sierra Club:

1. amended its complaint to challenge the proposed recreational development, supporting highway and overhead transmission lines on the grounds that such a development does not represent the highest and best use of a national, natural resource treasure; and

2. alleged that determination of the highest and best use of a national, natural resource treasure must utilize the methods of environmental systems science; and

3. brought the action on behalf of all the people of the United States, not only of this generation but of those generations yet unborn, who are entitled to the full, benefit, use and enjoyment of the national, natural resource treasure without degradation by reason of the failure of the federal agencies to determine the impact of their proposed public improvements upon such a national, natural resource treasure in accordance with the methods of environmental systems science;

4. then offered to prove by a fair preponderance of the substantial credible, scientific evidence that the proposed government action did, in fact, represent an imminent danger of serious, permanent and irreparable damage; standing would have been granted.

The evidence elicited in a trial on the merits may have induced Congress to re-examine the entire project in a manner similar to the President's reconsideration of the Cross-Florida Barge Canal in 1970.[21]

---

21. Environmental Def. Fund v. Corps of Engineers, 324 F. Supp. 878 (D.D.C. 1971). A few days later on January 19, 1971, President Nixon stated in a press release: "I am today ordering a halt to further construction of the Cross Florida Barge Canal to prevent potentially serious environmental damages. . . . A natural resource treasure is involved in the case of the Barge

B. Land Use Regulation

The growth of the American economy and steady urbanization of its population has been accompanied by increasing use of sovereign powers to protect the general welfare. New techniques of regulation were developed to manage the growth of towns occasioned in large part by industrialization. Building codes and zoning regulations were two such tools developed. Control of these techniques was delegated to local government, in the belief that each locality could best minister to its needs in accord with locally established priorities.

Euclidean or conventional rectilinear district zoning is essentially a system for dividing a community into zones to separate allegedly incompatible land uses. A locality divided into commercial, residential and recreational zones was first proposed by the New York City Fifth Avenue Association which wanted to separate poor persons from the rich carriage trade of New York society.[22] Today, the purpose of Euclidean zoning is to restrict density housing and to segregate use districts by establishing arbitrary fixed boundaries.

The problems of Euclidean zoning arise from the system's rigidity. Despite use restrictions the rectilinear districts are subject to taking claims brought by landowners of previously existing nonconforming uses as well as by those seeking special exceptions and variances. The arbitrary setting of boundaries and zoning reclassifications have increased the amount of land use litigation to protect property values.

Further, the district zoning program adopted in (Euclid and) the Standard Zoning Enabling Act was based upon a belief that rigid segregation of human activities was the best method to protect the public health, safety and welfare. Perpetuation of the belief in the effectiveness of Euclidean zoning has led to overcrowded suburban schools, overloaded sewage treatment plants, overburdened transportation systems and overtaxed homeowners.

Canal—the Ocklawaha River—a uniquely beautiful, semitropical stream, one of a very few of its kind in the United States, which would be destroyed by construction of the Canal. . . .

"The step I have taken today will prevent a past mistake from causing permanent damage. But more important, we must assure that in the future we take not only full but also timely account of the envrionmental impact of such projects—so that instead of merely halting the damage, we prevent it." Address by President Nixon, Jan. 19, 1971, in PUBLIC PAPERS OF THE PRESIDENT 43 (1971).

22. *See* S. TOLL, ZONED AMERICAN (1969).

The present district zoning ordinances and associated subdivision regulations which follow the exclusionary axioms underlying the Standard State Zoning Enabling Act of 1926 may be held unconstitutional by the courts. Several states now have statutes allowing local zoning classifications to be ignored in favor of regional or statewide concerns.[23] Many suburban communities must now face the very real possibility that within the next few years the courts may leave them without any of their conventional zoning tools to control new development.

Of course, this crisis in land use regulation represents both a danger and an opportunity. The danger is that old exclusionary techniques may be invalidated and not replaced. But opportunity is presented to develop new methods of control that account for regional needs and aspirations. Impact zoning represents one way to meet the immediate danger of unregulated development inconsistent with the public interest while affording municipalities the opportunity to use environmental systems science to develop enlightened regulatory programs for managing local development. The following account of two cities illustrates the dangers and opportunities presented by the necessity for accommodating regional interests.

C. The Petaluma Plan

On April 25, 1974, a United States District Court declared unconstitutional the attempt by the City of Petaluma, to implement a "no-growth" policy by means of a municipal ordinance which would limit new construction to no more than 500 residential dwelling units each year. The basic constitutional rule is that no city can regulate growth numerically so as to preclude residents of any other area from travelling into the region and establishing residence therein.[24] Unfortunately the District Court chose to base its ruling on the one ground—"the right to travel"—that would allow the Ninth Circuit Court of Appeals to reverse one year later. In the early 1960s Petaluma, within commuting distance of San Francisco, became the suburbia for the rapidly urbanizing Marin County.

Although within commuting distance of San Francisco and part of the San Francisco metropolitan region, it was not until the early

---

23. See F. BOSSELMAN & D. CALLIES, *The Quiet Revolution in* LAND USE CONTROL (1971).

24. Construction Indus. Ass'n v. City of Petaluma, 375 F. Supp. 574, 582 (N.D. Cal. 1974).

1960s when a combination of freeways, high taxes, and a water
shortage in rapidly urbanizing Marin County to the south swept
Petaluma from the rustic serenity of dairy and poultry farming into
suburbia. Initially Petaluma accepted the prevailing municipal assumption that growth is good. Tract homes inundated the eastern
portion of the city and uncontrolled growth became the development pattern for Petaluma.

In 1971, a "citizens committee" assisted by professional planners
drafted a suggested "Policy on Growth" which reflected the growing community sentiment towards limiting the future population of
Petaluma. The city council thereafter adopted a similar statement
whose preamble asserted:

> In order to protect its small town character and surrounding open spaces,
> it shall be the policy of the City to control its future rate and distribution
> of growth. . . .

The court believed that the city council sought to limit the demographic and market growth rate in housing to discourage immigra-
tion into the city. Permits to build the limited number of residential
housing units were allocated according to an intricate rating system.
The method of granting permits caused the Construction Industry
Association of Sonoma County, a nonprofit California trade group,
to challenge the "Petaluma Plan" in federal court on constitutional
grounds.

The Construction Industry Association did not attack the concept of a rating system, but contended that Petaluma's system resembled a "*Catch-22* operation." The Association argued that applicants for the limited number of building permits never knew the
criteria for granting the applications, how the criteria were to be
applied, or who was to grant the application.

The city contended that its "Plan" was to last only through 1977.
However, official attempts were made to perpetuate the program
through 1990 by limiting the city's contract with the County Water
Agency to amounts sufficient only to support the restricted population; sufficient water was, in fact, available to accommodate a
larger population.

An important aspect of the Petaluma case is the court's assumption of federal jurisdiction over a traditionally state and local question. The court found that housing in Petaluma and the San Francisco metropolitan region was "produced substantially through
goods, services and communication devices in interstate com-

merce." Although the Court of Appeals,[25] denied that a federal court is a "super Zoning Board," the judges reaffirmed the duty of the courts to determine whether the plan was arbitrary or unreasonable. "The reasonableness, not the wisdom, of the Petaluma Plan is at issue in this suit."[26]

The trial court found that Petaluma's claim of inadequate sewage and water treatment facilities was merely an a posteriori attempt to justify the "Petaluma Plan." the Court of Appeals disagreed. Nevertheless, both courts had to consider this fundamental question:

> . . . could the city establish by a fair preponderance of the substantial, credible, scientific evidence that any of its public facilities or societal services were in any way threatened by development at "market" or "demographic" growth rates?

Developers, municipal officials and concerned citizens who desire to limit the uncontrolled growth of a community or region should review the complex socioeconomic factors suggested by District Court Judge Burke:

> The . . . metropolitan region is generally self-contained and has a unitary housing market. Persons excluded from one suburb do not leave the region, but seek housing elsewhere in the area. . . .
>
> Limiting housing in the face of static or rising demand increases the cost of private housing and the rent structure of tenant housing. This increase is equally applicable in both the area practicing exclusion and elsewhere in the region where the rejected demand is felt.
>
> . . . Limits on housing supply in the suburbs tend to keep people who would otherwise move into those suburbs in the center cities.
>
> In any given period, a certain percentage of existing housing is in need of replacement, either because it is obsolete or substandard or because it is destroyed or damaged beyond repair.
>
> If the total housing demand in such a region be frustrated by a policy that limits the supply of housing to less than demand certain results will inevitably follow. Substandard and obsolete housing, which should be replaced will remain in the market to deal with the high demand and will partially fill it with low quality structures. The overall nature of the region's housing stock will decline. Tenant housing is as subject to this phenomenon as privately owned and occupied housing. Landlords will discover that they may leave substandard housing in the rental market and may ignore its need for maintenance and rehabilitation without suffering high vacancy rates, demand for such housing being unnaturally high.
>
> Growth throughout a metropolitan region takes place unevenly in certain "growth centers," areas having unused capacity which can be tapped or the ability to augment capacity to serve new residents. . . .

---

25. Construction Indus. Ass'n v. City of Petaluma, *supra* note 7.
26. *Id*. at 906.

If such growth centers curtail residential growth to less than demographic and market rates . . . serious and damaging dislocation will occur in the housing market, the commerce it represents, and in the travel and settlement of people in need and in search of housing. . . .

The public facilities, land, existing social advantages and access to the center cities and to other job centers that growth centers offer to a metropolitan region in need of housing cannot be adequately placed elsewhere to support local and regional housing needs. Although "new towns" can be constructed where none already exist, the initial cost would be prohibitive to build infra-structure, i.e., the basic public facilities necessary to serve the town. Experience in "new town" development has proved that the "front end facilities" cost in new towns makes them impractical at least as a source of housing for low and moderate income groups.

It is impossible to force housing out of growth centers and into rural areas without providing for public facilities. Some public facilities, i.e., fire protection, streets and schools, must be provided by the responsible government. Others, such as septic systems, water wells and private roads, tend to occupy large amounts of open space to provide for single family homes. In later years, . . . the cities are usually forced to add the old rural developments to city services . . . at substantially increased cost over the amount that would have been incurred, if the development had been originally incorporated into city services.

Moreover, it is not feasible to force housing out of growth centers and into the center cities. The destruction and reconstruction of center city housing raises many problems that have not been solved except in massive government-sponsored urban renewal projects—sometimes these have not been successful. . . .

As income rises, income earners tend to move into better housing. The housing they leave behind "filters down" to persons of lower income. . . .[27]

Although the Court of Appeals said that

The controversy stirred by the present litigation, and the complex economic, political, and social factors involved in this case are compelling evidence that resolution of the important housing and environmental issues raised here is exclusively the domain of the legislature,[28]

the district court reached certain conclusions of law which should serve as guidelines for developers interested in building and, paradoxical as it may seem, local officials interested in limiting construction of residential housing throughout the remainder of this decade. In particular, the court summarily resolved the issue of standing in favor of the regional Construction Industry Association and found no need for evidence establishing that any individual had actually been excluded by the plan. The lower court did not deny that the city had a right to respond to growth problems. However, local

27. Construction Indus. Ass'n v. City of Petaluma, *supra* note 24, at 579–80.
28. Construction Indus. Ass'n v. City of Petaluma, *supra* note 7, at 909 n.17.

government must choose the method of least interference with constitutionally protected activities to achieve its goals. Traditional powers to zone were upheld as constitutional methods to regulate development.[29] This is not to say that a municipality may not limit residential population growth upon scientific evidence which indicates, for example, that the total amount of available drinking water is only sufficient to support a certain number of people. Such natural limitations upon real property development can be utilized to support land use regulation outside of conventional zoning ordinances and subdivision regulations.

A key issue raised was the city's claim that under zoning powers, a municipality has the inherent right to "control its own rate of growth" to meet its citizens' desire to protect their "small town character." This furnished sufficiently compelling reasons to justify an ordinance which was patently exclusionary.

The district court relied on a decision of the Pennsylvania Supreme Court, which thwarted the attempt of a municipality to restrict residential housing to four-acre lots, to find the Petaluma Plan exclusionary.

> Zoning is a tool in the hands of governmental bodies which enables them to more effectively meet the demands of evolving and growing communities. It must not and cannot be used by those officials as an instrument by which they may shirk their responsibilities. Zoning is a means by which a governmental body can plan for the future—it may not be used as a means to deny the future . . . zoning provisions may not be used to avoid the increased responsibilities and economic burdens which time and natural growth invariably bring. . . .
>
> A zoning ordinance whose primary purpose is to prevent the entrance of newcomers in order to avoid future burdens, economic or otherwise, upon the administration of public services and facilities cannot be held valid. . . . It is clear . . . that the general welfare is not fostered or promoted by a zoning ordinance designed to be exclusive or exclusionary. . . .
>
> The implication of our decision . . . is that communities must deal with the problems of population growth. They may not refuse to confront the future by adopting zoning regulations that effectively restrict population to near present levels. It is not for any given township to say who may or may not live within its confines while disregarding the interests of the entire area.[30]

The principal defect of the Petaluma ordinance was the municipality's failure to confront the regional housing problem. Restricting the number of dwelling units in one city merely increases the housing problems of a neighboring community.

---

29. Construction Indus. Ass'n v. City of Petaluma, *supra* note 24, at 581–82.
30. *Id.* at 586.

> This case is a study in antiplanning, the refusal of a city to come to grips with the fact that it has joined a metropolitan complex and is no longer the sleepy small town that it once was. In a world in which nothing is as unchanging as change, Petaluma wants to stay the same. The means to that end is to draw up the bridge over the moat and turn people away. This is not the use of police power, but the abdication of that power.
>
> In a narrower sense, this case [holds] . . . that local police power may [not] be used to shift the burden of providing housing to other cities in a metropolitan region which have their own police power and their own problems . . . .
>
> The prospective resident turned away at Petaluma does not disappear into the hinterland, but presents himself in some other suburb of the same metroplex, perhaps in some town with as many problems or more than Petaluma . . . . By this means, Petaluma legislates its problems into problems for [nearby cities].[31]

Unfortunately, the district court ignored this misuse of delegated authority and instead ruled the Petaluma Plan an unconstitutional denial of the right to travel.

> In a large sense this case sets up the constitutional protections against a single small city passing laws to keep people away, to maintain "small town character" at the expense of depriving people of mobility, their right to travel, and of decent housing or perhaps any housing at all. . . .[32]

A better approach was used by the Supreme Court in *Boraas*[33] where the right to travel argument was limited to the peculiar circumstances of civil rights and welfare cases in which it was developed.

The Ninth Circuit Court of Appeals apparently construed *Boraas* to require automatic judicial approval of any local ordinance where the constitutional challenge asserts interference with the freedom to travel. Thus the opinion reversing the district court determination that the Petaluma "Plan" was exclusionary did not review the social or legislative adequacy of the Plan. Instead, the appellate court decision left municipalities the opportunity to redraft their ordinances in accordance with the comments of the New York Court of Appeals in Ramapo[34] or to adopt sophisticated techniques of land use regulation such as impact zoning.

D. Timed-Sequential Growth: Ramapo[35]

In 1968, the town of Ramapo, New York, amended its zoning ordinance to prohibit residential subdivision development except

---

31. *Id.* at 587.
32. *Id.*
33. Village of Belle Terre v. Boraas, 416 U.S. 1 (1974).
34. Golden v. Planning Board, *supra* note 8.
35. *Id.*

where a developer had obtained a special permit or variance. Issuance of a building permit was contingent upon the availability of five essential societal services:

- public sanitary sewers or approved substitutes,
- drainage facilities,
- improved public parks or recreational facilities including public schools,
- state, county or town roads,
- and firehouses.

The undisputed intent of these regulations was to provide for orderly growth through sequential development. The timing of development would be governed by the progressive availability of new public facilities and societal services or by the increase in capacity of those already existing.

The amendments were attacked as destroying the marketability of property, thereby invading private property rights. Opponents of the Ramapo plan also claimed that the objective to control growth was beyond the scope of the zoning enabling legislation.

The court acknowledged that the New York version of the Standard State Zoning Enabling Act of 1926 provided no specific authorization for "sequential development" or "timing" controls. Nevertheless, the court upheld the validity of the legislation controlling the sequence and timing of development as a means to address the problem of providing municipal facilities and services for an increasing population.

> . . . far from being exclusionary, the present amendments merely seek, by implementation of sequential development and timed growth to provide a balanced cohesive community dedicated to the efficient utilization of land. The restrictions conform to the community's considered land use policies as expressed in its comprehensive plan.

> Perhaps even more importantly, timed growth, unlike the minimum lot requirements recently struck down . . . as exclusionary, does not impose permanent restrictions upon land use. . . . Its obvious purpose is to prevent premature subdivision absent essential municipal facilities and to insure continuous development commensurate with the Town's obligation to provide such facilities . . . not to freeze population at present levels but to maximize growth by the efficient use of land, and in so doing testify to this community's continuing role in population assimilation. In sum, Ramapo asks not that it be left alone, but only that it be allowed to prevent the kind of deterioration that has transformed well-ordered and thriving residential communities into blighted ghettos with attendant hazards to health, security and social stability—a danger not without substantial basis in fact.

> We only require that communities confront the challenge of population growth with open doors. Where in grappling with that problem, the community undertakes, imposing temporary restrictions upon development, to

provide required municipal services in a rational manner, courts are rightfully reluctant to strike down such schemes. . . .

The Town . . . has utilized its comprehensive plan to implement its timing controls and has coupled with these restrictions provisions for low and moderate income housing on a large scale. Considered as a whole, it represents both in its inception and implementation a reasonable attempt to provide for the sequential, orderly development of land in conjunction with the needs of the community, as well as individual parcels of land, while simultaneously obviating the blighted aftermath which the initial failure to provide needed facilities so often brings. . .[36]

At the time of the litigation, all parties agreed that existing municipal facilities and services in Ramapo were inadequate to meet increasing demand. The court inquired whether the challenged amendments were within the parameters of the devices authorized and purposes sanctioned under the enabling legislation. The ability of the state statutory scheme to encourage effective land use policy and planning methods was more important to the court than the specific means suggested to municipalities in the general enabling legislation. The court concluded that the Ramapo amendments reflected legitimate public needs and were not veiled efforts at exclusion.

Under the Ramapo plan a capital budget was enacted to provide the necessary public facilities and services required to support the population expected by the end of the period of development restrictions. Of course, the court recognized that, similar to other municipalities, Ramapo cannot be certain that these commitments would be met over the years by subsequent municipal legislatures and paid for by succeeding generations of taxpayers.

The advantage of Ramapo is the plan's adoption of a "point system" where the suitability of an area for residential development at any particular time is identified. A reading of *Ramapo*,[37] *Petaluma*[38] and *Mt. Laurel*[39] indicates that the courts will uphold plans that in-

---

36. *Id.* at 369, 285 N.E.2d at 302–03, 334 N.Y.S.2d at 152–53.
37. Golden v. Planning Board, *supra* note 8.
38. Construction Indus. Ass'n v. City of Petaluma, *supra* note 7.
39. Southern Burlington County NAACP v. Township of Mount Laurel, 119 N.J. Super. 164, 290 A.2d 465 (Law Div. 1972), in which the court noted that "while it is proper to zone in certain instances against factories, it is improper to build a wall against poor-income people." (119 N.J. Super at 176, 290 A.2d at 472). "The patterns and practices clearly indicate that defendant municipality through its zoning ordinances has exhibited economic discrimination. . ." (119 N.J. Super. at 178, 290 A.2d at 473), and for this reason the zoning ordinance was declared invalid. The court then ordered the municipality to study housing needs and come up with a plan to eliminate this discrimination. The recent decision of the New Jersey Supreme Court, South-

clude criteria for metropolitan growth. The plan must inform a developer when and how much development of a particular parcel is permissible. Further, the plan should allow private financing of public services to mitigate delay, or provide tax relief through reduction of property value assessments in accordance with reduction in the market value of the property arising from the delay in development. Although Ramapo and Petaluma both sought to limit development to the capacity of municipal facilities and services, Petaluma did not permit the developer to provide facilities in order to advance the time when development would be allowed. An important element of the Ramapo ordinance, which apparently satisfied the court on the due process issue, was the provision that a prospective developer may advance the date of subdivision approval by agreeing to provide those improvements which will bring the proposed tract within the number of development points required by the [ordinance].[40]

A recent law review article argued that the court erred in upholding the Ramapo ordinance.[41] It contended that Ramapo cannot pass a law to bind the whole world. However, real estate developers and municipal officials should interpret *Ramapo* to mean that municipalities can regulate their population growth to a rate consistent with available resources and the carrying capacity of natural, social and economic systems. The public interest in air, water and other vital natural resources can be protected by limiting urban development. Reasonable limitations on land use can be sustained under the general police powers of local government:

> . . . The power to restrict and regulate conferred [by zoning enabling act] includes within its grant, by way of necessary implication the authority to direct the growth of population for the purposes indicated, within the confines of the Township. It is the matrix of land use restrictions, common to each of the enumerated powers and sanctioned goals, a necessary concomitant to the municipality's recognized authority to determine the lines along which a local development shall proceed, though it may divert it from its natural course.[42]

---

ern Burlington County NAACP v. Township of Mount Laurel, 67 N.J. 151, 336 A.2d 713 (1975), affirming the Superior Court has been proclaimed by civil rights groups throughout the United States as the death knell of the suburban exclusion of low income housing and multiple dwellings.

40. *Supra* note 8, 30 N.Y.2d at 373, 285 N.E.2d at 304, 334 N.Y.S.2d at 155.

41. Bosselman, *Can the Town of Ramapo Pass a Law to Bind the Rights of the Whole World?*, 1 FLA. ST. U.L. REV. 234 (1973).

42. *Supra* note 8, 30 N.Y.2d at 371, 285 N.E.2d at 297, 334 N.Y.S.2d at 146.

The significance of Ramapo for community planners is that land use tools beyond the rigid Euclidean zoning laws can be adopted to regulate community growth. Further, a city council's recognition that any local development program must include plans for regional growth is a prophetic insight towards the new trend in land use regulation. In the future the only proper exercise of sovereign powers by municipal governments will be that done in accord with regional needs. Planning for regional growth should incorporate conceptual models[43] and systems analysis[44] as well as create a common language[45] for land use regulation. Impact zoning, through regional

43. The ability to explain and simulate events clearly varies with their complexity. An architectural model, although a replica in miniature of a building, generally reflects only the formal and visual elements of the building while ignoring its structure. Nonetheless, it is a model of the building.

The same type of simulation is employed to represent new towns and urban redevelopment projects, and clearly these are abstracts. They remain unpopulated, but while the dynamics of natural and social processes may not occur, the "model" often permits some prediction of their dynamics.

Major regional subdivisions of the United States can be modeled in ways which describe the environmental systems and permit predictions to be made about the consequences of proposed changes within the region.

44. Systems analysis is a method for studying, or in the first instance, determining relationships among elements of interdependent systems which can be considered as sets because they behave as a unit, are involved in a single process, or contribute to a single effect.

The principal reason for using systems analysis in ecology, economics, and more recently the social sciences, is the complexity of environmental systems originating from a variety of causes: number of variables; number of different types of variables; different levels of organization of systems (populations, communities, trophic levels, cycles) and the non-homogeneous and non-uniform distribution of system elements throughout time and space.

Systems analysis has its roots in military and industrial operations research, applied mathematics, probability, statistics, computer science, engineering, econometrics and biometrics.

See V. Yannacone, Jr., How Shall We Generate Electricity? Criteria For Public Choice, in THE ENERGY CRISIS: DANGER AND OPPORTUNITY (V. Yannacone, Jr. ed. 1974); Watt, The Nature of Systems Analysis, in SYSTEMS ANALYSIS IN ECOLOGY (K. Watt ed. 1966); I. McHARG, DESIGN WITH NATURE (1970).)

45. There are certain terms commonly used in systems analysis with which planners, attorneys and concerned citizens should be familiar:

The controllable and partially controllable constrained inputs to a system are called *decision variables.*

When each decision variable has been assigned a particular value, the resulting set of decisions is called a *policy.*

A policy which does not violate any of the constraints imposed by the system is called a *feasible policy.*

The set of all possible feasible policies is termed a *policy space* and may vary with time in space of many dimensions. (For example, air, water, and animal communities would each be considered "dimensions" in this sense of the word).

The condition of the system at any time and place is represented by variables known as *state variables.*

Supplementing the state variables are the *system parameters* which may

planning is a constitutional tool to benefit the general welfare of a growing population.

E. Impact Zoning[46]

Impact zoning provides municipalities with an affirmative program for managing local growth while still accepting a fair share of regional growth. The basic elements of any community impact zoning program include:

1. Determination of the capacity of the ecological, societal, and economic systems of the community and its region to accommodate existing and future growth;
2. Identification and analysis of natural, societal and economic constraints upon development;

---

be constant or variable and are determined by considerations outside the system under immediate consideration.

State vectors are quantities which in addition to magnitude are characterized by direction: in time (past or future), in space (any direction in any dimension), or both, and must include all aspects of the system which are or can be affected by changes in the decision variables.

The concept of a "best decisions" decision set or policy implies the existence of criteria by means of which the effects of any feasible policy on the output of the system can be evaluated. Such criteria are called *overall objectives*, and in most instances consist of many component objectives, some of which are quantitative, while others are measurable at best in an ordinal or qualitative sense.

If two objectives can be measured or described in the same units or terms and to the same general relative degree of accuracy, they are said to be *commensurate*. *Non commensurate* objectives are those which cannot be expressed in common units or those in which the order of magnitude of the errors inherent of the evaluation of one variable may mask the significance of the magnitude of the other variables.

The *objective function* is a statement by means of which the consequences or output of the system can be determined, given the policy, the initial values of the state variables, and the system parameters. Athough conventional usage, particularly in economics, has limited the term objective function to quantitative objectives that are commensurate, many environmental systems include non-quantitative and non-commensurate objectives, which may account for the reluctance of many economists to consider environmental factors in cost-benefit and benefit-risk analyses.

46. Impact zoning is the designation of the sophisticated land use regulatory program developed over the years by the planning of Rahenkamp, Sachs, Wells & Associates. Descriptions of applications can be found in the following articles: "Logical Land Use Comes to the Fore," Savings Loan News, Sept., 1971; Rahenkamp, Sachs & Wells, *A Strategy for Watershed Development . . . That Beats the Bulldozer by Using Land-Sale Profits to Preserve Green Space*, LANDSCAPE ARCHITECTURE, April, 1971; *Flying Hills: An Open Space Community*, HOUSE & HOME, 1974; Wells, *The Power of Water in Planning*, LANDSCAPE ARCHITECTURE, Jan., 1974; *PUD Is Good for Everybody*, HOUSE & HOME, Sept., 1969; *The Town That Said NO to No-Growth*, HOUSE & HOME, 1974; *Here's A New System for Figuring Project Feasibility*, HOUSE & HOME, 1973; *Rezoning for the PUD*, HOUSE & HOME, Feb., 1971; *Impact Zoning*, HOUSE & HOME, Aug., 1972.

3. Formulation and enumeration of community goals for future growth and development;
4. Legal analysis of the extent of local land use regulatory authority.

A basic assumption of impact zoning is that regional and municipal systems have a maximum growth capacity. Community goals determine the substance of impact zoning regulations while state enabling legislation and legal limitations on municipal authority dictate its form and procedure.

Under impact zoning a prior assessment of the impact of a proposed project upon a community is made. The project assessment analyzes:

1. The community's growth capacity;
2. The amount of land available for development in the region;
3. The societal infrastructure of the community and region including public facilities and services;
4. The economy of the community and surrounding region, with emphasis on the cost to the community of increased services required for further housing developments and the additional tax revenues and other economic benefits which might be derived from such development;
5. Natural constraints, determinants and incentives for development.

A major advantage of impact zoning is the program's inherent flexibility. Unlike zoning ordinances and subdivision regulations promulgated under the Standard State Zoning Enabling Act, impact zoning provides a framework for orderly growth of a community aware of its regional obligations by suggesting a variety of acceptable land uses that accommodate the unique characteristic of each parcel of land.

Impact zoning is based on the concept that the full impact of any specific proposal for development on the natural, social and economic environment of a community can, and must, be evaluated. The findings of impact assessments can furnish the "fair preponderance of substantial, credible, scientific evidence" necessary to support planning, timing and management of development by local government in the courts. Through assessment, an enlightened private sector can direct community growth with minimal adverse consequences. The interrelated social, economic and scientific investigations, which are necessary elements of any impact zoning program provide the conceptual model for comprehensive municipal land use regulation and resource management.

Based on the capacity of existing natural, societal and economic systems, the extent of available resources, and constraints upon development inherent in the assayed limits to local growth, certain inappropriate land uses and development activities can be categorically prohibited in specific, well-defined areas.

In those areas otherwise suitable for development, the absence of adequate community services and societal infrastructure can delay development, or transfer the obligation for providing necessary community services and establishing the required societal infrastructure to the developer.

Analyzing the capacity of natural, social and economic systems should establish the natural, social and economic constraints upon development in a community, and necessarily reveal the intrinsic suitability of particular areas for specific uses, which if consistent with community goals, represent opportunities for development.

Impact zoning is not just another "Standard State Enabling Act" or a model zoning ordinance, but a concept to be implemented by local legislation adapted to the capacity and aspirations of each individual community.

Impact zoning represents a dynamic instrument for land use regulation and resource management in which the developer is given the opportunity for flexibility and innovation in design, while the community is furnished with sufficient information to rationally evaluate the impact of any proposed development. Impact assessment is a rational basis for regulating development to protect the public health, safety and welfare, and further the public interest.

A development proposal which might result in significant adverse effects may still be permitted; subject, however, to continuing, active municipal regulation and impact assessment including detailed consideration of alternatives.

1. *Evolution of an Impact Zoning Plan*

In any impact zoning program, the key parameters—capacity of the land and landscape, extent of natural resources, societal infrastructure, and economics should be quantified, thereby providing a common language by means of which developers, the community and the courts can communicate. After all, comprehensive planning is essentially a communications process.[47]

Development of an impact zoning program for any region begins with description and characterization of the operant natural processes—geologic, hydrologic, atmospheric, biologic—and the

---

47. Cerchione, *The Planning Bible: Vulgate or Vernacular?* and Cerchione & Black, *Planning: A Communications Process*, both in PLANNING, ENVIRONMENTAL SCIENCE, AVIATION (V. Yannacone, Jr. ed. 1974).

elements of the natural systems—soils, vegetation, wildlife. These factors attest an individual site's suitability for human activities. Key elements should be identified; aquifers (underground reservoirs) and their recharge areas; slopes so steep that any disturbance will uproot stabilizing vegetation, and unleash destructive erosion; water tables vulnerable to contamination; flood plains in which development could be periodically inundated, but which could be used wisely for agricultural purposes; soils of poor foundation quality or perhaps more suited for feeding the nation; and areas devastated by periodic wildfires, fractured by faults, or threatened by subsidence due to the improvident mining practices of another era.

After characterizing the natural environment of the area, the key parameters of impact zoning capacity of the land, extent of natural resources, societal infrastructure and economics of the community should be measured. A precise tabulation of resources provide a common language for communication between the courts, the community and developers. Communication is necessary for comprehensive planning.

A matrix relating each land use intrinsically suitable for the community or proposed by developers, to the natural, societal and economic resources of the community and the capacity of its land, landscape and environmental systems should be prepared. The assessment then can serve as a basis for an impact zoning ordinance, land use regulations, and community development timing controls.

2. *Capacity and Allocation*

The capacity of communities to absorb growth initially should be assessed. Planners should consider critical areas to be excluded from large scale development and resources subject to irreparable damage from particular kinds of development. Allocation of land depends upon using all developed or undeveloped land, which can be modified or altered without significant disruption of the community or adverse impact upon natural, societal and economic systems. Pro rata allocation must also accommodate the following factors: the capacity of each municipality to absorb growth in terms of its ability to provide new municipal services and societal infrastructures; accessibility of each municipality in terms of existing transportation systems; employment opportunities throughout the region; existing population density in each municipality; and the quantity and quality of housing stock in each municipality of the region.

3. Regional Housing Allocation

One of the basic elements of growth management in any impact zoning program is the *Housing Market Evaluation*[48] by means of which a community may determine its "fair share" of the regional housing need. [Housing Market Evaluation within the context of an impact zoning program is the only system suitable for local municipalities to allocate housing within a region.] Recent court decisions require individual communities to accept their "fair share" of regional housing demand. Otherwise, local zoning ordinances and subdivision regulations are invalidated as "exclusionary."[49] Further federal and state aid is denied until a community begins to accommodate a "fair share" of the regional housing needs.

Before a municipality can formulate plans, "fair share" must be defined. A community must examine:

- What is the region?
- What is the regional housing need?
- How should subregional allocations be made?
- What is a fair share for any particular municipality?

In large metropolitan areas, [the Standard Metropolitan Statistical Area (SMSA) defines a region to include a single economic and societal area.] In other areas, major government units such as counties or regional associations may define the logical area within which to make the allocation. Commuting patterns and commercial trading area studies can also provide substantial evidence of regional boundaries.

Determining "fair share" involves a comparison of the relative capacities of the ecological, social, and economic systems of the municipality and the surrounding region. The number of housing units to be approved or accepted each year in each community cannot be fixed by an arbitrary maximum scheme, as attempted by Petaluma, or by conventional district density zoning with acreage

---

48. Earlier work describing the Housing Market Evaluation Model developed by Rahenkamp, Sachs, Wells & Associates, includes Pennsylvania Housing Need and Allocation Model, a report prepared for the Pennsylvania Department of Community Affairs, by Walter S. Sachs, Jr., Project Coordinator, with Kathleen McLeister and Phillip J. Goldberg, all of Rahenkemp, Sachs, Wells & Associates. Other work includes a Spring, 1972, research project in the Department of City Planning of the University of Pennsylvania, under the direction of Assistant Professor Walter S. Sachs, Jr., and visiting lecturers Paul Davidoff and Neil Gold. *See also* Rahenkamp, *The Zoning Scene*, HOUSE & HOME, May, 1972.

49. *Supra* note 32.

minimums such as in Mt. Laurel. Rather, housing demand changes within the community and the region. The Housing Market Evaluation Model offers local government an accurate basis for planning to rationally assimilate growth. A regional housing allocation program offers a way of complying with the mandates of the federal courts in *Petaluma* and *Belle Terre* and the state courts in *Ramapo* and *Mt. Laurel.*

The Regional Housing Allocation Program proceeds through a number of stages:

1. Determination of regional housing needs;
2. Determination of regional housing supply and quality;
3. Determination of regional housing gap (the difference between need and supply adjusted for variations in social and economic conditions both within the region and outside the region);
4. Allocation of the regional housing gap among individual municipalities in terms of the land available for development and suitable for residential development;
5. Adjustment of the allocation to each municipality by considering
    (a) capacity of the societal infrastructure to accommodate growth by providing public facilities and community services;
    (b) accessibility in terms of existing transportation systems;
    (c) existing population density;
    (d) existing housing stocks;
    (e) natural and physical limits.

Regional housing need is determined by establishing the extent and character of the existing housing supply and then projecting future housing demand. Estimating regional housing need involves projecting regional growth in terms of new households, evaluating the existing need for replacement housing and surveying vacancy patterns throughout the region. Current regional housing need assessments should regularly be adjusted to incorporate new data.

In a regional housing allocation program, the municipalities in a region are compared in relation to their respective natural, social, and economic capacities to accommodate growth. Fair share calculations are based on the actual capacity of a community to accommodate development rather than mere pro rata extrapolations of immediate local demand.

Merely allotting a pro rata share of the regional housing need among the communities in proportion to the amount of land suitable for development is inconsistent with the public interest expressed in § 101 (a)[50] and § 101 (b)[51] of the National Environmental Policy Act:

---

50. 42 U.S.C. § 4331(a) (1974).
51. 42 U.S.C. § 4331(b) (1974).

SEC. 101(a) The Congress, recognizing the profound impact of man's activity on the interrelations of all components of the natural environment, particularly the profound influences of population growth, high-density urbanization, industrial expansion, resource exploitation, and new and expanding technological advances and recognizing further the critical importance of restoring and maintaining environmental quality to the overall welfare and development of man, declares that it is the continuing policy of the Federal Government, in cooperation with State and local governments, and other concerned public and private organizations, to use all practicable means and measures, including financial and technical assistance, in a manner calculated to foster and promote the general welfare, to create and maintain conditions under which man and nature can exist in productive harmony, and fulfill the social, economic, and other requirements of present and future generations of Americans.

(b) In order to carry out the policy set forth in this Act, it is the continuing responsibility of the Federal Government to use all practicable means, consistent with other essential considerations of national policy, to improve and coordinate Federal plans, functions, programs, and resources to the end that the Nation may—

(1) fulfill the responsibilities of each generation as trustee of the environment for succeeding generations;

(2) assure for all Americans safe, healthful, productive, and esthetically and culturally pleasing surroundings;

(3) attain the widest range of beneficial uses of the environment without degradation, risk to health or safety, or other undesirable and unintended consequences;

(4) preserve important historic, cultural and natural aspects of our national heritage, and maintain wherever possible, an environment which supports diversity and variety of individual choice;

(5) achieve a balance between population and resource use which will permit high standards of living and a wide sharing of life's amenities; and

(6) enhance the quality of renewable resources and approach the maximum attainable recycling of depletable resources.

Regional housing allocation as part of an impact zoning program permits a municipality to liberate land available for development from the twin evils of inflexible district zoning and special exceptions. Through impact zoning techniques municipal police power regulations can protect the public health, safety and welfare, and promote orderly growth consistent with the natural, societal, economic and resource limitations of the community.

The use of housing market evaluations and fair share regional allocation studies as a basis for comprehensive planning of residential development permits a municipality to refuse more than a fair share of regional growth; the community plan cannot then be banned by the courts as "exclusionary." Municipalities that use housing market evaluations to determine their fair share of housing responsibilities also should not be subject to the constant litigation confronting communities who continue to regulate land development by outmoded conventional zoning laws. Under the regional housing allocation program a community is protected from long term deterioration as a result of overwhelming residential development; instead, an adequate choice of suitable housing in desirable residential environment is offered to satisfy housing needs throughout a region.

Although the Regional Housing Allocation Program has been developed for use by individual municipalities in determining their own "fair share" of the regional housing gap, other political units may also benefit from this tool. Regular evaluation of the regional housing allocation can become a valuable procedure for geopolitical units such as school districts, recreation districts, and other special districts to estimate capital budget needs and to plan for expansion of community services.

Conclusion

The public is concerned with protecting the regional natural and sociological environment. This concern is reflected by the evolution in the exercise of sovereign powers. Communities, no longer able to hide behind myopic Euclidean zoning, must confront the ecological and social demands of their region. Many localities now recognize that the anachronistic tools of Euclidean zoning must be replaced by new techniques that can remedy the problems of increasing population and preserve irreplacable natural resources. Impact zoning is such a technique and one that can survive constitutional attack.

Through impact zoning, planners can evaluate the effects of proposed development programs and can estimate the maximum capacity of an area to absorb future growth. Already impact zoning has been used successfully in regional housing allocation programs where each locality assumes its fair share of regional growth. Extension of impact zoning techniques into other areas of land use concerns would provide a rational method to coordinate human and ecological demands. By using impact zoning government can continue to exercise its sovereign powers for the benefit of the collective good.

No-Growth and Related Land-Use Legal Problems: An Overview*

Ronald A. Zumbrun
President and Legal Director, Pacific
Legal Foundation; formerly Senior
Trial Attorney, California Department
of Public Works; B.A. Pomona
College; J.D. Boalt Hall School
of Law, University of California—
Berkeley.

Thomas E. Hookano
Assistant Chief, Land Use Section,
Pacific Legal Foundation; formerly
Deputy Attorney General, State of
California; B.A. University of
California; J.D. University of
California—Davis.

I. Introduction

CONTROLLED OR MANAGED MUNICIPAL GROWTH, whether it be by way of long-term, permanent, or short-term controls,[1] is the cause of widespread consternation and the subject of much creative legal debate. The rationale for growth control is often couched in terms of the results the process seeks to achieve, namely, orderly and attractive communities protected from the chaos of sprawl and geared precisely to the ability to provide supporting municipal services. The need to promote such community development remains largely undisputed, but the process which some identify as rife with racial and economic bias rages as a public controversy. That process is said to affect social and geographic mobility, the free enterprise system, balanced efforts to promote physical and social environmental well-being, housing supply and demand and integrated development.

---

*This is the printed version of an oral presentation made by Mr. Zumbrun at the National Association of Home Builders Legal Conference, in Anaheim, Calif. on April 24–25, 1975. The original presentation was prepared by Mr. Zumbrun and Mr. Hookano. It has been revised and edited to make it reflective of the current state of the law.

1. *See* Freilich, *Development Timing, Moratoria and Controlling Growth*, in Southwest Legal Foundation, INSTITUTE ON PLANNING, ZONING, AND EMINENT DOMAIN, Proceedings (1974).

To the novice, the growth control controversy can be numbing. This discussion is intended to provide an overview of the controversy and to provide the starting point for attorneys who may have the occasion to deal with legal problems associated with growth management. It is emphasized that the discussion herein is not meant to be exhaustive; it is precisely the purpose of the authors to provide an overview of the subject matter.

The discussion herein is divided into three parts: first, a survey of current attempts at growth control, with mention of the growth limiting effects of environmental legislation; second, a brief discussion of some socio-economic effects of growth management; and third, legal arguments related to growth management activity.

II. Survey of Current Growth Control Activity: Direct and Indirect

In *Golden v. Planning Board of the Town of Ramapo*,[2] the New York Court of Appeals judged the validity of Ramapo's timed and sequential growth control plan. The court stated:

> We only require that communities confront the challenge of population growth with open doors. Where in grappling with that problem, the community undertakes by imposing temporary restrictions upon development, to provide required municipal services in a rational manner, courts are rightfully reluctant to strike down such schemes . . .[3]

The *Ramapo* case exemplifies a judicial respect for communities which constructively grapple with problems brought on by growth. All communities, however, have not applied constructive measures in confronting the problems, nor have their methods earned such judicial respect. A survey of varying growth control measures reveals contrasting methods, motives, and approaches.

A. *Direct Local Control Activity*
1. THE RAMAPO PLAN—TIMING AND SEQUENTIAL CONTROLS

In 1966, the Town of Ramapo in New York adopted a general plan, and subsequentially a comprehensive zoning ordinance, whereby the development of residential units was conditioned upon obtaining a special permit. The permit could only be granted when an acceptable level of supporting facilities and services was available; namely, sewerage, drainage, park-recreation, schools, roads,

---

2. 30 N.Y.2d 359, 285 N.E.2d 291, 334 N.Y.S.2d 138, *appeal dismissed*, 409 U.S. 1003 (1972).
3. *Id.*, 285 N.E.2d at 302, 334 N.Y.S.2d at 153.

and firehouses. The rate of population growth was purposefully limited to match the ability of the city to provide services. A developer could accelerate his ability to use the land by agreeing to provide the necessary services at his expense.

The Ramapo Plan was challenged in *Golden v. Planning Board of the Town of Ramapo*. The plaintiffs contended that the plan was exclusionary and beyond the scope of the state enabling legislation. It also was alleged to be a taking without compensation. The Court of Appeals rejected plaintiffs' arguments by indicating that the goal of the plan was to phase development and growth so as to *maximize* population in an orderly manner. Characterized as such, the court had no problem finding that the plan was within the ambit of the existing enabling legislation and not exclusionary. As to the taking argument, the court stated that even if a parcel was restricted for the full 18-year life of the plan, it still fell short of a taking.[4] In reaching that conclusion, the court placed heavy emphasis on the fact that the plan was "a *temporary* restriction, promising that the property may be put to a profitable use within a reasonable time."[5] The United States Supreme Court subsequently denied an appeal for want of a substantial federal question.

The *Ramapo* case gives encouragement to communities which are confronted with the burdens of growth by indicating that some types of timing devices to regulate growth on a national basis can be upheld.[6]

2. THE PETALUMA PLAN: 500-UNIT LIMITATION

In Petaluma, California, a plan was adopted which established annual quotas on residential building permits. While the Petaluma Plan is similar in rationale and basic design to the Ramapo Plan, it has been argued that the Petaluma Plan does not maintain, as its basic purpose, mechanisms to accommodate contemporary demands brought on by population growth. It has been argued further that it does not seek to maximize population in an orderly fashion, but rather to limit it to protect the city's small-town character.

---

4. *Id.*, 285 N.E.2d at 300–303, 334 N.Y.S.2d at 150–154.
5. *Id.*, 285 N.E.2d at 303, 334 N.Y.S.2d at 154.
6. For further discussion of phased development controls, see: Clark, *Growth Control in California: Prospects for Local Implementation of Timing and Sequential Control of Residential Development*, 5 PAC. L.J. 570 (1974); Note, *A Zoning Program for Phased Growth: Ramapo Township's Time Control on Residential Development*, 47 N.Y.U.L. REV. 723 (1972); Bosselman, *Can the Town of Ramapo Pass a Law to Bind the Rights of the Whole World?* 1 FLA. ST. L. REV. 234 (1973).

In early 1971 a "citizens committee," along with a firm of professional planners, drafted a suggested growth policy for Petaluma. One of the motivating factors in the development of the Petaluma development policy was the sentiment of the local citizenry. A survey of local residents indicated a preference for limiting the increase of future residents. The City Council thereafter adopted a growth policy to correspond with that sentiment. The preamble of the city's official development policy stated that:

> In order to protect its small town character and surrounding open spaces, it shall be the policy of the City to control its future rate and distribution of growth. . . .[7]

The "Petaluma Plan" was devised to implement the official development policy. It contained, among other things, a limitation on the number of residential units to 500 per year and the creation of an "urban extension line" as a boundary for the city's expansion over the next 20 years. In effect, the city refused to annex or extend city facilities to land outside this "urban extension line." Within the "urban extension line" the city used density limitation and other techniques to set a maximum population for the city at 55,000 in 1985, compared with the 1962 projection of 77,000 for that same period. However, should the limitation on the number of units be lifted, the "urban extension line" would still act as a population growth limitation.

The Construction Industry Association of Sonoma County and local land owners challenged the validity of the Petaluma Plan in the United States District Court for the Northern District of California.[8] In the district court's opinion, certain elements of the plan were found to impose a burden on the fundamental interest in the right to travel. The court relied on a theory of equal protection and held that the plan must further a compelling governmental interest to be sustained. Finding that the plan was devoid of a compelling governmental interest, the court issued a permanent injunction enjoining its enforcement. The court's order was stayed, however, by Justice William O. Douglas, pending the city's appeal before the United States Court of Appeals for the Ninth Circuit.

The court of appeals reversed, holding that the Construction Industry Association and local land owners did not have standing to

---

7. Constr. Indus. Ass'n. v. City of Petaluma, 375 F. Supp. 574, *rev'd*, 522 F.2d 897 (9th Cir. 1975), *cert. denied*, 96 S. Ct. 1148, 47 L. Ed. 2d 342 (1976).
8. *Id.*

assert that the Petaluma Plan was unconstitutional as an infringement of the right to travel. The court stated that the plan was not a violation of substantive due process but a valid use of the police power to protect the public welfare. The court of appeals also said that the plan did not impermissibly burden interstate commerce. On February 23, 1976, the United States Supreme Court denied certiorari.[9]

While the district court decision was reversed, the decision is significant in that it marks the first time in which a land use program has ever been specifically invalidated on right to travel grounds.

3. BOCA RATON, FLORIDA: HOUSING CAPS

Boca Raton is an affluent retirement community in the State of Florida. In 1971, residents of Boca Raton voted by a narrow margin (7,722 to 5,626) to limit the number of dwelling units that can ever be built in the city to 40,000. At that time, the city already had 16,000 units.[10]

The Boca Raton growth limitation was to be implemented by downzoning vacant land to reduce population density. The municipal action was challenged as a violation of the right to travel by the Arvida Corporation, which originally requested zoning for a large housing development to accommodate 30,000 persons. In *Arvida Corp. v. City of Boca Raton*,[11] Arvida contends that there is a demand for moderately priced housing which can be met only by multiple units and that low-density zoning to implement the city's program will raise the cost of housing without any reasonable relationship to the city's ability to provide municipal services.

A federal court has abstained from the exercise of its jurisdiction on the federal constitutional issues pending the determination of the legality of the city's ordinance under state law.

It is notable that Boca Raton's growth control was implemented by a referendum. This mode of enactment is distinguished from the Petaluma Plan, for example, which was enacted by the City Council. Referenda or initiatives to adopt growth control measures are growing in popularity and appear to be constitutional.

---

9. *Id.*
10. *See* Boca Raton, Fla. Ordinance 1733, § 1, Oct. 3, 1972; Comment, *The National Land Use—Environmental Problem: Legal and Pragmatic Aspects of Population and Density Control*, 43 CINCINNATI L. REV. 377, 388 (1974); and LOCAL GROWTH MANAGEMENT POLICY, THE POTOMAC INSTITUTE 19–20 (1975).
11. 59 F.R.D. 316 (S.D. Fla. 1973).

4. *CITY OF EASTLAKE v. FOREST CITY ENTERPRISES:*
CONSTITUTIONALITY OF REFERENDUM ZONING

In May of 1971, Forest City Enterprises applied to the Eastlake, Ohio, Planning Commission for the rezoning of its property to permit multi-family, high-rise use. The City Planning Commission approved the Forest City application and the Eastlake City Council amended Eastlake's comprehensive zoning ordinance to permit the requested use.

Almost one year later, in April of 1972, Forest City Enterprises applied for a parking and yard approval which is a preliminary step to obtaining a construction permit. Section 3, Article VIII of the Eastlake City Charter requires that any ordinance which changes existing land use must be approved by a 55 percent vote in a city-wide referendum. Because Forest City did not obtain voter approval of the council's amendment to the comprehensive zoning ordinance, the Planning Commission denied the requested approval.[12]

Forest City challenged Section 3 of Article VIII of the Eastlake Charter on the grounds that the voter approval requirement violated Forest City's right to due process and the referendum provisions of the Ohio Constitution.[13]

The Ohio Supreme Court noted that "the zoning or rezoning of property is subject to the referendum process."[14] The court held, however, that the Eastlake referendum requirement denied Forest City Enterprises due process of law in that the reasonable use of property was made dependent upon "the potentially arbitrary and unreasonable whim of the voting public."[15] The court stated that the charter provision constitutes "an unlawful delegation of legislative power, thereby denying appellant due process of law."[16] The court also noted that no standards were established to insure that referendum requirement would be reasonable, rational and unarbitrary.[17]

The City of Eastlake petitioned the United States Supreme Court for a writ of certiorari. The United States Supreme Court held that the charter provision requiring proposed land use changes to be

---

12. An election was held in May of 1972, but Forest City failed to obtain the requisite voter approval of the zoning amendment.
13. Forest City Enterprises, Inc. v. City of Eastlake, 41 Ohio St. 2d 187, 324 N.E.2d 740 (1975).
14. *Id.*, 324 N.E.2d at 743.
15. *Id.*, 324 N.E.2d at 746.
16. *Id.*, 324 N.E.2d at 747.
17. *Id.*, 324 N.E.2d at 746.

approved by 55 percent of voters who participate in the referendum not to be violative of due process rights of the land owner.[18]

The *Eastlake* case seemed to involve the broad issue of growth control, i.e., making change in land use so burdensome as to be prohibitive. Justice Stern, of the Ohio Supreme Court, noted in his concurring opinion that the Eastlake Charter provision attempted "to exclude, build walls against the ills, poverty, racial strife, and the people themselves, of our urban areas."[19] He stressed that the inevitable effect of such provisions is to "perpetuate the de facto division in our society between black and white, rich and poor."[20]

While the need to promote comprehensive planning and to guard against arbitrary land use decision making was put before the United States Supreme Court, the Supreme Court decided the case primarily on the issue of the validity of the referendum as a means for direct political participation by the public. As zoning involves legitimate enactments, it appears that the *Eastlake* decision will allow broad application of the referendum process as a means of land use control. The uses of the referendum to control growth in a community that is anti-growth are almost limitless.

5. THE LIVERMORE SOLUTION: CONTROL BY INITIATIVE

The people of the City of Livermore, California, passed an initiative ordinance to control the issuance of building permits. The ordinance contained a recital declaring control of residential building permits necessary for the protection of the health, safety and general welfare of the citizens and as being a contribution toward solution of the city's air pollution problem. The ordinance had a definite growth control effect.

Residential building permits were defined to include single-family residential, multiple residential and trailer court building permits. The ordinance prohibited issuance of residential building permits until problems in the areas of educational facilities, sewage and water supply were solved.

The Associated Home Builders of the Greater Eastbay, Inc., were successful in overturning the city's initiative ordinance for failure to comply with California Government Code sections setting

---

18. City of Eastlake v. Forest City Enterprises, 96 S. Ct. 2358 (1976).
19. Forest City Enterprises, Inc. v. City of Eastlake, 41 Ohio St. 2d 187, 324 N.E.2d 740, 749 (1975).
20. *Id.*

forth the procedure for general law cities in enacting zoning ordinances.[21] The California Appellate Court rejected attempts by the city to classify the ordinance as an exercise of the police power akin to building codes. The court found the initiative to be a land use control measure which created a substantial interference with the use of land. As such, the court, relying on California case law precedents, required that there be notice and an opportunity to be heard before the ordinance could be enacted.[22] The California Supreme Court accepted the case for hearing on November 8, 1974. The matter is still pending.

6. SAN JOSE, CALIFORNIA—INTERIM CONTROLS BY INITIATIVE

The people of San Jose, a charter city, passed an initiative ordinance which prohibited zoning, prezoning or rezoning of any land for residential uses lying in school districts under certain conditions. If the total area of school building construction per pupil of estimated enrollment, including the estimated enrollment due to the proposed development, was less than the figure contained in a schedule set forth in the ordinance, zoning activity was precluded. The prohibition was to last two years from the date the ordinance was enacted. During the two-year period, the city, all entities responsible for community services within the city, and all concerned citizens were to undertake a study of problems connected with further residential development.

The ordinance contained a provision that the prohibition on zoning, prezoning and rezoning would not apply if the governing bodies of the school district filed with the City Council a written certification that the person seeking residential use has entered into a binding agreement to provide a satisfactory temporary alternative to permanent school construction. Finally, the ordinance contained a section which allowed the governing body of a school district to challenge a proposed zoning, rezoning or grant of a permit of any kind for residential use on submission of a written protest prior to the close of the City Council hearing on the zoning or permit. The written protest could be made only on the ground that the zoning or permit would cause impaction of schools within the district. Affirmative action on the zoning or permit was prohibited unless the City Council overruled the protest by a vote of five or more of

---

21. *See* Associated Home Builders, Etc., Inc. v. City of Livermore, 41 Cal. App. 3d 677, 116 Cal. Rptr. 326 (1974).
22. *Id.* at 685, 116 Cal. Rptr. at 332.

its members. The section pertaining to filing of a written protest by the governing body of a school district is not, by its terms, limited to a two-year duration.

The California Supreme Court upheld the San Jose initiative ordinance in *Builders Assn. of Santa Clara-Santa Cruz Counties v. Superior Court*.[23] Plaintiffs claimed:

1. The residents of a charter city could not constitutionally enact a zoning ordinance by initiative;

2. The ordinance unconstitutionally limits the power of a city council to rezone property;

3. The ordinance constitutes an unlawful delegation of the zoning authority to school districts;

4. The ordinance establishes an unreasonable classification in violation of the equal protection clause; and

5. The ordinance interferes with the constitutional right to travel.[24]

As to plaintiffs' first argument, the court merely referred to its opinion in *San Diego Building Contractors Association v. City Council of San Diego*,[25] wherein it held that the zoning ordinance was no more than a general legislative act and was neither quasi-judicial nor adjudicatory in nature. As such, the ordinance fell within the general rule which allows enactment of legislation without notice and hearing. Enactment of zoning ordinances through the initiative process was found to be authorized in the initiative and referendum provisions of both San Diego's and San Jose's charters.

With respect to plaintiffs' equal protection argument, the court found that the discrimination engendered by the ordinance was economic in character, and, as such, was valid if rationally related to a legitimate legislative purpose. In this case, the purpose was a thorough study of the problems of residential development and the voters' decision to allow such development, pending a study, in only those areas currently zoned residential, was deemed rational.[26]

As to an alleged infringement on the right to travel, the court found that plaintiffs had failed to demonstrate any noticeable or

---

23. 13 Cal. 3d 225, 118 Cal. Rptr. 158, 529 P.2d 582 (1974), *appeal dismissed* 44 U.S.L.W. 3745 (U.S. June 28, 1976).
24. *Id.* at 228, 118 Cal. Rptr. at 163, 529 P.2d at 587.
25. 13 Cal. 3d 205, 118 Cal. Rptr. 146, 529 P.2d 570 (1974), *appeal dismissed*, 44 U.S.L.W. 3745 (U.S. Jun. 28, 1976).
26. 13 Cal. 3d 225, 232–233, 118 Cal. Rptr. 158, 163, 529 P.2d 582, 587 (1974), *appeal dismissed*, 44 U.S.L.W. 3745 (U.S. June 28, 1976).

significant infringement on the right. The court found solace in the unchallenged finding of the trial court that the initiative had not in fact significantly reduced the supply of new housing in San Jose.[27]

The means of effecting growth controls chosen by Eastlake, Boca Raton, Livermore, and San Jose are important to note. These cases reflect citizen sentiment, as distinguished from the sentiment of local planning bodies, in favor of controlling the rate of growth. It may be that in the future, any opposition to such growth policies will have to be directed at the *total electorate*, rather than a planning commission or local city council. Opposition to "no-growth" measures submitted by way of referenda and the initiative process may thus involve the education of entire communities and become a formidible and costly undertaking.

B. *Indirect Local Control Measures*

Direct local growth control measures by initiative, referenda, or enactment by a representative body are supplemented by a variety of indirect and less comprehensive measures, including withheld municipal services and exclusionary zoning devices.

1. WITHHELD MUNICIPAL SERVICES

New urban development is commonly dependent upon an adequate water supply as well as sewerage capacity. The limitation of this capacity necessarily means a limitation on development. The degree of control over privately owned utilities and special water and sewer districts varies from community to community. It should be noted, however, that in some instances, utilities are being managed and regulated so as to influence the rate of growth.

For example, in early 1972, the Marin Municipal Water District located in Northern California, conducted town "meetings" in which the residents were encouraged to present their views on augmentation of the district's water supply to meet the projected growth in the district. The residents' views were somewhat conflicting but were generally interpreted to be negative as to augmentation for the purpose of meeting projected growth. A resolution was adopted in 1973 which declared that a *threatened* long-term water shortage existed.

The Marin County Superior Court, in *McCarthy Co. v. Marin Municipal Water District*,[28] found that there was no reasonable

---

27. *Id.* at 233, 118 Cal. Rptr. at 163, 529 P.2d at 587.
28. No. 66519, Marin County Superior Court, *appeal docketed*, No. 35543, Cal. Ct. App. 1st Dist., Aug. 8, 1974.

basis for the district to declare a water shortage emergency condition and, therefore, the action in imposing the moratorium was arbitrary, discriminatory and invalid.

McCarthy presents the interesting question of whether a specialized agency may usurp the planning function. Similar cases involving water district moratoriums have been filed in Southern California courts.[29]

The question of utility capacity was discussed both in *Ramapo* and *Petaluma*. The courts differed in their results. In *Ramapo*, it was agreed that the town's existing facilities were inadequate to meet the demands of natural population growth. In the *Petaluma* case, however, the district court found that the limitation in dwelling units did not correlate with the city's actual ability to supply services.

The stated purpose for the limitation (i.e., the rhetoric) and actual utility capacity are prime factors in determining the validity of withheld municipal services.[30]

2. ZONING DEVICES WITH EXCLUSIONARY EFFECTS

Zoning devices with exclusionary effects[31] are perhaps one of the most subtle means of achieving growth control. Large lot zoning, requirement of minimum square footage for dwelling units, prohibition of multi-family dwelling units, and overzoning for industrial uses are common means of effecting growth control by zoning. Several of these devices, however, have been invalidated where they have been found to be exclusionary. The most prominent cases have originated in the New Jersey and Pennsylvania courts.

In *National Land and Investment Co. v. Kohn*,[32] the four-acre minimum lot requirement of Easttown Township was declared unconstitutional. The court found that the purpose of the ordinance

---

29. *See also* Pomatto v. Goleta County Water Dist., No. 101404, Santa Barbara, California Superior Court, and Daggett v. Goleta County Water Dist., No. 104474, Santa Barbara, California Superior Court.

30. For additional discussion of growth control through limited utility extension, see Dewey, *Battle of the Heavyweights: In This Corner Environmental Rights and in the Far Corner Free Travel Rights*, 1 HAST. CON. L. Q. 153 (1974); Comment, *Control of the Timing and Location of Government Utility Extensions*, 26 STAN. L. REV. 945 (1974); and Comment, *Equal Protection in the Urban Environment: The Right to Equal Municipal Services*, 46 TUL. L. REV. 496 (1972).

31. The argument is often raised that all zoning is exclusionary. A noted advocate of "no-zoning" is Professor Bernard Siegan of the University of San Diego School of Law. He has authored the text, LAND USE WITHOUT ZONING (1972), and several articles on land use. *See* Seigan, *No Zoning is the Best Zoning*, LV(4) Cal. REAL ESTATE MAGAZINE 36 (1975).

32. 419 Pa. 504, 215 A.2d 597 (1965).

was exclusionary and as such, did not bear a substantial relationship to the proper police power purposes.[33]

Another Pennsylvania large lot zoning case of importance involved an ordinance of Concord Township which required two and three-acre minimum lots in certain residential areas. In *Appeal of Kit-Mar Builders, Inc.*,[34] Concord Township's minimum lot ordinance was struck down. The same court which decided the *National Land* case stated that "thinly veiled justifications for exclusionary zoning would not be countenanced by it."[35]

Perhaps the most significant recent case to invalidate zoning with exclusionary effects is *Southern Burlington County NAACP v. Township of Mount Laurel*.[36] The New Jersey Supreme Court, like the Pennsylvania Supreme Court, adopted an expanded concept of the general welfare to judge the validity of Mount Laurel's general zoning ordinance.

Mount Laurel was divided into three basic use categories: industrial, retail business and residential. The general zoning ordinance classified as industrial 4,121 acres, although only 100 acres were in actual industrial use. With respect to residential areas, minimum lot sizes, minimum floor areas and several restrictions on the development of multiple family dwelling units had the effect of placing housing in the township beyond the reach of low and moderate-income families, especially families with children. The New Jersey Supreme Court, agreeing with the trial court's finding stated:

> Mount Laurel 'has acted affirmatively to control development and to attract a selective type of growth' and that through its zoning ordinances has exhibited economic discrimination in that the poor have been deprived of adequate housing and the opportunity to secure the construction of subsidized housing.[37]

In *Mount Laurel* the principal question was whether a developing municipality may, by a system of land use regulation, validly make it physically and economically impossible to provide low and

---

33. The National Land case is discussed further, *infra*, with respect to the argument that any growth control measure must be consistent with a concept of general welfare which includes not only the interests of a municipality, but the contiguous region.

34. 439 Pa. 466, 268 A.2d 765 (1970).

35. *Id.* 268 A.2d at 770. An ordinance of Providence Township in Pennsylvania which did not provide for apartment buildings anywhere in the township met with the same fate as those in Concord and Easttown Townships. *See*, Appeal of Girsch, 437 Pa. 237, 263 A.2d 395 (1970).

36. 67 N.J. 151, 336 A.2d 713, *cert. denied*, 96 S. Ct. 18 (1975).

37. *Id.* 336 A.2d at 723.

moderate-income housing for those persons in need and thereby exclude such persons because of their income and resources.[38] The court concluded that Mount Laurel's ordinance was invalid in certain respects. The court noted that all zoning regulations, like any other police power enactment must promote the public health, safety, and general welfare. If it violates the general welfare, then it is an invalid attempted exercise of the police power. In this case, as in the aforementioned Pennsylvania cases, the court viewed the general welfare as encompassing the interests of the region and held that Mount Laurel and other *developing* communities, by their land use regulations, must make realistically possible the opportunity for a variety and choice of housing to all categories of people who may want to live there. The opportunity the municipality is obligated to provide encompasses its fair share of the present and prospective *regional* housing need. Thus, Mount Laurel's exclusionary zoning was struck down to the extent that it failed to be inclusionary.

The *Mount Laurel* case will be discussed further with respect to the argument for an expanded concept of the general welfare. It, however, like the Pennsylvania cases, represents a departure from the judicial attitude evidenced in *Lionshead Lake, Inc. v. Township of Wayne*,[39] wherein the New Jersey Supreme Court upheld locally imposed minimum-floor-area requirements. In *Lionshead*, the courts paid deference to local legislative judgments and evidenced a protectionist attitude. The recent change in judicial attitude, however, was stated by the court in the *Mount Laurel* case, to be mandated by "change in the world around us."[40]

C. *Regional Land Use and Federal Environmental Programs with Growth Control Effects*

A discussion of growth control mechanisms would be incomplete without a brief mention of regional land use controls and federal

---

38. *Id.* 336 A.2d at 724.

39. 10 N.J. 165, 89 A.2d 693 (1952).

40. 67 N.J. 151, 336 A.2d 713, 727, *cert. denied*, 96 S. Ct. 18 (1975). It should be noted that zoning which is racially motivated, resulting in invidious discrimination, and zoning with racially discriminatory effects, although not necessarily racially motivated, has been invalidated. *See* Kennedy Park Homes Ass'n. v. City of Lackawanna, 436 F.2d 108 (2d Cir. 1970), *cert. denied*, 401 U.S. 1010 (1971), and United States v. Black Jack, 508 F.2d 1179 (1974), *cert. denied*, 442 U.S. 1042, discussed *infra*. For additional discussion of exclusionary zoning devices see Sager, *Tight Little Islands: Exclusionary Zoning, Equal Protection, and the Indigent*, 21 Stan. L. Rev. 767 (1969); Aloi, *Recent Developments in Exclusionary Zoning: The Second Generation Cases and the Environment*, 6 S.W.U.L. Rev. 88 (1974).

environmental programs having growth control effects. These programs, emanating from both state and federal legislative enactments, superimpose controls over those imposed by local municipalities.

1. REGIONAL LAND USE CONTROL PROGRAMS

The San Francisco Bay Conservation and Development Commission (hereinafter referred to as BCDC) in California is an example
of a regional planning program having growth control effects.

The commission was created to regulate the filling and dredging
of the San Francisco Bay and adjacent tidelands. Prior to the creation of the commission, nine different counties and several cities
determined whether shallow portions of the Bay would be filled.
The BCDC has almost exclusive jurisdiction over development in
the Bay, and its powers are extensive. The California enabling
legislation requires a permit from the commission for all projects
in the Bay and on a 100-foot-wide strip around the Bay. While the
commission infuses a regional perspective into planning with respect
to the Bay, it leaves unresolved the issue of compensation for action which it takes. The California District Court of Appeals has
upheld the Commission's power to deny a permit for development
of privately owned property near Candlestick Park *without the payment of compensation.*[41]

A second example of a regional control agency is the bi-state
Tahoe Regional Planning Agency. That agency is the product of a
compact entered into by California and Nevada and ratified by the
Congress of the United States. The agency has a 10-member governing body appointed equally from the respective states. Finances
come from taxes levied upon the counties falling within the agency's
jurisdiction (an area of approximately 500 square miles).

The agency is mandated to prepare and adopt a regional plan
for the area within its jurisdiction and to implement it by adopting
all necessary rules, regulations, and ordinances. The rules, regulations, and ordinances are viewed as establishing a *minimum* standard applicable throughout the region.

The bi-state compact also provides that the agency police the
region to ensure compliance with the plan and its rules, regulations,
and ordinances. If it is found that a local jurisdiction is not enforc-

---

41. Candlestick Properties v. San Francisco Bay Conservation & Dev.
Comm'n, 11 Cal. App. 3d 557, 89 Cal. Rptr. 897 (1970). *See also* Baum,
San Francisco Bay Conservation and Development Commission, 2 LINCOLN
L. REV. 98 (1970), and Navajo Terminals Inc. v. San Francisco Bay Con-
servation and Dev. Comm., 46 Cal. App. 3d 1, 120 Cal. Rptr. 534 (1975).

ing the plan or rules, regulations or ordinances, the agency is authorized to bring court action to insure compliance. Whenever the agency is required by the compact or ordinance, rule or regulation to review or approve a public or private proposal, the agency is authorized to either approve, require modification, or reject the proposal.

As a result of the agency's general plan, many lawsuits have been filed by private property owners. During 1973 alone the Tahoe Regional Planning Agency was faced with 106 lawsuits for a total claim against the agency, States of California and Nevada and other governmental units of some $200 million.[42] The problem of compensation with regard to actions taken by the Tahoe Regional Planning Agency also remains unsettled.[43]

2. FEDERAL ENVIRONMENTAL LEGISLATION WITH GROWTH-LIMITING EFFECTS

While specialized and comprehensive state[44] and municipal regulatory measures comprise the first two layers of land use controls, federal environmental legislation undeniably "frosts the cake." A few examples of federal controls will be provided.

The National Environmental Policy Act of 1969 (hereinafter referred to as NEPA)[45] has broad implications in the field of land use regulation. The requirement of an environmental impact statement (hereinafter referred to as EIS) for governmental actions which may significantly affect the quality of the human environment has been interpreted to require EIS's for land development projects where there is government presence and the potential for a significant effect on the environment. Complying with NEPA procedures is often tricky and the opportunity for oversight great. While an adverse report is not a legal basis for denying a project

---

42. *See* Address by N. B. Livermore to Monterey County Planning Council. Land Use Controls and Their Effect on Private Property Rights, Mar. 3, 1973.

43. *See* Note, *Regional Government for Lake Tahoe*, 22 HAST. L.J. 705 (1971), and Brown v. Tahoe Regional Planning Agency, 385 F. Supp. 1128 (1973), opinion superseded by unpublished Order dated Jan. 10, 1975.

44. A discussion of state-wide land use legislation is not provided here. Such legislation is described by F. BOSSELMAN AND D. CALLIES in THE QUIET REVOLUTION IN LAND USE CONTROLS (1971) and HEALY, LAND USE AND THE STATE. Legislation in Hawaii, Florida and Vermont provide interesting examples. For federal legislative effects see Rose, *Government Role in Land Use Planning and Control is Growing*, 3(4) REAL ESTATE L.J. 809 (1974).

45. 42 U.S.C. § 4321, 35 seq. (1970).

permit, projects can be delayed almost indefinitely until all NEPA requirements are satisfied.

A few examples are worth citing. Walt Disney Production's Mineral King Project was intended to provide an intensified year-round recreational use of a 16,000-acre valley and mountains in the Sequoia National Forest. Although the project was approved in 1969, before NEPA was adopted, NEPA has provided Mineral King litigants with new ammunition to cause further delay. The adequacy of the United States Forest Service's EIS on the project is likely to be tested in the United States District Court for the Northern District of California.[46]

Other recent cases in which NEPA may have been used as a delaying tactic have involved dam construction. *Natural Resources Defense Council v. Stamm*,[47] involved the construction of Auburn Dam in California and *Environmental Defense Fund, Inc. v. Armstrong*[48] involved the construction of the New Melones Dam.

NEPA is seen by some as promoting no-growth by a morass of procedural requirements too burdensome and costly to comply with. The result is that some projects are abandoned or not initiated at all.

The Clean Air Amendments of 1970[49] superimposed additional controls over local land use. Pursuant to the Clean Air Amendments the Environmental Protection Agency adopted national air quality standards. Under the act, states are to adopt plans for implementation of the desired standard. If such plans are not adopted or unacceptable to the Environmental Protection Agency, the agency will impose its own. Plans are to consider "alternative control strategies" for attainment and maintenance of the national standards.[50] The definition of "alternative control strategies" includes:

---

46. *See* Sierra Club v. Morton, 405 U.S. 727 (1972).
47. 6 E.R.C. 1525 (E.D. Cal. 1974).
48. 352 F. Supp. 50 (N.D. Cal. 1972), 356 F. Supp. 131 (N.D. Cal. 1973), 487 F.2d 814 (9th Cir. 1973), *rehearing denied*, 419 U.S. 1041 (1974). An interesting sidelight in the New Melones case is that "environmentalists" were chastised by the Court in claiming that New Melones construction was unnecessary because the need would be met by Auburn Dam, while simultaneously alleging in the Auburn Dam case that Auburn Dam was superfluous because the need would be met by the New Melones Dam, 356 F. Supp. 131, 139, n. 7 (N.D. Cal. 1973).
49. 42 U.S.C. § 1857(b) et seq. (1970).
50. 40 C.F.R. § 51.10(a).

Closing or relocation of residential, commercial, or industrial facilities. . . .[51] [and]

[A]ny land use or transportation control measures not specifically delineated herein.[52]

The California experience with the Clean Air Amendments is instructive. On November 12, 1973, the Environmental Protection Agency, after rejecting three implementation plans drafted by the state, imposed its own control plan upon California.[53] The Environmental Protection Agency's plan included, in addition to strict motor vehicle controls, a number of indirect disincentives to vehicle use. These included: management of parking supply, requiring special permits for construction of new parking facilities of 50 spaces or more, or expansion of existing parking facilities; a heavy tax on free parking spaces whether provided by businesses or government—including on-street parking; and an escalating surcharge to be levied on paid parking spaces. To ensure strict compliance, the Environmental Protection Agency specified that any failure to comply with any of these provisions would subject an individual or government official to fines of $25,000 to $50,000 per *day* of violation or one to two years in prison. Within 30 days, 209 parties or groups of parties had filed suit against the Environmental Protection Agency in the United States Court of Appeals for the Ninth Circuit. The court of appeals held, among other things, that under the Clean Air Act, the EPA administrator does not have the power to impose sanctions on California or its officials for their failure to implement the EPA plan for the state.[54]

Some of the more onerous Environmental Protection Agency regulations, such as the parking surcharge provisions, were withdrawn under the pressure of this litigation. Subsequent action was taken by Congress in amending the Clean Air Act to prohibit such surcharges.[55] The validity of other provisions of the Environmental Protection Agency implementation plan is still being litigated.[56]

The implications in terms of land use control are staggering. The Environmental Protection Agency may, in the near future, be exer-

---

51. 40 C.F.R. § 51.1(n)(4).

52. 40 C.F.R. § 51.1(n)(9).

53. 40 C.F.R. § 52.223 et seq.

54. Brown v. EPA 521 F.2d 827 (9th Cir. 1975), *cert. granted*, 44 U.S.L.W. 3685 (Jun. 1, 1976). The Pacific Legal Foundation was a petitioner in this case.

55. Pub. L. No. 93–319 § 4(b)(2)(B) (1974).

56. *See*, e.g., City of Santa Rosa v. EPA, 8 E.R.C. 1929 (9th Cir. 1976).

cising a complete veto over development projects within a state and particular locality.

Regional, statewide and federal land use controls evidence an erosion of the traditional local control scheme. These additional controls undoubtedly contribute to the instability of the existing real estate market and the financial difficulties of the property owner.

III. A Brief Description of Primary Economic and Social Effects of Growth Control Measures

Growth controls necessarily have reverberating social and economic effects. Those effects should be considered when evaluating the validity of any no-growth measure.

A primary effect of growth controls is market uncertainty. For example, under the *Petaluma* annual 500-unit building limitation, uncertainty can stem from the fact that the property owner-developer may be precluded from ever knowing whether or not he may develop his land. It is difficult to ascertain the value of property when the developable uses remain uncertain. This is somewhat contrasted to the *Ramapo* plan of limited duration, wherein the property owner knows that at least within 18 years he will be allowed to use his land for a designated purpose.

Uncertainty in the market place is best seen in terms of the effects of environmental legislation. Professor Donald G. Hagman, noted authority on zoning in California, and Professor Dean Misczynski, University of California Research Economist, have written of the effects of market disequilibrium caused by the morass of federal controls imposed with regard to land use.[57]

Hagman and Misczynski point out that federal environmental laws affecting land use are, for the most part, new, controversial, and incompletely defined. Their newness and incomplete definition, however, are not the only reasons for market uncertainty. Confusion is generated because often special purpose oriented laws have been passed in disregard of one another. The result is paralysis; buyers and sellers immobilized by conflicting signals.

Hagman and Misczynski describe some of the specific effects of environmental legislation on the land market. The environmental impact report required under NEPA for projects where there is

---

57. *See* Hagman and Misczynski, *The Quiet Federalization of Land Use*, xv(4) CAL. REAL ESTATE MAGAZINE 14, 16 (1975).

some sort of federal presence often means considerable delay. As Hagman and Misczynski point out, some projects may be terminated, meaning a wipeout in land values, while others are relocated to minimize delay. NEPA can effect a geographical redistribution of values with no guarantee that the total real estate wealth created by the project will be increased.

The Clean Air Act can produce similar effects. A factory may be forced to shutdown due to air pollution with the resulting effect that it becomes relatively worthless real estate. The effects of the shutdown will reverberate throughout the community. A shopping center, for example, may be built to an inefficiently small scale in order to come within Environmental Protection Agency standards on air pollution. The result may be an inefficient use of land, reducing land values. It is startling to realize that the Clean Air Act Amendments could possibly stop growth both where the air is bad and where it is pure under the "non-degradation" rule.

The potential effects of the Federal Water Pollution Control Act Amendments of 1972 are similar to the Clean Air Act Amendments. New development is prohibited in areas with polluted water until such time as effluent and ambient water quality meets standards set by the Act. While underdeveloped areas may increase in value because they need less water pollution control abatement, moratoria will have the effect of lowering values in a polluted area for an indeterminable period of time.

Each of the federal environmental laws has the potential to impose constraints on development, as well as to shift market demand. During the implementation stages, they uniformly create uncertainty in land value. Superimposed on local growth control measures, the valuation of land by assessors and appraisers, as Hagman and Misczynski point out, can become a pure exercise of "intuitive conjecture."

While uncertainty in the market place due to increasing governmental regulation and growth control devices is a prime concern of landowners, it is also of concern to low and moderate-income persons because uncertainty is a factor which drives housing costs up. Those who weather the morass of local and federal controls ultimately will pass the cost associated with the risk of land development on to the consumer. As economist Paul Samuelson states:

> If people generally act like risk averters . . . they will prefer smaller steady incomes to erratic incomes even when those average out to a higher figure. Therefore, economic activities that involve much uncertainty and

risk . . . will be forced by comparative entry and exit of risk takers to pay, over the long run, a positive profit premium to compensate for aversion to risk. The yield on capital invested in such industries will involve, in addition to pure interest corresponding to safe investments, an extra element corresponding to positive profit.[58]

Those who bear the uncertainty must be paid their due.

It is not only uncertainty in the market place, but restrictive and exclusionary zoning practices which contribute to higher prices. In the New Jersey Supreme Court case of *Southern Burlington County NAACP v. Township of Mount Laurel*,[59] the court discussed the effect of Mount Laurel's exclusionary zoning practices. Those practices included minimum house size requirements; minimum lot size and frontage requirements; prohibition of multifamily housing; prohibition of mobile homes; and overzoning for nonresidential uses. The court found Mount Laurel's zoning ordinance to be so restrictive as to preclude single-family housing for not only low but moderate income families as well. The court noted that dwellings in the northeasterly and southwesterly corners of the township, where intensive development was taking place, but at a low density, had an average value in 1971 of $32,500.[60] In striking down the Mount Laurel general ordinance as contrary to the general welfare the court concluded, inter alia, that Mount Laurel impermissibly "permits only such middle and upper income housing as it believes will have sufficient taxable value to come close to paying its own governmental way."[61] Poor people and moderate income people, including many elderly and retired persons, were clearly excluded.

Mount Laurel is only one example of how exclusionary zoning ordinances drive costs upward to preclude access by lower income groups to either new or used housing. Such exclusionary zoning practices persist at a time when the need for better housing is acute. That need was documented in a study entitled *America's Housing Needs: 1970 to 1980*, by the Harvard-MIT Joint Center for Urban Studies. The study established that 6.9 million low and middle income American families live in physically inadequate homes. Another 700,000 reside in overcrowded units and 5.5 million pay exorbitant rents.

---

58. SAMUELSON, ECONOMICS: AN INTRODUCTORY ANALYSIS 604 (6th ed. 1964).
59. 67 N.J. 151, 336 A.2d 713, *cert. denied*, 96 S. Ct. 18 (1975).
60. *Id.* 336 A.2d at 719.
61. *Id.* 336 A.2d at 730.

The attainment of better housing is made difficult not only by high prices but by the fact that with "no-growth" policies, there are fewer new housing units available to stimulate moves.

A study of filtration resulting from new housing construction was conducted by the Survey Research Center at the University of Michigan.[62] The study was made in 17 metropolitan areas and involved more than 3,500 interviews. It reveals that the construction of one new unit makes possible a succession of 3½ moves to different and more likely better housing accommodations. New housing benefits more people indirectly than directly. For every 1,000 units built, there will be 2,500 moves to existing housing and 1,000 moves to new housing.

The survey also demonstrates that more than one-third of all those who move are likely to be in the low and moderate income categories. While most new construction occurs in outer parts of a metropolitan area, moves extend to the older areas near the center of the larger cities. The Michigan survey makes it clear that prohibiting new construction seriously harms the groups that are most in need of a better living environment and improved social surrounding.

Higher costs of housing due to market uncertainty and exclusionary zoning practices and the fact that under "no-growth" schemes fewer new housing units are available, contribute to the immobility of lower and moderate-income groups. While growth controls give cause for concern because of the negative effects on social and economic mobility, perhaps the most dangerous potential effect of indiscriminate growth controls is their proclivity to "balkanize the country."

In 1952, the New Jersey Supreme Court considered the validity of an ordinance of Wayne Township, New Jersey, imposing minimum floor area requirements. The requirement, in effect, created a social and economic barrier around the city. In subscribing to the prevailing judicial protectionist attitude of the times, the court sustained the living area requirement.[63]

The danger of growth controls is that surrounding communities may be forced to adopt similar measures to prevent a disproportionate share of the burdens incident to increasing population from descending upon them. The ultimate result would be a union of

---

62. J. LANSING, C. CLIFTON, J. MORGAN, NEW HOMES AND POOR PEOPLE, A STUDY OF MOVES (1969).
63. Lionshead Lake, Inc. v. Wayne Township, 89 A.2d 693 (N.J. 1952).

"hostile states and localities, each attempting to 'feather its own nest' at the expense of the others."[64]

The potential for "balkanization" is, however, less likely under a *Ramapo*-type plan where there is an effort to maximize population consistent with municipal services. This is contrasted to a *Petaluma*-type plan, where municipal services are geared down to serve only a limited population, or the Boca Raton Ordinance, which places an absolute limit on housing units.

IV. Legal Arguments Relative to "No-Growth" Activity

There have been a number of legal challenges to various growth control schemes in recent years. Much of the litigation has centered around an alleged violation of constitutional rights. Some of the more salient arguments will be discussed here.

A. *The Equal Protection Clause of the Fourteenth Amendment*

Challenges to zoning ordinances and no-growth plans as being a denial of equal protection have met with varying success. Failure to find a suspect class or any denial of fundamental right requires only that the municipality put forth some reasonable basis as supportive of the classification created by its enactments.[65] However, where there is a suspect class or a denial of a fundamental right, the courts examine the ordinance's rationale to determine if it promotes a compelling interest.[66] The most prevalent classifications in the areas of zoning and no-growth are race and wealth. The outcome of any class depends, for the most part, on which of these two classifications is present.

It is clear beyond a doubt that classifications based on race are suspect.[67] Allegations of racial discrimination have been a fruitful approach in overturning many municipal actions. In *United Farmworkers of Florida Housing Project v. City of Delray*, a refusal to

---

64. *See* Comment, *The Right to Travel: Another Constitutional Standard of Local Land Use Regulations*, 39 U. CHI. L. REV. 612, 630 (1972), wherein the author discusses cases in which the courts have attempted to prevent this "balkanization."

65. United States v. Maryland Savings-Share Ins. Corp., 400 U.S. 4 (1970).

66. San Antonio Independent School Dist. v. Rodriguez, 411 U.S. 1 (1973); *In re* Griffiths, 413 U.S. 717 (1973).

67. Brown v. Bd. of Ed., 347 U.S. 483 (1954); McLaughlin v. Florida, 379 U.S. 184 (1964).

allow a proposed housing project to tie into the city's existing water and sewer systems was overturned as being racially discriminatory.[68] The court found that once a municipality began to offer services outside its incorporated area, it could not refuse those services to others outside the area on the basis of race.[69] The city's claim that it had to remain faithful to its master plan and annexation policy, both of which had been riddled with exceptions, was deemed not to rise to the level of a compelling interest.[70]

Similarly, in *United States v. City of Black Jack*, the United States brought suit under the Civil Rights Act of 1968 alleging that the city had denied persons housing based on their race.[71] The city adopted a zoning ordinance prohibiting construction of multiple-family dwellings in an area in which a federally subsidized low and moderate-income integrated development was proposed. The appellate court reversed the district court's dismissal of the action holding that in making a prima facie case, plaintiffs need only show that the conduct of the defendant actually or predictably results in racial discrimination.[72] Thus, the court clearly indicated that plaintiffs in these types of cases are not saddled with the onerous burden of proving discriminatory motivation, they need only show that discrimination will be its effect.[73] The city's interests in road and traffic control, prevention of overcrowding of schools and prevention of devaluation of adjacent single-family homes were found not to be furthered by the ordinances in question and thus not compelling interests.[74] The decisions in *Norwalk Core v. Norwalk Redevelopment Agency*[75] and *Gautreaux v. Chicago Housing Authority*[76] should be noted for their similar findings on racial discrimination.

When ordinances or statutes in question engender a classification based solely on wealth, as distinguished from race, invalidation is more difficult. It appears from the decision in *San Antonio Independent School Dist. v. Rodriguez* that the United States Supreme Court is reluctant to find discrimination on wealth alone enough

---

68. 493 F.2d 799 (5th Cir. 1974).
69. *Id.* at 808.
70. *Id.* at 809.
71. 508 F.2d 1179 (8th Cir. 1974), *cert. denied*, 422 U.S. 1042 (1975).
72. *Id.* at 1184.
73. *Id.* at 1185.
74. *Id.* at 1186–1187.
75. 395 F.2d 920 (2d Cir. 1968).
76. 503 F.2d 930 (7th Cir. 1974).

to invoke the compelling interest analyses.[77] Additionally, it seems
that courts are unwilling to find racial discrimination where a statute discriminates against the poor and there is merely a statistical
correlation between poverty and race.[78]

The compelling interest analysis can be triggered where the statutory classification is based on wealth when its effect is a denial of
a fundamental right.[79] Unfortunately, the United States Supreme
Court has found that the right to housing of a particular quality
is not a fundamental right.[80] In cases where the effect of the ordinance is a population cap, it is arguable that the focus changes to
the right to any housing and perhaps the courts can be persuaded
to find this to be a fundamental right. If there is no denial of a
fundamental right, the court will consider the wealth classification
in light of the reasonable basis analysis.[81]

While it is clear that courts will not hesitate to strike down racially motivated classifications under an equal protection analysis,
the judicial attitude towards classifications based on wealth is more
lenient. Judicial reluctance at accepting statistical correlations between the poor and ethnic minorities and at finding a fundamental
right to decent housing are additional obstacles in the way of striking down discriminatory and "no-growth" zoning. For the present,
the most successful equal protection argument is likely to be one
tied to racial classifications.

B. *Right to Travel*

The argument that there is a constitutionally protected right to
travel has been made in several contexts. It is discussed here in a
limited setting: first, as it has been applied to exclusionary zoning
cases; and second, its utility in growth control cases.

While the right to travel is not explicitly mentioned in the Federal Constitution, it has been treated by the United States Supreme
Court as if it were one of the fundamental rights. The travel argument has been used to invalidate a number of state and local restrictions imposed to deny access to government benefits and privileges.

77. 411 U.S. at 28, 29.
78. Ybarra v. City of Town of Los Altos Hills, 503 F.2d 250, 253 (9th
Cir. 1974).
79. Harper v. Virginia Bd. of Elections, 383 U.S. 663 (1966).
80. Lindsey v. Normet, 405 U.S. 56, 74 (1972).
81. Ybarra v. City of Town of Los Altos Hills, *supra* at 250; Southern
Alameda Spanish Speaking Organization v. City of Union City, 424 F.2d
291, 295 (1970).

In *Shapiro v. Thompson*,[82] a leading right to travel case, the United States Supreme Court held that a state could not impose a one-year residency requirement as a condition for receipt of welfare assistance. In *Dunn v. Blumstein*,[83] the Supreme Court considered a Tennessee law which affected both interstate and intrastate travel by limiting voter registration only to those persons who, at the time of the succeeding election would have been residents of the state for one year and residents of the county for three months. The Court invalidated both durational residence requirements for the reason that they impinged on the exercise of the right to travel. In *Memorial Hospital v. Maricopa County*,[84] the court invalidated a durational residence requirement for the receipt of free medical care.

The right to travel argument logically can be extended to challenge growth control actions. It must be remembered that travel should not be treated as if it were an independent doctrine from equal protection or due process, but one of the fundamental rights which is implicitly protected by virtue of the due process and equal protection clauses of the fourteenth amendment of the United States Constitution. Thus, when examining state action which infringes on a fundamental right, the right involved and the applicable clause are intertwined into one doctrine. State action which serves to penalize travel in a discriminatory fashion is subject to review under the equal protection clause of the Fourteenth Amendment. Nondiscriminatory action is reviewed under the due process clause.

In structuring the argument it is argued first that the government regulation imposes a burden on the right to travel (either interstate or intrastate). Second, because travel is recognized as a fundamental right, and protected against both discriminatory and nondiscriminatory legislation, the compelling state interest test is urged upon the court. Failure to find the existence of a compelling state interest to support the regulation results in invalidating the legislation.[85]

---

82. 394 U.S. 618 (1969).
83. 405 U.S. 330 (1972).
84. 415 U.S. 250 (1974).
85. *See* the recent Supreme Court case of Village of Belle Terre v. Boraas, 416 U.S. 1 (1974), wherein a right to travel argument was raised before the Court in regards to a local ordinance prohibiting more than two persons not related by blood, marriage or adoption from occupying a detached house in a single family district.

C. *Expansion of the General Welfare Concept*

An argument that is emerging in the challenge of comprehensive measures to control the timing, character, and volume of development is that to be a valid exercise of the police power, such measures must be consistent with and promote the general welfare of the immediate region. In the landmark case of *Euclid v. Ambler Realty Co.*,[86] the United States Supreme Court validated the power of local municipalities to zone. The Euclid Court, nevertheless, warned:

> It is not meant by this, however, to exclude the possibility of cases where the general public interest would so far outweigh the interests of the municipality that the municipality would not be allowed to stand in the way.[87]

The court seemingly placed the "general public interest" over the interests of the municipality as a limitation on the exercise of the local police power.

There is the recognition that with urbanization, the impact of local land use decisions is not confined to municipal borders. Therefore, the municipality's responsibility to promote the general welfare should not be so confined. In assessing the validity of exclusionary zoning devices, courts are going beyond an examination of local justifications and examining the impact of regulations on the region.

Recent New Jersey and Pennsylvania cases have expanded the concept of the region being considered to include not one jurisdiction, but several.

In *National Land and Investment Co. v. Kohn*, the Supreme Court of Pennsylvania spoke of the obligation of Easttown Township to the region.[88] The court stated:

> The township's brief raises (but, unfortunately, does not attempt to answer) the interesting issue of the township's responsibility to those who do not yet live in the township and who are part, or may become part, of the population expansion of the suburbs. Four-acre zoning represents Easttown's position that it does not desire to accommodate those who are pressing for admittance to the township unless such admittance will not create any additional burdens upon governmental functions and services. *The question posed is whether the township can stand in the way of the natural forces which send our growing population into hitherto undeveloped areas in search of a comfortable place to live. We have concluded*

---

86. 272 U.S. 365 (1926).
87. *Id.* at 390.
88. 215 A.2d at 597.

not. A zoning ordinance whose primary purpose is to prevent the entrance of newcomers in order to avoid future burdens, economic and otherwise, upon the administration of public services and facilities can not be held valid. (emphasis added.)[89]

The court further stated:

> . . . zoning is a tool in the hands of governmental bodies which enables them to more effectively meet the demands of evolving and growing communities. It must not and cannot be used by those officials as an instrument by which they may shirk their responsibilities. Zoning is a means by which a governmental body can plan for the future—it may not be used as a means to deny the future.[90]

The court's message in the *National Land* case is that communities must cope with population growth and they may not adopt measures which will, in effect, abdicate that responsibility.

In another case, *Kit-Mar Builders, Inc. v. Township of Concord*,[91] the Pennsylvania Supreme Court invalidated minimum two and three-acre lot requirements on the ground that the effect of the large-lot zoning was to redirect growth pressures to other surrounding communities, which imposed a disproportionate share of the growth burden on those communities. The court referred to the *National Land* case in its decision and stated:

> The implication of our decision in *National Land*, is that communities must deal with the problems of population growth. They may not refuse to confront the future by adopting zoning regulations that effectively restrict population to near present levels. It is not for any given township to say who may or may not live within its confines, while disregarding the interests of the entire area. If Concord Township is successful in unnaturally limiting its population growth through the use of exclusive zoning regulations, the people who would normally live there will inevitably have to live in another community, and the requirement that they do so is not a decision that Concord Township should alone be able to make.[92]

In *Southern Burlington County NAACP v. Township of Mount Laurel*,[93] the court, relying on its interpretation of the New Jersey

---

89. *Id.* at 612.
90. *Id.* at 610.
91. 439 Pa. 466, 268 A.2d 765 (1970).
92. 268 A.2d at 768, 769.
93. 67 N.J. 151, 336 A.2d 713, *cert. denied*, 96 S. Ct. 18 (1975). Reference should be made to the case of Oakwood at Madison, Inc. v. Township of Madison, 283 A.2d 353 (1971), on remand 320 A.2d 223 (1974). In the first Oakwood case, the New Jersey court considered the effect of the township's zoning scheme on the region. Large-lot requirements together with minimum floor area requirements were the dominant zoning pattern. The court held that the ordinance was invalid because it failed to promote "reasonably a balanced community in accordance with the general welfare, unless it is defensible on some other ground" 283 A.2d at 358. The court did

constitution, concluded that Mount Laurel's ordinance, employing a variety of exclusionary devices, was invalid in certain respects. The court considered that land use regulation is encompassed within the state's police power and that all police power enactments must conform with state constitutional requirements of equal protection and due process. The court, in this regard, noted that all zoning regulation must, like any other police power enactment, promote the public health, safety, morals or the general welfare. If it fails to promote the general welfare, then it is in conflict with the state constitution. The court then went on to define the general welfare, and stated:

> . . . the general welfare which developing municipalities like Mount Laurel must consider extends beyond their boundaries and cannot be parochially confined to the claimed good of the particular municipality.[94]

Mount Laurel's ordinance was found clearly not to serve the general welfare of the region, which had a pressing need for low and moderate-income housing.

Mount Laurel is a significant recognition of the thought set forth in *Euclid* by the Supreme Court that the interest of the municipality must not be allowed to stand in the way of the interests of the general public.

General welfare is defined broadly by the *Mount Laurel* court to include the interest of the region. It may be argued, therefore, that a specific growth control plan is invalid to the extent that it sacrifices the interest of inhabitants of the region in favor of the municipality. It is a process of weighing local against the regional impact of local controls on growth. An argument can be made that it is the duty of a community to take only such growth control measures as are in harmony with the needs of the region, lest such action be invalidated.[95] While the judicial trend to expand the general

---

not find the existence of that other ground. The case was recently before the New Jersey Supreme Court for review of the township's amended ordinance. Oral argument took place on April 14, 1975.

94. Southern Burlington County NAACP v. Township of Mount Laurel, 336 A.2d at 727–728.

95. For further discussion of whether municipalities must consider regional needs in regard to land use regulation see: Comment, *Judicial Limitations on Parochialisms in Municipal Land Use Decisions: Scott v. City of Indian Wells*, 25 HAST. L.J. 739 (1974); Comment, *Validity of Local Ordinances Depends on Considerations of Regional, Not Merely Local, General Welfare*, 25 VAND. L. REV. 466 (1972); Walsh, *Are Local Zoning Bodies Required by the Constitution to Consider Regional Needs?*, 3 CONN. L. REV. 244 (1971); Roman Catholic Diocese of Newark v. Borough of Ho-Ho-Kus, 220 A.2d 97, 103 (N.J. 1966); Berenson v. Town of New Castle, 341 N.E.2d 236 (N.Y. 1975).

welfare concept in exclusionary zoning cases is gaining momentum, there is no consistent response in no-growth cases.

D. *Substantive Due Process*

The Fifth Amendment of the Federal Constitution provides that private property shall not be taken without just compensation. All but one of the states have similar provisions. Twenty-six states have added a clause which requires compensation not only for property taken, but "damaged" as well. The federal taking clause has received expanded interpretation to include governmental action that diminishes the value of property even though there is no physical appropriation.[96]

Land use regulations which unreasonably restrict the use and value of property cannot be upheld under the police power.[97] The courts have treated the taking question on a case-by-case basis. Due to the lack of a universal standard, there is much uncertainty and apparent inconsistency in the various jurisdictions. In this connection, Professor Arvo Van Alstyne stated the inadequacy of the judicial approach as follows:

> Judicial efforts to chart a usable test for determining when police power measures impose constitutionally compensable losses have, on the whole, been notably unsuccessful. With some exceptions, the decisional law is largely characterized by confusing and incompatible results, often explained in conclusionary terminology, circular reasoning, and empty rhetoric. Even the modicum of predictability which might otherwise inhere in the pattern of judicial precedents is impaired by the frequently reiterated judicial declaration that each case must be decided on its own facts.[98]

Out of the morass of cases, there are a number of fundamental principles that have emerged which should be considered in any challenge to a land use regulation alleged to be a taking.[99]

1. Is the regulation geared to prevent a noxious or nuisance type of private use? If so, it will generally be upheld even though there is great diminution in value.[100]

---

96. United States v. Kansas City Life Ins. Co., 339 U.S. 799 (1950).

97. Pennsylvania Coal Co. v. Mahon, 260 U.S. 393 (1922).

98. Van Alstyne, *Taking or Damaging by Police Power: The Search for Inverse Condemnation Criteria*, 44 S. CAL. L. REV. 2 (1970).

99. The conclusions set forth here are based primarily on California case law, but may be applicable in other states as well.

100. *See*, e.g., Consolidated Rock Products Co. v. City of Los Angeles, 57 Cal. 2d 515, 370 P.2d 342 (1962); Hadacheck v. Sebastian, 239 U.S. 394 (1915); Goldblatt v. Town of Hempstead, 369 U.S. 590 (1962).

2. Is the regulation an attempt to devalue property in advance of an impending public acquisition? If so, it will not be upheld.[101]

3. Does the regulation reasonably relate to a strong public health protection policy? If so, the regulation will be upheld so long as some reasonable use remains.[102]

4. Does the regulation involve an attempt to exact property (by way of dedication) in such a way that it does not reasonably relate to the purpose of a private project? If so, it will not be upheld.[103]

. 5. Is the regulation an attempt to effect architectural controls? If so, the regulation will be upheld so long as a reasonable use is left to the owner.[104]

6. Is the regulation an attempt to preserve or enhance a governmental resource? The regulation probably will not be upheld if the damage is permanent and severe.[105]

7. Is the land use device for planning only, as distinguished from a permanent regulation? If so, it will be upheld.[106]

8. Has the regulation interfered with a vested property right? If so, it will be invalidated.[107]

9. Is the regulation only temporary? If so, a greater degree of diminution in value will be tolerated than if it were permanent.[108]

---

101. Peacock v. County of Sacramento, 271 Cal. App. 2d 845, 77 Cal. Rptr. 391 (1969).

102. Turner v. County of Del Norte, 24 Cal. App. 3d 311, 101 Cal. Rptr. 93 (1972). The question of what is a "reasonable use" is a question for the trier of fact. *See* concurring opinion in McCarthy v. City of Manhattan Beach, 41 Cal. 2d 879, 264 P.2d 932 (1953).

103. Mid-Way Cabinet Etc. Mfg. v. County of San Joaquin, 257 Cal. App. 2d 181, 65 Cal. Rptr. 37 (1967). However, *see* Associated Home Builders Etc. Inc. v. City of Walnut Creek, 4 Cal. 3d 633, 94 Cal. Rptr. 630, 484 P.2d 606 (1971).

104. Bohannan v. City of San Diego, 30 Cal. App. 3d 416, 106 Cal. Rptr. 333 (1973). However, if the regulation is to solely promote aesthetic objectives, it will be invalidated. Varney & Green v. Williams, 155 Cal. 318, 100 P. 867 (1909); County of Santa Barbara v. Purcell, Inc., 251 Cal. App. 2d 169, 59 Cal. Rptr. 345 (1967).

105. *See*, e.g., Lutheran Church v. City of New York, 316 N.E.2d 305 (1974), denial of building permit to preserve a historical landmark; National Land and Investment Co. v. Kohn, 215 A.2d at 597, open space zoning invalid; *but compare* Just v. Marinette County, 201 N.W.2d 761 (1973).

106. Selby Realty Co. v. City of Buenaventura, 10 Cal. 3d 110, 109 Cal. Rptr. 799, 514 P.2d 111 (1973).

107. Such cases usually involve building permit revocations after the owner has expended funds in reliance upon permission to build. *See* Russian Hill Improvement Assn. v. Bd. of Permit Appeals, 66 Cal. 2d 34, 56 Cal. Rptr. 672, 423 P.2d 824 (1967).

108. State v. Superior Court, 12 Cal. 3d 237, 115 Cal. Rptr. 497, 524 P.2d 1281 (1974); Candlestick Properties, Inc. v. San Francisco Bay Conservation and Dev. Comm'n., *supra* note 41; Golden v. Planning Bd. of the Town of Ramapo, *supra* note 2.

10. Is the regulation acquisitory in nature? If so, it will be invalidated.[109]

In reaching the decisions in many of the cases cited in the foregoing footnotes, courts have discussed the issues in terms of whether there has been a violation of a property right. This mechanical approach has contributed to the complexity and confusion in cases involving a taking issue. Several cases, however, have forthrightly disregarded the property right-labeling analysis and approached the problem from the standpoint of public policy and a standard of fairness.[110]

A good example is *San Diego v. Miller* where the California Supreme Court rejected constrained notions of a labeling process of property interests.[111] In this connection, the court stated:

> Recent decisions, both of this and of the federal courts, have held the property-contract labelling process is not necessarily determinative in questions of due process compensation. *Instead, compensation issues should be decided on considerations of fairness and public policy.* "The constitutional requirement of just compensation derives as much content from the basic equitable principles of fairness . . . as it does from technical concepts of property law."

> [Citations omitted.] "[T]he right to compensation is to be determined by whether the *condemnation has deprived the claimant of a valuable right* rather than by whether his right can technically be called an 'estate' or 'interest' in land." (Emphasis added.)[112]

In *United States v. Willow River Power Co.*,[113] Justice Jackson recognized the actual issue stating:

> But not all economic interests are "property rights"; only those economic advantages are "rights" which have the law back of them, and only when they are so recognized may courts compel others to forbear from interfering with them or to compensate for their invasion. . . . We cannot start the process of decision by calling such a claim as we have here a "property right"; *whether it is a property right is really the question to be answered.* Such economic uses are rights only when they are legally protected interests. . . . (Emphasis added.)[114]

Although *Miller* involves direct condemnation, the principles are generally the same when applied to inverse condemnation.[115]

---

109. Sneed v. County of Riverside, 218 Cal. App. 2d 205, 32 Cal. Rptr. 318 (1963); Peacock v. County of Sacramento, *supra* note 104.
110. Bacich v. Bd. of Control, 23 Cal. 2d 343, 367, 144 P.2d 799 (1943).
111. 13 Cal. 3d 684, 119 Cal. Rptr. 684, 532 P.2d 139 (1975).
112. *Id.* at 143.
113. 324 U.S. 499 (1945).
114. *Id.* at 502–503.
115. *See* People v. Ricciardi, 23 Cal. 2d 390, 144 P.2d 799 (1943).

There is no reason why a standard of fairness should not be utilized in a land use regulation case involving the question of a taking.[116]

E. *Inverse Condemnation: A Postscript*

While the subject of inverse condemnation is much too broad for a thorough discussion here, it should be noted that downzoning action and open space regulatory actions motivated by a managed growth sentiment have given rise to several inverse condemnation lawsuits.

In *Arastra v. City of Palo Alto*,[117] Arastra, Limited, a partnership, brought an action in inverse condemnation in federal district court alleging that the defendant city's ordinance applying open space regulations to its property constituted the acquisition and taking of plaintiffs' real property located in the city. Arastra's property consisted of approximately 515 acres of unimproved land located in an area of the city known as "the foothills."

In 1967, at the time of acquisition, Arastra's property had been zoned for planned community development. A development plan contemplating a 10-acre commercial area and 597 residential lots in a total of 659 acres, including Arastra's land, had also been approved. Plaintiff Arastra subsequently in 1969, however, sought approval of an alternative development plan for the property which would permit, among other things, 1,776 housing units on 243 acres, a 150,000 square foot commercial site, an office complex and approximately 250 acres of open space. In the meantime, however, the city was undertaking a study as to the manner in which the entire foothills area should be developed.

As a result of several studies completed regarding the foothills, the City Council of Palo Alto ultimately voted to deny approval of plaintiffs' alternative development plan. Arastra believed that such action was motivated by the city's intent to purchase its property to preserve it in open space, for land banking purposes, and for a park addition.

The city had adopted an ordinance which added open space district regulations to the Palo Alto Municipal Code. The regulations, which applied to the Arastra property, were intended, *inter*

---

116. This is precisely the approach suggested by Professor Michelman in *Property, Utility and Fairness: Comments on the Ethical Foundations of "Just Compensation" Law*, 80 HARV. L. REV. 1165 (1967).

117. 401 F. Supp. 962 (N.D. Cal. 1975).

alia, to permit the reasonable use of open space land, while at the same time preserving the open space character to assure its continued availability for the containment of urban sprawl.[118] The city was ultimately responsible for designating plaintiff Arastra's land as permanent open space. The city defined "permanent open space" as "lands upon which development is to be permanently prohibited for reason of public health, welfare and safety."[119]

The city did not initiate any lawsuit to condemn Arastra's property, nor did it make any offer to purchase. Arastra thereafter commenced the lawsuit.

The trial court found that the effect of the city's actions was to render the subject property unmarketable for development, especially in light of actions taken just short of actual commencement of eminent domain proceedings. It found, in addition, that since November of 1970 the city had exhibited a policy of intending to acquire the property for the benefit of the community.

The issue which the Palo Alto court decided is as follows:

> If a city with power to do so, decides to acquire property to preserve scenic beauty, open space and the view from a public park and city roads, takes substantially all steps toward doing so, short of payment, leads the public and property owners to believe that the acquisition is inevitable, delays all development of the property while preparing for acquisition, and then, when it has determined that the cost is higher than hoped, on the pretense of protecting against non-existent hazards found to exist without substantial evidence, enacts a zoning ordinance, accomplishing all of the purposes of the acquisition, which purports to allow uses of property which are not economically realistic, with no inquiry as to the economic feasibility of the purported uses, is the resulting loss of value to the property affected compensable?[120]

The court answered in the affirmative. The court was essentially holding that there could be a valid exercise of the police power which requires compensation.

The decision of the *Arastra* court may be viewed narrowly as applicable only to a particular fact situation laden with a series of bad faith municipal actions. On the other hand, the *Arastra* case is precedent for the proposition that an inverse condemnation action may be brought where an open space regulation leaves the property owner with uses which are not economically realistic.

The counterpart to the *Arastra* case in the California state courts

---

118. *Id.* at 971.
119. *Id.* at 972.
120. *Id.* at 981.

is *Eldridge v. City of Palo Alto*.[121] In *Eldridge* the California Court of Appeal considered whether plaintiff Donald Eldridge could state a cause of action in inverse condemnation by alleging that his foothill property (750 acres) had been damaged by the City of Palo Alto's rezoning from single family residential to "open space." The Palo Alto ordinance expressly limited construction of single family dwellings to 10-acre minimum lots. The Court of Appeal reversed the trial court's decision with directions to set aside its order sustaining the demurrer without leave to amend. The *Eldridge* court held that the question of "[w]hether a zoning restriction is so 'arbitrary' or 'unreasonable' or 'burdensome' as to transcend 'proper bounds in its invasion of property rights,' is ordinarily *a question of fact to be determined by trial of the issue, and not by demurrer*."[122] Eldridge did not deny the validity of the ordinance, but sought only compensation for the city's action, which he argued had taken or damaged his property. The *Eldridge* court, like the *Arastra* court, thus held that a zoning ordinance could be a valid exercise of the police power yet require compensation if there were a taking of all reasonable use.[123]

The *Eldridge* case, however, must be viewed within the perspective of the California Supreme Court's ruling in *HFH, Ltd. v. Superior Court*.[124] In *HFH, Ltd.*, the California Supreme Court faced the issue of whether a complaint, alleging that a zoning action taken by a city had reduced the market value of land, stated a cause of action in inverse condemnation. Plaintiffs, HFH and Von's Markets, alleged that the rezoning of their property from commercial to residential resulted in a devaluation from approximately $400,000 to $75,000.[125] The HFH and Von's property is located on one of the quadrants of a four-corner intersection with the three remaining quadrants zoned or in commercial use.

The California Supreme Court held that a mere reduction in market value will not support an action in inverse condemnation. Footnote 16 of the *HFH* decision provides, however, that

> This case does not present, and we therefore do not decide, the question of entitlement to compensation in the event a zoning regulation forbade

---

121. 57 Cal. App. 3d 613, 129 Cal. Rptr. 575 (1976).
122. *Id.* at 628.
123. *Compare*, Dale v. City of Mountain View, 55 Cal. App. 3d 102 (1976).
124. 15 Cal. 3d 508, 125 Cal. Rptr. 365, 542 P.2d 237 (1975), *cert. denied*, 96 S. Ct. 1495 (1976).
125. *Id.* at 512.

substantially *all* use of the land in question. We leave the question for another day.[126]

The *Eldridge* case appears to be the type of case the Supreme Court was describing in footnote 16. It is noted that the California Supreme Court denied a hearing in *Eldridge* after the *Eldridge* court rendered its second opinion, and subsequent to the *HFH, Ltd.*, opinion.

If there are any tentative conclusions to be drawn, one certainly must be that there is a definite distinction in California courts as between complaints in inverse condemnation alleging a mere diminution of value as a result of zoning action and those alleging a total loss of all beneficial use. It appears at present that only the latter case has any chance of success.

While the cases of *Eldridge v. City of Palo Alto* and *Arastra v. City of Palo Alto* are certain to generate more litigation as to the question of what constitutes a loss of all beneficial use of the land, they do give renewed vitality to the United States Supreme Court's admonition, in *Pennsylvania Coal Co. v. Mahon*, to the effect that while property may be regulated, "if regulation goes too far it will be recognized as a taking."[127]

V. Conclusion

In this presentation, an attempt has been made to summarize existing developments in the area of growth control. The subject, however, is a dynamic one and requires constant attention to remain current. It is influenced by ever-changing environmental, economic, and legal developments. Comprehensive state and federal legislation is just as likely to change the rules of the game as are pronouncements made by the courts of the land. Nevertheless, the mandatory preoccupation is worthwhile when it is considered that legitimate growth management action can help produce a better overall living environment. "No-growth" policies, which are synonymous with zero community growth, are an avoidance of the challenge to balance economic, environmental and energy goals. As such they are intolerable. The contemporary pursuit of growth management which is limited to a genuine correlation of resources to population, however, may mean possible salvation from total environmental, social, and economic imbalance.

---

126. *Id.* at 518.
127. 260 U.S. 393, 415 (1922).

Air Rights are "Fertile Soil"

Eugene J. Morris

B.S.S. (C.C.N.Y. 1931), L.L.B. (St. Johns 1934), a partner in the New York law firm of Demov, Morris, Levin & Shein. Mr. Morris has lectured and written widely. He is currently the Chairman of the Special Committee on Federal Navigation Servitude of the Section of Real Property and Probate Trust Law and a member of the Special Committee on Housing and Urban Development, both of which are A.B.A. committees.

I. Introduction

Building one structure on top of another — using air space — is an old idea: the ancient Romans built dwellings on top of aqueducts; from the sixteenth to the eighteenth century houses lined London Bridge; the Rialto Bridge in Venice and Ponte Vecchio in Florence, of even earlier vintage, still have thriving shops and residences. But in the past thirty or forty years, as a result of important technological and legal developments responding to pressing urban needs, the concept of air space utilization has grown into a complex, significant and expanding field.[1]

When we speak of the use of air space or air rights, we refer to the ownership and development of a specified space, located above the ground, independent of and apart from the land or the structure on which it rests. Simply erecting buildings on vacant land does, of course, involve utilization of air space but where there is only a single fee title and the land is developed as both a legal and physical entity with the building or buildings erected on it, we do not have what is characterized as an "air rights" project. Conventional buildings rest on the right to build on land; air rights projects rest on the right to build in air space above some existing independent structure or use, except that one structure rests upon

---

1. Thus, in 1930 one writer commented that the technique had been applied "in transactions so spectacularly important that everyone to whom the underlying theory has been explained has felt in consequence a stirring of the imagination." Ball, *Division Into Horizontal Strata of the Landspace Above the Surface,* 39 YALE L.J. 616, 651 (1930).

the other, or on a platform above a differing use and may share some facilities in common. The key factor in an air rights arrangement is that each of two or more parties has separate and distinct ownership or control of real property located in different horizontal strata yet resting on the same two-dimensional plot of land, and each puts the same plot of land to separate and legally independent uses at the particular strata at which ownership exists.

Many air rights projects have accounted for dramatic and spectacular transformations of whole sections of a city and its skyline. One of the earliest air rights developments in this country was the conversion of New York City's Park Avenue. Once a singularly ugly street blighted by the above ground tracks of the New York Central Railroad, it became a splendid avenue lined by luxurious office and apartment buildings through the expedient of depressing the tracks below street level, and then developing the air rights space above them. Later, in Chicago in 1927, Marshall Field & Co. pioneered in the air rights field by constructing the Merchandise Mart, then the world's largest building,[2] over the tracks of the Chicago and Northwestern Railroad. Soon after, several other buildings were erected over acres of open tracks in the Chicago Loop area: the Chicago Daily News Building, the Chicago Post Office, and the Chicago Sun-Times Building. More recently, Chicago's Prudential Building and

the two cylindrical towers of Marina City were built on air rights over the railroad tracks or over water. In New York City the 59-story Pan Am Building with its heliport stands atop Grand Central Station, as does the new Madison Square Garden sports arena and a 29-story office building on top of the Pennsylvania Railroad's New York terminal.

Although, heretofore, air rights developments have usually been limited to the space above railroad tracks, more recently use has been made of the air space over other buildings, highways and waterways: in Illinois, many "roadside" restaurants have been built, and independently leased, over the state tollway; in Boston, an air rights arrangement has permitted construction of an extension of the state highway system underneath the new Prudential Center; Baltimore's Mercy Hospital has a new 14-story section overhanging an older hospital; and in New York City, the Bridge Apartments (consisting of four 32-story buildings and almost 1,000 apartments) were built over the new approach to the George Washington Bridge. Currently, newly-enacted legislation has permitted the Board of Education of the City of New York to experiment with a plan for the construction of schools with apartment, office and/or industrial buildings above them, utilizing stratified horizontal ownership.[3]

Such projects promise more economic use of land which would otherwise be unproductive and unavail-

---

2. Schmidt, *Public Utility Air Rights*, 54 A.B.A. Rep. 839, 844 (1929).
3. N.Y. ED. LAW, §§ 450-471. (McKinney Supp. 1969). *See* also E.J., Morris, *School Air Rights Development Fund Will Stimulate Building Construction*, Real Estate F., March, 1967, p. 36, April 1967, p. 74.

able for development, thus, helping to meet the pressing need for space in our cities. Air rights' development can mean both convenience and saving for the superjacent or subjacent occupiers in addition to providing increased revenues for the community. Taking advantage of air rights can make some public projects such as schools, hospitals, courthouses and auditoriums more feasible and less costly, cutting the loss of public revenue by preserving taxable property, and often concealing the blighting effects of such improvements as highways, bridge approaches, and railroad rights of way. Thus, the employment of air rights is rapidly developing into an important technique of great value to urban land planners as well as to private developers.

This article will trace the legal basis and current status of air rights, survey generally the characteristics and reasons for air rights' utilization, discuss current developments in the field, and examine some of the legal techniques and problems involved in the development of air rights. There are several articles dealing with the legal basis of air rights and still others which are non-legal treatments dealing with the significance of air rights in urban development.[4]

II. Legal Aspects

1. ANCIENT ORIGINS

The doctrine that horizontal strata of air space may be separately owned and developed as real estate is not inherent in our common law; it developed only quite recently in response to the needs of an increasingly urbanized society.

While air rights are a relatively new concept to the common law, the condominium, adopted by the Anglo-American legal systems from the civil law system, has been traced back as far as the Babylonian law of 2,000 B.C.[5] Currently, at least forty-nine states, the District of Columbia and Puerto Rico, have enacted condominium statutes which provide for the creation, enjoyment and transfer of estates above the surface of the ground.[6]

At common law, air rights were determined according to the familiar maxim, *Cujus est solum, ejus est usque ad coelum,*[7] that is, whoever owns the soil has dominion over the land "up to the skies." Thus, a landowner had the exclusive right to occupy the space above his lands and

---

4. *See, e.g.,* Ball, *supra,* note 1: Ball, *The Jural Nature of Land,* 23 ILL. L. REV. 45 (1928); Ball, *The Vertical Extent of Ownership in Land,* 76 U.PA. L. REV. 631 (1928); Bell, *Air Rights,* 23 ILL. L. REV. 250 (1928); and with the specifics of actual air rights development, *see, e.g., Conveyance and Taxation of Air Rights,* 64 COLUM. L. REV. 338 (1964). Liebman, *Development of Air Rights,* N.Y.L.J. NOTES AND VIEWS, Nov. 12, 13, 14, 15, 1968.

5. *See* Bernard, Urban Land Institute, Technical Bull. #46 (1963); Dalton, N.Y. Times, April 26, 1964, § VIII, p. 1, col. 8, Kerr, *Condominium,* A.B.A. Sec. of Real Property, Probate and Trust Law, Proceedings, p. 19 (1965); Burke, *Condominium Housing for Tomorrow,* MANAGEMENT REPORTS, p. 5 (1964).

6. For a list of such statutes, *see* ROHAN & RESKIN, CONDOMINIUM LAW & PRACTICE, (1966) (appendix B-1). (Vermont is the only state, at the time of this writing, which has not yet enacted such a statute.)

7. COKE, COMMENTARIES ON LITTLETON, § 4a(1670); BLACKSTONE, 2 COMMENTARIES, 18 (1836) KENT COMMENTARIES, 621 (1896).

was entitled to legal recourse when anyone else intruded into his airspace.[8] However, it is some distance from *cujus est solum* to the idea of transferring title to empty space above the ground and to trace its derivation requires a closer examination of the development of the legal meaning of the ownership of land.

The Roman concept of ownership of real property included such rights as *ius disponendi, ius utendi, ius abutendi, ius fruendi,* etc.[9] In English law, it has been defined as a "right indefinite in point of user, unrestricted in point of disposition, and unlimited in point of duration, over a determined thing."[10]

A property owner may, of course, carve out portions of his fee by granting leases, easements and other estates in real property, but the basic ownership of the fee remains perpetual. Air rights are one part of the bundle of rights included in "ownership" of land but what had to be resolved was whether air rights were distinguishable "property rights" that could be independently conveyed.

In resolving this question, two basic competing interpretations of the *cujus est solum* principal arose, namely:

a) the appurtenant theory holding that air rights are appurtenant to ownership of land, and the surface-owner may exercise these rights in the full enjoyment of his land; and

b) the homogeneous space theory stating that air space itself is owned just like the soil, and a title in fee consists of three-dimensional homogeneous space, part of it filled with soil and the remainder air space, to be measured in the two-dimensional terms of "land surface area" for convenience only.

Upon examination of these two interpretations and their implications, it is apparent that the latter is essential to the doctrine of horizontal stratification of ownership of real estate.

2. THE "APPURTENANT" THEORY

The view that air rights are appurtenant to ownership of the land surface has ancient roots. In an agricultural society where the surface level of the land, give or take a few feet, was the source of the value of the land, the early focus of land law was logically, on the surface of the soil. Particularly was this so in a society of limited technology which offered almost no way to make use of the

---

8. The advent of air travel has, of course, necessitated a modification of this doctrine. Congress has declared that "there is recognized and declared to exist in behalf of any citizen of the United States a public right of freedom of transit through the navigable air-space of the United States" (49 U.S.C. § 1304 (1964), and the Supreme Court has declared:
 ... The ancient idea that landlordism and sovereignty extend from the center of the world to the periphery of the universe has been modified. Today the landowner no more possesses a vertical control of all the air above him than a shore owner possesses horizontal control of all the sea before him. The air is too precious an open road to permit it to be "owned" to the exclusion or embarrassment of air navigation by surface landlords who could put it to little real use.
(Northwest Airlines v. Minnesota, 322 U.S. 292 302-03 (1944) (concurring opinion of Jackson, J.)
 9. Ball, *The Vertical Extent of Ownership in Land,* 76 U. PA. L. REV. 631, 645 (1928).
 10. Austin, 2 LECTURES ON JURISPRUDENCE, 817, (3rd ed. 1869).

space much above or below the surface.[11] Thus, in discussing the definition of land, Blackstone writes at length about the solid surface and treats *cujus est solum* almost as an afterthought.[12]

In ancient law, a landowner had rights because they were necessary for the full enjoyment of the surface he owned. Professor Wigmore stated, as recently as 1912, that the proprietary right in realty includes not only the basic right to the surface but "also includes such appurtenant elements as serve to make the land safe for habitation and completely available for economic use as a fixed headquarters of individual activity."[13] Heading his list of "appurtenant elements" is "the space superjacent to the land . . ., without limit as to distance upwards."[14] Since this view, of necessity, was the basis of air rights, it was adopted by the United States Supreme Court in *Causby v. U.S.*[15] in 1946, but in a radically modified form. It held that:

> . . . the airspace is a public highway. Yet it is obvious that if the landowner is to have full enjoyment of the land, he must have exclusive control of the immediate reaches of the enveloping atmosphere . . . The landowner owns at least as much of the space above the ground as he can occupy or use in connection with the land . . . We think that the landowner, as an incident to his ownership, has a claim (to the superjacent airspace) . . .[16]

An invasion of airspace was considered a trespass on real property not because the space was "real property" per se but rather because the invasion had possible effects upon the landowner's freedom to use the surface of the land.[17] In 1815 Lord Ellenborough, C.J., in view of the absurdity of making balloon enthusiasts guilty of trespass, ruled that interference with air space is not a trespass and that "if any damage arises from the object which overhangs the close, the remedy is by an action on the case, not one in trespass."[18] In 1912 Wigmore wrote that whether air space is protected "against any invasion, regardless of damage done, is a question of law still open."[19] In the *Causby* case the Supreme Court did hold that invasions of air space ". . . are in the same category as invasions of the surface,"[20] but the Court failed to distinguish in principle between an invasion that did negligible damage and one that did grave damage.

---

11. Ball. *supra* note 9, at 637.
12. BLACKSTONE. *supra* note 7.
13. WIGMORE SELECT CASES ON TORTS, 855 (1912).
14. *Id.*
15. Causby v. U.S.. 328 U.S. 256 (1946).
16. *Id.* at 264.
17. Ball, U.PA. L. REV., *supra* note 4, at 636.
18. Pickering v. Rudd, 4 Camp. 219, 1 Stark. 581, [K.B.](1815).
19. WIGMORE, *supra* note 13, at 856.
20. Causby v. U.S., *supra* note 15, at 265.

To support the appurtenant theory, then, the distinction between air rights and air space is vital. Space is not owned, only land surface can be owned, but with its ownership goes the right to use the space above and below it. If one does not own land then one cannot own and transfer title to airspace. This position is more clearly demonstrated when we note that among his "appurtenant elements" Wigmore lists the property owner's right to light, air and access. The light-air-access rights are of the same class as air rights; they are part of the package included in owning land-surface. Much as one cannot transfer the year warranty that comes with a new car unless one transfers the car as well, the property owner may not transfer his light-air-access rights without the land to which the rights are appurtenant. Though he may lease his property, he may not, independently, lease his light-air-access rights.[21] The right to occupy air space does not run with air space; it runs with, and is inseparable from ownership of the land (*i.e.*, the surface). The *cujus est solum* maxim is taken literally; airspace belongs to the surface-owner and no one else. In short, then, under this first construction of the maxim, conveyance of "air-rights" cannot be legally accomplished.

The fallacy in the "appurtenant rights" view lies in its origin, namely, the presumption that land is valuable only insofar as its surface may be put to a socially or economically productive use. Urbanization has changed the measure of land value from one based on what the land surface will produce, to a value measured not exclusively by the productivity of the soil, but the location of the land and its physical relationship to other areas of the city.

3. THE "HOMOGENEOUS SPACE" THEORY

The two-dimensional view of land utility, represented by the "appurtenant" theory, has been replaced in our industrial-urban society by a three-dimensional view. Land no longer offers merely a surface to exploit but a trinity of surface, sub-surface and air space which demands to be put to an economic use. Today, the first step in making use of much urban real property is often to eliminate the surface by digging a huge pit for the building foundation. Indeed, the surface area is frequently the least significant creator of value, since the ground floor of so many office buildings serves only to permit access to the more economically productive upper floors. Neither the rentable commercial office space in the new Pan American Building nor the functioning part of the Grand Central Terminal beneath it are located at the land surface. In contrast to the old view, land surface is of value only insofar as it makes possible the use of air space and subsurface space.

Further, more than ever before, modern engineering enables man to move the "surface" at will, levelling and raising mountains and hills and

---

21. New York Elevated R.R. Co. v. Kernochan, 128 N.Y. 559, 29 N.E. 65, (1891); *but see In Re* Elevated R.R. Structures in Forty-Second St., 265 N.Y. 170, 192 N.E. 188 (1934), and *In Re* Third Avenue R.R. Bridge, 27 A.D.2d 135, 276 N.Y.S.2d 674 (1967).

totally changing the contour of the land.[22] Is the law to tell us that every stroke of the bulldozer fundamentally alters the subject of a man's legal title to real property? Much of what distinguishes real property from personal property is its permanence, but then urban real property lacks permanence in a world where today's technologies are available to modify it and the uses to which it can be put both above and below the surface.

Clearly, then, if "land" is to be something of value and have permanence, it cannot be defined in terms of ground, air, or the boundary between ground and air. Contrary to the traditional measurement or delimitation in the two-dimensional terms of "land surface area," the real "land" in law must be three-dimensional space, including surface, air and subsoil, regardless of what fills it. If, in the view of the law, air space is as much "real property" as an acre of farmland, then real property can just as easily be subdivided into horizontal as well as vertical planes.[23]

4. DEVELOPMENT INTO MODERN LAW

Historically, as the economic focus of real estate shifted from agriculture to high-rise building construction it is interesting to trace the evolution of the common law from the appurtenant theory to the homogeneous space theory. The change was gradual and involved an evaluation of whether air space was sufficiently separable from the soil to divide it into horizontal strips which could be conveyed independently of the land or of any other strip.

Early in English Common Law history, there are indications that the society was so land-based that the courts refused to recognize that one could own an apartment or upper chamber of a building and not own the land on which the building was situated.[24] But, once again, necessity reared its head—oddly enough in connection with the problem of providing accommodations for attorneys in England. Originally,

---

22. A dramatic illustration is the excavation in the construction of the World Trade Center in downtown New York City. A huge pit was dug for the foundation of the new structure and the "land" was sold and carted a few blocks away to provide fill for the creation of 21 acres of new "land" along the adjacent shore of the Hudson River. No one today would contend that the newly created land, where the river existed before, belongs to anyone but the owner of the bed of the river while it was still covered with water. The land (or, more accurately, the soil) became personalty when it was excavated, and being sold as such, lost its character as land (or real property).

23. This modern interpretation is subtly, but significantly, different from the older interpretation of Salmond which states that one owns land as well as the space above and below it. Salmond, in JURISPRUDENCE, 7th ed. § 155 (1924), refers to it as "a determinate portion of the earth's surface, the ground beneath the surface down to the center of the world, and the column of space above the surface ad infinitum." The Salmond view ties the ownership of space to the ownership of the land, but the space is more than a mere appurtenant right. It is not owned as a fee in and of itself but, instead, is part and parcel of the fee itself. Thus, a sector of that air space cannot be carved out and owned independently. It goes with the land. He who owns the land, granted, owns the air space and that ownership is absolute (unlike the Wigmore or "appurtenant" theory as was shown in the *Causby* case), but he may not separate the soil from the air.

24. Ball, *supra* note 1, at 619, referring to a case in the year book of 5 Hen. VII 9, where "in answer to a suggestion that a man might have a frank tenement in an upper chamber, it was said that such could not be, for it could not continue, since if the foundation failed, the chamber would be gone."

the Inns of Court in London leased their chambers to tenants but by Coke's time, began to sell them outright.[25] However, the English courts were prompt to stress that if the building were destroyed, the fee would vanish. One owned an apartment in fee, but as yet one was unable to own space in fee without first owning the land below that space, and Ball wryly observed, "His ownership was of fee dignity, although subject to untimely dissolution."[26]

American courts also asserted this condition and, in the Oregon case of *Hahn v. Baker Lodge*,[27] the court held that when a building burned down, the rights of the tenants to their space in the building were lost whether they be fee or leasehold rights; although in the 1860's Illinois and Iowa courts upheld instances of separate ownership of upper and lower stories, and ruled that the parties were not joint tenants, tenants in common, or coparceners, but rather were adjoining owners, each with sole title to a portion of the premises.[28]

A major step was taken in 1870 when an English court treated horizontal strips of air as separate properties in the landmark case of *Corbett v. Hill*.[29] In that case part of plaintiff's property projected over defendant's land (on the second story) above defendant's one-story building. Plaintiff and defendant both took from a common grantor and the overlap was not apparent until defendant sought to build second and third stories on his structure which would be next to, and above, the projecting part of plaintiff's building—forming a kind of interlocking joint. Plaintiff asked for an injunction to prevent defendant from building the additional stories on the theory that he had acquired rights to all the air space above his projection. Defendant maintained that he had the rights to all the space over his section of the land and that the plaintiff's projection itself, was, in fact, illegal. The court indicated that it could not rule that either had an absolute right to the air space. Certainly, plaintiff had no right to air space over the land which he did not own initially. On the other hand, defendant's counterclaim to ownership of all the air space was unrealistic. The court ruled that plaintiff's holding was restricted to the projection itself, but that he did own the air space represented by the projection in fee; a fee carved out of the defendant's air space by the common grantor. The court therefore ruled that defendant could build the floors, but not take plaintiff's holding. Thus, in effect, the court recognized the principle that one could own space quite independently of a building and the land on which it rested. Ball, commenting on the case, observed:

as a consequence of these views, the court in effect recognized that here a vertically limited portion

---

25. *Id.* at 621, citing Coke on Littleton, "A feoffment may be made of an upper chamber over another man's house beneath."

26. *Id.* at 625.

27. 21 Ore. 30, 27 P. 166 (1891).

28. McConnel v. Kibbe, 43 Ill. 12 (1867); McCormick v. Bishop, 28 Iowa 233 (1869).

29. L.R. 9 Eq. 671 (1870).

of the space was the subject of an ownership distinct from that of the space above and below it.[30]

A further step was taken in the English case of *Reilly v. Booth*[31] in 1890 where a building was constructed with a passageway running through its lobby from the street to a garden in back of the house. Plaintiff sold defendant the garden and the rights to "exclusive use of the gateway (to the garden)." Defendant proceeded to decorate the gateway in a manner which offended plaintiff. Plaintiff sued alleging that the decorations had nothing to do with the use of the gateway which was all he had granted. The court ruled that "ownership, not an easement had passed since there is no easement known to the law that gives exclusive and unrestricted use of a piece of land." Thus, the court held that the defendant actually did own a strip of space running through the center of plaintiff's building and could do anything he wished with it.

A major step was taken in 1912 in the United States in the Iowa case of *Weaver v. Osborne*[32] where defendant sold only the second floor of his structure to plaintiff in fee simple. The contract of sale indicated that plaintiff owned in fee the space thirteen feet above the ground to the top of the building. Shortly after the agreement the entire building burned to the ground. Defendant sought to rebuild the structure without granting any space in his new building to plaintiff. Plaintiff brought suit to prevent the construction of the new structure on the ground that he owned the space thirteen feet above the ground in fee simple absolute regardless of the fate of the specific building. He alleged that the space represented by the second floor of the former building still belonged to him, even though that building no longer existed. In what has become a landmark case, the court held that plaintiff had a right to the space and the law thus came full circle from the literal interpretation of the *cujus est solum, ejus est usque ad coelum* maxim. The courts had finally held that one could own space independently of any building or other ground-based structure. Air space itself could now be conveyed and owned, not merely the rights to air space appurtenant to ownership of a piece of land.

The focus of the legal system as applied to real property had shifted to the concept of "space" rather than "land."

Following this breakthrough, in 1915, a South Carolina court upheld an instance of deliberate horizontal stratification of property. The court indicated that if one could make a grant of a mine (subsurface space) one could make a grant of air space and concluded that the defendant was "sovereign of the air over the Watson store which lay above the fourteen foot line.[33] That same year

---

30. Ball, *supra* note 1, at 629.
31. 44 Ch. D. 12 (1890).
32. 154 Iowa 10, 134 N.W. 103 (1912).
33. Pearson v. Matheson, 102 S.C. 377, 382, 86 S.E. 1063, 1065 (1915).

a Montana court held that "the right of an owner to carve out of his property as many estates of interests (perpendicular or horizontal, perpetual or limited) as it may be able to sustain cannot be open to doubt."[34] Eight years later, a Washington court surprisingly called horizontal division of air space a "well-recognized common law right."[35]

From the cases, then, it would seem that the homogeneous space concept of the *cujus est solum* maxim and of the legal nature of land is now accepted and that the conveyance and development of air rights, or air space, has firm legal grounding. In addition, the air rights principle has received recognition in the statute books.

5. EARLIER STATUTORY RECOGNIZATION OF AIR RIGHTS

The nation's first air rights law, adopted by Illinois in 1927,[36] provided that railroads owning real estate in fee may sell, convey, transfer, and lease estates above and below the surface. In 1938, New Jersey adopted a substantially similar provision[37] and went even further by declaring that:

> . . . estates, rights and interests in areas above the surface of the ground whether or not contiguous thereto, may be validly created in persons or corporations other

than the owner or owners of the land below such areas, and shall be deemed to be estates, rights, and interests in lands.[38]

Thus air rights estates are to have the same legal status, in terms of rights, applicability of law, etc., as land estates. Colorado followed suit in 1953[39] and the California Civil Code reflected this change in common law most dramatically when it amended its former statutory definition of land as "the solid material of the earth, whatever may be the ingredients of which it is composed, whether soil, rock, or other substance."[40] In 1963, this law was amended, deleting the word "solid" and adding:

> and includes free or occupied space for an indefinite distance upwards as well as downwards, subject to limitations upon the use of air space imposed, and rights in the use of air space granted by law.[41]

6. MODERN STATUTORY DEVELOPMENTS

The trend established by case and statute law developments up to now is being accelerated as a result of increasing pressure for more buildable space in urban areas. At the Federal level this trend became manifest in 1958, when Congress acted to permit state and local governments:

---

34. Cobban Realty v. Donlan, 51 Mont. 58, 63, 149 P. 484, 487, (1915).
35. Taft v. Washington Mutual Savings Bank, 127 Wash. 503, 508, 221, P. 604, 606 (1923).
36. ILL. REV. STAT. Ch. 114, § 174a (1959).
37. N.J. REV. STAT. § 48: 12-13.
38. *Id.* at § 46:3-19 (1938).
39. COLO. REV. STAT. ANN §§ 118-12-1 (1953).
40. Cal. Civil Code § 659 (1872).
41. *Amended by* Cal. Stats. 1963. Ch. 860 § 5.

To use the air space above and below the established grade line of the Interstate Highway System for the parking of motor vehicles pursuant to agreement between the Federal government and the state highway department, and provided that the parking facility does not interfere with the operation and safety of the highway.[42]

The Bureau of Public Roads of the Department of Commerce has indicated, however, that there will be no grants of air space over the rights-of-way, but only revocable permits or leases.[43]

In the field of housing, the Federal Housing Administration has agreed that a mortgage on air space falls within the scope of the National Housing Act which provides for first mortgages on "real estate, in fee simple or on a leasehold."[44] Similarly, the Urban Renewal Administration of the Housing and Home Finance Agency has issued regulations indicating that § 110(c) of the Housing Act of 1949, as amended, permits the acquisition of air rights for urban renewal projects.[45] In the 1964 Amendments to that act, Congress took a major step by establishing that urban renewal projects may include:

. . . air rights in an area consisting principally of land in highways, railway or subway tracks, bridge and tunnel entrances, or other similar facilities which have a blighting influence on the surrounding area and over which air rights sites are to be developed for the elimination of such blighting influences and for the provision of housing (and related facilities and uses) designed specifically for, and limited to, families and individuals of low or moderate income. . . .[46]

It also provided that the standard definition of an "Urban Renewal Area" requiring that projects be located in a "slum area or blighted, deteriorated or deteriorating area" need not apply. The 1964 amendment has a double significance. It contains the first use of the term "air rights" in any legislation and it encourages the employment of air rights to accomplish one of the purposes for which it is uniquely suited—the covering over of necessary but unsightly and community-blighting facilities.

The Urban Renewal Administration has issued an interesting set of guidelines for these projects which prescribes rules relating to acquisition and re-use value of such sites and outlines four methods for acquiring the air rights: (a) fee support; (b) easements back; (c) perpetual easement for the project and its support; and (d) long term lease, which generally must provide for a single payment in advance for the entire term of the lease. For the purposes of such projects, "air rights" is defined to include "air-

---

42. Federal-Aid Highway Act of 1961 § 104, 23 U.S.C. § 111.

43. *See* B or PR Instructional Memorandum 21-3-62, *Use of Airspace on the Interstate System,* cited by O'Carroll, *Thin Air,* 28 NYS BJ 130, 133. (April 1966).

44. *See also* Crawford, *Some Legal Aspects of Air Rights and Land Use,* 25 Fed. B.J. 167 (1965).

45. *Id.,* at 171.

46. Pub. L. No. 88-560, 42 U.S.C. § 1460 c(1)(iv)(1964)(Housing Act of 1964).

space or development rights above a specified horizontal plane and such surface rights . . . and land" needed for support and access for the structure and to ensure compatability with the subjacent use.[47]

An outstanding example of state and local legislation for implementation of the air rights principle is the recent New York State law providing for use of air rights in connection with school construction.[48] The statute creates the New York City Educational Construction Fund, a new state agency or authority with independent financing powers and authorization to develop schools as part of combined occupancy structures. Under this arrangement, a developer builds the school on the site acquired by the city and owned by the Fund and employs the air rights over the school for the construction of a residential, commercial or industrial building or any combination of these. The capital funds required for the acquisition of the land and construction of the school are obtained by the Fund as a result of the sale of tax exempt five-year short term construction bonds and notes and tax exempt forty-year long term bonds and notes. The debt service retirement on these bonds and notes will be paid by tax equivalency and rental payments called for by the utilization of the air rights above the school structure.

In some instances, where the property is located in a prime area, these air rights payments may ex-

ceed the sum needed to retire the bonds. This surplus can be made available to the Fund and used for other projects which, because of their location, may be unable to produce sufficient revenue to retire the bonds in order to pay for the cost of land acquisition and construction of the school building. Thus, it is estimated that the Fund will be able to pay for the full cost of land acquisition and school construction out of air rights uses on a broad basis in all areas of the city.

In addition to the revenue derived from utilizing air rights on tax exempt property, the concept offers many social advantages and opportunities. Not only does it permit the development of a modern school campus with its attendant advantages, but it also affords opportunities to use precious land in areas where it is badly needed and would not otherwise be available and to diversify the occupancy in a manner which would not otherwise be possible. For one example, vocational schools located beneath related commercial or industrial establishments could offer the enrichment of observation and on-the-job training practice and employment.[49]

Another form of air rights development is the condominium concept of ownership of real property which in the United States grew out of a desire to improve on the cooperative idea. Although the earliest forms of condominiums appear in Babylonian and Roman law and have been commonly used in Civil

---

47. Urban Renewal Administration, Local Public Agency Letter (#324) (February 15, 1965).

48. *Supra* note 3.

49. For a full discussion of this program *see* Liebman *Development of Air Rights,* N.Y.L.J., Notes and Views, Part Four, Nov. 15, 1968.

Law countries for many years, they were relatively new and untried in the United States until early in the 20th Century when cooperative forms of real estate ownership became popular in certain areas and, shortly after World War II, became widespread, particularly in New York City and other large urban centers.

Under the cooperative form of ownership, the real estate (usually a multiple dwelling) is owned by a corporation whose sole stockholders are the tenant-"owners" of the individual apartments they occupy under the terms of occupancy agreements or proprietary leases. Although this form of ownership gained widespread acceptance, both as a means of avoiding the impact of rent control and as a means of developing new luxury or middle income housing, its legal form left much to be desired. Consequently, when the condominium idea was introduced legal scholars and practitioners immediately recognized that the cooperative's purposes could be achieved on a much more practical basis and rest upon a more solid legal foundation.

The condominium, which is really a type of air rights development, is a form of ownership whereby an individual acquires title in fee to an apartment in a multiple dwelling along with the right to participate in the use of the common facilities needed for operation of the multiple dwelling. Thus, in effect, the condominium owner really acquires a fee to air space and is entitled to use that ownership in any

way he sees fit, so long as it is consistent with the contractual requirements involved in the employment of the common facilities needed by all of the tenants in connection with the operation of the property.

The owner, then, is given the opportunity to buy and sell the fee to his property freely, subject only to prior contractual arrangements with other owners in the same building. He is also afforded the right to work out any financing or mortgaging arrangements he desires and to pay his own taxes directly to the taxing authority, altogether independently of other owners in the same building. In all respects, this type of ownership constitutes the ownership of air rights and, in view of its immediate and widespread popularity, within the last few years statutes have been passed formalizing arrangements for condominium ownership and the common facilities requirements in practically all states of the union.[50]

The various statutes serve to simplify and unify the procedure for the development of condominiums and we may anticipate a considerable development of the condominium form in future real estate ventures, most particularly, in housing.

A dramatic illustration of the advantages of the condominium form of air rights ownership is furnished by a study of the United Nations Plaza building in New York City, where air rights ownership of a multiple-use building was arranged on the basis of conventional legal documents without employment of the condominium statute which, at the

---

50. *See supra* note 6.

time the building was developed, had not as yet been enacted into law in the State of New York.[51] The structure consists of four separate units of ownership (a garage, an office building and two separate residential cooperative towers) and was built on the basis of each of the separate and distinct ownerships entering into covenants and agreements with the co-owners which prescribed and delineated the rights of the cooperative owners to the common facilities contained in the building and with respect to each other. These agreements, consisting of four deeds, totalling more than six hundred printed pages, spell out minute detail all of the reciprocal rights of the four owners and delineate in three-dimensional terms the area owned by each of the participants in the venture. Adding to this complex situation is the fact that two of the owners are separate cooperative apartment houses in each of the towers operating under totally independent ownership and with all the attendant rights and obligations of each having to be spelled out in detail. In all likelihood, had the condominium form of ownership been possible when this project was developed, the documents could have been far shorter and simpler, resulting in greater clarity and ease in ascertaining the rights of the various parties to the total project. Instead, the property is generally re-

garded as one of the most complicated air rights developments worked out in this country up to now.

Air rights projects are not restricted to space over solid land; space over rivers, lakes and bays may often be adapted to new construction through the use of supporting piers or caissons.

One restriction, however, upon utilization of air space above navigable waterways is the existence of the legal doctrine of "navigation servitude."[52] This doctrine, implicit in the commerce clauses of the Federal Constitution, states that navigable waterways used in interstate commerce are in the public domain and that the federal government may seize or order the removal of any structure located in a navigable waterway without having to pay damages to its owner.[53] The severity in applying this doctrine is mitigated in part by a procedure whereby Congress declares that a particular section of a navigable waterway, upon which some structure is sought to be erected, is henceforth "non-navigable"[54] — constituting, in effect, a waiver of the government's right to seize or remove a structure without compensation to the owner. Nevertheless, even after a Congressional declaration of "non-navigability," title insurance for an air rights project over water may be difficult to obtain[55] with the

---

51. N.Y. REAL PROP. LAW, §§ 337-39(c)(McKinney Supp. 1967).
52. *Underwater Land and the Navigation Servitude"* COLUM. J. OF L. & SOCIAL PROBLEMS, pp. 5-6 May 2, 1966.
53. Greenleaf-Johnson Lumber Co. v. Garrison, 237 U.S. 251 (1915).
54. *See, e.g.,* 33 U.S.C. § 27 (1964).
55. Schlitt, *Waterfront Renewal Held Back by Obscure Legal Impediment,* 156 N.Y.L.J. 1s (Sept. 12, 1966).

result that private development in this area is, for all practical purposes, barred.[56]

The posture of the law today, then, is that "real property" is simply three-dimensional space defined by two-dimensional border lines running from the center of the earth "to the skies" (*i.e.*, to just below the navigable air space)[57] and the landowner may convey any part of his three-dimensional land whether contiguous to the surface of the soil or not.

Increasingly, public policy is resorting to the air rights principle as a tool for helping to achieve such diverse benefits as urban renewal, community development, better education, more effective employment of waterfront areas and increased revenues. Clearly, an appreciation of the value and usefulness of air rights is growing and federal, state and local governments are now seeking actively to take advantage of the principle.

Let us now turn to a consideration of the practical methods of conveyancing air rights.

III. The Air Rights Transaction

Once the need and legal foundation for separate air rights ownership became firmly established, lawyers sought ways to effectuate the conveyance, ownership and use of these rights. The rights themselves are, of course, no different than other rights affecting real property in general. The same principles of statute and case law govern; the only variations are those resulting from the physical differences created by the ownership of air space, such as three-dimensional descriptions, reciprocal easements, common facilities and the need for physical support of the structures.

1. CONVEYANCES OF AIR RIGHTS

The conveyance of air rights (i.e., the transfer of the right to own or use a certain volume of air space above a limiting plane or planes) is accomplished by an instrument which describes the condition and duration of the specific air rights conveyed, the method of supporting and servicing the structures to be built, and the configuration of the air space being transferred.

Three basic methods of conveying air rights are currently in use: A) The Lease, B) The Fee Simple Absolute, and C) The Easement Back.

(A) THE LEASE:

The lease for a period of years is the most frequently employed method of conveying an interest in air space, and is the one used in the development of the air rights over the New York Central Railroad's tracks on Park Avenue in New York City for more than fifty years. An air rights' lease in many ways resembles a conventional real estate lease.[58] In addition to the usual pro-

---

56. Currently, the Special Committee on the Navigation Servitude of the American Bar Association's Section of Real Property, Probate and Trust Law, is seeking enactment by Congress of a statute to modify the doctrine of the navigation servitude, but at the time of this writing, no bill has yet been introduced in Congress.

57. Congress has declared that "there is recognized and declared to exist in behalf of any citizen of the United States a public right of freedom of transit through the navigable air space of the United States" (49 U.S.C. § 1304 (1964)).

58. Brennan, *Lots of Air–A Subdivision in the Sky,* 12 TITLE NEWS 1, (Jan. Feb. 1957).

visions involved in conventional long-term leases, an air rights lease makes provision to insure adequate support for any new structures planned for the air space. A general easement of support, analogous to the common law easement of support from subjacent (*e.g.,* mines) and adjacent lands, will probably be necessary as a matter of course.[59] Moreover, specific provision should be made for the placement of columns and footings for lateral support of the air rights structure. The subjacent owner may require that provisions be included for access to the surface, maintenance facilities, and perhaps, as was the case in Park Avenue, the right to run ventilation shafts up through the air rights structures and to maintain special equipment relating to the supporting use below, such as power lines for railroads or illumination for a highway. Likewise, the air rights user must make adequate provision for ingress and egress and for utilities such as gas, electric, heat, air conditioning, sewers, water, and other essential elements.

To render the project feasible, the leasehold must be mortgageable, which means that liens on the subjacent property must either be subordinated or excluded from the air rights areas. The New York Central Railroad used an elaborate system of grants, leases and holding companies in order to clear up title to the air rights it conveyed.[60] Generally, in leasing air space, the description of the space is simple if it is above a railway or highway but becomes more complex if it is located above an existing building or one about to be constructed, since the description and survey must delineate the three-dimensional space boundaries with precision.

(B) THE FEE SIMPLE ABSOLUTE:

It is frequently desirable or necessary that the entire fee to the space above a certain plane be transferred. The various fee methods differ, of course, with the nature of the interest in the land conveyed and the nature and quantity of the air rights conveyed.

(1) *The Support Easement Method*

Here, the subjacent owner conveys title to the air space in fee and retains title to all the space beneath the specified plane, while granting to the air rights developer an easement to run support columns and related structures through the space beneath the plane, as well as easements to the common facilities required for each of the fee holders. As in the case of a lease, the placement of supports is precisely spelled out in advance. If such precision is not possible, provision must be made for agreeing on their locations. For example, the agreements for the Washbridge Apartments, built over the entrance to the George Washington Bridge in New York City, provided that the means of support would be determined by the City of New York with the approval of the Chief Engineer of the Port of New York Authority.[61] Un-

---

59. *Conveyance and Taxation of Air Rights, supra* note 4.
60. *Id.* at 343.
61. *Id.* at 349.

der a support easement arrangement, the air space owner does not get actual ownership of the space occupied by his support structures although, of course, he owns the structures themselves and the air space which has been conveyed to him in fee.

(2) *The Fee Support Method*

The fee support method, which is one of the earliest techniques used, is extremely complex and demands the utmost degree of precision. The classic example of its use is the Chicago Merchandise Mart of the Marshall Field Company, built over the Chicago & Northwestern Railroad's tracks. In the fee support conveyance, the air space owner obtains fee title to cylinders or columns of "ground space" through which he may run his supports. Circles, squares or other appropriate configurations corresponding to the shape of the supporting members are designated on the plat and the deed states that the air space owner is granted all the space above and below those configurations or "ad coelum et ad inferno," as Blackstone would have it. Also, as a practical matter, the builder is frequently granted some extra space for the "belling out" of his columns at their base for additional support or space needed during the construction period. The plat for the Merchandise Mart, in addition to marking out several "air lots" included no less than 296 cylinder and prism lots for support.[62] Needless to say, a fee support conveyance requires the expert skills of lawyers, architects and engineers in its preparation and execution.

(C) THE EASEMENT BACK:

In the easement back method, the air rights developer becomes the fee owner of the entire parcel but grants to the subjacent user a permanent easement or a lease for a term of years. Sometimes, of course, the distinction between a support easement and an easement back agreement may be only a matter of semantics. For example, the deed for the Chicago Daily News Building over the Chicago Union Station conveyed to the News "the entire interest in the property . . . excepting therefrom the space below a designated plane, and excepting from the exception the right to run columns and foundations through the excepted space." However, in a conventional easement back deed, the subjacent owner would not retain title to the subsurface space, but only an easement to that part which it needed for its operation, with counter easements for support for the superjacent structure.

2. COMPARISON OF METHODS

The choice of a particular method of conveyance may be in some part a matter of personal predilection but ordinarily it will be determined by the particular circumstances encountered in each project, including financing requirements and the tax and other needs of the parties to the transaction. Among any number of possible factors, the nature of the ownership of the land involved, the laws governing the surface or sub-

---

62. Bell, *supra* note 4, at 261.

surface user, mortgaging and other financing arrangements, and architectural and engineering considerations must all be taken into account in drawing up the instrument of conveyance in an air rights project.

Sometimes the choice between lease and fee may be dictated by statute. For example, Congress has allowed the construction of various facilities on the air rights of the Interstate Highway System[63] but the Bureau of Public Roads of the Department of Commerce has ruled that only leases and not grants of fee can be allowed.[64] On the other hand, since some financing agencies have been reluctant to advance funds on a lease, acquisition of title would be required if such funds are needed.[65]

Real estate taxes and assessments are other considerations that must be kept in mind in arranging an air rights transaction. The method of conveyance will, to a large degree, determine the assessment of taxes on the parties involved. If the conveyance is by lease or an easement back method, then only one "landowner" is on the property and hence there would be in most instances only one assessment. In such cases, an agreement would have to be worked out between the two occupying parties. For example, in the case of the Chicago Daily News-Union Station development, it was agreed that if the properties were not taxed separately, the station would pay one-third of the tax on the fee and the News would pay two-thirds. Each was to pay for assessments on his own improvements, and the News was to pay all special assessments.[66] However, with a fee support or support easement deed, there are actually two separate property owners and two parcels of property. Land taxation is rooted in the concept of two-dimensional land, but there is little reason why tax assessors cannot become accustomed to the idea of splitting the bill between two or more property owners on the same lot, each "property" being valued as a separate parcel of realty. New York City retains the right to "apportion any assessment in such manner as it shall deem just and equitable,"[67] and, in general practice, the City follows apportionments provided in contracts or requested by both parties.[68]

The method of allocating the assessed value of the real property to the subjacent and superjacent areas can vary from jurisdiction to jurisdiction. The main problem is one of determining the correct assessment of the total fee simple absolute, and then allocating that amount to the various estates in real property, including the air rights use on the basis of ordinary principles of real estate valuation. The problem would, of course, be complicated by situations where part of the use, either in the air rights or the subjacent use, involves tax exempt property. For example, in the Bridge Apartments Project in New York City,

63. 23 U.S.C. § 111.
64. *Supra* note 43.
65. *Conveyance and Taxation of Air Rights, supra* note 4, at 343.
66. Bell, *supra* note 4, at 262.
67. N.Y.C. ADM. CODE § 172-1.0 (1957).
68. *Conveyance and Taxation of Air Rights, supra* note 4, at 351.

the air rights development is located above a tax exempt use -- consisting of a highway approach to the George Washington Bridge — amounting to a privately owned taxable apartment house constructed in the air space above a public road. In such case the same principles of allocation of value are required, but then one part of the allocated value is exempted as required by law.

3. PROBLEMS

We can get a clearer view of the problems involved in an air rights transaction if we focus our attention, for a moment, on the case of the air space over railroad tracks and facilities. In an air rights transaction, the goal is to put the air rights clearly and securely into the hands of someone capable of developing them and in a condition suitable for development. Especially in the case of railroads, but similarly for other properties, the legal problems may be divided into four main categories: (a) questions of title, (b) mortgages and other encumbrances on the property, (c) competing needs of the railroad and its superjacent neighbor, and (d) land and code enforcement requirements.

In our large cities, the railroads generally need to occupy considerable amounts of land for track rights-of-way, yards and terminals. Since terminals and converging tracks are often located in the core of the business district (or the business district has tended to grow up around the railroad terminal), this land is prime real estate.[69] Land held by railroads, however, is often restricted by statute to be used for railroad activities,[70] and constructing housing and office buildings can scarcely be considered a proper railroad activity. In order to develop this air space, it may be necessary to transfer it to an outside developer. However, where the railroad does own the land in fee, free of restrictive covenants or limitations, it may readily sell, lease, or otherwise transfer parts of that land, including air space, to another party for development. Although the approval of governmental public service or commerce commissions having jurisdiction may be required, railroads are generally permitted to dispose of property not required for railroad purposes.

Frequently, however, a railroad is not the fee owner of the land in its right-of-way. The land is sometimes held by lease, license, easement, or, at best, by a determinable fee. In such cases, of course, the railroad cannot sell the air space since it does not own a conveyable interest in it. At the same time, the owner of the reversionary interest cannot develop the air rights over the railroad, since the railroad usually has "the exclusive right to the use and possession of the property, during the term of its corporate existence and for the purpose of its corporation."[71] In many instances a railroad has rights to the air space only during the period of its operation as a railroad but, since the

---

69. Urban Land Inst. Tech. Bulletin, *supra* note 5.
70. *See, e.g.,* the New York Railroad Act of 1850, *as amended.*
71. Kip v. N.Y. Cent. R.R. Co., 40 Misc. 62, 250 N.Y.S. 5,9 (1931) referring to land acquired by the railroad through condemnation.

railroad might quite conceivably discontinue operations as no longer profitable, a long term lease under this type of ownership would be technically unfeasible because the lease would fall with the discontinuance of the railroad's right to operate.

Similar problems arise from mortgages and bonds on the railroad's property. Railroads are financed by mortgages covering all their property, including their air space. With such a lien on the property, it would be difficult to obtain financing for the construction of an office building or housing project.

These problems of title and mortgage liens on air space require careful attention and solution before a project can begin, but they are not insurmountable. Where the railroad does not own the fee to its land, an arrangement may be worked out whereby the developer of the air space can acquire a sufficient interest in the property to permit development. One method is for the railroad to purchase the reversionary interest from the fee owner.[72] Similarly, various kinds of joint agreement among the railroad, the remainderman, and the would-be air space developer can be worked out for transferring title to the air space. This method might involve a sale, or a lease from both the railroad and the holder of reversionary interest. Whatever specific technique is used, "the owner of the fee and the railroad company must join in the grant."[73]

Bonds and mortgages on railroad property generally provide for a release of the property from the lien of the mortgage (if the trustees are willing) in the event that the railroad sells or contracts to sell portions of its real estate, such as air space, not needed for the operation of the railroad. However, such a release may not be permissible on a mere lease of property; consequently, in this situation, a sale would be required.[74]

In all of the kinds and varieties of transactions suggested so far, it is important that the operation of the railroad itself not be impaired, lest the interests of the railroad's owners or mortgage-holders be detrimentally affected. This is especially true in providing for physical support for, and access to, the air rights project. The developer must obtain enough air, surface and subsurface space to meet his needs, but no property necessary to the operation and maintenance of the railroad may be taken. The problem involved is not only legal but architectural and engineering as well, and must be resolved prior to the time the instrument of conveyance is drafted.

Local land use and code requirements can also create problems in air rights conveyancing. For example, where the nature of the uses differ, zoning suitable to the subjacent use (as for a railroad) would often bar the proposed superjacent use and either a zoning change or a variance might be required. More-

---

72. Corning v. Lehigh RR, 14 App Div. 2d 156, 217 NYS 2d 874 (4th Dept. 1961).
73. Schmidt, *supra* note 2, at 842.
74. *See* Becker, *Subdividing the Air-A New Method of Acquiring Air Rights*, CHI-KENT L.R. 40, 41 (Extra vol. 1931), and Ball, *supra* note 1, at 652.

over, the nature of the subjacent use might give rise to code requirements which would not be applicable if the subjacent use were different or were not there at all. Thus, for example, the fire retarding requirements for housing could be quite different if it is built above an operating railroad.

IV. Conclusion

Many of the problems we have outlined are by no means unique to air rights transactions and, as is also the case in similar fields, the problems vary greatly from case to case and require custom-tailored solutions each time. Available to the lawyer today is the pioneering experience in handling air rights projects in Chicago and New York thirty to fifty years ago and examples of how similar cases have been dealt with, but he will find ample room in the air rights field for bold, imaginative, creative, work and thought. Few valid generalizations can be made, since the details and circumstances of an air rights transaction are just as complex and varied as those in conventional real property transactions. The lawyer must know the facts in the case, the needs and wishes of the parties involved, and the kinds of techniques that have been used in the past and start from there.

Transfer Development Rights—
A Pragmatic View

Hershel J. Richman

Bean, DeAngelis and Kaufman; Solicitor,
Bucks County Planning Commission, Doylestown,
Pennsylvania, November, 1974 to March, 1976;
presently environmental consultant to Bucks
County, Pennsylvania; Adjunct Professor of
Environmental Law, Graduate School, Drexel
University; J.D., Villanova Law School (1967);
B.A., B.S., Pennsylvania State University (1964).

Lane H. Kendig

Director, Lake County Department of Planning,
Zoning and Environmental Quality, Waukegan,
Illinois; Director of Community Planning, Bucks
County Planning Commission, Doylestown,
Pennsylvania (1972–76); Masters of Regional
Planning, University of North Carolina (1968);
Bachelor of Architecture, University of
Michigan (1962).

I. Introduction

THE TRANSFER OF DEVELOPMENT RIGHTS (TDR) has exploded on
the planning scene. Although interest started slowly, law and planning scholars began to spread the word in the early 1970s, and
many communities started to seriously consider TDR.

The interest in TDR is primarily related to its potential in avoiding the eminent domain—taking deadlock[1] which has received widespread discussion in recent years. Despite all the scholarly rhetoric,
however, there is a relative paucity of adopted ordinances which
can be used to evaluate TDR. Our purpose here is not to add to the
basic discussion of TDR in theory, but to share our experiences as
consultants who have written a working TDR zoning ordinance for
Buckingham, one of Bucks County's townships, and to identify legal and planning problems and our solutions.

---

1. A major discussion of this is F. BOSSELMAN, J. CALLIES & BAUTA,
THE TAKING ISSUE (1973); *See also* Costonis, *Whichever Way You Slice It,
DTR* (Development Transfer Rights) *Is Here To Stay*, PLANNING (July,
1974).

II. Buckingham—The Setting and
Planning for Agriculture

Bucks County lies in the Boston-Washington megalopolis and shares a common boundary with the city of Philadelphia. Buckingham Township is a suburban fringe township approximately 25 miles from the center of Philadelphia. In 1970, about 24 percent of the Township's 21,000 acres of land had been consumed by low-density suburban development, often known as urban sprawl, and two-thirds of the residents lived in subdivisions with lot sizes varying from one to five acres. There remained some 13,000 acres of good, productive agricultural land which most farmers wanted to continue farming.

Bucks County had been the fastest growing county in Pennsylvania since 1950, and heavy pressure for urbanization was being focused on that portion of the county around Buckingham. This pressure raised land values and taxes making it impossible for farmers to hold or buy land for agricultural purposes. When the farmers began selling out and leaving, the new suburban residents, fearing destruction of the rural atmosphere, sought ways to keep it, and became even more vocal in support of agricultural preservation than the farmers and large landowners. In the Comprehensive Plan[2] which was adopted by the Planning Commission on March 19, 1974, and by the Board of Supervisors on April 10, 1974, the Township identified as one of its primary goals to "protect and preserve the Township's agricultural industry," although it recognized the difficulty in achieving that goal.

The Plan noted that farmers and landowners have investments in their land, and that preservation of agriculture could not be accomplished without first arriving at a fair method of compensating individuals for any loss in their investment. In order to accomplish the twin objectives of preservation and compensation, the Planning Commission planned to complete a detailed analysis of alternatives, to hold public hearings, and to submit recommendations to the Township which would then adopt land use control in the form of a new zoning ordinance. Studies of these proposals would be carried out by a subcommittee on agricultural zoning composed of five to seven members. The majority of the agricultural subcommittee was to be farmers or large landowners. Additional groups could

---

2. BUCKS COUNTY PLANNING COMM'N. STAFF, BUCKINGHAM TOWNSHIP COMPREHENSIVE PLAN (1974).

have been formed to research special areas of concern. The programs to be investigated or worked on included: farmland assessment methods, a public development rights acquisition program, the concept of transferring development rights, and alternative, less restrictive zoning methods.

The Comprehensive Plan set a general framework for the Township's land use, although it did not finalize policy for the agricultural district. In general, the plan divided the Township into two basic districts: a development district designed to accommodate the twenty-year growth of the Township in keeping with regional population projections, and a rural area. The development district was further divided into conventional use and density classifications. The rural area contained both an agriculture and a resource protection zone. After a heated debate between the farmers and the civic groups, a combination of a voluntary TDR system and performance zoning[3] for agricultural preservation was developed. Both options were designed to balance two views of the land: land as a commodity and land as a resource. The landowner (farmer) was permitted to transfer the potential to develop his land to parcels held by other landowners (development district).[4] Performance zoning, the second option available to the landowner if he chose not to transfer his development rights, is an extreme form of clustering. This clustering permits a gross density of .5 dwellings[5] per acre but requires that 90 percent of the land be set aside as permanent open space.

III. Why TDR?

Over the past decades planners have explored many ideas to supplement zoning to reach preservation goals. The use of easements was one method which was examined closely by Buckingham officials since a notable early effort had been the beautifully-done (but never implemented) 1968 plan to preserve the Brandywine River's floodplains and stream corridors. That plan called for the purchase of easements on some 11,000 acres at $180 per acre.[6] That same

---

3. BUCKS COUNTY PLANNING COMM'N., PERFORMANCE ZONING 40–41 (1973).

4. BUCKS COUNTY PLANNING COMM'N, THE URBAN FRINGE (1970).

5. In Buckingham, one-acre lots have been yielding an average .75 dwellings per acre because of soils, parcel shape and size and other natural features.

6. CHESTER COUNTY WATER RESOURCES AUTH., THE BRANDYWINE PLAN 3 (1968).

year, the Pennsylvania General Assembly passed the Conservation and Land Development Act, Public Law 442,[7] which specifically authorized the Department of Forest and Waters (superseded by the Department of Environmental Resources) and the Department of Agriculture, as well as the counties of the Commonwealth, to use the power of condemnation to protect open space and conserve natural resources "including farmland, forests, and a pure and adequate water supply."[8] The Conservation and Land Development Act did not specifically authorize townships, such as Buckingham, to use this particular power of condemnation, and there is no specific authorization within the condemnation powers granted to the township for purchase of development rights or easements. The inability of Buckingham to use Public Law 442, however, was not the main impediment to its adopting the purchase of development rights or easements (as used in Suffolk County, New York), since a cooperative arrangement with Bucks County to implement such a scheme probably could have been worked out. The main impediment was cost. The initial cost to the community of Public Law 442, or similar techniques to preserve land with easements, most likely would be between 80 and 90 percent of full market value, an amount beyond the reach of the community given any acceptable level of public indebtedness.

The farmers suggested preferential taxation as a solution to the problem. The preferential tax systems, although helpful to farmers, are not really a land use control device but simply a means of altering the economics of farming in urban areas. The real cause of the loss of farm land, the differential between the values of land for urban and agricultural uses, remains unchanged with preferential assessment so that at its best it is only an incentive to avoid premature conversion. The ultimate rate of conversion to urban use is not affected.

Various types of zoning were examined for their potential to protect agriculture. Conventional zoning into minimum size lots will preserve agriculture only if the lots are extremely large, at least 40 acres. Although there is nothing specifically within the Municipalities Planning Code[9] which grants a right to classify by size, the broad general purposes of the Municipalities Code (Section 105)

---

7. Act of January 19, 1968, Pub. L. No. 442.

8. Act of January 19, 1968, Pub. L. No. 442.

9. Pennsylvania Municipalities Planning Code; Act 247 of 1968, *as amended by* Act 93 of 1972.

and the references specifically to the zoning purposes and classifications as contained in Article VI of the Municipalities Planning Code provide an umbrella under which such a classification could be justified.[10]

In light of the judicial decisions by the California and Utah courts in *Gisler v. County of Madera*[11] and *Morgan County v. Stephens*[12] there could be judicial support for a zoning classification to effectuate the preservation and protection of agricultural lands and activities. However, large-lot zoning faces a tough battle in Pennsylvania because of the series of exclusionary zoning cases starting with the *Girsh Appeal* in 1970.[13] The real issue is whether such zoning promotes agriculture or housing. Realistically, the result is housing rather than the preservation of agriculture. Large-lot zoning requires the withdrawal of huge acreages to house a few families and is actually counter-productive.

Just as with easements, large-lot agricultural zoning has to overcome political and economic barriers which again are more formidable than the questions of legality. Experience shows that this alternative is unacceptable to farmers in many urbanizing areas due to the differential between existing land values (with potential for urban development) and the agricultural use values.

The third program considered was a scheme to transfer development rights. Although there is no specific enabling legislation contained within the Municipalities Planning Code or in other legislative enactments, it is believed that the transfer of developmental rights plan could be legitimately established under the Municipalities Planning Code. The Pennsylvania Supreme Court in its landmark "exclusionary zoning" cases has supported the municipality's right to adopt innovative zoning ordinances[14] to more effectively meet the demands of evolving growing communities.[15] Although the Supreme Court of Pennsylvania has never faced a zoning scheme

---

10. In addition, PA. CONST. art. A, § 2 (b)i, and the Pennsylvania Farm Land and Forest Land Assessment Act of December 19, 1974, Pub. L. No. 973, 72 Pa. Stat. 5490.1, and the Act of January 13, 1966, Pub. L. No. 1292, *as amended*, 16 Pa. Stat. 11941 (commonly referred to as Act 515) deal with the preservation of agricultural lands.

11. 38 Cal. App. 3d 305, 112 Cal. Rptr. 919 (1974).

12. 520 P.2d 1340 (Utah 1974).

13. 437 Pa. 233, 263 A.2d 416 (1970).

14. Girsh Appeal, 437 Pa. 233, 263 A.2d 416 (1970); National Land Inv. Co. v. Easttown Township Bd. of Adjustment, 419 Pa. 504, 215 A.2d 597 (1965).

15. National Land Inv. Co. v. Easttown Township Bd. of Adjustment, 419 Pa. 504, 215 A.2d 597 (1965).

utilizing transfer of development rights from one parcel to another, it has faced a similar dilemma when planned unit developments were in their infancy. In *Cheney v. Village 2 at New Hope*,[16] the validity of planned unit development was upheld before the adoption of enabling legislation. The court stressed the power of local legislative bodies to be creative in their pursuit of good regulations. Thus, if a council reasonably believed that a given district could contain all types of structures, with no density limitations and with no adverse affects on health, safety and morals, such a district could be created.

At the time of our review of the transfer of development rights scheme, we did not have the benefit of the New York Court of Appeals decision in *Fred F. French Investing Co., Inc., v. City of New York*[17] which supported a transfer of development rights scheme even though the municipal ordinance itself was unacceptable.

> It is recognized that the "value" of property is not a concrete or tangible attribute but an abstraction derived from the economic uses to which the property may be put. Thus, the development rights are an essential component of the value of the underlying property because they constitute some of the economic uses to which the property may be put. As such, they are a potentially valuable and even a transferable commodity and may not be disregarded in determining whether the ordinance has destroyed the economic value of the underlying property.[18]

Thus, the broad enabling legislation in Pennsylvania (Municipalities Planning Code), as well as case law establishing the wide latitude available to municipalities in establishing its land use regulations, led us to the conclusion that transfer of development rights in Pennsylvania was a legitimate use of the zoning powers of a municipality.

After the determination that both agricultural zoning districts and a transfer of development rights scheme were legally possible, the choice of method to preserve agricultural land was left to the community. Our dilemma in Buckingham was that extreme resource protection does not permit an acceptable economic use. The root of the problem is the economic differential between agricultural value and development value. TDR is the bridge which enables the community to regulate under the police power while assuring a new method for the private market place to compensate the landowner

---

16. 429 Pa. 626, 241 A.2d 81 (1968).
17. 39 N.Y.2d 587, 350 N.E.2d 381, 385 N.Y.S.2d 5 (1976).
18. *Id.* at 11.

(farmer) for the difference between regulated value and a reasonable use value. As a device to preserve the land and protect its value, the Pennsylvania Farmers Association has endorsed the concept of transfer of development rights and urged its implementation on a statewide basis for purposes of preserving agricultural soils.[19]

The transfer of development rights requires a mechanism which changes an intangible property right (the right to develop property) to an economic, saleable asset. The theory is simple. A restricted landowner is given certificates embodying his development rights which can be used for building on other land in the municipality. In selling the certificates, the landowner receives compensation for the severed development value of his property. The landowner still retains ownership, and the land still retains some residual value, even though it is now permanently restricted to agricultural use.[20] Buckingham Township has chosen to use TDR for agricultural preservation. TDRs could also be used to preserve other resources such as scenic areas, large floodplains or wetlands.

IV. How Much Will It Preserve?

TDR is not a panacea; it depends on the private real estate market, hence the amount of land that can be preserved will be directly related to a community's expected growth and the price of land. For example, Buckingham had a development area that could accommodate 3,000 additional dwellings. How many acres could TDR preserve? Certainly, it could not support the 13,000 acres of farmland remaining. In Buckingham, the land values were at a level which required the allocation of one certificate per acre of restricted farmland to arrive at a fair compensation. If land had been twice as expensive, we would have had to allocate about three certificates per acre of farmland, and only 1,000 acres could have been preserved. Thus, land value at the inception of a TDR system is a critical factor affecting how much can be preserved.

Buckingham's willingness to absorb 3,000 additional dwellings in one area of the Township, over and above the 1,700 which would be permitted as a matter of right, is also important in determining how much will be preserved. Our experience indicates that the pub-

---

19. THE PENNSYLVANIA FARMERS ASS'N, REPORT OF THE COMPREHENSIVE LAND USE PLANNING STUDY COMM'N, PFA Policy 1 (1975).

20. On the first sale of deed-restricted agricultural land in Buckingham, the price was in excess of $1,500 per acre, although $1,000 is a more reasonable price for most agricultural uses.

lic needs to be convinced of the value of a trade-off: development by right for preservation of agricultural land. In addition, there will probably be extensive pressure to lower or eliminate any development by right. This obviously has exclusionary and economic implications. It is recommended that the zoning should be able to stand on its own as being non-exclusionary and not depend entirely on TDR.

There is a third very important factor to consider regarding the capacity of a development area: the housing market in the municipality. We estimated, based on the county's housing plan, that it would take approximately 25 to 30 years for the Buckingham market to absorb 4,700 new dwellings. Thus, even if the Township had set aside land for 13,000 dwellings over and above that allowed by right, the time period required to absorb that number of units would be an important factor in the ability of a TDR system to fairly compensate landowners.[21]

Planners can only guess as to whether people will speculate on development rights in a very low housing demand situation; if they do not, serious trouble would arise within a mandatory TDR plan. This problem is less serious with a voluntary system. In Buckingham, the farmers have been disappointed in the small demand for development rights, a problem aggravated by lack of sewer capacity and the recent housing slump.

We believe that TDR would have limited value in very rural communities which have low land values and little development pressure. If agricultural zoning with very large lots cannot be achieved, TDR on a voluntary basis should be set up so that maximum advantage can be taken of the small differential between development and agricultural values. TDR appears to work best in the rapidly

---

21. There are several concerns relating to a by-right density. In strong exclusionary zoning states such as Pennsylvania or New Jersey, the fair share of regional growth must be identified, and the zoning without TDR should not be exclusionary. A market study was examined as another alternative to regional housing plans but was rejected in Buckingham as too expensive. Basic economic fairness is another concern; TDR seeks to maintain existing values for farmers. Land in a development district is more valuable because of proximity to sewers and other services. If these services are not in the area, it should not be a development district. The values created by existing zoning must likewise be given full consideration. It would be unfair to set the by-right zoning in the development area so low as to decrease land values while trying to maintain them in the agriculture district. These concerns may not be a legal necessity but are vital economic and political concerns. Ideals in planning are often ignored because planners failed to recognize these realities and TDR is no exception to this rule.

growing fringe areas where the demand for housing can sustain substantial preservation goals. In urban situations, the price of land makes it difficult to preserve anything but small areas. As land values increase, more certificates must be given to each acre of preservation land, requiring more development to preserve a given acreage.

TDR will probably be a partial, rather than a total, solution to the preservation problem for most municipalities. For this reason, a voluntary TDR system which has legal advantages (as discussed later) also has advantages from the planning, political and economic point of view. These advantages relate to a TDR program's ability to preserve only a portion of large conservation or agricultural districts. A voluntary system can be used in combination with other land use controls to give landowners more alternatives.

V. Back-Up for TDR

If TDR cannot achieve all of a community's land preservation goals, how are they to be met? Conventional large-lot zoning will not work. Very large-lot zoning (40 acre) is impractical in many metropolitan areas.[22] Preferential taxation is helpful but does not deal with basic land use issues. Purchase, like TDR, can realistically do only part of the job, and in Pennsylvania it is questionable whether municipalities have the power to purchase land for agricultural preservation. Performance zoning which utilizes an extreme form of clustering remains as an alternative.

Buckingham has utilized both TDR and performance zoning. A landowner in the agricultural (or any other residential) district may build any type of housing from single-family detached houses to garden apartments. However, 90 percent of the land must remain as open space in the agricultural district and only 10 percent of the land is available for development. The gross density on the entire site is .5 of a dwelling per acre. In order to achieve this density on the 10 percent of the land allowing buildings, it is necessary to

---

22. This is an alternative on the fringes of metropolitan areas where development land values are very close to agricultural values. The key element is a farm population which recognizes that any development will inevitably lead to an increase in land values, which in turn will bring economic pressures, higher taxes and inability of farmers to purchase land at agricultural values. A community which recognizes that once development begins, farming becomes increasingly difficult, may choose to take that first step.

build at a rate of five dwellings per acre. Although the permitted density (.5 dwellings per acre) is below what one typically expects from one-acre zoning (approximately .75 dwellings per acre), the farmer still retains 90 percent of his land which has considerable value for agricultural purposes. Thus, like the TDR concept, performance zoning allows a reasonable economic return on the property at the same time that it meets environmental protection goals. The development value under performance zoning plus the agricultural value (just as TDR value plus the agricultural value) equal the development value which existed under the previous one-acre zoning. With the development district selected in Buckingham, TDR would have preserved 23 percent of the 13,000 agricultural acres. The civic groups worked to minimize the size of the development district adopted; thus TDR's use probably could not be used to preserve more acreage. With the combination of performance zoning and TDR, it was estimated that 92.3 percent of the agricultural land could be preserved. Performance zoning alone would have preserved 90 percent. What TDR did was provide approximately one-fourth of the landowners with an option other than development, thus, freedom of choice.

VI. Setting up a TDR System

In writing a TDR ordinance, planners must be far more rigorous than usual. Any TDR ordinance has to meet the acid test of the marketplace. No TDR system will achieve its goal unless it works for both the buyer (developer) and seller (farmer). For a willing buyer and willing seller to conclude a sale, the expectations of the seller must be equal to or lower than the budget of the buyer. Developable land in Buckingham Township was selling for $3,500 to $5,000 per acre, although farmers often sold at lower prices to speculators, because of poor soil conditions and the absence of sewer facilities. In order to provide adequate compensation, TDR had to return $2,000 to $3,000 per acre to the Buckingham farmer.

The other side of the economic equation involves the builder who was permitted to build a variety of housing types in Buckingham. The price he typically would pay for land on a per dwelling unit basis is as follows:[23]

---

23. These values were determined by staff from talking to realtors, builders and architects familiar with housing in the Buckingham area. The information was collected in 1974–75 while drafting the ordinance.

Single-family, one acre	$5000–$7000
Single-family, small lot	5000
Duplex or Patio House	4000
Atrium, Townhouse, or 4-Plex Units	3000
Garden Apartments	2000

Because performance zoning requires a mix of housing types, it was necessary to test a variety of housing mixes to determine maximum and minimum prices builders would pay for the certificates. These prices ranged from $2,600 for a concentrated development of apartments to $3,400 for one which concentrated on single-family detached units. In working out the allocation formula in Buckingham, we were conservative, building in a cushion to insure that the system would work. Our formula required that buyers be willing to pay more than sellers expected. This calculation was worked out for allocations of from .8 of a certificate per acre to more than one certificate per acre. For two reasons, Township officials chose one certificate per acre even though an allocation of .9 certificates per acre would have been adequate to meet our test. First, the elected supervisors had not shown much interest in the details of the ordinance until it came to hearing and were confused by the complexity of the various calculations. Second, the farmers and the civic association were still fighting and arguing in meetings for one-acre zoning or no development. The supervisors were closely associated with the farmers and raised the allocation as a gesture of support.

There is still a lack of understanding of TDR in Buckingham. In writing other similar ordinances, planners should devote more time to education of the public officials and farmers. We developed a simple game to illustrate the principle and to show the impact of different allocation formulas on the ability of TDR to work, but we never got to illustrate it because of the ongoing disputes between the farmers and the civic association. Many issues were resolved by vote only to be re-argued endlessly by the losers.

Although some legislation requires the use of assessment records in determining land values,[24] we chose to distribute certificates on a

---

24. Assembly Bill No. 3192, N.J. S. REP. (November 24, 1975) requires the use of the assessment records in determining land valuations. Depending on the quality of assessment records, this may or may not be a viable alternative.

uniform one per acre basis. Individual assessment of each parcel has two drawbacks: first, the higher cost of setting up the system, and second, the certainty of numerous appeals caused by the differences in individual allotments of development certificates. It should be noted that even with the formula allocation used, some municipalities—Buckingham was not one of these—have areas where access to roads, services or differences in zoning would result in differing allocations. Existing land values should provide the planner with the information needed to determine whether several allocation rates are needed.

VII. Legal Constraints in Buckingham

During the course of the planning process which resulted in the Buckingham Township Zoning Ordinance, there were some legal problems which forced the consultants and the Township to exercise unusual care regarding certain issues. Eight landowners filed "curative amendments"[25] demanding that they be permitted to develop townhouses, apartments and/or mobile homes on their parcels of property. This challenged the then existing zoning, not the ordinance containing Transfer of Development Rights. When a landowner believes the zoning ordinance is substantively unconstitutional, (not providing for all types of housing or "fair share" housing) he has the right to file a petition with the municipality suggesting a *cure* to the zoning ordinance to overcome such substantive unconstitutionality. A decision by the municipality on the proposed cure is judicially reviewable. These eight "curative amendments" caused a realization that the challenged ordinance (prior to the ordinance including Transfer of Development Rights) did not provide for adequate housing to meet the standards established by the Pennsylvania Supreme Court. As consultants to Buckingham, we believed, and a majority of the Township fathers concurred, that it was absolutely essential to adopt a zoning ordinance that would "by right" provide for housing in a density that could be considered *inclusionary* and would survive review by the Pennsylvania Supreme Court. Our development rights scheme as contained in the ordinance is, in reality, a modified version of a pure developmental rights ordinance. The ordinance is voluntary. After they sell their development rights, landowners in the agricultural district have certain residuary rights

25. Pennsylvania Municipalities Planning Code Act 247 of 1968, *as amended by* Act 93 of 1972.

to develop one house per 25 acres, or to the right to develop .5 dwelling units per acre in a cluster using 10 percent of the parcel. The ordinance also provides a "by right" density of 2.5 dwelling units per acre in the development district. Densities in the development district, with the use of development rights certificates, are permitted to increase to 5.5 dwellings per acre. All types of dwelling units, single family, twins, townhouses and apartments are permitted in all districts. A minimum open space and a mix of dwellings is required so that the zoning is similar to a planned unit development. This permits all kinds of housing to be built at lower densities and with higher amenity value than would be possible with conventional zoning.

Another major consideration by Buckingham was whether the system should be voluntary or mandatory. A mandatory system would require the landowners in the agricultural district to accept the development right certificates in lieu of any right to develop and require them to transfer these development right certificates to landowners in the development district. Implementation would require that the Township have powers of condemnation. It was feared the landowners in the agricultural district could challenge the "value" of the development certificates as compensation for forfeiture of the right to develop. An issue was whether or not certificates could be given in lieu of cash, and further, whether they could be given as long as there was available money for those individuals who did not desire to have development certificates.[26]

In a voluntary system, landowners in the agricultural district must elect whether or not to accept the option to sell the development rights to a landowner in the development district. It was the view of the legal counsel for the Township that the landowners in the agricultural district only should be eligible for certificates. As soon as a landowner in the development district was identified, a certificate should be issued and immediately affixed to the land in the development district. Therefore, the development rights are not

---

26. J. SACKMAN, NICHOLS' THE LAW OF EMINENT DOMAIN (3d ed. 1974) Vol. III, 8.2 at 17, states "While the constitutions of the states do not ordinarily prescribe the medium by which compensation shall be paid, that compensation must be in money is a qualification that has been read into the phase now under consideration by all the courts in which the question has arisen." Although there are few cases in which it has been held that distribution of certificates in lieu of cash is appropriate, this issue has not been resolved in Pennsylvania.

"floating" and are treated as running with the land and as an interest in the land.[27]

Another factor which concerned us was the tax impact of TDR on the community and special districts. TDR could have problems if certificates owned by a developer were taxed as personal property rather than real property. In Pennsylvania, the school districts cannot tax personal property, and the maximum rates for other taxing bodies are much lower for personal property than real property. Thus, preservation of the tax base required assignment of the rights to a specific property where its development value could be taxable as real estate.

Yet another issue that confronted the Township was the perpetuation of the development rights scheme for future generations. It was believed that a compromise between an absolute deed restriction (perpetual limitations) and merely a legislative limitation, which could be amended by any subsequent board of supervisors, was appropriate.[28] Thus, a deed restriction must be incorporated on any

---

27. This conclusion has been supported by the Fred F. French Inv. Co., 77 Misc. 2d 199, 352 N.Y.S.2d 762 (Sup. Ct. 1973), aff'd, 39 N.Y.2d 587, 350 N.E.2d 381, 385 N.Y.S.2d (1976).
   Put another way, it is a tolerable abstraction to consider development rights a part of the solid land from which as a matter of zoning they derive. But severed, the development rights are a double abstraction until they are actually attached to a receiving parcel, yet to be identified, acquired, and subject to the contingent future approvals of administrative agencies, events which may never happen because of the exigencies of the market and the contingencies and exigencies of administrative action.
28. The distribution of Development Rights shall be made to a property owner in Buckingham Township so designated by the landowner upon the submission of the following: (a) An agreement of sale for said certificates by the parties. (b) The landowner selling said Development Rights filing of record with the Recorder of Deeds a restrictive covenant running with the land, as set forth herein, effecting the parcel of land of said landowner from which the Development Rights have been transferred. The restrictive covenant shall be as follows:
   Under and Subject, nevertheless, that said premises described herein shall not be used, at any time, for those uses designated as not permitted ("N") in the Agricultural Preservation District as set forth in Article IV of the Buckingham Township Zoning Ordinance adopted on March 6, 1975; and further, construction and/or placement of buildings or facilities on said premises shall only be permitted if it is in accordance with the standards established in Section 502 relating to the Agricultural Preservation District of the Buckingham Township Zoning Ordinance adopted on March 6, 1975, and not inconsistent with the permitted uses within the Agricultural Preservation District as provided for in said Ordinance adopted on March 6, 1975, provided, however, additional uses may be permitted and/or alternate standards established for said premises provided said uses and/or standards are authorized by an amendment to the Township Zoning Ordinance which is enacted following: (1) the adoption by the Township Supervisors of a legally and constitutionally valid revision to the

parcel of land from which a development right has been transferred. In order to encourage the use of TDRs, other private uses permitted as conditional uses in residential areas, such as neighborhood shopping in developments with more than 40 acres of residential use, private recreational facilities, or golf courses, were required to obtain the maximum number of development certificates (the same number a residential developer would buy to achieve the maximum density) as the condition for approval. Additionally, the maximum impervious surface ration in the planned industrial district (buildings and parking) could be increased from 55 percent to 70 percent if the developer bought certificates.

VIII. Public Reaction

TDR appeared suddenly and offered an apparent panacea to resource preservation, but an in-depth exploration exposes many problems. Even a brief examination by planners and lawyers will generate a tangle of unanswered questions sufficient to discourage elected officials. Although there are not answers for all questions, strategies can be developed to reduce the risks to an acceptable level. A system that is unworkable or is declared unconstitutional leaves the community in a position no worse than it was in the beginning. Because most of the alternatives have been unable to cope with environmental problems, there is much to gain and little to lose.

A major problem is that some people either cannot or will not take the time to understand the complexities and subtleties of the problem. In Buckingham, the laymen, mostly members of the civic association, demanded that zoning and especially TDR protect *all*

Township's Comprehensive Plan consistent with the provisions of Article 1, § 27 of the Commonwealth of Pennsylvania Constitution, and (2) said revision to the Comprehensive Plan is approved by a majority of the registered voters of the Township in a duly authorized and held referendum.

And the grantee, for himself, his heirs and assigns, by the acceptance of this indenture, agrees with the grantor, his heirs and assigns, that said restrictions and condition shall be a covenant running with the land, and that in any deed of conveyance of said premises or any part thereof to any person or persons, said restrictions and conditions, when modified pursuant to the provisions contained herein shall be incorporated by reference to this indenture and the record hereof or as fully as the same are contained herein.

Upon the sale or transfer of the Development Rights from a designated parcel of land, said land shall then automatically be designated Agricultural Preservation ("AP") and subject to the limitations and restrictions imposed by said designation in this Zoning Ordinance as well as the limitations and restrictions imposed on said land by virtue of any restrictive covenants.

the land. Economics, equity, exclusionary zoning, and other factors were ignored. The planners and lawyers who did the comprehensive planning in Buckingham were accused of foot-dragging, or of being on the "take" from developers. The effect of this was that the farmers became violently antagonistic to anything suggested by the local civic association. They sensed that the civic association members, who were newcomers to the community, wanted stewardship of the farmers' land. We faced the conflict which occurred between those who wish to save the land and those whose land was to be preserved.

A second obstacle that must be overcome when attempting an innovative program is "fear of the unknown." In Buckingham, the lack of trust between farmers and civic groups made this fear a real problem. The planner, in order to convince people to try something new, should show a successful working example of the proposal. TDR, still basically theoretical, is difficult to document. A recent report[29] listed seven TDR ordinances adopted around the country; yet most had no actual transfer experience. During the next five years, use of TDR will be breaking new ground. The planner must, through his own persuasive powers, try to logically demonstrate a workable system.

IX. Conclusion

Even though TDR is in its infancy, we believe it has the potential to contribute to preservation of key environmental areas including natural features such as swamps, floodplains, and agricultural zones as well as man-made resources such as historic buildings. In retrospect, the development of a model ordinance which had a strategy built into it to avoid the most troublesome legal and planning issues was easy. It was far more difficult to overcome the human problems and to sell the concepts to the various factions in Buckingham. Within the Bucks County Planning Staff, there was a group of planners who would still be studying TDR to see if it would work. Fortunately, one of Buckingham's two lawyers supported the innovations even though he had no supportive case law. In other municipalities in Bucks County, we were stymied by the unwillingness of the local solicitor to support the concept or to admit his uncertainty about the legality.

---

29. M. BENNETT, TRANSFER OF DEVELOPMENT RIGHTS (1976).

Selling an innovative concept is time consuming. Two-thirds of our costs in creating the Buckingham Plan and ordinance was consumed in attending meetings, in preparing material to demonstrate operations to the public, and in answering specific questions. Perseverance and a willingness to debate issues at length are essential assets to planners who propose an innovative idea such as TDR.

Institutionalizing the Revolution: Judicial Reaction to State Land-Use Laws

David E. Hess
University of Illinois, M.A. (1976);
Shippensburg State College, B.A.
(1974).

SINCE BOSSELMAN AND CALLIES described state land-use laws as a "revolution in land-use controls,"[1] courts have been busily transforming revolutionary ideas into everyday fare.

Judicial reaction to statewide, shoreland and regional land-use programs has been overwhelmingly favorable and supportive. Courts have uniformly upheld state land-use programs as legitimate attempts to control environmental and growth-related problems.

To better understand the breadth of the transformation, it is necessary to look at judicial reaction to key state land-use programs.

Six years have passed since the revolution was first proclaimed and in that time the number of states enacting land-use controls has risen. Ten states now have some form of statewide land-use law.[2] Eleven states have coastal or shoreland management statutes.[3] The four regional agencies continued their land-use control functions.[4]

---

1. F. BOSSELMAN AND D. CALLIES, THE QUIET REVOLUTION IN LAND USE CONTROL (1971).

2. Colorado—COL. REV. STAT., art. 65; Florida—FLA. STAT. ANN., ch. 380 (1972); Hawaii—H. I. REV. STAT., ch. 205 (1961); Maine—MAINE REV. STAT. ANN., Tit. 38, § 481; MAINE REV. STAT. ANN., Tit. 12, § 685–A; MAINE REV. STAT. ANN., Tit. 5, § 3310 (1970); Maryland—A.C.M., Tit. 8 (1974); Minnesota—MINN. STAT. ANN. § 16.01 (1973); Nevada—NEV. REV. STAT. § 321.640 (1973); Oregon—ORE. REV. STAT. § 215.055 (1973); Vermont—VT. STAT. ANN., Tit. 10, ch. 151, § 6001; Wyoming—WYO. STAT. § 9–160.40.

3. California—West's Public Res. Code § 27000 (1972); Delaware—DEL. CODE ANN. § 7–7000 (1971); Maine—MAINE REV. STAT. ANN., Tit. 12, § 4811 (1971); Michigan—MICH. STAT. ANN § 13.1831 (1970); Minnesota—MINN. STAT. ANN., § 105.485 (1969); New Jersey—N.J. STAT. ANN., 13:9A–1 (1973); North Carolina G.S.N.C. 113A–100 (1974); Rhode Island—GEN. LAWS 46–23 (1971); Vermont—U.S.A., Tit. 24, ch. 91, § 4301; Washington— R.C.W.A. § 90.54.010 (1971); Wisconsin—WIS. STAT. ANN. 59.971 (1965).

4. Adirondack Park Agency—E.C.L. 9.0301 (McKinney Supp. 1971); Hackensack Meadowlands Development—N.J.S.A. 13:17–1 (1968); San Francisco Bay Conservation—WEST'S ANN. GOV. CODE § 66600 (1969); Tahoe Regional Planning Agency—WEST'S ANN. GOV. CODE § 66800 (1967).

Gauging judicial reaction to all state land-use programs is not possible for a number of reasons. First of all, the statewide programs in Maryland, Nevada, Oregon and Wyoming are in the early planning or initial regulatory phase, consequently, there has been very little opportunity for a court test; secondly, the shoreland statutes in Michigan, Minnesota, North Carolina and Vermont allowed a long lead time for developing and implementing shoreland regulations. In some instances the deadline for enacting regulations has just passed. As a result, as with the statewide programs, there has simply not been enough time for issues to arise which require judicial disposition. For example, Florida recently designated several controversial areas of critical state concern under its Environmental Land and Water Management Act. A number of challenges to those designations are making their way slowly through the courts.[5] In Maine no suits have been filed against the state's program to regulate critical areas.[6] Minnesota has been able to gingerly negotiate its way through enforcement problems by settling disputes out of court.[7]

Statewide Land-Use Management

Statewide land-use laws are victims of many of the difficulties noted above, but court reaction can be sampled through four programs: Colorado's Land Use Act (1974), Hawaii's Land Use Law (1961), Maine's Site Location of Development Act (1970) and Vermont's Act 250 (1969). Although Act 250's judicial history is less well known, it is chosen for review here because it was recently given a clean bill of health by the Vermont Supreme Court.

Vermont created a system of nine district commissions and a single statewide Environmental Board. The system was given authority to develop a State Land Use Plan and to administer a permit program for land uses over ten acres in size or above 2500 feet in elevation.

Within the permit program, the district commissions are the first to hear permit applications. The applicant has the option of appealing the district's decision to the Environmental Board if he is not satisfied. Permits may only be approved if local governments ac-

---

5. Telephone interview with Tom Harris and Jim Whisenand, Florida's Attorney General's Office, January 9, 1976.

6. Telephone interview with Harry Tyler, Maine State Planning Office, January 30, 1976.

7. Telephone interview with Yo Jouseau, Minnesota State Planning Agency, January 30, 1976.

quiesce to the project and if the development is found not to be detrimental to the public's health, safety and welfare. The Board does have the option to deny permits even if the local government approves a project.

The Vermont Supreme Court has consistently upheld the Act's constitutionality and the Environmental Board's discretion to administer the Act.[8] Schuyler Jackson, chairman of the Board, has said that the latest decision, *In re Wildlife Wonderland, Inc.*,[9] "shut the door" to future court challenges; provided the Board follows proper procedures.[10] *Wildlife Wonderland* affirmed the Board's authority to enforce the Act so long as it does so within the Act's guidelines and supports each decision with substantial evidence. Further, the court held that the permit applicant has the burden of showing that his proposed action complies with the Act."[11]

In other cases, the court has insisted that the Board's permit procedure insure that all interested parties be given an opportunity to participate.[12]

All four statewide land-use laws under consideration have been upheld as valid exercises of the police power.[13] These successes are more significant in view of the variations in purpose and administrative structure among the states. (See Figure 1.)

Shoreland Management

Eleven states have coastal or shoreland management statutes but only four have been judicially reviewed. California's Coastal Zone Conservation Act, Delaware's Coastal Zone Act, Washington's Shoreline Management Act and Wisconsin's Shoreland Zoning Requirement represent the only measure of court reaction to shoreland management laws.[14]

---

8. Great Eastern Building Co., Inc., 326 A.2d 152 (Vt. 1974); *In re* Quechee Lakes Corporation, 296 A.2d 190 (Vt. 1972).

9. 346 A.2d 645 (Vt. 1975).

10. Telephone interview with Schuyler Jackson, chairman of Vermont's Environmental Board, January 9, 1976.

11. This holding concurred with the earlier decision, *In re* Baker Sargent Corporation, 313 A.2d 669 (Vt. 1973).

12. Cases involving due process include: *In re* State Aid Highway No. 1, Peru, Vermont, 328 A.2d 667 (Vt. 1974); *In re* Quechee Lakes Corp., 296 A.2d 190 (Vt. 1972); *In re* Preseault 292 A.2d 832 (Vt. 1972).

13. Colorado—City of Louisville v. District Court in and for County of Boulder, 543 P.2d 67 (Col. 1975); Hawaii—Town v. Land Use Comm'n, 524 P.2d 84 (Hawaii 1974); Maine—*In re* Spring Valley Dev., 300 A.2d 736 (Me. 1973); Vermont—*In re* Wildlife Wonderland, Inc., 346 A.2d 645 (Vt. 1975).

14. *See* note 3, *supra*.

FIGURE 1: Statewide Land Use Statutes

	Colorado (critical areas)	Florida (DRI's) (critical areas)
Date Enacted	1974	1972
Purposes	encourages planned orderly development within land's character and adaptability	protect environmental rights, water resources management
State Plan Required	NO	NO
Special Structure Created	YES	NO
Jurisdiction over Land Uses[1]	wide	narrow wide
State Veto of Local Approval[2] (without court action)	NO	possible on appeal possible on appeal
State Override of Local Denial[2] (without court action)	NO	possible on appeal possible on appeal
Burden of Proof in Permit Review	local government	local/regional agencies local
Enforcement of Regulations	local government	local local
# of Decisions	1	4 pending
Major Issues	Commission authority to request local hearing and to enjoin development if hearing not held	designation

Under California's shoreland statute a series of six regional commissions and a single state-level Coastal Zone Conservation Commission were created by voter initiative in 1972. The initiative gave the commissions planning and permit authority in the state's coastal zone. Permit administration is similar to Vermont's general land-use program. The regional commissions handle the initial application while an option is available to appeal to the state-level commission. The commissions have full authority over land use in a special coastal permit area. To issue a permit, the commissions must find that the development will not have an adverse environ-

Hawaii (districts) (special permit) 1961		Maine 1970	Vermont 1969
protect agricultural land, control public costs of growth, tax incentives to desired development		control environmental impact of large developments	insure land use is compatible with natural capability—especially larger developments
by amendment		NO	YES
YES		NO	YES
relatively wide		narrow	narrow
(N.A.)	YES	(N.A.)	YES
(N.A.)	NO	(N.A.)	NO
applicant	regulator	applicant	divided—applicant has major burden
state	local/state	state	state
6 major/several pending		4 major/1 pending	7 major
classification/ procedural		grandfather clause/ broadside	parties to process/ court's role/jurisdiction/broadside

[1]This is a general characterization meaning: *wide*—practically no limits on size or location of development coming under the program's jurisdiction; *narrow*—just the opposite.
[2]Approval or denial of land development.

mental impact and that it conforms to the enabling Act's policies. Unlike Vermont's program, however, both planning and permit authority will end on January 1, 1977 unless the state legislature approves the coastal plan now before it.

By far the two most important cases upholding the Coastal Zone Conservation Act have been *CEEED v. California Coastal Zone Conservation Commission*[15] and *State v. Superior Court of Orange County.*[16] These two cases approved the Act's purposes, its pro-

15. 118 Cal. Rptr. 315 (Cal. App. 1974).
16. 115 Cal. Rptr. 497, 524 P.2d 1281 (Cal. 1974).

cedures[17] and the state's right to regulate land use without violating constitutional guarantees of equal protection, due process or the right to travel. *CEEED* also affirmed the state's authority to protect state interests in local home rule jurisdictions.

The issue of exemption from the permit process, either by virtue of the Act's grandfather clause or the vesting of rights, has been a primary issue for review.[18] Oddly enough none of the decisions indicated whether the adoption of the Act by voter initiative had any bearing on the outcome.

The judicial treatment of the other three shoreland management laws is very similar. The laws of Delaware, Washington and Wisconsin were all held to be proper exercises of police power despite the differences in objectives and administrative approaches.[19] (See Figure 2) The key characteristics of the laws were upheld, i.e., discretion of the regulatory agency, the reasonableness of placing the burden on the applicant of proving compliance with the statutes, limiting judicial review to determining if the agency acted within its authority and whether the agency decision was supported by "substantial evidence."

Regional Agencies

Laws creating all four major regional land-use regulatory agencies have been subjected to court tests. The Adirondack Park Agency, Hackensack Meadowlands Development Commission, San Francisco Bay Conservation and Development Commission and the Tahoe Regional Planning Agency have all been regulating land use

---

17. Klitgaard and Jones, Inc. v. San Diego Coast Regional Comm'n, 121 Cal. Rptr. 650 (Cal. App. 1975), agreed here also.

18. Avco Community Developers, Inc. v. South Coast Regional Comm'n, 122 Cal. Rptr. 810 (Cal. App. 1975); Urban Renewal Agency of the City of Monterey and City v. California Coastal Zone Conservation Comm'n, 121 Cal. Rptr. 446 (Cal. App. 1975); California Central Coast Regional Coastal Zone Conservation Comm'n. v. McKeon Constr., 112 Cal. Rptr. 903 (Cal. App. 1974); Environmental Coalition of Orange County, Inc. v. Avco Community Developers, Inc., 115 Cal. Rptr. 59 (Cal. App. 1974); Transcentury Properties, Inc. v. State, 116 Cal. Rptr. 487 (Cal. App. 1974); County of Orange v. Heim, 106 Cal. Rptr. 825 (Cal. App. 1973); San Diego Coast Regional Comm'n for San Diego County v. See the Sea, Ltd. 109 Cal. Rptr. 377, 513 P.2d 129 (Cal. 1973).

19. California—CEEED v. California Coastal Zone Conservation Comm'n, 118 Cal. Rptr. 315 (Cal. App. 1971); Delaware—Kreshtool v. Delmarva Power & Light Co., 310 A.2d 649 (Del. 1973); Washington—Department of Ecology v. Ballard Elks Lodge No. 827, 527 P.2d 1121 (Wash. App. 1973); Wisconsin—Just v. Marinette County, 201 N.W.2d 761 (Wis. 1972).

FIGURE 2: Shoreland Management Statutes

	California 1972	Delaware 1971	Washington 1971	Wisconsin 1965
Date Enacted				
Purposes	protection of natural resources, scenic areas, marine fisheries and delicate ecological balance	protect an area crucial to the state's quality of life—economic and environmental—encourage recreation and tourism	coastal areas are among most valuable and fragile natural resources—must be managed in the public interest	control pollution of navigable waters
Coastal Plan Required	YES	YES	Local—YES	YES
Special Structure Created	YES	YES	YES	NO
Regulated Area	within 1,000 yards of mean high tide	varies, about 5,280 yards from mean high tide	within 333 yards of ocean or lake, 100 yards of rivers + associated wetlands	within 333 yards of lakes or ponds, 100 yards of rivers
Jurisdiction over Land Uses[1]	wide	narrow	wide	wide
State Veto of Local Approval (without court action)[2]	(N.A.)	YES	possible on appeal	NO
State Override of Local Denial (without court action)[2]	(N.A.)	NO	possible on appeal	NO
Burden of proof in Permit Review	applicant	applicant	applicant	local government
Enforcement of Regulations	state	state	local/state	local
# of Decisions	13 major/100 pending	1	11	2
Major Issues	constitutionality/procedures/grandfather clause—vested rights	purpose/"substantial evidence"	definition of "shoreline"/exemption/procedures	constitutionality/taking

[1] This is a general characterization meaning: *wide*—practically no limits on size or location of development coming under the program's jurisdiction; *narrow*—just the opposite.

[2] Approval or denial of land development.

on a regional basis for some time, and survived judicial attack.[20] While any one of the four agencies would provide a good illustration, the Hackensack Meadowlands Development Commission has withstood the more interesting court challenges.

The Commission has assumed all land-use control functions within its jurisdiction. Local governments may require land-use permits, but developers (and the Commission itself) view the regional agency as the body with statutory authority.[21] In addition to land-use regulation, the Commission is responsible for planning in the region and has authority to manage solid waste and to undertake its own redevelopment and reclamation projects by issuing revenue bonds. It also administers a tax sharing program between municipalities so that they all may benefit from planned growth.

Meadowlands Regional Development Agency v. State[22] represents the first and possibly the strongest affirmation of the Meadowlands Commission's authority by the state supreme court. The Commission was challenged on equal protection and due process levels, as well as an abuse of legislative discretion to designate a region for special attention, and as an intrusion into local affairs to protect regional interests. Each challenge was rejected by the court and the Commission's authority was sustained.

However, the Commission has not enjoyed absolute judicial success. In a case involving the construction of a natural gas plant the Commission's permit authority was held to be an interference with interstate commerce.[23] The staff attorney to the Commission feels the decision does not place a major restriction on granting future permits,[24] because only those facilities coming under the jurisdiction of federal regulatory agencies should be affected.[25]

The court has upheld the Commission's authority to approve or disapprove land uses proposed by other governmental agencies,[26]

---

20. *See* note 4, *supra.*

21. Telephone interview with Jerry Rosenweig, staff attorney for Hackensack Meadowlands Development Commission, February 13, 1976.

22. 270 A.2d 418 (N.J. 1970), *appeal dismissed* 414 U.S. 991 (1973).

23. Transcontinental Gas Pipe Line Corp. v. Hackensack Meadowlands Dev. Comm'n, 464 F.2d 1358 (3d Cir. 1972).

24. *See* Note 21, *supra.*

25. *Id.*; Note: Hackensack Meadowlands Dev. Comm'n, v. Municipal Sanitary Landfill Authority, 348 A.2d 505 (N.J. 1975) also involved an alleged interference in interstate commerce. The Commission banned out of state garbage from landfills within its jurisdiction and the original plaintiffs contended that garbage was an article of commerce. The court disagreed.

26. Bergen County Sewer Authority v. Hackensack Meadowlands Dev. Comm'n, 324 A.2d 108 (N.J. 1974).

its tax sharing program,[27] and challenges involving uncompensated taking.[28]

The other three regional agencies closely parallel the Meadowlands Commission's record under judicial review. All have been upheld as legitimate exercises of the police power for the objectives they seek to accomplish; notwithstanding the difference between programs.[29] (See Figure 3) The vital features of each were upheld, i.e. legislative designation of the region for special attention and the discretion of the administrative agency in enforcing permit requirements.

Legal Guidelines

To the state planner involved with existing land-use control programs, or to those considering programs, the courts have produced several legal guidelines which may be summarized briefly:

1. A precisely drafted enabling statute can eliminate litigation on conflicting provisions.[30]

2. A simple, clearly worded grandfather clause can minimize litigation. (Avoiding all litigation on the subject is impossible.)[31]

3. The administering body must develop "substantial evidence" on the record of its proceedings to avoid being overturned upon judicial review.[32]

4. Whatever the procedures, the regulator must follow the provisions of the law in every detail to avoid being reversed by court action.[33]

---

27. Meadowlands Regional Dev. Agency v. State, 304 A.2d 545 (N.J. 1973), *appeal dismissed* 414 U.S. 991 (1973).

28. Meadowlands Regional Development Agency v. Hackensack Meadowlands Dev. Comm'n, 293 A.2d 192 (Super. Ct. N.J. 1972), *appeal denied* 229 A.2d 69 (N.J. 1972).

29. Adirondack—McCormick v. Lawrence, 372 N.Y.S.2d 156 (1975); Meadowlands Regional Dev. Agency v. State, 270 A.2d 418 (N.J. 1970); Bay Commission—Candlestick Properties Inc. v. San Francisco Bay Conservation and Dev. Comm'n, 89 Cal. Rptr. 897 (Cal. App. 1970); Tahoe—People ex rel Younger v. County of El Dorado, 487 P.2d 1193 (Cal. 1971).

30. *In re* Preseault, 292 A.2d 832 (Vt. 1972).

31. King Resources Co. v. Environmental Improvement Comm'n, 270 A.2d 863 (Me. 1970); San Diego Coast Regional Commission for San Diego County v. See the Sea, Ltd., 109 Cal. Rptr. 377, 513 P.2d 377 (Cal. 1973); Putnam v. Carroll, 534 P.2d 132 (Wash. 1975).

32. *In re* Maine Clean Fuels, Inc., 310 A.2d 736 (Me. 1973); *In re* Wildlife Wonderland, Inc., 346 A.2d 645 (Vt. 1975); Kreshtool v. Delmarva Power & Light Co., 310 A.2d 649 (Del. 1973); Department of Ecology v. Ballard Elks Lodge No. 827, 527 P.2d 1121 (Wash. App. 1972).

33. Town v. Land Use Comm'n, 524 P.2d 84 (Hawaii 1974); King Resources Co. v. Environmental Improvement Comm'n, 270 A.2d 863 (Me. 1970); *In re* Quechee Lakes Corp., 296 A.2d 190 (Vt. 1972).

FIGURE 3. Regional Land-Use Agencies

	Adirondack Park Agency	Hackensack Meadowlands Development Comm.	San Francisco Bay Conservation and Development Comm.	Tahoe Regional Planning Agency
Date Enacted	1971	1968	1969	1969
Purposes	protect an area of national and international environmental significance	protect a fragile marshland in the face of development	planning for the Bay as a unit to protect the Bay as a valuable natural resource	protect the Tahoe Basin—its environmental quality and economic productivity
Plan Required	YES	YES	YES	YES
Special Structure Created	YES	YES	YES	YES
Regulated Area	state park with 6,000,000 acres	marshland—18,000 acres	shoreline + 100 foot wide strip on shore	drainage basin
Jurisdiction over Land Uses[1]	wide	wide	wide	unclear
State Veto of Local Approval[2] (without court action)	YES—certain types of development	(N.A.)	YES	NO
State Override of Local Denial[2] (without court action)	YES—certain types of development	(N.A.)	YES	NO
Burden of Proof in Permit Review	Agency	Commission	Commission	Agency
Enforcement of Regulations	Agency/Local	Commission	Commission	Local/Agency
# of Decisions	4 major	10 major	4 major	7 major
Major Issues	home rule/purposes/standing in hearings	constitutionality/interstate commerce/regional issues?	taking/grandfather clause/jurisdiction	taking (inverse condemnation) constitutionality/regional concerns?

[1]This is a general characterization meaning: *wide*—practically no limits on size or location of development coming under the agency's jurisdiction.

[2]Approval or denial of land development.

5. Everyone having a legitimate interest in the outcome of a permit decision must have an opportunity to participate in the permit process.[34]

6. Regulatory agencies following points #3, #4 and #5 will find that the courts, in all but the most extreme factual situations, will not reverse their decisions on the basis of the denial of equal protection, due process or declare an uncompensated taking.

7. It is acceptable to the courts if the burden of proving compliance with the statute is on the applicant rather than the regulator.[35]

8. The courts will approve a wide variety of environmental and aesthetic public objectives and regulatory configurations so long as they are reasonably related.[36]

9. A land-use program enacted by voter referendum seems to be on equal footing with non-referendum based laws in subsequent court tests.[37]

10. State regulation of land uses of state or regional interest does not intrude into municipal affairs; even in home rule jurisdictions.[38]

11. State attempts to regulate federally licensed land uses may be preempted.[39]

---

34. Town v. Land Use Comm'n, 524 P.2d 84 (Hawaii 1974); Great E. Bldg. Co., Inc. 326 A.2d 152 (Vt. 1974); Klitgaard & Jones, Inc. v. San Diego Coast Regional Comm'n, 121 Cal. Rptr. 650 (Cal. App. 1975); Natural Resources Defense Council, Inc. v. Adirondack Park Agency, 359 N.Y.S. 2d 718 (1974).

35. *In re* Maine Clean Fuels, Inc., 310 A.2d 736 (Me. 1973); *In re* Baker Sargent Corp., 313 A.2d 669 (Vt. 1973); *In re* Wildlife Wonderland, Inc., 346 A.2d 645 (Vt. 1975); CEEED v. California Coastal Zone Conservation Comm'n, 118 Cal. Rptr. 315 (Cal. App. 1971).

36. City of Louisville v. District Court in and for the County of Boulder, 543 P.2d 67 (Col. 1975); Town v. Land Use Comm'n, 524 P.2d 84 (Hawaii 1974); *In re* Spring Valley Dev., 300 A.2d 736 (Me. 1973); *In re* Wildlife Wonderland, Inc. 346 A.2d 645 (Vt. 1975); CEEED v. California Coastal Zone Conservation Comm'n, 118 Cal. Rptr. 315 (Cal. App. 1971); Kreshtool v. Delmarva Power & Light Co., 310 A.2d 649 (Del. 1973); Department of Ecology v. Ballard Elks Lodge No. 827, 527 P.2d 1121 (Wash. App. 1974); Just v. Marinette County, 201 N.W.2d 761 (Wis. 1972); McCormick v. Lawrence 372 N.Y.S.2d 156 (1975); Meadowlands Regional Dev. Agency v. State, 270 A.2d 418 (N.J. 1970); Candlestick Properties, Inc. v. San Francisco Bay Conservation and Dev. Comm'n, 89 Cal. Rptr. 897 (Cal. App. 1970); Younger v. County of El Dorado, 487 P.2d 1193 (Cal. 1971).

37. CEEED v. California Coastal Zone Conservation Comm'n, 118 Cal. Rptr. 315 (Cal. App. 1974); Eastlake Community Council v. Roanoke Associates Inc., 513 P.2d 36 (Wash. 1973).

38. CEEED v. California Coastal Zone Conservation Comm'n, 118 Cal. Rptr. 315 (Cal. App. 1974); Wambat Realty Corp., v. State, 378 N.Y.S.2d 912 (1975); Meadowlands Regional Dev. Agency v. State, 270 A.2d 418 (N.J. 1970); Younger v. County of El Dorado, 487 P.2d 1193 (Cal. 1971).

39. Transcontinental Gas Pipe Line Corp. v. Hackensack Meadowlands Development Commission, 464 F.2d 1358 (3rd Cir. 1972).

It is clear from this review of court reaction that the revolution first identified by Bosselman and Callies in 1971 is rapidly becoming accepted and institutionalized through state and Federal court opinion.

Statewide Land Use Planning in Oregon with Special Emphasis on Housing Issues

Terry D. Morgan

J.D., University of Missouri–Kansas
City School of Law (1975); Research
Editor, *The Urban Lawyer* (1975); Legal
Counsel, Housing Resources Corporation.

John W. Shonkwiler

J.D., Northwestern School of Law (1975);
Member, Committee on Land Use, Planning
and Zoning; ABA Section of Local Government
Law (1977–78); Executive Director,
Housing Resources Corporation.

I. Introduction

UNTIL VERY RECENT TIMES, Oregon was primarily a rural state. Immense natural resources, particularly agricultural and forestry lands, combined with a mild maritime climate and vast recreational opportunities, have made the state an attractive home for immigrants from states east of the Rocky Mountains. Consequently, Oregon has experienced tremendous growth pressures in the last decade.[1]

Growth and accompanying urbanization have necessarily posed conflicts with continued cultivation of the natural resource base. In 1973, the Oregon legislature enacted SB 100,[2] which provided for statewide land use planning. This unique legislation created a Land Conservation and Development Commission and Department,[3] which were responsible for the promulgation of planning goals which all cities and counties in the state must observe. In response, local governments have undertaken intensive planning efforts to revise comprehensive plans, zoning and subdivision ordinances to comply with the statewide goals.

---

1. Although its population is still relatively small, since 1970, Oregon's population has increased at a rate twice as great as the national average. BUREAU OF GOVERNMENT RESEARCH AND SERVICE, UNIVERSITY OF OREGON, OREGON POPULATION SHIFTS IN THE 1970s, at 1 (1978).

2. SB 100, ch. 80, 1973 Or. Laws.

3. OR. REV. STAT. § 197.030 (1977 Rep. Pt.).

This article examines Oregon's legislative scheme and the administrative and judicial responses to it. Part II focuses on the statutory framework of the goals against the backdrop of judicial decisions concerning land use. This section also describes regional planning legislation for the Portland metropolitan area as an adjunct of statewide planning.

Part III explores the effect of statewide planning on the provision of housing. The state housing goal is compared in effect to the *Southern Burlington County NAACP v. Township of Mount Laurel*[4] and *Oakwood at Madison, Inc. v. Madison Township*[5] decisions by the New Jersey Supreme Court. Finally, this section offers recommendations for assuring the effectiveness of the housing goal in meeting state housing needs.

II. The Goals of Statewide Planning

A. *The Judicial Framework: Primacy of the Comprehensive Plan*

The Oregon Supreme Court gained nationwide attention with its decision in *Fasano v. Board of County Commissioners*.[6] In evaluating the approval of a zoning change by the county board, the court refused to apply the traditional arbitrary/capricious standard of review. The court distinguished two basic kinds of land use decisions by local governments: legislative and quasi-judicial.

Legislative land use actions, the court stated, are those which establish general policies which apply to many decisions. A reviewing court may only overturn such actions upon a showing that the decision-making body abused its discretion arbitrarily. Quasi-judicial decisions, on the other hand, involve determinations of the use of particular pieces of property through the application of general policy statements.[7] Upon review, a court may apply more exacting scrutiny.

---

4. 67 N.J. 151, 336 A.2d 713 (1975).
5. 72 N.J. 481, 371 A.2d 1192 (1977).
6. 264 Or. 574, 507 P.2d 23 (1973).
7. *Id.* at __, 507 P.2d at 26–27. The court noted that zone changes are normally quasi-judicial in nature. However, comprehensive planning activities are not necessarily legislative actions, nor are zoning decisions necessarily quasi-judicial actions under Oregon case law. In Culver v. Dagg, 20 Or. App. 647, 532 P.2d 1127 (1975), the court of appeals characterized zone changes affecting large areas and large numbers of people as legislative acts. On the other hand, in South of Sunnyside Neighborhood League v. Board of Comm'rs, 280 Or. 3, 569 P.2d 1063 (1977), comprehensive plan changes which precede zone changes and which apply only to specific properties were characterized as quasi-judicial in nature.

The second principle established by *Fasano* is the subordination of zoning decisions to the comprehensive plan for the community. The court defined the relationship as follows:

> It is clear that under our statutes the plan adopted by the planning commission and the zoning ordinances enacted by the county governing body are closely related; both are intended to be parts of a single integrated procedure for land use control. The plan embodies policy determinations and guiding principles; the zoning ordinances provide the detailed means of giving effect to those principles.[8]

Proponents of a zone change must prove conformance with the comprehensive plan according to the following principles: "(1) There is a public need for a change of the kind in question and (2) that need will be best served by changing the classification of the particular piece of property in question as compared with other available property."[9]

The court's willingness to examine quasi-judicial decisions in more detail was not unlimited. In *Dickinson v. Board of County Commissioners*,[10] the court of appeals clarified that a reviewing court would not substitute its judgment for that of the local planning agency. Rather: "The scope of judicial review is limited to an examination of the administrative record for the purpose of ascertaining that: (1) the proper procedures were followed; (2) the relevant factors were considered by the agency; and (3) there was reliable, probative and substantial evidence to support the decision of the agency."[11]

The supreme court elaborated upon the relationship between the comprehensive plan and its implementing measures in *Baker v. City of Milwaukie*.[12] In *Baker*, a property owner brought an action in mandamus to compel the city to conform its zoning ordinance, which was adopted prior to the comprehensive plan for the city, to the policies in the comprehensive plan. The plaintiff also sought

---

8. 264 Or. at __, 507 P.2d at 27.

9. *Id.* at __, 507 P.2d at 28. *Fasano* also established procedural requirements for processing zone change applications:

Parties at the hearing before the county governing body are entitled to an opportunity to be heard, to an opportunity to present and rebut evidence, to a tribunal which is impartial in the matter—i.e., having had no pre-hearing or ex parte contacts concerning the question and issue—and to a record made and adequate findings executed.

Id. at __, 507 P.2d at 30. The legislature has incorporated these procedures for county planning and zoning hearings involving "quasi-judicial" matters. OR. REV. STAT. § 215.402–.422 (1977 Rep. Pt.).

10. 21 Or. App. 98, 533 P.2d 1395 (1975).

11. *Id.* at __, 533 P.2d at 1396.

12. 271 Or. 500, 533 P.2d 772 (1975).

to invalidate the granting of a variance made pursuant to the zoning ordinance.

Citing *Fasano*, the supreme court likened the comprehensive plan to a constitution for development within the city, and ruled that the comprehensive plan was the controlling land use planning document. The court further instructed:

> Upon passage of a comprehensive plan a city assumes a responsibility to effectuate that plan and conform prior conflicting zoning ordinances to it. We further hold that the zoning decisions of a city must be in accord with that plan and a zoning ordinance which allows a more intensive use than prescribed in the plan must fail.[13]

In *Green v. Hayward*,[14] the supreme court retreated from the precepts of *Baker* but further defined the principles of *Fasano*. Area residents had successfully challenged the county's order rezoning property from agricultural to heavy industrial use on the ground that it failed to conform with the agricultural provisions of the comprehensive plan for the county. In reversing, the court noted the conflicting textual statements of the comprehensive plan which were applicable to the tract in question:

> Nearly every individual zoning decision could reasonably be said to conform to or support one or more of the generally-stated goals or objectives in a typical modern comprehensive plan. On the other hand, we are not authorized, and do not wish, to prescribe de novo court review of these decisions on the merits. The proper concern of the courts in these cases is to ascertain whether adequate procedures were followed and proper legal standards were applied.[15]

The court further stated that the local governing body was in the best position to make "an initial interpretation of a comprehensive plan and a determination whether a proposed change complies with the specifics of the plan as properly interpreted . . ."[16] Since a reviewing court must base its ruling on a properly documented record, the court instructed that a local government support its quasi-judicial decisions with adequate findings of fact and a statement of reasons for the determination. Without such a basis for review, the

---

13. *Id.* at ___, 533 P.2d at 779. The 1977 legislature codified the *Baker* precepts as follows: "Zoning, subdivision or other ordinances or regulations and any revisions or amendments thereof shall be designed to implement the adopted county comprehensive plan." OR. REV. STAT. § 215.050(2) (1977 Rep. Pt.). This section also provides that the comprehensive plan and ordinances shall be in conformity with the statewide planning goals.
14. 275 Or. 693, 552 P.2d 815 (1976), *rev'g*, 23 Or. App. 310, 542 P.2d 144 (1975).
15. *Id.* at 704, 552 P.2d at 821.
16. *Id.* at 706, 552 P.2d at 822.

court would remand the decision for establishment of findings and reasons.

B. *Statewide Planning Legislation*

While appellate decisions established the primacy of the comprehensive plan in land use planning, the appropriateness of the contents of a comprehensive plan had not been litigated. The 1973 legislation establishing statewide planning called for the preparation and adoption of statewide planning goals by January 1, 1975.[17] All comprehensive plans and implementing ordinances and regulations adopted by a state agency, city, county or special district were required to be in conformity with the statewide goals within a year from the date of approval.[18] The Land Conservation and Development Commission (LCDC) was created to promulgate statewide goals and to review local plans and ordinances for compliance with the goals.[19]

The LCDC initially adopted fourteen statewide goals.[20] But the local government task of revising existing plans and ordinances proved enormous. By the statutory date for compliance, not a single jurisdiction had been acknowledged as in conformance with the goals. Several important issues have emerged during this initial phase of statewide planning.[21]

---

17. OR. REV. STAT. § 197.225 (1977 Rep. Pt.).
18. OR. REV. STAT. § 197.250 (1977 Rep. Pt.).
19. OR. REV. STAT. § 197.040 (1977 Rep. Pt.).
20. Or. Adm. R., ch. 660, § 10, app. A (1975). These were: Citizen Involvement (Goal 1); Land Use Planning (Goal 2); Agricultural Lands (Goal 3); Forest Lands (Goal 4); Open Spaces, Scenic and Historic Areas, and Natural Resources (Goal 5); Air, Water and Land Resources Quality (Goal 6); Areas Subject to Natural Disasters and Hazards (Goal 7); Recreational Needs (Goal 8); Economy of the State (Goal 9); Housing (Goal 10); Public Facilities and Services (Goal 11); Transportation (Goal 12); Energy Conservation (Goal 13); Urbanization (Goal 14). The commission subsequently adopted five additional goals relating to preservation of the Willamette River and coastal areas. Or. Adm. R., ch. 660, § 20 (1975); § 30 (1977). The 1977 legislature imposed a two-year moratorium on enactment of any new statewide goals. SB 570, ch. 664, § 16a, 1977 Or. Laws.
21. It is beyond the scope of this article to discuss all the ramifications of the statewide planning legislation. Several issues not covered here have been of passing importance, while other provisions of the statute which are of potential importance have not thus far received attention. For example, the 1973 legislation required the commission to promulgate "guidelines" as well as statewide planning goals. Ch. 80, § 33, 1973 Or. Laws. Prior to the 1977 legislative session, it was unclear whether local governments were obliged to comply with guidelines as well as goals. Definitions of "goals" and "guidelines" were appended to the 1973 legislation providing that goals were mandatory standards while guidelines were advisory. OR. REV. STAT. §

1. *Dual Standards for Development.* While the enabling legislation required cities and counties to adopt comprehensive plans and implementing ordinances which conformed with the statewide goals, it did not deal directly with the applicability of the goals to individual development decisions by local governments. The statutes did state that cities and counties "shall exercise their planning and zoning responsibilities" in accordance with the statewide planning goals.[22] However, another provision stated that "comprehensive plans and zoning, subdivision, and other ordinances and regulations . . . shall remain in effect until revised . . ."[23] The latter provision could be interpreted to mean that the *Baker* principles govern development actions during the interim between adoption of the goals and acknowledgment that the comprehensive plan was in conformity with the goals.

The interpretation was further clouded by the fact that "a land conservation and development action" taken by a state agency, city, county or special district could be appealed by another governing body or state agency as in conflict with the statewide planning

---

197.015 (7)(b) (1977 Rep. Pt.). All references to guidelines were eliminated from obligatory provisions of the statute as well.

The discussion in the text treats only issues relating to planning responsibilities of cities and counties. The statutes also require state agencies and special districts to carry out their "planning duties, powers and responsibilities and take actions that are authorized by law with respect to programs affecting land use . . ." in accordance with statewide planning goals. OR. REV. STAT. § 197.180, .185 (1977 Rep. Pt.). State agencies must submit cooperative programs to the Land Conservation and Development Department. OR. REV. STAT. § 197.180 (1977 Rep. Pt.) Special districts operating within cities and counties are required to enter into cooperative agreements with the city or county, stating when the district intends to bring its plan or programs into conformity with the statewide goals and listing the tasks required to achieve compliance. OR. REV. STAT. § 197.185 (1977 Rep. Pt.). These agreements will affect the city or county's compliance with the public facilities goal and will probably become the subject of litigation in the future. Planning actions by state agencies and special districts are subject to petition for review of goal violations to the LCDC, and these entities have standing to petition for goal violations of other jurisdictions. OR. REV. STAT. § 197.300 (1977 Rep. Pt.).

The LCDC also has the power to designate "activities of statewide significance" including siting of public transportation facilities, siting of public sewerage systems, water supply systems and solid waste disposal sites, and siting of public schools. OR. REV. STAT. § 197.400 (1977 Rep. Pt.). Additional activities of statewide significance and areas of critical state concern may be designated by the commission under statutory procedures, OR. REV. STAT. § 197.405 (1977 Rep. Pt.); and activities so designated cannot be developed until a planning and siting permit is issued by the commission. OR. REV. STAT. § 197.410, .415 (1977 Rep. Pt.).

22. OR. REV. STAT. § 197.175 (1977 Rep. Pt.).
23. OR. REV. STAT. § 197.275(1) (1977 Rep. Pt.).

goals.[24] Other interested parties could only appeal "a comprehensive plan provision or any zoning, subdivision or other ordinance or regulation alleged to be in violation of statewide planning goals."[25]

The temptation to equate the term "land conservation and development action" with the judicial definition of "quasi-judicial action" was great. Without defining a land conservation and development action, the 1977 legislature confined application of the goals to such actions *post acknowledgment* "only through the acknowledged comprehensive plan and implementing ordinances."[26] The 1977 amendments also authorized the LCDC to "direct the city or county to apply specified goal requirements in approving or denying future land conservation and development actions" prior to acknowledgment of compliance under certain specified conditions.[27]

The confusion over whether quasi-judicial decisions were subject to conformity with both the comprehensive plan and with the statewide goals, was resolved, in part, in the case of *South of Sunnyside Neighborhood League v. Board of Commissioners.*[28] The case involved a comprehensive plan change which permitted the establishment of a sixty-five-acre planned commercial center. The court characterized the change as quasi-judicial in nature and emphasized that changes in the comprehensive plan map must be compared for consistency with goals and policy statements in the text of the comprehensive plan.

---

24. OR. REV. STAT. § 197.300(1)(b) (1977 Rep. Pt.).
25. OR. REV. STAT. § 197.300(1)(a), (c)-(e) (1977 Rep. Pt.).
26. OR. REV. STAT. § 197.275(2). There are two specified exceptions: (1) "the acknowledged comprehensive plan and implementing ordinances do not control the action or annexation under consideration;" or (2) "substantial changes in conditions have occurred which render the comprehensive plan and implementing ordinances inapplicable to the action or annexation." *Id.*
27. OR. REV. STAT. § 197.252(1) (1977 Rep. Pt). The commission must first find that

[P]ast approvals or denials would have constituted violations of the statewide planning goals and: (a) the Commission finds that the past approvals or denials represent a pattern or practice of decisions which make continued utilization of the existing comprehensive plan, ordinances and regulations ineffective in achieving the statewide planning goals to performance of the compliance schedule; or (b) the Commission finds that a past approval or denial was of more than local impact and substantially impairs the ability of the city or county to achieve the statewide planning goals to the performance of the compliance schedule.

Id. These sanctions can only be applied by a commission at the time of annual progress review, approval of a planning assistance grant, or revision of a compliance schedule. *Id.* § (2).
28. 280 Or. 3, 569 P.2d 1063 (1977).

In discussing the relationship of statewide planning goals to quasi-judicial decisions, the court noted that the majority of the goals "are directed primarily to the overall planning process. With some few exceptions, they are not designed to guide decisions about the permissible uses of particular pieces of property. The comprehensive plan is expected to provide that guidance."[29] Insofar as the overall plan is in compliance with the statewide goals, there is no necessity to test the plan amendment for compliance with each of the goals.

On the other hand, the court reasoned, a comprehensive plan amendment involving a particular piece of property cannot be assumed to comply with provisions of statewide planning goals which specifically govern the kind of decision under consideration. In such circumstances, the proponent of the plan amendment must show compliance with these specific site goals.[30]

Subsequent cases have established that the approval of subdivision plats is a quasi-judicial process subject to the applicability of site-specific goals.[31] An important qualification, however, was added in *1000 Friends of Oregon v. Board of County Commissioners.*[32] Petitioners therein challenged the validity of a subdivision approval both for nonconformance with the county's comprehensive plan and as a violation of the agricultural lands goal. The court of appeals theorized that the statewide goals form the apex of a pyramid that included the comprehensive plan, zoning laws and subdivision ordinances, stating, "It is implicit in the statutory scheme of Senate Bill 100 that LCDC goals are in effect the 'constitution' for local government comprehensive plans."[33]

In denying relief, the court conceded that local governments could not be expected to observe each goal to the fullest extent. "Compliance is achieved if local governments can adequately demonstrate that an amendment results in a plan which considers and

---

29. *Id.* at ___, 569 P.2d at 1073.
30. *Id.* at ___, 569 P.2d at 1074.
31. Bienz v. City of Dayton, 29 Or. App. 761, 566 P.2d 904 (1977). The court held that *Fasano* standards apply to tentative subdivision approvals, since a subdivision plan was quasi-judicial in nature in that it applied to specific individuals and involved the application of general rules to individual interests. The court also cited the statutory provision requiring subdivision ordinances to be in compliance with the statewide planning goals in concluding that a subdivision approval was a land use decision.
32. 32 Or. App. 413, 575 P.2d 651 (1978).
33. *Id.* at 422, 575 P.2d at 656.

accommodates as much as possible all applicable planning goals."[34]
Thus, insofar as statewide goals are applicable to individual land use
decisions, the court will still defer to the balancing process among
goals applied by the local government in approving the development proposal.

   2. *The Role of the LCDC.* The Land Conservation and Development Commission plays two important roles under the statewide
planning legislation.[35] Each is unique in the field of land use planning. In its planning supervisory role, the LCDC functions as over-
seer of the comprehensive planning process at the local level.[36] The
relationship between the agency and the local government is viewed
as contractual in nature.[37] The intended outcome is a comprehensive plan and implementing ordinances which are "acknowledged"
by the commission to be in compliance with the statewide goals.[38]

   The city or county operates under a "compliance schedule"
which is based on a work program designed to achieve compliance. If the local government stays on schedule, it is deemed to be
making "satisfactory progress" toward realization of the goals. Prior
to 1977, failure to make satisfactory progress could be sanctioned
through the assumption of planning responsibilities by the commission.[39] Although the power was never invoked, its existence caused
sufficient consternation among local governments to precipitate
legislative amendments under which the commission must now issue an order requiring the delinquent city or county to conform its
plan or ordinances to the statewide goals and must seek enforcement through a court order.[40]

---

34. *Id.*, 575 P.2d at 657 (quoting South of Sunnyside Neighborhood
League v. Board of Comm'rs, 27 Or. App. 647, 654, 557 P.2d 1375, 1381
(1976)).

35. *See* OR. REV. STAT. § 197.040 (1977 Rep. Pt.).

36. *Id.* § (2)(e).

37. OR. REV. STAT. § 197.251(2)(a) (1977 Rep. Pt.). The section states:
The city or county shall agree to complete the tasks as listed in the compliance schedule in consideration of the Commission's agreement to recognize that the city or county is making satisfactory progress toward preparing and adopting a comprehensive plan or implementing ordinances or
regulations in conformity with the statewide planning goals.

38. *Id.* § (1). The commission is required to evaluate the plan and ordinances within 90 days and to formulate a "clear statement of findings which
sets forth the basis for the approval or denial of the request." *Id.*

39. *Compare* OR. REV. STAT. § 197.325(1) (1975 Rep. Pt.) *with* §
197.320 (1977 Rep. Pt).

40. OR. REV. STAT. § 197.320 (1977 Rep. Pt.). In order to enforce its
order, the commission must have "good cause to believe" that the city or

The second major function of the LCDC is to act as an appellate body for determining alleged goal violations by local governments.[41] The statutes grant standing to cities, counties, special districts, state agencies and "any person or group of persons whose interests are substantially affected" to challenge "a comprehensive plan provision or any zoning, subdivision or other ordinance or regulation adopted by a state agency, city or county or special district" which is allegedly in violation of the statewide goals.[42] The commission reviews the petition on the "administrative record" of the proceeding below and must issue an order containing "a clear statement of findings setting forth the basis for the Commission's determination . . ."[43] The commission may seek court enforcement of the order.[44]

This appellate scheme confers broad authority on the LCDC over planning and zoning decisions by local governments. The commission's jurisdiction extends both to legislative and quasi-judicial decisions under the legislation. The statutes contain an express directive that the commission shall not substitute its judgment for a finding of fact in a quasi-judicial proceeding.[45] Through rulings the commission has extended the notion of review "on the administrative record" to review of legislative decisions by requiring a statement of findings and reasons before determining goal violations.

---

county is not making satisfactory progress on its compliance schedule or that a comprehensive plan or ordinance is not in conformity with the goals by the date for compliance. *Id.* § (1). The city or county has the right to a hearing on the matter, with review of the commission's order for the hearing to the court of appeals. *Id.* § (3). As part of its order for noncompliance, the commission can prevent "some or all categories of land conservation and development actions in one or more specified geographic areas" of the city or county. *Id.* § (4).

41. OR. REV. STAT. § 197.300–.315 (1977 Rep. Pt.).

42. OR. REV. STAT. § 197.300(1) (1977 Rep. Pt.). This section actually establishes four different categories of standing. Three categories pertain to appeals by governmental entities. In addition to alleging that a comprehensive plan or zoning ordinance violates statewide goals, these petitioners can assert that a land conservation and development action by another government body violates the statewide goals or is outside the authority granted in the statewide planning legislation.

43. OR. REV. STAT. § 197.305(1), .310(3) (1977 Rep. Pt.). The matter is first referred to a hearings officer, who has 45 days to make a ruling as to whether the commission has jurisdiction over the matter. *Id.* § 197.310(1). Once jurisdiction is assumed, the hearings officer conducts evidentiary hearings and proposes a final order within 90 days after the date of receipt of the petition by the commission. *Id.* § 197.310(3).

44. *Id.* § 197.310(6).

45. OR. REV. STAT. § 197.305(1) (1977 Rep. Pt.).

The extension was established in the case of *1000 Friends of Oregon v. CRAG,*[46] in which the petitioners alleged that the agricultural lands goal and the urbanization goal had been violated by the establishment of a regional urban growth boundary which contained too much land for the accommodation of urban needs. The commission refused to reach a determination on substantive violations of the goals. Rather, it ruled that the regional boundary designations were unreviewable because CRAG had not furnished an adequate statement of "results" as required by the urbanization goal. The case was remanded to CRAG for completion of the "consideration" of factors enumerated in the goal and for a written statement of results.

The commission's position parallels that taken by the Oregon Supreme Court in the *Green* decision. The *Green* rationale that quasi-judicial decisions be accompanied by a statement of findings was extended to cover statewide goal considerations in the case of *Peterson v. Mayor of Klamath Falls.*[47] The issue before the court was the applicability of statewide goals to annexation proceedings by a city.[48]

The supreme court concluded that annexations were decisions which fell within the statutory category of "planning responsibilities" which cities had to exercise in accordance with statewide planning goals. The court went further to characterize annexations as quasi-judicial in nature, "since the consideration of the statewide goals and the determination that a particular annexation proposal does or does not comply with those goals necessarily involves the application of general standards to a specific situation and to specific individuals."[49]

At the same time, annexations possess aspects of actions that have traditionally been characterized as legislative in nature. Since

---

46. LCDC 77–004 (Final Order, March 10, 1978), *appeal docketed*, No. 10242 (Or. App. April 7, 1978). The urbanization goal requires that urban growth boundaries should be "based upon consideration" of seven enumerated factors. "The results of the above consideration shall be included in the comprehensive plan." Or. Adm. R., ch. 660, § 15–000(14).
47. 279 Or. 249, 566 P.2d 1193 (1977).
48. The applicability of statewide goals to annexations was a highly debated issue before the 1977 legislature. The sections interpreted by the court in its opinion were amended during this session to expressly provide that cities and counties must observe the statewide goals in the annexation of unincorporated territory. Or. Rev. Stat. § 197.175(1) (1977 Rep. Pt.). The LCDC has since adopted a rule governing the applicability of the goals to annexations. Or. Adm. R., ch. 660, § 010–300 to –315 (1978).
49. 279 Or. at 255–56, 566 P.2d at 1196.

the "threshold determination" as to conformity with the statewide planning goals was quasi-judicial in nature, the court reasoned, the city's decision must be supported by adequate findings and a statement of reasons.[50] The court remanded to the city, instructing that "[t]hose findings should be sufficient to demonstrate that in reaching its decision the city has considered the relevant planning goals and has applied those general standards to the specific facts of the case before it."[51]

The commission's action in *CRAG* differs from the result in *Petersen*, in that designation of the regional urban growth boundary is clearly legislative in nature. If the commission can require local governments to support legislative decisions with findings and reasons in order to evaluate compliance with the statewide goals, it is logical to assume that a court may also do so. Indeed, the *Petersen* rationale is easily extended to purely legislative actions, such as the declaration of a moratorium, in that the "threshold determination" as to applicability of the goals is one which must necessarily be made in all land use decisions. If the court takes this position, it must distinguish between standards of review for quasi-judicial and legislative proceedings if the *Fasano* distinctions are to remain viable.

3. *Prioritization of Goals.* In both its supervisory and appellate roles, the LCDC has given priority to the agricultural lands goal and the urbanization goal.[52] Instructions to local governments concerning the revision of comprehensive plans to comply with the goals required early attention to the preservation of agricultural land and to the construction of urban growth boundaries.[53] At the same time, the commission evolved a theory of applicability for the agricultural goal in its appellate opinions.

In one of the first cases decided under the statewide goals,[54] the commission concluded that a county had failed to follow the proper procedures in designating approximately 11,000 acres of non-urban

---

50. *Id.* at 255–57, 566 P.2d at 1196–97.

51. *Id.* at 257, 566 P.2d at 1197 (footnote omitted).

52. JOINT LEGISLATIVE COMMITTEE ON LAND USE, REPORT ON STATE-WIDE PLANNING 6 (1976).

53. The commission staff initially conducted progress reviews of the planning efforts of local governments on an informal basis. The agricultural lands goal and the urbanization goal were treated together and received considerable comment. Other goals were summarily noted in the staff reports to the commission.

54. 1000 Friends of Oregon v. Board of Comm'rs. LCDC 75–006 (March 2, 1977).

land as other than an exclusive farm use district. Once it was determined that the subject land fell under the definition of agricultural land in the goal, the county was required either to zone the land for exclusive farm use or justify the need for non-farm use under an exacting exceptions procedure provided for in the land use planning goal. The commission subsequently formalized its position that local governments must use an exceptions procedure when agricultural land is not zoned for exclusive farm use by administrative rule.[55]

The commission's emphasis on the agricultural lands goal necessarily posed problems for developers in the populous Willamette Valley, which is comprised almost entirely of agricultural land under the goal definition.[56] For urban areas, the commission considered the urbanization goal as the conflict resolution mechanism among competing land uses and hence among competing goal considerations.[57] The urbanization goal requires the establishment of urban growth boundaries separating "rural" from "urbanizable" land. By definition, rural lands lie outside the urban growth boundary and urbanizable lands lie inside the urban growth boundary. The establishment of the boundary is accomplished through consideration of seven specific factors, which in effect incorporate other applicable goals.[58]

---

55. *See* LAND CONSERVATION AND DEVELOPMENT COMMISSION, EXCEPTIONS POLICY PAPER § 2(A) (March 15, 1978). The exceptions procedures are set forth under the land use planning goal (Goal 2). In order to justify an exception to a goal, "compelling reasons and facts" must be set forth and included in the comprehensive plan as follows:
    (a) Why these other uses should be provided for; (b) what alternative locations within the area could be used for the proposed uses; (c) what are the long-term environmental, economic social and energy consequences to the locality, the region or the state from not applying the goal or permitting the alternative use; (d) a finding that the proposed uses will be compatible with other adjacent uses.
Or. Adm. R., ch. 660, § 15–000(2). Use of the exceptions process is limited to "those statewide goals which prescribe or restrict certain uses of resource land." EXCEPTIONS POLICY PAPER, *supra*, at § 2(A). As the commission notes, the finding requirements for establishing an exception for a quasi-judicial action are similar to the *Fasano* standards. *Id.* at § 14.
56. The agricultural lands goal defines agricultural land by using a soil capability classification system employed by the United States Soil Conservation Service. In western Oregon, lands of predominantly Classes I through IV are presumed to be agricultural. The river valleys where the population is centered are comprised almost entirely of such soils.
57. EXCEPTIONS POLICY PAPER, *supra* note 55, at § 2(B).
58. The language of Goal 14 anticipates other goals. Thus Factor 2 refers to the need for housing (Goal 10), and employment opportunities (Goal 9). Factor 3 requires consideration of the "orderly and economic provision

The relationship between the urbanization goal and the agricultural lands goal was clarified in an LCDC opinion involving the establishment of the regional urban growth boundary in the Portland metropolitan area.[59] The commission reasoned that lands within a legally sufficient and validly enacted urban growth boundary would be insulated from the substantive and procedural requirements of the agricultural lands goal. Hence development which was consistent with other applicable goals could proceed without conformity to agricultural lands policy. Conversely, in the absence of a valid urban growth boundary, vacant and uncommitted land is subject to the provisions of the agricultural lands goal and proponents must demonstrate that the need for urban uses outweighs the need to preserve agricultural lands.[60] These rulings have reinforced the commission's policies that the construction of urban growth boundaries be given priority in local planning efforts.

C. *The Second Phase*

As planning jurisdictions conclude their efforts to bring comprehensive plans and implementing ordinances into compliance with the statewide goals, the issues which have occupied attention during the initial phases of statewide planning are destined to give way to other concerns. The importance of the statewide goals in local land use decisions should be reduced following acknowledgment of compliance. The 1977 legislative revisions expressly provide that the "goal shall apply to land conservation and development actions and annexations only through the acknowledged comprehensive plan and implementing ordinances . . ."[61]

Unless the exceptions swallow the rule, one could anticipate that the *Fasano-Baker* principles may again come into their own: (1) the comprehensive plan may resume its "constitutional" status; and (2) scrutiny of land use planning decisions may once again vary according to quasi-judicial/legislative characterization.

---

for public facilities and services" (Goal 11). Factor 5 refers to energy consequences (Goal 13) and Factor 6 refers to the retention of agricultural land (Goal 3). LCDC 77–004 (Final Order, March 10, 1978), *appeal docketed*, No. 10242 (Or. App. April 7, 1978).

59. *Id.*

60. The commission subsequently adopted a rule exempting lands within cities from the requirements of the agricultural lands goal. Or. Adm. R., ch. 660, § 010–300 to –315 (1978). *See* discussion in text accompanying note 63 *infra*.

61. OR. REV. STAT. § 197.275(1) (1977 Rep. Pt.).

Once the majority of comprehensive plans are acknowledged as in compliance with the goals, the role of the LCDC is also likely to change. In its supervisory capacity, the commission may turn to a monitoring program to assure that comprehensive plans are in fact meeting goal objectives. The volume of appeals should also be reduced, especially appeals of quasi-judicial matters, as the LCDC confines itself to review of comprehensive plan amendments or those actions which are not controlled by the comprehensive plan. It may also be anticipated that the commission will increase its presently undeveloped role of designating "activities of statewide significance" and "areas of critical state concern."[62]

The approach of the time for compliance should also be accompanied by attention to development-related goals. This was presaged in the *CRAG* opinion, which exempted cities from the requirements of the agricultural lands goal. In a subsequent rule, the commission declared lands within city limits to be "urban" or "urbanizable" per se.[63] The presumption that cities will ultimately be developed underscores municipal responsibilities under the goals in accommodating future population growth.

D. *Regional Planning Legislation*

A review of statewide planning in Oregon would be incomplete without reference to unique regional planning legislation which was enacted by the 1973 legislature.[64] For the Portland metropolitan area only, the regional planning district (CRAG) has the following land use planning powers:

1. Adoption of regional planning goals and objectives.[65] In concept, the goals and objectives are analogous to the statewide planning goals.

2. Development of a comprehensive plan for the region.[66] While each member jurisdiction is required to develop its own comprehensive plan pursuant to the statewide planning goals, CRAG has authority to develop a distinct plan for the region.

3. Designation of areas and activities having significant impact on the region.[67] This power is akin to the LCDC's power to designate areas and activities of statewide significance.

---

62. *Id.* § 197.400–.430.
63. Or. Adm. R., ch. 660, § 010–300 to 315 (1978).
64. SB 769, ch. 482, 1973 Or. Laws.
65. Or. Rev. Stat. § 197.755(1) (1977 Rep. Pt.).
66. *Id.* § 197.755(2).
67. *Id.* § 197.755(3).

4. Review of local comprehensive plans for conformance with regional goals and objectives.[68]

5. Coordination of land use planning activities of member jurisdictions.[69]

6. Discretionary review of local government land use decisions for conformity with goals and objectives.[70]

CRAG's uniqueness lies in its ability to enforce its goals and objectives.[71] Local governments in the Portland area must not only conform their comprehensive plans to the statewide planning goals but to regional policies as well. This dual obligation of local governments has led to a number of problems.

In an appellate opinion, the LCDC established that CRAG itself is subject to the statewide planning goals despite distinct enabling authority.[72] This was interpreted to mean that regional goals and objectives as well as the regional comprehensive plan must conform to the statewide goals.

While consistent, this holding does not resolve the ambiguity of local government obligations under state and regional policies. CRAG has determined that it must abide by its regional goals and objectives, but these apply only indirectly to member jurisdictions. A local government achieves compliance with regional goals and objectives, according to the scheme, by conforming its comprehensive plan to the regional plan.[73] However, the compliance schedules for CRAG and its members are at variance, so that some cities and counties will have acknowledged plans prior to the completion of the regional plan.

---

68. *Id.* § 197.755(4).

69. *Id.* § 197.755(5). Outside of the metropolitan Portland area, counties are assigned the responsibility of coordinating "all planning activities affecting land uses within the county" under the statewide planning legislation. OR. REV. STAT. § 197.190 (1977 Rep. Pt.) The urbanization goal (Goal 14) requires that cities and counties cooperate in the establishment and change of urban growth boundaries.

70. OR. REV. STAT. § 197.755(6) (1977 Rep. Pt.).

71. Pursuant to its review of local comprehensive plans for conformance with regional goals and objectives, CRAG has the discretion to "recommend or require, as it considers necessary, changes in any such plan to assure that the plan conforms to the goals and objectives. . . ." *Id.* § 197.755(4). Likewise CRAG can "assure conformity with the goals and objectives" when exercising its discretion to review ordinances, regulations and actions taken by its members. *Id.* § 197.755(6).

72. LCDC 77–004 (Final Order, March 10, 1978), *appeal docketed*, No. 10242 (Or. App. April 7, 1978).

73. COLUMBIA REGION ASS'N OF GOVERNMENTS, GOALS AND OBJECTIVES, Objective II, Section 1(C) (1976).

The LCDC has attempted to reduce such discrepancies by requiring urban growth boundaries of constituent jurisdictions to coincide with the regional urban growth boundary.[74] The commission has also emphasized the importance of regional policies in determining a member's compliance with the statewide housing goal.[75] It is further contemplated that a "rider" will be attached to the acknowledged comprehensive plans of CRAG's members requiring revision of such plans to conform with regional policies as these are developed.[76]

These problems may be partially resolved as a result of the merger of CRAG into the Metropolitan Service District (MSD), effective January 1, 1979.[77] This agency will be responsible for "metropolitan aspects" of water and sewerage facilities, public transportation and land use planning.[78] While the enabling legislation preserves the majority of CRAG's land use planning powers, it

---

74. 1000 Friends of Oregon v. City of Sherwood, LCDC 76–021 (March 10, 1978). CRAG set about establishing a regional urban growth boundary pursuant to the urbanization goal prior to implementation of other goals. Objective II relating to planning processes defines an "elemental" approach to planning as follows:

> The regional plan shall be developed and administered incrementally and the elements and all adopted elements together shall constitute the regional plan . . . each element shall implement and conform to certain objectives designated in the element. When local plans conform to a regional plan element, they shall also be deemed to comply with the objectives designated in that element.

Goals and Objectives, *supra* note 73.

The first element to be adopted by CRAG was the Land Use Framework Element (adopted in 1976; revised in 1977). The element contemplates classification of all areas within the region as Urban Areas, Rural Areas and Natural Resource Areas. By definition, Urban Areas lie inside the regional growth boundary.

The *Sherwood* appeal was decided at the same time as the *CRAG* appeal, LCDC 77–004 (Final Order, March 10, 1978), *appeal docketed*, No. 10242 (Or. App. April 7, 1978), by the LCDC. Since the latter opinion established that the regional boundary was insufficient under the urbanization goal, Sherwood's boundary—which coincided with the regional urban growth boundary—fell at the same time.

75. Seaman v. City of Durham, LCDC 77–025 (April 18, 1978).

76. Columbia Region Ass'n of Governments, *Introduction to Proposed Compliance Schedule*, LCDC 77–004 (Final Order, March 10, 1978), *appeal docketed*, No. 10242 (Or. App. April 7, 1978) (submitted pursuant to interlocutory order, Dec. 19, 1977).

77. HB 2070, ch. 665, 1977 Or. Laws. The measure did not become law until it was approved by the voters of the affected counties at the primary election on May 23, 1978. The measure abolishes CRAG and transfers the majority of its functions to an expanded metropolitan service district, an existing agency responsible for public services provisions in the Portland area. *See* OR. REV. STAT. §§ 268.010–.630 (1977 Rep. Pt.).

78. HB 2070, ch. 665, §§ 10A, 17, 1977 Or. Laws.

eliminates the power to maintain and develop a comprehensive plan
for the region and the power to review land use actions of local
jurisdictions.[79] Rather, the MSD is charged with the preparation
and adoption of "functional plans" relating to "areas and activities
having significant impact upon the orderly and responsible development of the metropolitan area. . . ."[80]

These legislative changes may facilitate the regional district's
ability to coordinate land use planning activities among its members and may serve to eliminate some of the duality with which
local jurisdictions are presently faced. In any event, it is certain that
regional policies will play an important role in determining compliance of individual planning jurisdictions with the statewide goals.

III. The Effect of Statewide Planning on the Provision of Housing

The implications of statewide land use planning can be best understood by a closer look at the operation of the goals and the inter-
relationships between the legislation, its administration and judicial
enforcement. The following materials examine the operation of
the statewide housing goal.

A. *Housing Crisis in Progress*

As in other areas of the country, Oregon has experienced sharply
increased housing prices in recent years.[81] The crisis has many in-

---

79. The tri-county government commission, which was responsible for
authoring the measure, was explicit in its intent to abolish the agency's power
to devise a regional comprehensive plan:
> To reduce duplicative efforts, the commission recommends that the re-
> gional level not be involved directly in preparing a detailed comprehensive
> land use plan for the region. Instead, it should prepare functional plans
> for major area-wide activities, such as water, sewerage and transportation
> that would serve as framework guidelines for local comprehensive plans.
> Local comprehensive plans will still have to conform with area wide land-
> use policies and goals and the broader functional plans, but the duplicative
> detailed comprehensive planning at the regional level would be eliminated.
TRI-COUNTY LOCAL GOVERNMENT COMM'N, MEMORANDUM TO HOUSE
COMM. ON INTERGOVERNMENTAL AFFAIRS, 1977 SESS., at 15 (Jan. 28, 1977).
The distinction between detailed comprehensive planning and "functional"
plans may be related to a regional map. If this interpretation is made, then
the MSD will not be able to construct and enforce a regional urban growth
boundary. Local governments in the region must, of course, comply with the
urbanization goal, and the MSD would be responsible for coordinating planning efforts in establishing local urban growth boundaries. HB 2070, ch. 665,
§§ 17(3), 19, 1977 Or. Laws.
80. *Id.* § 18. Under this provision, functional plans can at least be developed for air quality, water quality and transportation.
81. In the Portland metropolitan area, the average price of a new home
rose 69% during the period from 1972 to 1977; the average price of an ex-

dicators. Disposable incomes have not kept pace with rising housing costs. Significant changes in tenure have occurred, as fewer families are able to afford the minimum priced new or used home. These changes in the marketplace also affect urban densities and lifestyles, as households are forced to shift to smaller single family units or to multi-family units.

At the same time that housing prices have increased, regulatory measures affecting the costs of housing have proliferated.[82] The interrelationship between governmental regulation and housing costs is receiving increased public attention.[83] Governmental regulations contribute to housing costs in at least the following ways:[84]

1. Requirements for site development and manner of construction. Subdivision regulations, including design review criteria, and building codes are the chief sources of regulatory impact. These regulations may be imposed at any level of government.[85]

2. Administrative procedures which govern the length of time required to process development applications. Subdivision and partitioning ordinances typically establish procedures for approving development applications.[86] These measures often require review by departments and agencies other than the decision-making body. The complexity of appellate procedures also lengthens the time for

---

isting home rose 83% during the same period. From 1970 to 1977, estimated median family income rose only 62%. Those households able to purchase the average priced new home decreased from 75% to 64%. Average monthly contract rent increased 33% during the period from 1973 to 1977. COLUMBIA REGION ASS'N OF GOVERNMENTS, INITIAL HOUSING POLICIES, AFFORDABLE HOUSING 19–21 (1978).

82. *See generally* R. Freilich, *Awakening the Sleeping Giant: New Trends and Developments in Environmental and Land Use Controls*, in INSTITUTE ON PLANNING, ZONING, AND EMINENT DOMAIN 1 (1974).

83. *See generally* U.S. DEP'T. OF HOUSING AND URBAN DEVELOPMENT, FINAL REPORT OF THE TASK FORCE ON HOUSING COSTS (1978). The Oregon legislature has convened a joint interim task force on housing costs which held seven meetings ending October 11, 1978. A Joint Interim Task Force Report on housing costs is projected to be published and presented to the 1979 Oregon Legislative Session.

84. Many schemes have been devised to classify regulatory impacts on housing costs. *See, e.g.*, Ellickson, *Suburban Growth Controls: An Economic and Legal Analysis*, 86 YALE L.J. 385 (1977). *But see* Freilich, *Editor's Comments: Land Use Controls and Growth Management: The Need for a Comprehensive View*, 9 URB. LAW. v (Summer 1977).

85. In Oregon, for example, there is a state building code. OR. REV. STAT. § 456.750–.890 (1977 Rep. Pt.). As a result of a recent state supreme court decision, municipalities are free to enact more restrictive building code requirements. *See* discussion in text accompanying notes 93–95, *infra*.

86. U.S. DEP'T. OF HOUSING AND URBAN DEVELOPMENT, *supra* note 83 at 28–34. *See generally* R. FREILICH & P. LEVI, MODEL SUBDIVISION REGULATIONS (1975).

development approval,[87] as does negligent administration of the process.

3. Exclusion of housing types. This occurs primarily at the local government level. It may occur directly as where a city or county prohibits some types of units or subjects them to burdensome procedural requirements. Exclusion may also result indirectly, by means of restrictions on number of bedrooms, size of residential lots, or multi-family density limitations.[88]

4. Land availability constraints. This category refers to the availability of sites for the kinds of uses which are authorized by the city or county. Housing costs are increased when demand for an authorized use significantly exceeds the supply of land available for the use. This occurs not only through mapping deficiencies but also as a result of service moratoriums, quota systems or phasing devices which retard the provision of services in relation to the demand for the type of housing.[89]

---

87. The adoption of statewide planning legislation has added complexity to the appeals process. The statewide goals themselves provide potentially aggrieved parties with a new arsenal with which to attack development decisions. *See* discussion in text accompanying notes 22–34, *supra*. This has considerable impact prior to the acknowledgment of comprehensive plans, since the term "land conservation and development action" can apply to several decisions in the course of obtaining a development approval. For instance, prior to acknowledgment of the comprehensive plan for the jurisdiction, an application for a zone change of vacant agricultural land to a residential designation would be subject to the exceptions procedure under the land use planning goal. *See* discussion in text accompanying notes 54–55, *supra*. Once secured, a separate appeal on the basis of the agricultural lands goal could be made at the time of preliminary plat approval for a subdivision. 1000 Friends of Oregon v. Board of County Comm'rs, 32 Or. App. 413, 575 P.2d 651 (1978).

An appellant has his choice of forums. He may challenge a development decision on the basis of goal violations either in the circuit court under a declaratory judgment or mandamus proceeding, or he may choose to appeal the decision to the LCDC. Prior to the 1977 legislative session, an appellant could potentially bring appeals in both forums. Amendments now require him to elect between the circuit court and the LCDC. OR. REV. STAT. § 197.300(3). It is unclear whether this limitation applies only to a single appellant or whether it pertains to the facts that give rise to the cause of action.

88. For a general discussion of exclusionary land use policies and case summaries, *see* URBAN LAW INSTITUTE, FAIR HOUSING AND EXCLUSIONARY LAND USE (1974). As noted therein, much of the exclusionary land use litigation has involved challenges to the exclusion of federally assisted housing. The scheme presented here pertains primarily to regulatory practices that affect the operation of the nonassisted housing market.

89. *See* Ellickson, *supra* note 84. In the Portland area, the cost of improved lots increased 200% from 1973 to 1977, while the cost of unimproved land increased 211% per acre. COLUMBIA REGION ASS'N OF GOVERNMENTS, *supra* note 81, at 11.

While the effect of regulation varies among communities with local government policy, much of the impact stems from statutory requirements or from regional and state policies that condition the planning and zoning functions of cities and counties. The effect of this regulatory scheme on housing costs is cumulative, so that households are priced out of a particular housing market or are forced to contribute an increasing proportion of their income to shelter needs.[90]

B. Oregon's Response

Oregon's legislature has dealt in a piecemeal fashion with some of the regulatory causes of housing cost increases. Thus it has provided that state agencies must utilize a "one-stop" permit procedure for processing development applications.[91] The 1977 Legislative Assembly also enacted a joint resolution, stating: "The cost of all state and local regulatory legislation should be measured against the benefits to the occupants . . . (a) Health and safety requirements should be interpreted narrowly rather than broadly, in making such measurements . . ."[92] The Oregon courts have had little occasion to deal with the relationship between governmental regulation and housing costs. The result has generally been to up-

---

90. Expenditures of more than 25% of gross family income for housing costs is considered excessive by many authorities. The U.S. Department of Housing and Urban Development uses this percentage in its market analysis. *See* FHA TECHNIQUES OF HOUSING MARKET ANALYSIS (1970). Oregon uses this percentage in determining "lower income families" for its own subsidy programs. OR. REV. STAT. § 456.615(12) (1977 Rep. Pt.).

91. OR. REV. STAT. § 447.800–.865 (1977 Rep. Pt.). The legislature recognized the cost impacts of procedural delays. "The Legislative Assembly further finds that state agency processes in making decisions regarding issuance of permits for projects may impose unnecessary cost on project developers and deny citizens the opportunity for effective participation in the decision making process." *Id.* § 447.085(2). Under the procedure, permit applicants need submit only a single application to the Executive Department, which then notifies other state agencies of the pending application. *Id.* § 447.820. Agencies not responding within 30 days cannot require a permit of the applicant. *Id.* § 447.820(4), (5).

At the local government level, each city or county is required to publicize a list of all development charges and permits issued by the city or county describing the nature of the fee and the agency from which the permit may be obtained. *Id.* § 447.875, .880.

92. 1977 Or. Laws, Resolutions, HJR8, at 1094–95. The Oregon Department of Commerce also contains a Housing Division, OR. REV. STAT. § 456.550–.610 (1977 Rep. Pt.), which has the power to "undertake and carry out studies and analysis of housing needs within the state and ways of meeting such needs . . ." and "submit proposed legislation . . . to alleviate any existing housing shortage or detrimental housing conditions . . ." found to exist thereby. *Id.* § 456.625(1), (2).

hold regulatory action by local governments. In *Haley v. City of Troutdale*,[93] the supreme court authorized the use of local building code requirements exceeding that of the state's building code. The defendant city had adopted an ordinance requiring double-wall construction on single-family dwellings, wherein the state Building Code permitted both single-wall and double-wall construction.[94] The state of Oregon challenged Troutdale's ordinance, claiming that the state's provisions preempted the building specifications. In rejecting the state's position, the court held that state requirements were "basic" and "minimum safety standards" above which local governments were free to enact more restrictive measures.[95]

The appellate courts have also decided a series of cases which deal with the exclusion of mobile homes by local governments. In *Clackamas County v. Ague*,[96] the court of appeals upheld the county's declaration of a mobile home as a nuisance. Although the comprehensive plan stated that mobile homes should be encouraged "as a means of fulfilling limited income housing needs,"[97] county ordinances permitted mobile homes only as conditional uses in a few zones. The court could find no conflict between the existing plan and the ordinance.

The court also rejected plaintiff's equal protection theory on the ground that only a minimum rationality was required to uphold the county ordinance.[98] A distinction such as the difference in appreciation values between mobile homes and conventionally constructed homes was found a sufficient basis for discriminating between the uses.

In *Clackamas County v. Dunham*,[99] a divided court of appeals vacated an injunction granted by the trial court for the removal of a mobile home in an area which was not zoned for mobile home use. The court based its decision on ordinance interpretation, ruling that the term "trailer house" used in the ordinance did not apply to the modern mobile home.

The supreme court reversed *Dunham*, holding that the 1960 ordinance did encompass modern mobile homes: "[A]s it leaves the

---

93. 281 Or. 203, 576 P.2d 1238 (1978).
94. These terms refer to the thickness of siding and sheathing required in the construction of units.
95. 281 Or. at 211, 576 P.2d at 1243 (1978).
96. 27 Or. App. 515, 556 P.2d 1386 (1976).
97. *Id.* at ___, 556 P.2d at 1388.
98. *Id.* at 518, 556 P.2d at 1388.
99. 282 Or. 419, 579 P.2d 223 (1978), *rev'g*, 30 Or. App. 595, 567 P.2d 605 (1977).

manufacturer, a 'building' which is a mobile home is forever a mobile home."[100] Justice Howell, in a dissenting opinion, pointed out the distinction between modern mobile homes and those contemplated by the county's ordinance. He also concluded without explanation that the county ordinance as construed by the majority violated the statewide planning goals.

C. Scheme of the Statewide Housing Goal

The statewide housing goal was adopted by the Land Conservation and Development Commission in 1975, along with 13 other statewide goals. The goal reads as follows:

> To provide for the housing needs of the citizens of the state. Buildable lands for residential use shall be inventoried and plans shall encourage the availability of adequate numbers of housing units at price ranges and rent levels which are commensurate with the financial capabilities of Oregon households and allow for flexibility of housing location, type and density.[101]

The goal is, of course, result oriented; it envisions stability of unit prices in the marketplace and the achievement of consumer preference. Achievement of the goal necessarily requires local governments to attend to all categories of regulatory impacts on housing costs. Affirmatively, cities and counties must make available sufficient buildable lands to accommodate housing needs. On the other hand, jurisdictions must examine and amend local ordinances and administrative practices which unnecessarily increase housing costs.

The cornerstone of the housing goal is the buildable lands inventory.[102] The goal clearly requires local governments to approach the issue of residential land supply in a market sense; the supply of developable land by housing type must keep pace with demand for housing if a stable housing market that satisfies consumer preference is to be achieved. Policies and practices which limit the supply of serviced land for residential use or which result in inflated land prices clearly contravene the goal.

---

100. *Id.* at 426, 579 P.2d at 226 (footnote omitted).

101. Or. Adm. R., ch. 660, § 15–000(10).

102. The term "buildable lands" under the goal is defined as "lands in urban and urbanizable areas that are suitable, available and necessary for residential use." Or. Adm. R., ch. 660, § 15–000(10). This term appears to be all-inclusive, requiring that vacant and developable lands be identified with respect to service capabilities as well as with reference to zoning designation.

D. *Judicial Activism in Other Jurisdictions: A Comparison*

1. Mount Laurel. Before exploring the promise of the state housing goal in minimizing adverse regulatory impacts on housing, it is well to examine judicial action in other jurisdictions where similar issues have been presented.[103] The New Jersey Supreme Court has gone the farthest in analyzing the economic exclusion of lower income households as a result of local government policy.[104] In *Southern Burlington County NAACP v. Township of Mount Laurel,* the court held that a developing municipality "must, by its land use regulations, presumptively make realistically possible an appropriate variety and choice of housing" for low- and moderate-income households.[105] It must, therefore, "affirmatively afford such persons the opportunity to acquire such housing at least to the extent of the municipality's fair share of the present and prospective regional need therefor."[106]

The township of Mount Laurel had large quantities of vacant land zoned exclusively for single-family dwellings, with relatively large minimum lot size requirements. The town also contained large areas which were zoned for industrial use. The resulting scheme allowed only for homes within the financial reach of persons of at least middle-income.

In finding Mount Laurel's zoning ordinance contrary to the general welfare, the court discounted the town's theory that fiscal and environmental reasons justified the zoning scheme.[107] The munici-

---

103. Not considered here are federal cases which devolve upon the issue of exclusionary intent. Following the U.S. Supreme Court's decision in Village of Arlington Heights v. Metropolitan Hous. Dev. Corp., 429 U.S. 252 (1977), the equal protection clause of the fourteenth amendment does not protect suspect classes of persons from municipal housing practices which create racially disproportionate impacts. Rather, such persons must show "that a discriminatory purpose has been a motivating factor" in the decision to exclude them from the community.

104. Other states have also invalidated municipal zoning ordinances which create adverse regional impacts. Surrick v. Zoning Hearing Bd., 476 Pa. 182, 382 A.2d 105 (1977); Berenson v. Town of New Castle, 38 N.Y.2d 102, 341 N.E.2d 236, 378 N.Y.S.2d 672 (1975); *see also* Associated Home Builders of the Greater East Bay, Inc. v. City of Livermore, 18 Cal. 3d 582, 557 P.2d 473, 135 Cal. Rptr. 41 (1976).

105. 67 N.J. 151, ___, 336 A.2d 713, 724 (1975).

106. *Id.*

107. The township had argued that the unavailability of services to much of the vacant land area justified large minimum lot sizes. The court stated that the township could require improvements by developers or use special assessment procedures to install appropriate facilities. In view of exclusionary impacts of the zoning scheme, the court stated that "the danger and impact [from urban development] must be substantial and very real (the

pality had failed to meet its substantive and procedural burden in overcoming the presumption that its ordinance was invalid. The court gave the town ninety days to revise those parts of its zoning ordinance found to conflict with the principles set forth in the opinion.

The court grounded its analysis in the equal protection and due process provisions of the New Jersey Constitution.[108] The importance of housing in providing for the general welfare raised the case to constitutional importance, the court commented.[109] Insofar as land use regulations contravened the ability of low- and moderate-income households to acquire shelter, they were impermissible exercises of the police power and were constitutionally invalid.

The court stressed that the general welfare that must be considered by a municipality was that of the region in which the municipality was located. The applicable "region" would vary from situation to situation. Once determined, the municipality must "bear its fair share of the regional burden of providing for low- and moderate-income housing needs."[110]

---

construction of every building or the improvement of every plot has some environmental impact)—not simply a makeweight to support exclusionary housing measures or preclude growth—and the regulation adopted must be only that reasonably necessary for public protection of a vital interest." *Id.* at ___, 336 A.2d at 731. *See* discussion in text accompanying notes 137–144, *infra.*

108. The court avoided basing its decision on the minority status of the plaintiffs or the exclusionary intent of the municipality, stating: "We will, therefore, consider the case from the wider viewpoint that the effect of Mount Laurel's land use regulation has been to prevent various categories of persons from living in the township because of the limited extent of their income and resources." *Id.* at ___, 336 A.2d at 717. *Cf.* Village of Arlington Heights v. Metropolitan Hous. Dev. Corp., 429 U.S. 252 (1977) (focusing on intent).

The constitutional basis of the decision protects lower income households against legislative measures designed to reestablish the status quo disturbed by the court's decision. *See* Rose, *Mount Laurel: Is it Based on Wishful Thinking?*, 4 REAL EST. L.J. 61, 67–68 (1975).

109. The court did not go so far as to declare housing as a "fundamental interest." This approach has been adopted by the United States Supreme Court. *See, e.g.,* San Antonio School Dist. v. Rodriguez, 411 U.S. 1 (1973). In Robinson v. Cahill, 62 N.J. 473, 303 A.2d 273, *modified on rehearing,* 67 N.J. 333, 339 A.2d 193 (1975), the court defined its role in determining a constitutional violation to be as follows: "Ultimately, a court must weigh the nature of the restraint or denial against the apparent public justification, and decide whether the state action is arbitrary." *Id.* at 492, 303 A.2d at 282. In *Mount Laurel,* however, the court did not frame its opinion in these precise terms.

110. Southern Burlington County NAACP v. Township of Mount Laurel, 67 N.J. 151, ___, 336 A.2d 713, 733.

2. *Oakwood at Madison.* The principles of *Mount Laurel* were clarified and extended in the case of *Oakwood at Madison, Inc. v. Township of Madison.*[111] The township had been the subject of previous litigation stemming from its exclusion of multi-family dwellings. The township amended its zoning ordinance to provide for smaller lot zoning, more multi-family development and planned unit developments. The trial court found that the municipality still fell short of its regional fair share, in that the proportion of new housing units affordable to lower income households was less than the present population of such households and the township had not taken into account prospective needs for lower priced units.

The supreme court began its analysis by reiterating the principles of *Mount Laurel:* developing municipalities must by their zoning regulations serve the general welfare of the region in providing for the needs of lower income households through the assumption of a "fair share" of such housing. A municipality fulfills its obligation through "bona fide efforts toward the elimination of minimization of undue cost-generating requirements" in the zoning ordinance.[112] The court then made a significant qualification: municipalities are *not* required to "devise specific formula for estimating their precise fair share of lower income housing needs of a specifically demarcated region."[113]

The reasons for this qualification, the court explains, are twofold. First, numerical housing goals are not "realistically translatable into specific substantive changes in a zoning ordinance" and hence are merely incidental to effective housing relief.[114] Second, courts are not equipped to regulate housing distribution for a region. Housing quotas for individual municipalities are properly the province of "administrative agencies acting under legislative authorization."[115]

The court's reasoning is sound. Since municipalities are not engaged in the building of housing, and since the private market cannot construct new housing for lower- and moderate-income households without subsidization, it is probable that a new housing market will not accommodate a municipality's fair share of the regional need for lower income housing. However, the court ex-

---

111. 72 N.J. 481, 371 A.2d 1192 (1977).
112. *Id.* at ___, 371 A.2d at 1200.
113. *Id.*
114. *Id.*
115. *Id.* at ___, 371 A.2d at 1200–01.

plained, lower income households can acquire lower priced housing through the "filtering" process, whereby families of lower income acquire units vacated by higher income families seeking newly constructed housing.[116]

For the filtering process to work, the court held, a municipality must "adjust its zoning regulations so as to render possible and feasible the 'least cost' housing, consistent with minimum standards of health and safety, which private industry will undertake, and in amounts sufficient to satisfy the deficit in the hypothesized fair share." In analyzing Madison's revised ordinance, the court found it quantitatively and qualitatively deficient. "Insufficient areas are zoned to permit such housing, and the zoning restrictions are such as to prevent production of units at least cost consistent with health and safety requirements."[117]

3. Pascack Association, Ltd. Still further qualifications were placed on the *Mount Laurel* principles in the case of *Pascack Association, Ltd. v. Mayor of Washington.*[118] Unlike the communities of Mount Laurel and Madison, Washington Township contained only 2.3% vacant land. The majority of the land was occupied by single-family dwellings, and the remaining vacant acreage was primarily single-family. Five of eight municipalities in the region had no multi-family units whatsoever. In light of these facts, the trial court held that the township had not provided its fair share of multi-family housing and invalidated the ordinance as exclusionary.

In reversing, the supreme court emphasized that the *Mount Laurel* decision was based on constitutional principles therein protecting low- and moderate-income households. While courts must apply constitutional principles to municipal zoning schemes that do not accommodate the needs of such persons, a court may not interfere with legislative actions by municipalities that do not impact this class. The court's review in such instances is limited to whether the zoning scheme is "clearly arbitrary, capricious or unreasonable, or plainly contrary to fundamental principles of zoning or the statute."[119] The court found that the particular development under consideration did not address the needs of lower- and moderate-income households.[120]

---

116. *Id.* at ___, 371 A.2d at 1207–08.
117. *Id.* at ___, 371 A.2d at 1208.
118. 74 N.J. 470, 379 A.2d 6 (1977), *rev'g*, 31 N.J. Super. 195, 329 A.2d 89 (1974).
119. *Id.* at ___, 379 A.2d at 11.
120. *Id.* at ___, 379 A.2d at 10.

Appellants argued that municipalities must zone "for an appropriate variety and choice of housing" for all categories of the population under *Mount Laurel*. The court rejected this notion, commenting that such an idea was realizable only in a developing municipality. As a developed municipality, the court reasoned, Washington Township was free to maintain its single-family character.[121] The court further noted that the need for affordable housing of all kinds for the general population" was not a proper subject for judicial scrutiny in the absence of statutes that imposed regional housing obligations on municipalities.[122]

E. *Housing Goal Revisited*

Each of the New Jersey decisions exhorts the legislature to adopt laws that remedy social problems stemming from inadequate housing where judicial scrutiny of local zoning ordinances under constitutional principles cannot provide solutions.[123]

Oregon's statewide planning legislation is arguably such a legislative scheme. The language of the housing goal in fact reflects the *Mount Laurel* directive that municipalities must make available an appropriate variety and choice of housing.[124] The statewide housing goal is universal in its application to all Oregon households, and is not addressed only to the provision of lower income household needs.

The correspondence of the statewide housing goal with the New Jersey decisions has not escaped the Land Conservation and De-

---

121. *Id.* at ___, 379 A.2d at 13. The court stated:
Thus, maintaining the character of a fully developed, predominantly single family residential community constitutes an appropriate desideratum of zoning to which a municipal governing body may legitimately give substantial weight in arriving at a policy legislative decision as to whether, or to what extent, to admit multi-family housing in such vacant land areas as remaining in such a community.
In some respects, the court's decision is ambiguous. The discussion on the role of the court in reviewing for constitutional violations is clearly linked to the impact of the regulations on lower income households. Had the developer been able to provide such housing, the court may have scrutinized the exclusion of apartment units more closely.
122. *Id.* at ___, 379 A.2d at 15. The court stated: "The sociological problems presented by this and similar cases, and of concern not only to our dissenting brother, but ourselves, call for legislation vesting appropriate developmental control in state or regional administrative agencies." *Id.*
123. *Id.*
124. Compare the edict of *Mount Laurel*—to "make realistically possible an appropriate variety and choice of housing" 72 N.J. 481, ___, 371 A.2d 1192, 1200, with the language of the housing goal—"the availability of

velopment Commission. In *Seaman v. City of Durham*,[125] the commission identified the goal directives with the principles of *Mount Laurel* and *Oakwood at Madison*. The case involved the city's attempts to reduce permitted densities on vacant and developable land by increasing minimum square foot requirements of dwelling units. The commission determined that the housing goal required local governments to plan for regional needs rather than for parochial interest:

> Goal 10 speaks of the housing needs of Oregon households, not the housing needs of Durham households. Its meaning is clear: planning for housing must not be parochial. Planning jurisdictions must consider the needs of the relevant region in arriving at a fair allocation of housing types. Goal 10 represents the broader interest of all Oregon households.[126]

In the absence of regional determinations allocating "fair share" housing responsibilities, the commission would embrace a "least cost" doctrine of the *Oakwood at Madison* decision, requiring that the jurisdiction "do its part toward solving the housing needs of the area's residents of all income levels, as far as is reasonably possible given the constraints of land, materials, and similar costs."[127] The commission found that the increases in square footage requirements violated the principle by adding to the minimum cost of new housing and by constraining flexibility in housing type. The city's ordinance was invalidated and the matter remanded pending allocation of fair share by CRAG.

The *Seaman* opinion illustrates one of the weaknesses in the "least cost" principle in *Oakwood at Madison*. Under that case, a municipality has an obligation to render "least cost" housing only to the extent of its fair share of the regional need.[128] The *Oakwood* court discussed at some length factors which are relevant in determining an appropriate "region" and regional fair share.[129] It indicates that an official fair share housing allocation by a group of counties might merit "prima facie judicial acceptance."[130]

---

adequate numbers of housing units . . ." and "flexibility of housing location, type and density."
    125. Seaman v. City of Durham, LCDC 77–025 (April 18, 1978).
    126. *Id.* at 9.
    127. *Id.* at 13.
    128. 72 N.J. 481, __, 371 A.2d 1192, 1207.
    129. *Id.* at __, 371 A.2d at 1217–23. The court adopted the trial judge's definition of the appropriate region as "the area from which, in view of available employment and transportation, the population of the township would be drawn, absent invalidly exclusionary zoning." *Id.* at __, 371 A.2d at 1219.
    130. *Id.* at __, 371 A.2d at 1220.

Such fair share plans usually embrace only subsidized housing.[131] The court fails to explain how a review of zoning schemes for least cost housing violations will result in a filtering process that arrives at the municipality's fair share. There are as many "imponderables between a zone change and the actual production of housing on sites as zoned"[132] inherent in the dynamics of filtering as there are in the market production of new housing units for lower income families following an assignment of fair share. In short, *Oakwood at Madison* does not provide a method for getting from least cost scrutiny to the constitutional objective of providing for lower income housing needs.

The LCDC's opinion in *Seaman* perpetuates this confusion. On one hand, the opinion seems to contemplate a regional allocation of housing needs irrespective of income class. Yet the term "fair share" was interpreted by New Jersey courts to apply only to lower income housing allocations. Furthermore, allocation plans underway for the region encompassed only assignment of a fair share of assisted housing.[133]

Logically, regional allocation of housing responsibilities under Oregon's housing goal should achieve "the ideal of the well-balanced community, providing all kinds of housing for a cross section of the regional population pattern" referred to in the *Pascack* case.[134] In fact, this kind of determination may be essential to an effective filtering process.[135] Under such a system, the demand for

---

131. Regional allocation schemes are most often associated with the development of an Area Wide Housing Opportunity Plan, which is the device used by the U.S. Department of Housing and Urban Development as the basis for distributing housing assistance funds. 24 C.F.R. § 891.102(c) (1978). The plan must contain "an area wide assessment . . . of the housing assistance needs of lower income households. . . ." *Id.* § 891.503. Needs by household type are to be identified for each county and for each jurisdiction of over 25,000 persons. *Id.*

In the CRAG area, the regional level allocation is made on the basis of housing need and employment opportunities for low- and moderate-income households in the jurisdictions. Projections of each category are made annually and for a three-year goal. COLUMBIA REGION ASS'N OF GOVERNMENTS, DISCUSSION DRAFT, AREA WIDE HOUSING OPPORTUNITY PLAN (1978).

132. 72 N.J. 481, ___, 371 A.2d 1192, 1200.

133. *Supra* note 131.

134. 74 N.J. 470, ___, 379 A.2d 6, 14 (1977).

135. An effective filtering process in theory requires a stable and well functioning new housing market. Higher income families must vacate older structures in search of affordable new units. To the extent that new housing construction is limited in some areas of the region, other jurisdictions which facilitate construction may become overburdened in periods of heavy demand for housing. If facilities become temporarily overloaded, or growth control devices are imposed to regulate the rate of growth in such communities, the

housing units and the supply of developable land would be allocated among the jurisdictions of the region. The housing demand forecast would be specified by unit type and price range. Land supply would be specified by housing type and by acreage.[136]

As indicated previously, local governments also contribute to housing cost increases through substantive and procedural requirements for processing development applications. The least cost doctrine of the *Seaman* opinion must necessarily extend to local ordinances and regulations which have this effect. A municipality's obligations under the goal, thus, will not be exhausted following a regional allocation of housing responsibilities. Prior to acknowledgment of compliance of the local comprehensive plan, a municipality should be required to demonstrate that its ordinance scheme is designed to achieve least cost housing for all Oregon households.

F. Problems and Recommendations

1. Role of the Judiciary. The Oregon courts have not been called upon to interpret the statewide housing goal. Review of a zoning scheme for housing goal violations will be, in most instances, a statutory exercise in which the court considers other applicable planning goals in addition to the housing goal.[137] This balancing

---

region will be unable to rechannel demand into other communities which have artificially limited new housing supply.

136. The U.S. Department of Housing and Urban Development (HUD), as well as the state of Oregon's Housing Division, employs a market analysis procedure which generates the demand for housing units by price range or rent level. The model is contained in HUD's *Techniques of Housing Market Analysis* (1970). CRAG is developing these figures by jurisdiction for the Portland region.

CRAG has also identified a system for allocating this demand to vacant and developable land by jurisdiction. The first step is a buildable lands survey for the region pursuant to the Housing Goal. *See* discussion, *supra* note 102. Single family dwellings are allocated according to a holding capacity variable (based primarily on vacant land zoned for single family use) and according to a variable defining accessibility of vacant residential land to new basic employment opportunities. Multi-family units are allocated according to five variables: accessibility of vacant residential land to population; share of single family dwelling units; change in accessibility to population; share of future manufacturing employment; and housing value. CRAG, "First Round" Regional Growth Allocation for the CRAG Transportation Study Area Year 2000 at 15–17 (1978).

137. Both the *Green* decision, 271 Or. 500, 533 P.2d 772 (1975), and the *Benton County* case, LCDC 77–004 (Final Order, March 10, 1978), *appeal docketed*, No. 10242 (Or. App. April 7, 1978), indicate that policy decisions by local governments are essentially balancing processes and that a reviewing court must not substitute its judgment for local decision makers. The comprehensiveness of the statewide planning goals assures that housing

process must be guided by a set of standards for establishing housing goal violations.[138]

One obvious solution is to ground the least cost principle of the housing goal in the Oregon Constitution for low- and moderate-income households. The constitutional approach of the New Jersey Supreme Court has the advantage of guaranteeing housing availability for economically deprived households regardless of the status of state legislation on the subject.

The equal protection clause of Oregon's constitution is well-suited to afford this minimum protection for lower income households.[139] In *Olsen v. State*,[140] a case involving an equal protection challenge to the Oregon system of school financing, Justice Linde cited the New Jersey Supreme Court's decision in *Robinson v. Cahill*[141] in framing the equal protection test under Oregon's constitution:

> We prefer the approach made by the New Jersey Court in *Robinson v. Cahill* [citation omitted]. Its approach could be termed a balancing test. Under this approach the court weighs the detriment to the education of the children of certain districts against the ostensible justification for the scheme of school financing. If the court determines the detriment is much greater than the justification, the financing scheme violates the guarantee of equal protection.[142]

The Oregon Supreme Court should again follow the lead of the New Jersey Supreme Court in declaring that housing for lower income families is of fundamental importance. The municipality's interest in justifying effectively exclusionary land use regulations would vary according to the goal objective used to justify the re-

---

policies will not be promulgated at the expense of other valid planning objectives.

138. In Sun Ray Drive-In Dairy, Inc. v. Oregon Liquor Control Comm'n, 16 Or. App. 63, 517 P.2d 289 (1973), the court stated: "It is not for the court, but for the administrative agency with its statutory mandate and its expertise to develop standards." *Id.* at ___, 517 P.2d at 294. Without standards, the court could not avoid substituting its judgment for that of the administrative agency whose decision was under review.

Under the statewide planning legislation, a land planning decision can be challenged either by appeal to the LCDC or by a petition in the circuit court. *Supra* note 44. A determination by the LCDC is subject to the right of appeal to the court of appeals. The principles of *Sun Ray* are directly applicable to this form of review.

139. OR. CONST. art. I, § 20. Oregon's due process clause—art. I, § 10—does not have the constitutional breadth of the equal protection clause. *See* Linde, *Without Due Process*, 49 OR. L. REV. 125 (1970); *cf.* Surrick v. Zoning Hearing Bd., 476 Pa. 182, 382 A.2d 105 (1977).

140. 276 Or. 9, 554 P.2d 139 (1976).

141. 62 N.J. 473, 303 A.2d 273 (1975).

142. 276 Or. at ___, 454 P.2d at 145.

strictions. The municipality would operate under a presumption that its ordinance scheme was invalid.[143]

Where land use regulations prevent the achievement of least cost housing for other income classes, the LCDC must specify minimum obligations of local governments under the housing goal. The housing goal imposes essentially affirmative duties which must be executed by local governments before the plan and ordinances can comply with the goal.[144]

2. *Role of the Commission.* If least cost housing is to be effected in Oregon, it is essential that the LCDC establish procedures and criteria for evaluating the structure of local comprehensive plans and implementing ordinances for compliance with the housing goal. Courts can be expected to defer to local zoning schemes which have been acknowledged by the commission as in compliance with the statewide planning goals.[145] The specter of premature acknowledgment could come to haunt judicial proceedings involving allegations of housing goal violations. The presumption of validity attaching

---

143. In *Mount Laurel,* the court stated:
We have spoken of this obligation of such municipalities as "presumptive." The term has two aspects, procedural and substantive. Procedurally, we think the basic importance of appropriate housing for all dictates that, when it is shown that a developing municipality in its land use regulations has not made realistically possible a variety in choice of housing . . . a facial showing of violation of substantive due process or equal protection under the state constitution has been made out and the burden, and it is heavy one, shifts to the municipality to establish a valid basis for its action or non-action. . . . The substantive aspect of "presumptive" relates to the specifics, on the one hand, of what municipal land use regulation provisions, or the absence thereof, will evidence invalidity and shift the burden of proof and, on the other hand, of what basis and considerations will carry the municipality's burden and sustain what it has done or failed to do. . . .
67 N.J. 151, __, 336 A.2d 713, 728 (1975).
144. The *Seaman* decision, LCDC 77–025 (April 18, 1978), directs that local governments must examine their plans for consistency with the least cost principle, without specifying the extent of the obligation. Contrast the affimative duties under development-related goals with the negative obligation under preservation-related goals. The LCDC has prescribed that the agricultural lands and forest lands goals, together with certain shoreline goals, require local governments to meet the procedural burdens of the exception process before authorizing development actions which potentially conflict with the goals' objectives. EXCEPTIONS POLICY PAPER, *supra* note 55, at § I(3).
145. Prior to acknowledgment, existing zoning ordinances are subject to the application of all the goals. Post acknowledgment, the goals apply only through the comprehensive plan for the jurisdiction. OR. REV. STAT. § 197.275(1) (1977 Rep. Pt.). Of course, a zoning ordinance could still come under one of the two exceptions to this rule. *See* discussion, *supra* note 26. Given the possibility of deference, it may be that the LCDC's orders of compliance will become the focal point of litigation.

to plans and ordinances which have been acknowledged by the LCDC could operate to diminish even constitutional scrutiny by the courts.

The issue assumes immediate importance in view of the fact that the commission has scheduled review of urban growth boundaries of certain cities, counties and of CRAG prior to submission of comprehensive plans and ordinances by these jurisdictions. An urban growth boundary which is established without adequate consideration of land needed for housing during the relevant planning period contributes directly to housing cost increases through its effect on land prices. The commission can avoid such consequences through timely promulgation of standards for housing goal compliance which are applicable to all plan elements which are submitted for acknowledgment.

IV. Conclusion

Oregon's land use legislation offers a comprehensive solution to a housing crisis which is in part fueled by governmental regulation. Administratively, the statewide housing goal has been linked with principles established by New Jersey courts. If Oregon's citizens are to be availed of a full range of housing remedies, Oregon courts should supplement these principles with appropriate constitutional interpretations. The effectiveness of judicial scrutiny is dependent, however, on the diligence of the LCDC in establishing standards of review for housing goal violations.

The Public Control of
Land Use:
An Anglophile's View

Victor Moore, LL.M.*

Visiting Professor, University of Missouri-Kansas
City, School of Law 1977; Senior Lecturer in Law,
University of Reading, Reading, England; Visiting
Lecturer, Inns of Court School of Law, London,
England; Assistant Editor, Journal of Planning and
Environment Law and Encyclopedia of Land
Development (Sweet and Maxwell, London,
England). The article is substantially the author's
presentation of the annual John B. Gage Lecture
on Urban Affairs given by him at the University of
Missouri-Kansas City School of Law in April, 1977.

I. Introduction

BEFORE THERE WAS ANY PUBLIC CONTROL over the use and development of land, landowners were free to use their land in any way
they wished, subject only to limitations contained in their individual
grant and to obligations placed upon them at common law. In essence, therefore, provided an owner acted within the limitations of
his estate and committed no nuisance or trespass against his neighbor's property, he was free to use his land for the purpose for which
it was economically best-suited. Today, most societies desire, indeed, many require, not only that this freedom should be restricted
for the public good, but also that land use in general should be
determined by the long-term interests of communities as a whole
rather than as a consequence of the incidence or spread of individual land ownership.[1]

In this paper, I shall attempt to look at the legal methods used or
proposed to be used to achieve those ends. Although I feel com-
pelled to refer to the British experience as a committed Anglophile,
it is not because Britain is regarded by many as the cradle of land-
use planning, but rather that the problems of land-use control in

---

*My thanks are due to Professor Robert Freilich for his considerable help
in the preparation of this paper and for his guidance which enabled me to
focus on some essentials of the American land use system and to those who
participated in the seminars on Urbanization and Metropolitan Government
at UMKC for their individual (and collective) insight and wisdom.

1. *See* RECOMMENDATIONS FOR NATIONAL ACTION, REPORT OF HABITAT:
UNITED NATIONS CONFERENCE ON HUMAN SETTLEMENTS, VANCOUVER, 1976.

societies with mixed economies vary only in degree, and because the solutions to those problems, and, in turn, the problems created by those solutions, tend to have a number of common features.

II. Legal Structure of Land Use Control: Britain v. United States

Insofar as I pursue a comparative approach, I will highlight the main characteristics of our respective systems. In the United States, the legal perimeters of land-use control are to be found within the tough structure of its written constitution; namely, in the provisions requiring due process of, and equal protection under the law, and that prohibiting the taking of private property for public use without just compensation. Britain, on the other hand, is neither enriched nor enslaved by any similar constitutional document. With one qualification, which for this purpose has no immediate consequence, Parliament is supreme and, in theory at least, this omnipotence would allow it to abolish the Monarchy with the same ease as it could pass or repeal an Act for the Protection of Birds.[2]

The British land use system has been imposed by Parliament. Its twin pillars are a development plan prepared for an area and a prohibition against the carrying out of any development of land unless and until a permit for that development has been granted by the appropriate municipal authority. The development plan may have two parts or tiers: an upper tier "structure plan" which it is compulsory for a county authority to prepare and a lower tier "local plan" which may be prepared eithei by the county authority or a district authority, the latter being a lesser but autonomous municipality within the geographic area of a county.

The function of each part of the plan and the relationship between them is critical. The upper tier structure plan does not deal with detailed land use. Its purpose is to indicate with a fairly broad brush the long-term strategy for a wide area, in terms of the policies applicable to major land uses in the area, such as industry, housing, transport and communications. In the normally accepted sense of the word, the structure plan is not a plan at all. As a strategy, its form must inevitably be that of a written document. The lower tier local plan, on the other hand, is concerned with detailed land use.

---

2. The qualification arises as a result of Britain's adhesion to the European Economic Community by the European Community Act of 1972. In the field of land use, the influence of community legislation on domestic law has been minimal.

It is prepared in response to development or redevelopment pressure in any area. It will zone land for a particular purpose, but always within the context of the land use policy for the area as set out in the structure plan.[3] As with the American system, the identification of land in a development plan as suitable for a particular use is a guide rather than a guarantee that a permit will be issued to allow an owner to use it for that new purpose. Unlike the American system, there is no later adoption of a zoning ordinance which translates the guide into a guarantee.[4]

At first sight, you may view the British system as arbitrary. It is saved from this label by the requirement of wide citizen participation in the preparation of both tiers of the development plan, the need for a structure plan to be approved by Central Government before it takes effect, the presumption that a permit will be issued for any development in accordance with proposals in the development plan and the power of Central Government to intervene to issue a permit for development if for no valid reason the local authority has refused to do so. The British people have lived with this system for more than thirty years and usually have accepted and supported its terms.

If land-use control in Britain has been imposed from above, in the United States it has sprung from grass roots. Its main mechanisms are the comprehensive plan and the zoning ordinance. The comprehensive plan is a single document, its prime intent being to prevent haphazard or piecemeal zoning. It too is a blueprint which guides municipalities in the exercise of their zoning or subdivision power. The zoning ordinance is a distinctive legislative act which ultimately confers legal rights and the vehicle by which the local municipality determines both the use of land and the type, density and position of buildings within each zoning district. Flexibility is built into the system by the ordinance allowing an owner considerable latitude in the type of development which may be permitted, as for example, by devices such as overlay zones and holding zones;

---

3. The two-tier development plan system described here is the new system introduced in 1968 to gradually replace the single "all-purpose" development plan which has constituted the basic planning document in England since 1948.

4. In the second major critique of land-use planning and development control in England and Wales within three years (the first being the Review of the Development Control System by George Dobry, Q.C., (H.M.S.O.)) the REPORT OF THE ENVIRONMENT SUB-COMMITTEE OF THE EXPENDITURE COMMITTEE OF THE HOUSE OF COMMONS (Report H.C. 359–1; Session 1976–77), suggested consideration be given to development plans bestowing a legal right to develop, subject to safeguards.

by contract and conditional zoning; and by cluster or planned unit development. This device stands somewhere between zoning and subdivision control and allows an owner of more than one lot who wishes to develop an entire tract of land to have regard to its total area, insuring its comprehensive development as opposed to piecemeal treatment on a lot by lot basis. Furthermore, the whole system is given additional flexibility by the power vested in zoning board of appeals to issue variances and special exceptions from any strict zoning ordinance requirements. How then, one might ask, does the system work in practice?

Traditionally, the application of the police power as seen in the American law of zoning has been used to meet problems associated with health, safety, morality or welfare. Although zoning ordinances which cause reductions in property values are not necessarily invalid[5] their constitutionality as applied to particular land requires that the property restricted be left with a reasonable use. One application of this principle demonstrates that zoning must not be used to give protection to property where to do so leaves adjacent property with no reasonable use. This is seen in *Spaid v. Board of County Commissioners for Prince George's County*,[6] where, for the benefit of residential development on the east side of a turnpike, an attempt was made to create a buffer zone of land lying between industrial development and the west side of the turnpike. In directing reclassification of the buffer zone land to an industrial zoning, the Court of Appeals of Maryland, quoting from *Hoffman v. Mayor and City Council of Baltimore*, said:

> If a residential neighborhood desires protection by a border of unused property, necessarily it must provide its own property, not appropriate its neighbors', for this purpose. . . . Property owners in a residential district cannot create a "no man's land" at the border of their district by forbidding one property owner in an adjoining district from making any use at all of his property, or any use for which it is "peculiarly suitable."[7]

This case can be contrasted with the English case of *RMC Management Services Ltd. v. Secretary of State for the Environment*[8] where a permit was refused for the erection on land of a ready-mixed concrete-batching plant, because it would generate an abnormal level of airborne abrasive dust. It was held that although the level of dust would not amount to even a common law nuisance, it would,

---

5. *See* Euclid v. Ambler Realty Co., 272 U.S. 365 (1926).
6. 259 Md. 369, 269 A.2d 797 (1970).
7. 197 Md. 294, 79 A.2d 367 (1951).
8. 22 E.G. 1593 (1972).

nevertheless, affect adversely the operation of four neighboring establishments who had been attracted to the area by the clean air necessary for the high-precision scientific and engineering work in which they were engaged. In refusing to upset the decision, the High Court said, ". . . [the] Minister is entitled to ask himself whether the proposed development is compatible with the proper and desirable use of other land in the area." The risks to four special clean air neighbors, thus, were a consideration properly to be taken into account in restricting the use of the adjacent property.

Contemplating what the decision would have been in the alternate counties if the facts of the cases had been transposed, one would hope that the Maryland Court of Appeals would have held that the continued zoning for agricultural purposes (of the land planned for the concrete-batching plant) did not deprive the owner of any reasonable use of his land and, thereby, amounted to neither an abuse of due process nor a taking without payment of just compensation; and that the Secretary of State for the Environment would have allowed an appeal against the refusal to allow industrial development on the buffer strip on the ground that such restriction was unnecessary in view of the existing buffer which was provided by the turnpike.

There can be no doubt that during the last three decades, in response to changing conditions brought about by increasing urbanization, the scope of the police power in the United States has expanded considerably from the traditional "Euclidian" base. In 1954, in *Berman v. Parker*, the Court said, "It is within the power of the legislature to determine that the community should be beautiful as well as healthy, spacious as well as clean, well-balanced as well as carefully patrolled."[9] More recently, the Supreme Court in the *Village of Belle Terre v. Boraas* upheld a zoning ordinance intended to exclude group student housing from a community, and said, "A quiet place where yards are wide, people few, and motor vehicles restricted are legitimate guidelines in a land use project addressed to family needs. . . . The police power is not confined to the elimination of filth, stench and unhealthy places."[10]

Other areas in which zoning ordinances have been upheld include the preservation of the historic character of a locality,[11] the preservation of a rural environment[12] and the safeguarding from

9. 348 U.S. 26, 33 (1954).
10. 416 U.S. 1, 9 (1974).
11. Maher v. City of New Orleans, 235 So. 2d 403 (La. 1970).
12. Ybarra v. Town of Los Altos Hills, 503 F.2d 250 (9th Cir. 1974).

exploitation of a state's water resources.[13] Of recent developments, however, perhaps the most significant is the acceptance by the New York Court of Appeals in *Golden v. Planning Board of Ramapo*,[14] of the legitimacy of the police power to facilitate the sequential control of urban growth. There, in order to overcome the problem of private development outstripping public resource, the ordinances sought to link the former to the provision of the latter. Under the scheme, private development could only take place where a lot could be shown to be within a minimal distance of public services such as roads, parks, drainage, sewers and fire protection facilities. In upholding the validity of the ordinance the Court said:

> [W]here it is clear that the existing physical and financial resources of the community are inadequate to furnish the essential services and facilities which a substantial increase in population requires, there is a rational basis for "phased growth" and hence, the challenged ordinance is not violative of the Federal and State Constitutions.[15]

Having looked at some of the cases in which the police power has been held to be validly exercised, may we find courts holding the reverse? The constitutional principle of equal protection under the law ensures that the police power should not be used to overtly foster or maintain racial discrimination. In the 1975 case of *United States v. City of Black Jack*,[16] the court invalidated an ordinance which rezoned land so as to prevent the construction of federally subsidized low-income multi-family housing in an area. In the more recent case of *Village of Arlington Heights v. Metropolitan Housing Development Corporation*,[17] however, the Supreme Court upheld the refusal of a village to rezone land to allow for multi-family housing where its action was based not on any racial discriminatory intent but upon the preservation of property values and the integrity of the existing zoning pattern. Quite clearly, motivation is to be the yardstick by which future courts will distinguish between "racial" land use regulations which are unconstitutional and "socio-economic" land use regulations which are not.

Perhaps the more significant fetter on the exercise of police power is that of the fifth amendment (as applied to the states through the Fourteenth Amendment), prohibiting the taking of private property for public use without just compensation. The

---

13. Just v. Marinette County, 201 N.W.2d 761 (Wis. 1972).
14. 30 N.Y.2d 359, 334 N.Y.S.2d 138, 285 N.E.2d 291 (1972), *appeal dismissed*, 409 U.S. 1003 (1972).
15. *Id*. at 303.
16. 508 F.2d 1179 (8th Cir. 1974), *cert. denied*, 422 U.S. 1942 (1975).
17. 429 U.S. 257 (1977).

problem here may be summed up in the phrase "take, and you must compensate; regulate, and you need not." Hence, landowners who find that the value of their property has been reduced by the exercise of police power are moved to show that the regulation amounts in fact to a taking and that, accordingly, they should be compensated.

One of the earliest cases to consider the issue was *Pennsylvania Coal Co. v. Mahon*,[18] where the Supreme Court declared unconstitutional as an undue regulation of the company's property Pennsylvania's Kohler Act which was enacted to prevent coal mine subsidence from destroying towns on the surface by regulating the amount of coal which could be mined. Mr. Justice Holmes propounded his much quoted but generalized test, "[T]he general rule at least is, that while property may be regulated to a certain extent, if regulation goes too far it will be recognized as a taking." The case shows that in determining whether the regulation has, in fact, gone too far, the courts will weigh the public benefit flowing from the regulation against the extent of the loss of property value. No doubt there were many who on the facts preferred the dissenting judgment of Mr. Justice Brandeis. He believed that the state only prevented a noxious use of private property and that the Act validly regulated property rights under the aegis of the police power to protect public welfare.

What the conflicting judgments in the Pennsylvania case do presage is the perennial difficulty of determining in any particular situation whether or not a taking can be said to have occurred. Not surprisingly, the courts have struggled constantly with the issue, and their decisions are both confusing and difficult to rationalize.[19] Indeed, until last year the only conclusion that it seemed safe to draw from them was: a regulation does not amount to a taking *merely* because it causes depreciation in the value of the affected property. Now the law has been somewhat clarified as a result of the decision in *Fred F. French Investing Co., Inc. v. City of New York*.[20] There the New York Court of Appeals had to consider whether the rezoning of potential private parks exclusively as parks open to the public constituted a deprivation of property rights without due process of law in violation of constitutional limitations. In possibly the clearest exposition of the demarcation line between the

---

18. 260 U.S. 393 (1922).
19. *See* F. BOSSELMAN, D. CALLIES, & J. BANTA, THE TAKING ISSUE (1973).
20. 39 N.Y.2d 587, 385 N.Y.S.2d 5, 350 N.E.2d 381 (1976).

exercise of police power and eminent domain, Chief Judge Breitel said "[a] zoning ordinance is unreasonable if it frustrates the owner in the use of his property, that is, if it renders the property unsuitable for any reasonable income productive or other private use for which it is adapted and thus destroys its economic value, or all but a bare residue of its value."[21]

III. An Anglophile's View of the Effectiveness of United States Land Use Controls

Having examined the legal techniques for security the public control of land use, we may now consider their effectiveness in the light of the concern expressed about them by government agencies, public officials and professional and other expert bodies. In this respect, there seems to be three aspects of land and its use most likely to make an impact on a visitor to the United States from Western Europe. (1) the country's immense vastness, which gives it a range of options not available to most Western European nations; (2) the dereliction in the core of most older industrial cities; and (3) its uncontrolled urban sprawl, an urban sprawl *in excelsis.*

As regards the dereliction of inner cities, the problem in the United States seems more grave than that in Britain, where there has not yet been a significant racial overtone which constitutes a feature of the American scene. Cities have resulted from men's desire to communicate with each other, a communication which is not now always welcome and which has now taken a different form with the growth of the freeway, cheap energy and telecommunications. Occasionally, one sees the view pressed that the rejuvenation of inner cities is as difficult as making the desert bloom—so why do we try? Quite apart from being a philosophy of despair, the view ignores the fact that the problems of inner cities are no longer land use but social problems and that as such they are unlikely to go away without treatment. In Britain, we recently have been taking a fresh look at the inner-city problem. Even if one ignores any social engineering motivation for change, the plain fact which Britain cannot ignore is that its population density is nine times that of the

---

21. *See also* HFH, Ltd. v. Superior Court of Los Angeles County, 15 Cal. 3d 508, 125 Cal. Rptr. 365, 542 P.2d 237 (1975), where it was held that a mere downzoning gave no constitutional right to compensation. The court left to another day the question of entitlement to compensation if a zoning regulation forbade all use of the land in question. *See* the splendid discussion of the many issues in this case in HAGMAN, 1976 LAND USE LAW AND ZONING DIGEST No. 2, at 5.

United States and that living as we do, cheek by jowl, all land is a vital commodity. America also faces this problem. We just cannot afford to let any city resemble a doughnut of the variety which has a hole in its middle. The British Government's recent *White Paper*, "Policy for the Inner Cities,"[22] sees the framework of its policy as including the strengthening of the economies of inner areas, improving their physical fabric and environment, alleviating social problems and securing a new balance between inner areas and the rest of the city region in terms of population and jobs. To help achieve these ends, it proposes introducing legislation to enable municipalities to make loans of up to ninety percent to companies for the purchase of land and erection or improvement of industrial buildings. In addition, over the next two years, the Government is making available £100,000,000 for construction work in selected inner-city areas.

Although it must now be clear that wherever they are situated, the regeneration of inner cities requires a long term financial commitment from governments; the speed of regeneration may well depend upon the presence or otherwise of other techniques. In Britain, one of those techniques is central governmental control of industrial development, whereby such development is not allowed to take place unless the developer has been granted an "industrial development certificate." A developer should now be more likely to obtain that certificate if the development proposed is within the inner city. It must also not be forgotten that a land use policy which imposes restrictions on development outside the perimeter of an existing town, is likely to result if universally applied, in the development pressure being transferred to within the perimeter. This is one bonus which can flow from the control of urban sprawl; another is the safeguarding of valuable agricultural land.

On this subject, it is significant that the Department of Agriculture's Economic Research Service has estimated that of the 400 million acres of cropland in the United States, about two million acres are being "irreversibly lost" each year to urban build up and that an additional one million acres are being used for ponds, lakes and reservoirs. The conclusion drawn from these facts and others by the Soil Conservation Service of the Department "is that the days of complacency about America's cropland supply are over."

I would suggest that there are two major hurdles to be overcome before the United States will feel it possesses an acceptable, real-

---

22. Cmnd. 6845 (H.M.S.O.).

istic and effective land-use system. First, there needs to be much greater regional, state and federal involvement in both the determination of land use policy and in securing its implementation, together with public acceptance of their need to do so. One must seriously question whether decisions are being made at the level at which they ought to be made. Second, a solution must be found for dealing with the financial windfalls and wipeouts which are respectively bestowed or inflicted on landowners as a result of land use regulation. Initially, it seems relevant to make a number of observations which, although trite, are often forgotten by many who should know better, in particular, politicians. To begin with, save for the lowest levels of political jurisdiction, land use regulation does not involve the question of whether there should be growth or no growth. It is predominantly a question of whether growth should be controlled, and, if so, how, where and when. In any mixed economy, planners cannot act as Canute. Land use regulation and policies must thus accept both the influence of market forces and an increasing gross national product and accommodate or plan around them. Furthermore, it must be recognized that most land use decisions are concerned with the resolution of conflict. There are many developments necessary for national, state or local wellbeing which nobody wishes as a neighbor, but which must be located somewhere. Recognition of what is perhaps obvious, has tremendously important implications for citizen participation in the planning process. So, too, does the fact that although some kind of development is fixed as to where it is to take place (e.g., mineral exploration), other developments frequently pose a range of options, all of which may be equally favorable from the state's point of view, but each of which would be distasteful to the community receiving the development.

A. *Greater Regional, State and Federal Involvement*

This must inevitably mean a loosening of the iron grip of many of lesser authorities. At the moment, in addition to the federal government and fifty states, there are about 3,000 counties, 18,000 municipalities and 17,000 townships, each of which has the power in some way to plan or regulate land use. That is an average of about 760 per state. Fortunately, there is now a growing recognition that certain aspects of land use must be dealt with on a national or regional basis. Perhaps it may be too much to hope that national involvement will ever extend beyond cooperation between federal agencies and state governments and the use of federal financial assistance to achieve national goals.[23] The states, however, have the constitutional power to regulate their own land use and it must be an encouraging sign for the future that many of them are now beginning to do so.

One of the first examples was the Land Use Law of the state of Hawaii which in 1961 created a comprehensive statewide zoning plan dividing the state into agricultural, conservation, urban and rural districts. Under that legislation, the state determines its overall policy for development, but allows a local input into the administration of the zoning program. Then in 1970, the state of Vermont adopted a comprehensive Environmental Control Law whereby residential subdivision involving lots of more than 10 acres, substantial commercial and industrial development or development exceeding 2,500 feet was to be conditional upon a permit being obtained from the state's Environmental Agency. There are also many states which now exercise control over areas of critical concern such as power plants siting, surface mining, and the management of coastal zones and wetlands. The American Law Institute's Model Land Development Code, which states have been reluctant so far to adopt, while giving to local government the power of zoning and subdivision control allows it to be superceded and exercised by the state in certain key areas.[24]

The British (and indeed the continental) experience suggests that, forward looking though some of these approaches might be, they are not entirely satisfactory, since for land use planning to be effective it must begin with integrated state planning and end with local planning rather than vice versa. I have already made the point that there can be no absolutes in land-use planning and that the detail of land use must be structured upon the choice of options made at some higher level. This makes it imperative, therefore, for that choice to be made democratically. A local community would be bound to feel aggrieved, if, for example, a policy of growth was imposed upon it by the state when it would have pre-

---

23. The Council of State Governments is beginning to do much encouraging work in this respect.

24. Perhaps the closest analogy to the concept of areas of critical concern is the system being adopted in Scotland which varies somewhat from the system in England and Wales. In Scotland, too, legislation provides for integrated structure plans and detailed local plans. In Scotland, however, if the proposed development is one of eleven categories likely to raise nationally important issues, the matter must be referred to Central Government.

ferred one of no-growth and it had been given no opportunity to participate in the decision-making process.[25]

In Britain, we have begun to deal with that problem in this way. Before a county authority submits its structure plan to the Secretary of State for his approval it must have publicized the matters it was proposing to include in the plan and it must alert people who might wish to make representations about those matters to the fact that they may do so and it must give them adequate opportunity to do so. The result is that when the plan is submitted for approval to the Secretary of State it should contain what the county authority believes should be the favored option and one that the majority of the population are prepared to countenance.[26] If the Secretary of State then approves the plan, which he may do so only after considering any objections to it, the district authority's way is then clear to prepare local plans which dovetail into the policies contained in the structure plan. It is significant that most countries on the continent of Europe have also adopted systems for "split-level" development plans (some of which are multi-tiered) as each seeks to translate national economic and social goals into local detailed land-use regulation.

There is another reason for greater state involvement. Land-use regulation is no longer regarded solely as an exercise in physical planning. It is fast becoming part of a jigsaw in which economic, social and environmental policies are coordinated and implemented. It is right that that coordination should begin at the level at which those policies are adumbrated.

B. *How to Deal with the Windfalls Which Accrue to an*
   Owner of Land Allowed to Develop It and the Wipeouts
   Which Are Suffered by Those Not Allowed to Do So

In Britain since 1947, the police power has been used to prevent any development of land where central or local government decrees

---

25. But local democracy can "rule" only in local circumstances. In Britain, for example, a proposed route for a major road to bypass a busy market town may show a number of alternatives alongside the authorities "preferred route." Local feeling may then persuade the authority to select an alternative route. This is the closest one can get in Britain to the plebiscite situation, as seen in City of Eastlake v. Forest City Enterprises, 426 U.S. 668 (1976), where the charter of the city had been amended to require a change of zoning to be subject to a plebiscite and to be approved by fifty-five percent of the voters before becoming effective.

26. This is the theory, but it has not yet worked in practice. In the first instance the separation of strategic (structure plan) matter from local matters

that it should not be developed. In those circumstances, no compensation is generally payable.[27] It is a state of affairs now recognized as a permanent feature of British land use planning. It is accepted by all, and the market generally reflects that acceptance. Attention over the years, thus, has focused on the other side of the coin, namely the windfall profits which accrue to those allowed to develop. These windfalls arise from two major sources: (1) the diversion of the development pressure from the land which is restricted from development to that where it is allowed; and, (2) the presence in the value of developed land of an element which is due to public expenditure or other community action.

Windfall recapture has for long been a political football. Now, after many unsuccessful attempts to deal with the problems, twin legislation has been passed which it is claimed will be a "final solution" to the problem of land values. Under the Development Land Tax Act of 1976, a tax of eighty percent is levied on any development value in land which an owner realizes. The tax is paid by the owner to the national exchequer. Under the Community Land Act of 1975, local authorities are given wider power to acquire land considered suitable for private development (whether by agreement or eminent domain) on special terms. The terms are that the authority pays the seller the net sum he would have received had he sold the land privately and subsequently paid the eighty percent to the state. In short, the local authority *may* now buy undeveloped land cheap and then either sell for the development purpose or develop the land itself and then sell. At some later date, the tax will rise to one hundred percent and local authorities will be *required* to purchase all land needed for major private development before the development takes place.

What is the American position?[28] First, regarding wipeouts: here (as in Britain) no compensation is paid for loss of value where land

has proved difficult to observe. In the second, there has been a marked reluctance on the part of the public to become involved with structure plan preparation. Interest in development is really generated only when the development is closer to home. *See* 1976 JOURNAL OF PLANNING AND ENVIRONMENT 469.

27. Compensation is paid for very limited development which is regarded within an owners "existing-use" rights and for the loss of development value due to planning restrictions where the value existed in 1948. Development value arising after 1948, therefore, is not compensated where that value cannot be realized due to the restrictions.

28. The text for many years to come for all interested in this area is the work by D. HAGMAN & D. MISCZYNSKI, WINDFALLS FOR WIPEOUTS. The authors give the area a comprehensive treatment and examine many of the techniques used for recapturing windfalls and mitigating wipeouts, both in the United States and other countries.

use regulation prevents an owner from putting his land to its best economic use. The difficulty which has no parallel in Britain occurs where control is exercised in areas where previously there was none, or where existing control is made more severe. The plain fact is that although the legitimacy of land use regulation was originally based upon a nuisance analogy and the protection of private property, from the beginning its effect has often been to provide a public benefit at private cost. It seems quite legitimate that where the police power is used to eliminate filth, stench and unhealthy places, compensation should not be paid to an owner who is unable because of it to put his property to its best economic use. Here, the power is based on reasonably objective criteria and its application is generally universal. It is otherwise, however, where the police power is concerned with land-use regulation such as zoning, since its incidence and effect so often depends upon the making of a choice between a number of options.

No doubt the absence of a general code of compensation for land use regulation may be explained as part of the country's traditional attitude to land ownership as once fostered by those who drove America's frontiers westward to California. Today, however, it can be justified only on the basis that land ownership remains a lottery.[29] This philosophy is most unlikely to persuade those living next to a freeway or those who have bought their property at an enhanced value for later building development, to accept the need for a land use policy which restricts the land to its existing agricultural use. Unfortunately, it seems that before changes can be made in this direction, constitutional obstacles may need to be overcome, namely those provisions to be found in some state constitutions which prohibit the use of public funds for private purpose.

As regards windfall recapture in the United States, there are a number of techniques in current use. They include a special capital gains tax on land (as in Vermont), special assessments, exactions and fees on development permissions, advance eminent domain purchases and transferable development rights, this last technique being one which is capable of avoiding a wipeout whilst at the same time recapturing the windfall. Although the techniques are plentiful in variety, they are regarded either as impracticable or as not taking from the landowner a sufficient percentage of the windfall profit. In Britain, current legislation is geared to eventually taking

---

29. It may also be justified where the state takes all the development value (e.g., by levying a tax on it at a rate of 100 percent) thus reducing the value of all land to its value for existing use purposes.

all the windfall, so removing from the landowner any increment in the value of land which is due to the development process. One suspects that given its constitutional history a similar arrangement would be anathema to the American scene. Nevertheless, no effective and acceptable land use system is likely to be established until the problem of land values has been solved. Fortunately, there is room for optimism.

As Chief Judge Breitel has said:

> The legislative and administrative efforts to solve the zoning and landmark problem in modern society demonstrate the presence of ingenuity. . . . That ingenuity further pursued will in all likelihood achieve the goals without placing an impossible or unsuitable burden on the individual property owner, the public fisc, or the general taxpayer. These efforts are entitled to and will undoubtedly receive every encouragement. The task is difficult but not beyond management. The end is essential but the means must nevertheless conform to constitutional standards.[30]

---

30. Fred F. French Investing Co., Inc. v. City of New York, 39 N.Y.2d 587, 385 N.Y.S.2d 5, 350 N.E.2d 381 (1976).

Table of Cases

A

Abbott House v. Village of
Tarrytown, 8

Agins v. City of Tiburon, 4, 40, 41,
43, 44

Almquist v. Town of Marshan, 34

Ambler Realty Co. v. Village of
Euclid, 7

Arastra v. City of Palo Alto, 192,
193

Arlington Heights v. Metropol.
Hous. Dev. Corp., Village of,
11, 17, 49, 270, 271, 286

Arnel Dev. Co. v. City of Costa
Mesa, 10

Arvida Corp. v. City of Boca Raton,
165

Associated Homebuilders of Greater
East Bay, Inc. v. City of
Walnut Creek, 2, 37, 190

Associated Homebuilders, Inc. v.
City of Livermore, 3, 9, 14, 16,
37, 168, 270

Aurora v. Burns, City of, 2

Avco Community Developers, Inc.
v. South Coast Regional
Comm'n, 40, 240

B

Bacich v. Board of Control, 193

Baker v. City of Algonae, 78, 249

Baker Sargent Corp., *In re,* 237, 245

Beaver Gasoline Co. v. Zoning
Hearing Bd., 26, 76, 77

Belclaire Holding Corp. v. Klingher,
25, 75

Belle Terre v. Boraas, Village of, 3,
8, 16, 20, 148, 185, 285

Berenson v. Town of New Castle,
14, 16, 28, 188, 270

Bergen County Sewer Auth. v.
Hackensack Meadowlands
Dev. Comm'n, 242

Berman v. Parker, 38, 40, 285

Bienz v. City of Dayton, 254

Binkowski v. Township of Shelby, 78

Board of Appeals v. Housing
Appeals Comm., 12

Board of County Comm'rs v.
Casper, 63

Board of County Comm'rs v.
Ralston, 24, 76

Board of Supervisors v. DeGroff, 13

Boca Villas Corp. v. City of Boca
Raton, 9, 35, 36

Bohannan v. City of San Diego, 190

Boomer v. Atlantic Cement Co., 2,
45

Bristow v. City of Woodhaven, 8, 78

Brown v. Board of Educ., 182

Brown v. EPA, 177

Builders Ass'n of Santa Clara–
Santa Cruz Counties v.
Superior Court, 169

C

California Coastal Zone Conservation Comm'n v. McKeon
Constr., 240

Cameron v. Zoning Agent, 8, 78

Candlestick Properties v. San
Francisco Bay Conservation &
Dev. Comm'n, 174, 190, 243,
245

Causby v. United States, 201

CEEED v. California Coastal Zone
Conservation Comm'n, 239,
240, 245

Cheney v. Village 2 at New Hope,
Inc., 2, 37, 223

Chisholm v. Georgia, 130

Chrobuch v. Snohomish, 25, 75

Citizens for Washington Square v.
City of Davenport, 9

City of . . . (See city name)

Clackamus County v. Ague, 268

Clackamus County v. Dunham,
268, 269

Coalition for Los Angeles County
Planning v. Board of
Supervisors, 9, 35

Cobban Realty v. Donlan, 206

Concord Township Appeal, 88

Consolidated Rock Products Co. v.
City of Los Angeles, 189

Construction Indus. Ass'n v. City of

Petaluma, 3, 9, 19, 35, 36, 132,
   143, 145, 146, 147, 148, 150,
   164, 165
Corbett v. Hill, 204
Corning v. Lehigh, 216
County Council v. District Land
   Corp., 41
County of Orange v. Heim, 240
County of Santa Barbara v. Purcell,
   Inc., 190
Crow v. Brown, 11, 62
Culver v. Dagg, 248

D
Daily v. City of Lawton, 62
Dale v. City of Mountain View, 194
Data Processing Services v. Camp,
   19
Day-Brite Lighting, Inc. v. Missouri,
   39
DeCaro v. Washington Township,
   8, 35
Department of Ecology v. Ballard
   Elks Lodge No. 827, 246, 243,
   245
Derry Borough v. Shomo, 8
DeSimone v. Greater Englewood
   Hous. Corp., 8, 78
Dickinson v. Board of County
   Comm'rs, 249
Dillon Companies, Inc. v. City of
   Boulder, 26, 77
Douglaston Civic Ass'n v. Galvin, 9
Dunn v. Blumstein, 185

E
Eastlake Community Counsel v.
   Roanoke Assocs., Inc., 245
Eastlake v. Forest City Enterprises,
   Inc., City of, 9, 10, 25, 26
   167, 180
El Cortez Heights Ass'n v. Tucson
   Hous. Auth., 11
Eldridge v. City of Palo Alto,
   194, 195
Elevated R.R. Structures, *In re,* 202
Environmental Coalition of Orange
   County, Inc. v. Avco Com-
   munity Developers, Inc., 240
Environmental Defense Fund, Inc.
   v. Armstrong, 176
Environmental Defense Fund v.
   Corps of Engineers, 141
Euclid v. Ambler Realty Co.,

Village of, 2, 6, 24, 39, 53, 76,
   121, 129, 186, 284
Exton Quarries, Inc. v. Zoning Bd.
   of Adjustment, 77

F
Farrelly v. Town of Ramapo, *In re,*
   78, 125
Fasano v. Board of County
   Comm'rs, 2, 10, 21, 24, 25, 75,
   77, 78, 79, 88, 248, 249, 250
Feliciano v. United States, 31
Fiore v. City of Highland Park, 10
Flemming v. City of Tacoma, 26, 77
Fletcher v. Romney, 78, 125
Floyd v. New York State Urban
   Dev. Corp., 12
Forest City Enterprises, Inc. v. City
   of Eastlake, 26, 166, 167
Fred F. French Investing Co., Inc.
   v. City of New York, 2, 40, 41,
   42, 224, 231, 287, 295

G
Gautreaux v. Chicago Hous. Auth.,
   11, 67, 183
Girsh, *In re.*, 2, 6, 8, 10, 63, 77,
   125, 222
Gisler v. County of Madera, 8, 222
Glenview Dev. Co. v. Franklin
   Township, 14, 15
Goldblatt v. Town of Hempstead,
   39, 44, 190
Golden v. Planning Bd. of Ramapo,
   2, 3, 9, 34, 40, 49, 78, 87, 121,
   126, 132, 134, 148, 150, 151,
   162, 163, 190, 286
Great E. Bldg. Co., Inc., 237, 245
Green v. Hayward, 250, 277
Greenwald v. Town of Ramapo,
   In re, 78, 125
Griffiths, *In re,* 182

H
Hackensack Meadowlands Dev.
   Comm'n v. Municipal Sanitary
   Landfill Auth., 242
Hadacheck v. Sebastian, 2, 189
Hahn v. Baker Lodge, 204
Haley v. City of Troutdale, 268
Harper v. Virginia Bd. of Elections,
   184
Hartford v. Town of Glastonbury,
   City of, 9

Herman v. Parker, 20
HFH, Ltd. v. Superior Court, 41, 43, 194, 288
High Meadows Park, Inc. v. City of Aurora, 8
Hills v. Gautreaux, 11
Hoffman v. Mayor and City Council of Baltimore, 284
Home Builder's League, Inc. v. Township of Berlin, 8
Hunter v. Erickson, 9
Huttig v. City of Richmond Heights, 13

I
In re . . . (See party name)

J
James v. Valtierra, 9, 28
Jehovah's Witnesses v. Mullen, 25, 75
Johnson County Planning Comm'n v. Fayette Bldg. Corp., 8
Jones v. Alfred H. Mayer Co., 46
Just v. Marinette County, 2, 3, 9, 40, 45, 190, 240, 245, 286

K
Kaiser-Aetna v. United States, 41
Kennedy Park Homes v. City of Lackawanna, 62, 173
King Resources Co. v. Environmental Improvement Comm'n, 243
Kip v. N.Y. Cent. R.R., 215
Kit-Mar Builders, In re, 8, 63, 125, 128, 172
Kit-Mar Builders, Inc. v. Township of Concord, 187
Klitgaard and Jones v. San Diego Coast Regional Comm'n, 240, 245
Kreshtool v. Delmarva Power & Light Co., 240, 243, 245
Kropf v. City of Sterling Heights, 8

L
Lake Country Estates, Inc. v. Tahoe Regional Planning Agency, 4, 41, 47
Lawton v. Steele, 3, 40
Leonard v. City of Bothell, 10
Lindsey v. Normet, 184

Lionshead Lake, Inc. v. Township of Wayne, 173, 181
Louisville v. District Court, City of, 29, 237, 245
Lutheran Church v. City of New York, 190
Lynch v. Household Finance Corp., 41, 47

M
Mahaley v. Cuyahoga Metropol. Hous. Auth., 11
Maher v. City of New Orleans, 285
Maher v. Gagne, 48
Maine Clean Fuels, Inc., In re, 243, 245
Maine v. Thiboutot, 48
Malmar Assocs. v. Board of Comm'rs, 8
McCarthy v. City of Manhattan, 190
McCarthy Co. v. Marin Mun. Water Dist., 170
McConnel v. Kibbe, 204
McCormick v. Bishop, 204
McCormick v. Lawrence, 243, 245
McLaughlin v. Florida, 182
Meadowlands Regional Dev. Agency v. Hackensack Meadowlands Dev. Comm'n, 243
Meadowlands Regional Dev. Agency v. State, 242, 243, 245
Memorial Hosp. v. Maricopa County, 185
Metropolitan Hous. Dev. Corp. v. Village of Arlington Heights, 18
Meyer v. Lord, 8
Middlesex and Boston St. Ry. Co. v. Newton, 13
Midkif v. Tom, 38
Mid-Way Cabinet Etc. Mfg. v. County of San Joaquin, 190
Molino v. Borough of Glassboro, 8
Monell v. Dept. of Social Servs., 41, 47
Moore v. City of East Cleveland, 17
Morgan County v. Stephens, 222
Mount Laurel v. Southern Burlington NAACP, Township of, 116
Mugler v. Kansas, 2

N
National Land Inv. Co. v. Easttown

Township Bd. of Adjustment, 222
National Land Inv. Co. v. Kohn, 8, 171, 186, 190
National Resources Defense Council,, Inc. v. Adirondack Park Agency, 245
National Resources Defense Council v. Stamm, 176
Navajo Terminals, Inc. v. San Francisco Bay Conserv. & Dev. Comm'n, 174
Nectow v. City of Cambridge, 3, 39, 40
New Orleans v. Duke, 40
New York Elevated R.R. v. Kernochan, 202
Norwalk Core v. Norwalk Redev. Agency, 183

O
Oakwood at Madison, Inc. v. Township of Madison, 8, 13, 15, 187, 248, 272, 273, 275, 276
Olson v. State, 278
1000 Friends of Ore. v. Board of County Comm'rs, 254, 255, 258, 263, 266
Owen v. City of Independence, 41

P
Park View Heights Corp. v. City of Black Jack, 12
Pascack Assoc., Ltd. v. Mayor of Washington, 15, 273, 274, 276
Peacock v. County of Sacramento, 190, 191
Pearson v. Matheson, 205
Penn. Cent. Transp. Co. v. City of New York, 4, 40, 41, 44
Pennsylvania Coal Co. v. Mahon, 40, 44, 189, 194, 287
People v. Ricciardi, 191
People ex rel. Younger v. County of El Dorado, 243
People of Puerto Rico v. Eastern Sugar Assocs., 38
Peterson v. Mayor of Klamath Falls, 257, 258
Pomatto v. Goleta County Water Dist., 171
Preseault, In re, 237, 243
Putnam v. Carroll, 244

Q
Quechee Lake Corp., In re, 237, 243

R
R. v. Hillington London Borough Council ex. p. Royco Homes, Ltd., 13
Ranjel v. City of Lansing, 9
Reilly v. Booth, 205
Reitman v. Mulkey, 9
Ridge Realty Co. v. Oldham County Plan. Comm'n, 8
Riverdale v. Town of Orangetown, 13
RMC Mgmt. Servs., Ltd. v. Secretary of State, 284
Robinson v. Cahill, 271, 278
Robinson v. City of Boulder, 37
Rodgers v. Village of Tarrytown, 76
Rodo Land, Inc. v. Board of County Comm'rs, 35
Roman Catholic Diocese of Newark v. Borough of Ho-Ho-Kus, 188
Rubin v. McAlevey, 123
Russian Hill Improvement Ass'n v. Board of Permit Appeals, 190

S
Salamar Builders Corp. v. Tuttle, 9
San Antonio Indep. School Dist. v. Rodriguez, 182, 271
San Diego v. Miller, 191
San Diego Building Contractors Ass'n v. City of San Diego, 169, 170
San Diego Coastal Regional Comm'n v. See the Sea, Ltd., 240, 243
Santa Rosa v. EPA, City of, 177
Save a Valuable Environment v. City of Bothell, 14, 16
SAVE Centennial Valley Ass'n v. Schultz, 8, 41
Seaman v. City of Durham, 263, 275, 279
Selby Realty Co. v. City of Buenaventura, 190
Serrano v. Priest, 64
Shannan v. Department of HUD, 11, 63, 67
Shapiro v. Thompson, 77, 185
Sierra Club v. Morton, 19, 140, 176
Simmons v. City of Royal Oaks, 78
Slaughter House Cases, 133

Smith v. County of Washington, 76
Smoke Rise, Inc. v. Washington
    Suburban Sanitary Comm'n, 9
Sneed v. County of Riverside, 191
Snyder v. City of Lakewood, 10
South of Sunnyside Neighborhood
    League v. Board of Comm'rs,
    253, 254
Southern Alameda Spanish Speaking
    Organ. v. City of Union City,
    63, 184
Southern Burlington NAACP v.
    Township of Mount Laurel, 2,
    7, 14, 18, 28, 150, 172, 173,
    180, 187, 188, 248, 249, 279
Spaid v. Board of County Comm'rs,
    284
Spring Valley Dev., *In re,* 29, 237,
    245
Spur Indus., Inc. v. Del E. Webb
    Dev. Co., 2
State v. Superior Court, 190, 239
State Aid Highway No. 1, *In re,* 237
Steel Hill Dev., Inc. v. Town of
    Sanbornton, 8, 35, 36, 87
Suffolk Hous. Servs., Inc. v. Town
    of Brookhaven, 9
Sun Ray Drive-In Dairy, Inc. v.
    Oregon Liquor Control
    Comm'n, 278
Surrick v. Zoning Hearing Bd.,
    14, 270

T
Taft v. Washington Mutual Savings
    Bank, 206
Third Ave. R.R. Bridge, *In re,* 202
Topanga Ass'n for a Scenic
    Community v. County of
    Los Angeles, 10, 22
Toso v. City of Santa Barbara, 43
Town v. Land Use Comm'n, 29,
    237, 243, 245
Town of Bedford v. Village of
    Mt. Kisco, 87
Township of . . . (See township
    name)
Trancentury Properties, Inc. v.
    State, 240
Transcontinental Gas Pipe Line
    Corp. v. Hackensack

Meadowlands Dev. Comm'n,
    242, 245
Turner v. County of Del Norte, 190

U
United States v. City of Black Jack,
    12, 17, 173, 183, 286
United States v. Kansas City Life
    Ins. Co., 189
United States v. Maryland Savings-
    Share Ins. Corp., 182
United States v. Willow River Power
    Co., 191
Urban Renewal Agency v.
    California Coastal Zone
    Conservation Comm'n, 240

V
Varney & Green v. Williams, 190
Vickers v. Gloucester Township,
    63, 127
Village of . . . (See village name)

W
Wambat Realty Corp. v. State, 245
Ward v. Village of Skokie, 25, 75, 77
Warth v. Seldin, 9, 19
Washington v. Davis, 12, 18, 28
Weaver v. Osborne, 205
West v. City of Portage, 10
Westwood Forest Estates, Inc. v.
    Village of South Nyack, 128
Wilcox v. Zoning Bd. of Appeals, 36
Wildlife Wonderland, Inc., *In re,*
    29, 237, 243, 245
Williston v. Chesterdale Farms, Inc.,
    28
Wilmington v. Lord, City of, 9
Wilson v. Hidden Valley Mun.
    Water Dist., 37
Wrigley Properties, Inc. v. City of
    Ladue, 13

Y
Ybarra v. Town of Los Altos Hills,
    8, 36, 184, 285
Young v. American Mini Theatres,
    4, 24, 40
Younger v. County of El Dorado,
    245

Application to the Section of Urban, State and Local Government Law

DIVISION OF LEGAL PRACTICE AND EDUCATION

Section of Urban, State and
Local Government Law
American Bar Association
1155 East 60th Street
Chicago, Illinois 60637

☐ Enclosed is check for $15.00, payable to
American Bar Association
for annual membership*
in the Section of Urban, State and Local Government Law, which entitles me to a subscription to THE URBAN LAWYER.

*Attorneys who are not members of the ABA will be sent an application for such membership, which is a prerequisite to Section membership.

Section Committee in which I am

interested _____

_____

☐ Since I am not eligible for membership in the
American Bar Association
but desire to subscribe to
THE URBAN LAWYER, I enclose my check for $22.50, payable to American Bar Association,
for a one-year subscription, beginning with the next issue ($27.50 for subscriptions mailed outside the United States and its possessions).

☐ Enclosed is check for $6.00 payable to American Bar Association for a copy of the

_____, 19 _____

issue of THE URBAN LAWYER.

NAME_____

STREET_____

CITY_____ STATE_____ ZIP_____

The Land Use Awakening

A comprehensive overview of recent zoning law
Edited by Robert H. Freilich and Eric O. Stuhler

Over the past decade, a remarkable awakening of interest in land use law d practice has occurred. **The Land se Awakening: Zoning Law in the eventies** brings together statements m prominent attorneys, law profes- rs, planners, and architects who have en in the forefront of this activity.

Originally published in The Urban wyer, these articles examine the ajor cases involving **exclusionary ning, procedural reform, growth anagement, flexible zoning,** and the ate role in land use planning.

In addition, the editors have prepared introduction, *especially for this vol- 1e,* which summarizes the key events the decade—linking them to related intemporary issues— and analyzes the fect of subsequent decisions.

This forty-page introduction, together th these twelve seminal articles, make le **Land Use Awakening** the most imprehensive overview of the subject w available.

The Land Use Awakening is a publi- ation of the Urban, State and Local overnment Law Section of the ABA.

Contents include:

Legal Assaults on Municipal Land Use Regulation *by Ira Michael Heyman*

Some Observations on the American Law Institute's Model Land Development Code *by Fred P. Bosselman et al.*

Golden v. Town of Ramapo: Establishing a New Dimension in American Planning Law *by Robert H. Freilich*

Impact Zoning: Alternative to Exclusion in the Suburbs *by Victor J. Yannacone, Jr. et al.*

No-Growth and Related Land Use Prob- lems: An Overview *by Ronald A. Zum- brun and Thomas E. Hookano*

Air Rights Are "Fertile Soil" *by Eugene J. Morris*

Institutionalizing the Revolution: Judicial Reaction to State Land Use Laws *by David E. Hess*

The Public Control of Land Use: An Anglophile's View *by Victor Moore*

February 1981   300 pages (est.)   6 × 9   Paper